JOURNAL FOR THE STUDY OF THE NEW TESTAMENT
SUPPLEMENT SERIES
69

JSOT Press
Sheffield

Rhetoric and Reference in the Fourth Gospel

Margaret Davies

Journal for the Study of the New Testament
Supplement Series 69

In memory of my father, Herbert Davies,
and of my uncle, Clifford Cleeves.

Published by JSOT Press
JSOT Press is an imprint of
Sheffield Academic Press Ltd
343 Fulwood Road
Sheffield S10 3BP
England

Typeset by Sheffield Academic Press
and
Printed on acid-free paper in Great Britain
by Biddles Ltd
Guildford

British Library Cataloguing in Publication Data

Davies, Margaret
Rhetoric and Reference in the Fourth Gospel. - (JSNT Supplement Series, ISSN 0143-5108; No. 69)
I. Title II. Series
226.5

ISBN 1-85075-345-8

CONTENTS

PREFACE

This study attempts a comprehensive reading of the Fourth Gospel, as a particular kind of narrative written at the end of the first century or at the beginning of the second, which makes sense of its theology, anthropology and history within that period. Part I is an elucidation of the type of narrative, Part II is a detailed exploration of its theological themes and metaphors, and Part III concerns questions of historical reference and reception. I have taken up the most valuable insights of structuralism and reader-response criticism, without ignoring what those methods ignore, namely, questions of theological and historical reference. History, theology and aesthetics are intrinsically related in the Fourth Gospel itself. Moreover, a just appreciation of the text requires us to recognize that particular historical situations affect the nature of any narrative.

When writing, I had two different audiences in view. The first audience was scholars who have written on the Fourth Gospel. I hope my own reading will challenge them to justify their alternative interpretations, in particular, to explain more clearly what they think the theological and anthropological perceptions of the Gospel are, and how these would fit into the probable period of its origin, rather than into the third, fourth or even fifth century. I also seek to correct some commentators' polemical and unjustified statements about Judaism in the first century. In addition, I would like to make people more aware of the difficulties faced by women who read the Gospel and the majority of commentaries and studies. But I have eschewed quoting other peoples' writings just to point out prejudices or errors, and have chosen, rather, to give my own constructive account.

The second audience was postgraduates, undergraduates and others who already have some knowledge of critical Gospel studies. For them I have provided background material with which scholars will already be familiar. I have tried to make the style and arguments transparent and positive.

Since readers will need constantly to refer to the text of the Fourth Gospel, it would be too irksome for them also to interrupt their reading by looking for other references at the end of the book, so I have included those references which are pertinent to an argument in brackets within the text.

I would like to acknowledge my debt to the many commentaries, studies and articles available today, some of which are not even listed in the bibliography, but which have helped me to form my own understanding of the text. I am also grateful to another group of people, to third year undergraduates and postgraduates at Bristol who have studied the Fourth Gospel with me over the last eight years. Their conscientious questionings and their arguments in discussions and essays have helped to illuminate the narrative.

Vicki Jones typed the original manuscript. Her interest in the work and her exceptional skills were a great support. The former editor of the series, David Hill, offered helpful suggestions which I was glad to accept, and the desk editor, Steve Barganski, worked diligently in guiding the text through the press. My thanks to all three.

Margaret Davies, Bristol 1992

ABBREVIATIONS

AB	Anchor Bible
BA	*Biblical Archaeologist*
BETL	Bibliotheca ephemeridum theologicarum lovaniensium
BJRL	*Bulletin of the John Rylands University Library of Manchester*
FRLANT	Forschungen zur Religion und Literatur des Alten und Neuen Testaments
HTR	*Harvard Theological Review*
IEJ	*Israel Exploration Journal*
JBL	*Journal of Biblical Literature*
JSNT	*Journal for the Study of the New Testament*
JTS	*Journal of Theological Studies*
NCB	New Century Bible
NovT	*Novum Testamentum*
NovTSup	*Novum Testamentum*, Supplements
NTS	*New Testament Studies*
OTL	Old Testament Library
SBLDS	SBL Dissertation Series
SBLMS	SBL Monograph Series
SBT	Studies in Biblical Theology
SNTSMS	Society of New Testament Studies Monograph Series
TDNT	G. Kittel and G. Friedrich (eds.), *Theological Dictionary of the New Testament*
VT	*Vetus Testamentum*
VTSup	*Vetus Testamentum*, Supplements
WUNT	Wissenschaftliche Untersuchungen zum Neuen Testament

INTRODUCTION

When we read texts, we discover that some are immediately appealing, either because of their closeness to our own concerns or because of their exotic strangeness. Those in our own language and from our own time are naturally more immediately comprehensible and some of them seem to speak directly to us. Those in foreign languages or from ancient times, whatever their initial appeal, are more difficult to understand, and we have to familiarize ourselves not only with their linguistic conventions but also with their literary strategies and cultural traditions before we can fully appreciate them. The Fourth Gospel was probably written at the end of the first century CE and its language is a form of Hellenistic Greek. But that Greek has been influenced by a literature whose authority the text assumes, its Scripture, taken over from Judaism. It is one of the tasks of this book to explore relations between the Fourth Gospel and its Scripture and to come to an understanding of the work's genre.

The Fourth Gospel is a short work, but it is quite long enough to allow different readers to select and emphasize different parts as especially important to its overall force. Naturally, in reading we form the work into a comprehensible whole, but a full and careful reading has to avoid noticing only those matters which correspond to our own interests while ignoring others. Even if we exercise care, however, we soon discover that our own readings differ from those of other people. No two commentaries on the Fourth Gospel agree in detail. A brief summary of those matters which distinguish my own reading from that of another and opposed reading may help to orientate those who want to make their own study of the Fourth Gospel.

Meir Sternberg's subtle elucidation of the poetics of the Hebrew Bible (1985) illustrates the ways in which ideology, history and aesthetics combine to enhance the readers' understandings of God and creation. He accepts that readers may ignore or recognize what is implicit as well as explicit in the narrative, and hence he supposes that individual readers may be more or less competent. They under-read when they fail to fill in the gaps with what is implied, but they may also over-read by filling out the text inappropriately, as some allegorists do. Nevertheless, he is confident that the Hebrew Bible never leaves readers bereft of judgment. Rather 'full-proof composition' ensures that, while the narrative may be over-read or under-read, it cannot be counter-read. This 'full-proof composition' engages the reader's sympathy to recognize not facile but coherent norms, and to judge accordingly (see Sternberg 1985: esp. pp. 41-57, 234-35).

Sternberg's study does not encompass New Testament narratives, which he regards as less subtle than their Hebrew precursors. But he raises an interesting general issue by suggesting that biblical narratives cannot be counterread. In the case of the Fourth Gospel, this seems not to be true, as the following discussion illustrates.

We know that the Gospel was popular in Christian Gnostic circles in the second and third centuries, and since we also know a good deal about Gnostic teachings from their own writings and from those of their opponents, it is not hard to see what occasioned that popularity and something of how Gnostics must have read the Fourth Gospel (see Wiles 1960: ch. 6). No doubt the opening of the Gospel, which encourages us to contemplate the eternal life of God and which is so unlike the beginnings of the Synoptic Gospels, provided Gnostics with an opportunity to fill out the brief Johannine intimations with more definite theological doctrines (e.g. *The Apocryphon of John*). But as the Prologue proceeds, it makes a statement which could have caused difficulty for any Gnostic. It asserts that 'the λόγος became or was flesh' (1.14). In my reading, this forms the first climax of the Prologue and is understood to draw attention to the vulnerability of the human being who embodied the λόγος. Since Gnostics taught that the eternal and transcendent could have nothing to do with temporal material existence, they would have placed 1.14 in the background or would have interpreted 'flesh' differently. For example, the second century Gnostic *Gospel of Philip* (ch. 23), interprets the 'flesh' mentioned in Jn 6.51-58 in this way: 'His flesh is the λόγος and his blood is the holy spirit'. Such an interpretation of 'flesh' in 1.14 would overcome its offensiveness to Gnostics (see also Irenaeus, *Against Heresies* 1.8.5). For them Jesus was really an emissary from the transcendent realm who only appeared to be a human being in order to impart his esoteric knowledge to others whose divinity had become entangled temporarily in an ultimately unreal material prison.

In reading the Fourth Gospel, therefore, they would interpret the miracles as signs of Jesus' divine origin, manifestations of his divine majesty and power (δόξα). His discourses, in which he sometimes speaks as the Wisdom of God, claiming, 'I am the light of the world' or 'I am the way, the truth and the life', would further evidence his transcendent nature. Gnostics would highlight the ways in which Jesus' special knowledge suggests he is not limited to normal human perceptions. He knows about his own origins and destiny and has insights into other peoples' characters and histories. His references to 'truth' would be understood to refer to transcendent reality (e.g. *The Gospel of Truth*).

Since Gnostics believed that Jesus was not really a human being, they naturally inferred that he could not die. They would have noticed that, compared to the Markan passion narrative, the Johannine account of Jesus' crucifixion lacks a sense of human agony and instead creates the atmosphere of a religious ceremony which Gnostics could interpret as a colourful account of Jesus' progress back to the transcendent realm. Finally, the resurrection narrative could be understood in metaphorical terms (e.g. *The Epistle of Rheginos*).

The Gnostic reading is diametrically opposed to my reading, which will follow in the rest of this book. I have to grant that the Gnostic reading has force, not least in drawing attention to the lack of realism in the Johannine portrait of Jesus. In the Fourth Gospel, Jesus reflects on the significance of his completed mission, even before he has finished it, and in this he becomes the mouthpiece of the author. Nevertheless, the Fourth Gospel seems deliberately to compensate for this peculiar feature by emphasizing Jesus' full humanity and vulnerability, even in the Prologue, while in the narrative, Jesus' dependence on God is constantly reiterated in his words, 'I can do nothing from myself'. What is stressed is Jesus' complete obedience to God, even in suffering death by crucifixion. So, in my reading, δόξα means not 'divine splendour' but the 'honour' appropriately accorded Jesus for his obedience. He is not honoured by most people, but he is honoured by the Father and by the disciples. When Jesus is utterly humiliated by his opponents, tortured to death in public on the cross, he is honoured by God and his obedience becomes exemplary for his followers: 'Greater love has no one than this, that a person lays down his life for his friends' (15.13).

Again, in my reading, 'truth' means 'genuineness' and 'fidelity', as it does in the Gospel's Scripture, rather than 'transcendent reality'. And Jesus' fidelity leads to a martyr's death. His last words from the cross, 'It is finished or completed' (19.30), represent his death as the climax of his mission. Chapter 20 provides the essential aftermath of this climax. God sets his seal on Jesus' obedience by raising him from the dead, and the resurrection appearance stories picture the transfer of responsibility for the mission from Jesus to his disciples, who are endowed with God's spirit as Jesus was.

I have contrasted my reading with a Gnostic reading to show that it is possible for texts to be understood in diametrically opposed ways. And it is not difficult to find at least a partial reason for the opposition. Most Gnostics did not accept the Jewish Scriptures as authoritative. Rather they understood them to provide knowledge of the creator of the world, who was not their transcendent God. They were therefore disinclined or unable to interpret the Fourth Gospel in the literary and theological context which Scripture provides. My reading, on the other hand, recognizes and argues for the Gospel's dependence on Scripture. It is Scripture which provides most of the vocabulary, literary motifs and theology.

Outside of a few Gnostic communities in California, modern commentators are inclined to reject Gnostic readings of the Fourth Gospel. I have used them to illustrate an extreme case: that counter-readings of the same text are possible. But anyone who compares my reading with those in modern commentaries by Barrett, Brown, Schnackenburg and Lindars, to mention only the most influential, will also notice marked disagreements. It is because I have become increasingly unconvinced by their readings that I have written my own. For example, all these commentaries use the word 'Incarnation' with a capital letter. But that word is used appropriately when referring to the orthodox doctrine which was formulated in the Chalcedonian Definition of the Faith in 451 CE. The Definition reads as follows:

> Following then the holy Fathers, we all unanimously teach that our Lord Jesus Christ is to us one and the same Son, the self-same perfect in Godhead, the self-same perfect in Manhood; truly God and truly man; the self-same of a rational soul and body; consubstantial with the Father according to the Godhead, the self-same consubstantial with us according to the manhood; like us in all things, sin apart; before the ages begotten of the Father as to the Godhead, but in the last days, the self-same, for

> us and our salvation, (born) of Mary the Virgin Theotokos as to the manhood; one and the same Christ, Son, Lord, only-begotten; acknowledged in two natures unconfusedly, unchangeably, indivisibly, inseparably; the differences of the natures being in no way removed because of the union, but rather the property of each nature being preserved, and (both) concurring into one πρόσωπον and one ὑπόστασις; not as though he were parted and divided into two πρόσωπα, but one and the self-same Son and only-begotten God, Word, Lord, Jesus Christ; even as from the beginning the prophets have taught concerning him, and as the Lord Jesus Christ himself has taught us, and as the symbol of the Fathers has handed down to us (see Bindley 1950: 234-34, 192-93).

It is clear that this doctrine of Christ's two natures depends on the doctrine of the Trinity and that 'Son of God' in the definition refers both to the eternal Son and to the man Jesus. This formulation represents the fruit of centuries of theological debate in a cultural environment in which Platonism and Stoicism both provoked new questions and provided new categories in which to formulate answers. This new context had already led to the development of a λόγος Christology which owed much more to Stoic and Platonic philosophy than to the Prologue of the Fourth Gospel (see Wiles 1960: 98-99). Moreover, once the Fourth Gospel was read in terms of Greek philosophy, as it was from the second century onwards, it could be taken for granted that 'Son of God' referred to Jesus' divinity. Although second and third century opponents of Gnosticism insisted that the Johannine Christ is human, they shared with Gnostics the view that he is divine. 'Father' and 'son' were no longer understood metaphorically in terms of the relationship between God and Israel or Israel's messiah, but in terms of a transcendent relationship. The ways in which this transcendent relationship was expressed varied through the third, fourth and fifth centuries, as different theological controversies brought different issues into sharp focus. At each stage, appeal was made to Johannine statements in support of a wide range of heretical views (see Wiles 1960: chs. 7 and 8). For example, in the fourth century, reading 'Son of God' in a transcendent sense seemed most obviously to bolster the Arian view, since the Gospel repeatedly emphasizes the Son's dependence on and subordination to the Father. Fifth-century commentators like Cyril of Alexandria tried to counter such views, while interpreting the Gospel to support their own side in the dispute over Christ's two natures.

Throughout these centuries the Fourth Gospel was read, not in its own terms, in its first-century historical context, but to provide answers to these new questions. Allegorical methods of interpretation, practised especially in Alexandria, allowed answers to be found.

In the twentieth century, we are much more aware of historical developments and the gaps these open up between old texts and later communities, and we are more inclined to try to read ancient texts in terms of the language and cultural realities at the time of their composition. We do not bridge the gap by means of allegorical interpretations. Nevertheless, most modern commentaries underestimate the breadth of the gap and telescope doctrinal developments. Their use of 'Incarnation' makes this clear. I do not think that they assume the Fourth Gospel encapsulates the doctrine of the two natures of Christ as defined exactly at Chalcedon, but they assert that the Johannine Christ is both divine and human. They interpret 'Son of God' to refer to the transcendent reality of God's eternal existence and make 'Son of God' synonymous with their interpretation of λόγος. They do not spell out, however, the implications of their assertions for the Johannine understanding of 'God' or 'humanity'.

The Johannine Prologue accepts its Scripture's conception of the transcendent God who creates all things, including human beings. People are understood as creatures, entirely dependent upon their creator. Moreover, human beings, including Jesus, are made of flesh, are vulnerable and mortal. It is precisely this difference between the transcendence of the Creator God and the creaturely nature of human beings which presented such problems for Christians, when they wanted to say that Jesus Christ is divine. They could do so, either by denying Jesus' humanity, as Docetism in all its popular forms did in the first four centuries, or by denying God's transcendence as the Arians did in the fourth century, or they could abandon Scripture and develop their own theologies and anthropologies as the Gnostics did. The formulation of the doctrine of Christ's two natures in the fifth century allowed Christians for the first time to assert that Jesus Christ is both God and man, without denying either God's transcendence or humanity's creatureliness.

Only two studies of the Fourth Gospel draw out clearly the implications of reading 'Son of God' as an attribution of divinity. Käsemann (1968) notices that to do so means that the Fourth Gospel is Docetic (see the criticisms of Käsemann's thesis by Thompson 1988).

Haenchen (1984) notices that to do so means that the Fourth Gospel is subordinationist.

In the book which follows, I shall argue that the Fourth Gospel's Christology is neither Docetic nor subordinationist because 'Son of God' refers to Jesus' status as a Jew and as the Jewish messiah, not to his divinity. 'Son of God' is not synonymous with λόγος. λόγος is the eternal expression of God's purpose. Jesus, the Son of God, is the human being whose whole life expresses that purpose because he is obedient to God. The Gospel's Christology is not subordinationist, as Haenchen asserts with his Arian predecessors, because Jesus' dependence on God is that of a human being, not of the second person of the Trinity.

Two other dissatisfactions with contemporary commentaries have prompted my writing this book. The first is that they share the Gospel's apparent anti-Judaism. Although they recognize that the Gospel's portrait of Judaism is inaccurate for the time of Jesus, they assert that it is accurate for the time when the Gospel was written. But what we know of Judaism during the first two centuries CE from its own sources suggests, on the contrary, that the Fourth Gospel's portrait, taken at face value, is a gross caricature. Judaism's twin concerns, to love God and to love fellow human beings, has much more in common with the Johannine depiction of its ideal community than the Fourth Gospel countenances. And how could it be otherwise, when both communities accepted the same Scripture as authoritative? For example, Jews recited and recalled the Shema morning and evening (*m. Ber.* 1.1-3):

> Hear O Israel; the Lord our God, the Lord is one; and you shall love the Lord your God with all your heart, and with all your soul, and with all your might. And these words which I command you this day shall be upon your heart; and you shall teach them diligently to your children, and you shall talk of them when you sit in your house, and when you walk by the way, and when you lie down, and when you rise. And you shall bind them as a sign upon your hand, and they shall be as frontlets between your eyes. And you shall write them on the doorposts of your house and on your gates (Deut. 6.4-9).

Josephus, the first-century Jewish historian, refers to the Jewish practices of acknowledging God's bounties at dawn and before sleep, and of inscribing 'the greatest of the benefits which they have received from God' on their doors, and displaying them on their arms and head, 'so that people may see on every side the loving care with which God surrounds them' (*Ant.* 4.212-13).

The Nash Papyrus (second or first century BCE) contains the Shema and the ten commandments. This single sheet seems to have served as a reminder of what was essential. And the ten commandments themselves summarize relationships between human beings and God, and amongst people (Exod. 20.1-17; Deut. 5.6-21). Leviticus 19 further summarizes relations between people, adding to those in the ten commandments requirements to leave gleanings from the harvest 'for the poor and the sojourner' (19.9-10), and to love the sojourner as yourself (19.34).

First-century Jewish writers therefore express these twin concerns. Philo, for example, places Jewish ancestral customs under two headings, 'one of duty to God as shown by piety and holiness, one of duty to people as shown by love of humanity and justice' (*Spec. Leg.* 2.63; see also *Rev. Div. Her.* 168-73). He goes on to explain that

> God asks nothing from you that is heavy or complicated or difficult, but only something quite simple and easy. And this is just to love Him. . . to serve Him. . . with your whole soul. . . and to cling to His commandments (*Spec. Leg.* 1.299-300)

and that 'the Law stands pre-eminent in enjoining fellowship and humanity' (*Spec. Leg.* 1.324). The second concern is also expressed negatively: 'What a man would hate to suffer he must not do to others' (*Hypothetica* 7.6; see Tob. 4.15).

Similarly, Josephus often links piety and justice (e.g. *Ant.* 9.16; 10.50; 18.117). His apologetic work, *Against Apion*, aims to demonstrate that 'we possess a code excellently designed to promote piety, friendly relations with each other, and humanity towards the world at large, besides justice, hardihood and contempt for death' (2.146). This code teaches 'not impiety, but the most genuine piety' and invites people 'not to hate their fellows, but to share their possessions', to become 'foes of injustices and scrupulous for justice' (2.291). Hence, at the sacrifices in the Temple, where Josephus had officiated as a priest before the war of 66-70 CE,

> prayers for the welfare of the community must take precedence over those for ourselves; for we are born for fellowship, and he who sets its claims above his private interests is specially acceptable to God. We should beseech God not to give us blessings, for He has given them spontaneously and

> put them at the disposal of all, but for capacity to receive, and, having received, to keep them (2.196-97, and see 2.211-214 which emphasizes consideration for enemies; see the discussion in Sanders 1990: 67-81).

Josephus, writing in Greek to educated pagans in the Graeco-Roman world, considered that this link between theology and ethics was uniquely conceived by Judaism. He explains:

> For Moses did not make religion a department of virtue, but the various virtues—I mean, justice, temperance, fortitude, and mutual harmony in all things between the members of the community—departments of religion. Religion governs all our actions and occupations and speech; none of these did our lawgiver leave unexamined or indeterminate (*Apion* 2.171).

It is precisely this conception of the relationship between theology and ethics which the Fourth Gospel adopts from its Scripture. Love of God determines love of fellow human beings.

What divided Jews and Christians was the question whether Jesus was the messiah. Since the Fourth Gospel asserts that Jesus is the messiah, albeit a messiah who has much more in common with the prophet Moses than the king David, and that his life, death and resurrection creates the pattern for a human life which is truly obedient to God, it incorporates a perception of the worth of human suffering and martyrdom which is more central than it is for Judaism, though Judaism, too, honours its martyrs. For the Fourth Gospel martyrdom is the hallmark of sonship and discipleship, the paradigm of what it means to love friends. For Judaism persecution is a temporary punishment by God for the infidelity of the people, borne not by those who are unfaithful, but by the righteous who will be rewarded at the resurrection (e.g. 2 Macc. 7). Judaism can therefore look backwards and forwards to times when loving God and neighbours does not require martyrdom, whereas the Fourth Gospel seems to exclude such a possibility from historical existence and reserve it for the post-mortem resurrection community.

From other New Testament writings, especially Paul's epistle to the Romans, chs. 9–11, we know that most Jews rejected Jesus' messiahship. Judaism continued and developed without reference to Jesus as the Christ. Although some Jews became Christians, soon the majority of Christians were non-Jews, converts and the children of converts from various Graeco-Roman cults. This Jewish rejection is dramatically depicted and polemically explained in the Fourth Gospel, in which 'Jews' oppose Jesus at every turn. Whether their reasons for doing so are correctly represented by the Fourth Gospel will be a matter for examination in Part III, but the fact of rejection affords the author the opportunity for presenting and countering opposition to Jesus within the narrative of Jesus' ministry.

The final dissatisfaction with most modern commentaries arises from the fact that commentators share the Gospel's patriarchal language and outlook and hence repeatedly refer to believers as masculine, and they fail to notice or discuss the restricted role which the Gospel assigns to women. Many of them are male clerics who belong to churches which deny to women the clerical function men perform. But not even Barrett, who belongs to a Methodist church which ordains women, seems to be aware that the patriarchal assumptions are alienating, even positively offensive to some women readers. Among the most influential commentators, only Brown (1979: Appendix 2) has corrected the male myopia of his earlier commentary by discussing the roles of women in the Fourth Gospel. Actually, he rather overcompensates by exaggerating their importance. In fact, to accept the Fourth Gospel's teaching as worthy of serious consideration, a twentieth-century western woman has to deny the subservient role the Gospel tries to foist on her, and to include herself alongside the male disciples as a fully responsible human agent. In doing this, however, women cannot overlook that the Fourth Gospel is one of many texts which has lent its authority to the subordination of women in societies where it has been read.

The study which follows is divided into three main parts. The first part seeks to elucidate the nature of the narrative itself in order to discover its literary strategies. The second part examines the content of the narrative, its theological themes and metaphors. The third part concerns historical reference and is structured by asking and answering what the text implies about the author and his knowledge of history, and about the original readers' role. These divisions are made for convenience and are essentially artificial. How a story is told determines what is foregrounded and what is backgrounded or omitted, and this affects the content. Similarly, any historical mistakes affect the persuasive force of the rhetoric.

Part I

Aspects of the Rhetoric of the Fourth Gospel

Chapter 1

FOCUS

The Fourth Gospel attempts to persuade readers to recognize the importance of Jesus of Nazareth, and, more precisely, to 'believe or continue to believe that Jesus is the Christ, the Son of God' (20.31). We shall be looking first at various ways in which it focuses its message, and we shall do this by answering questions like: who speaks and how? who sees and from what angles? The questions are answered under two main topics, recounting and representation, and perspective.

1. *Recounting and Representation*

Narratives may relate events more or less concretely. The more that physical characteristics are detailed, the more mimetic the effect, the more representational the narrative. Otherwise, the narrative merely recounts rather than represents what is told. Mimesis is achieved in narrative both by the description of the physical attributes of characters and places, and by the use of direct rather than indirect speech.

1.1. *Concentration on Speech rather than Appearance*

In the Fourth Gospel no depiction of the appearance of characters is allowed to distract from concentration on their speech. We remain ignorant of what Jesus looked like, how old he was, except that he was 'not yet fifty years old' (8.57), how he dressed, where he slept, what he ate. And this is equally true of all the other characters in the Gospel. Only the briefest identifying descriptions are given: that Jesus was from Nazareth, was a son of Joseph (1.45), that he accompanied his mother to a wedding at Cana (2.1-2) and afterwards stayed with her and his brothers in Capernaum (2.12); that the named disciples in ch. 1 are presumably Jews, some of whom came from Galilee (1.43); that Nicodemus was a Pharisee and ruler of the Jews in Jerusalem

(3.1); that John was baptizing at Bethany across the Jordan (1.28), then at Aenon near Salim (3.23); that a woman was a Samaritan from Sychar (4.5); that a royal official came from Capernaum to Cana in Galilee (4.46-47); that a man at the sheep pool in Jerusalem had been ill for 38 years (5.2-5); that Jesus' brothers, their number and names unspecified, lived in Galilee, went to Jerusalem for the Feast of Tabernacles, and did not believe in Jesus (7.1-5); that a man in Jerusalem had been blind from birth (9.1); that Lazarus lived with his sisters, Mary and Martha, in Bethany, near Jerusalem (11.1); and that Joseph was a Jewish disciple from Arimathea (19.38).

Similarly, the setting of incidents is indicated as briefly as possible, and in general only those details essential to the action or the dialogue are noted—in the hills by the Sea of Tiberias where no bread could be bought (6.1), at a wedding in Cana where there were six stone water-containers for Jewish purification (2.6), at Aenon near Salim where there was water for baptism (3.23), in the Temple courtyard where animals were sold and money exchanged (2.14), or in Jerusalem at the time when crowds were attending feasts (chs. 7–10, 12–20). It is difficult to discover any detail which is incidental to the account, and, because incidental, heightens the sense of representation.

Perhaps 5.2 contains details which are hardly necessary for an appreciation of the healing story: 'Now there is in Jerusalem by the sheep pool, that which in Hebrew is called Bethzatha, which has five porticoes'. (Some manuscripts read 'Bethzatha', others 'Bezatha', 'Belzetha', 'Bethsaida' or 'Bethesda', and it is impossible to discover which reading was original.) Marsh (1968) shows some ingenuity in finding a symbolic meaning for each detail—'Sheep gate' (his translation supplies the word 'gate') points forward to ch. 10 in which Jesus describes himself as the Good Shepherd (and also the Door, though Marsh misses this possible connexion), the five porticoes symbolize the 'five books of the law in which Jews should have found the way to fulness of life', the man's 38 years (5.5) mirror the 38 years of Israel's wanderings in the wilderness (Deut. 2.14), so that the whole section serves 'to contrast the barrenness and sterility of the Mosaic law in Jewish tradition, with the quickening, life-giving word of Jesus' (p. 250). These suggestions have failed to convince other commentators. It is likely that in this case the details provide, unusually, an exact location for the incident. Again, in 6.10, 'now there was much grass in the place' is an incidental detail which plays no important part in the story, but I have found no other examples. At 9.7 a translation of the Hebrew name 'Siloam, which means sent' seems to highlight the theme of Jesus' mission from the Father and his commission to disciples.

1.2. *Symbolic References to Time*

Similarly, when times are noted, they usually serve a symbolic function. Nicodemus visits Jesus at night and remains unenlightened (3.20), and Judas leaves the supper table at night to betray Jesus (13.30). The timing of the events in the final week of Jesus' life (chs. 12–19) relates his death to the sacrifice of the Passover lamb (see immediately below) and his resurrection to the third day, the decisive day which marks a new beginning, the first day of the week (chs. 20–21). There are, nevertheless, a few exceptions to this rule. Jn 4.6, 'Jesus, wearied as he was with his journey, sat down beside the well. It was about the sixth hour' could prefigure the time of the crucifixion (19.14), which depicts, more completely than the reference to Jesus' weariness here, the vulnerability of his existence, but it is more likely that his travelling at midday provides an explanation for his tiredness. In the same way, in 1.39, 'and they stayed with him that day, for it was about the tenth hour', the reference to the late afternoon explains why the disciples stayed with him. Similarly, 'it was winter' (10.23) confirms the progression of time between the Feast of Tabernacles in the autumn (7.1–10.21) and the Feast of Renewal (10.22).

1.3. *Gaps to Be Filled from Scripture*

There are, however, some surprising omissions of details. When Jewish feast are named, their ceremonies are not described, even when they provide the themes of discourses or are pertinent to details in the narrative. For example, of the features which link the sacrifice of the Passover lamb and Jesus' death, its timing (19.14), the presence of hyssop (19.29), the failure to break the bones of his legs (19.31-33) and the removal of the corpse before morning (19.38), only the third is made explicit (19.36) and the others have to be discovered from Exodus 12. These are gaps in the Johannine narrative which have to be filled from Scripture to provide a full understanding. By contrast, when incidents are depicted on the Sabbath, the narrative makes plain on each occasion that Jews were forbidden to work, but that Jesus did not allow the prohibition to interfere with his ministry (5.9-10; 9.13-17). This detail is, however, necessary to explain the disputes which arose from the incidents.

1.4. *Dialogue and Monologue*

The general absence of descriptive details allows concentration on what is said by the characters, rather than what is seen. The narrative is dominated by dialogue and monologue. There are few examples of indirect speech (e.g. 4.47, 51-52; 12.12, 29; 13.29; 18.14, 27; 20.18; 21.23) and some of these recap what had already been given in direct speech (e.g. 18.14, 27; 20.18). The attribution of direct speech makes a formal distinction between narrator and character, and creates a more immediate and mimetic effect, but characters in the Fourth Gospel do not use their own peculiar vocabulary or style of speech. Even the main character, Jesus, does not talk in a way which distinguishes his words from the narrator's. His discourses explain key terms from the narrator's Prologue: life, light, witness, the world, true and truth, believing, his own and honour. These same terms are used by other characters: life by Peter (6.68); witness by John (1.34); world by the Samaritans (4.42), the 'Jews' (6.14), Jesus' brothers (7.4) and the Pharisees (12.19); truth and true by the crowds about John (10.41) and by Pilate (18.38); believing by the Samaritans (4.42), the crowd (6.30), Peter (6.69), the man born blind (9.36, 38), Martha (11.27), and the disciples (16.30); and honour by the 'Jews' who question the man born blind (9.24).

Sometimes, characters use the same term in slightly different ways, which allows for various nuances to be explored. For example, the crowd in 6.30 challenges Jesus: 'Then what sign do you do, that we may see and *believe* you? What work do you perform?', showing by their question that they had not perceived the significance of the feeding miracle or the walking on the water (6.1-21). They request the kind of sign which would force them to believe, but forced belief is not what Jesus requires. Rather, his mission is to inspire faith like that which Peter voices after the crowds and even some of the disciples had abandoned Jesus at the end of his Galilaean ministry, when he had hinted at his imminent death in his remarks about giving his flesh (6.52-58). Peter declares, 'You have the words of eternal life; and *we have believed* and have come to know that you are the Holy One of God' (6.68-69). This faith is more than trust in an otherwise unknown benefactor. It is recognition of who Jesus is.

There are, moreover, genuine disagreements and misunderstandings in the dialogues. Johannine dialogues sometimes convey a sense of talking at cross purposes, as Jesus' discussion with Nicodemus well illustrates (3.1-15). Nicodemus fails to grasp the significance of Jesus' statements about being born again or born from above. The misunderstandings allow Jesus to define his meaning more clearly. The same technique, but with more success, is used in Jesus' discussions with the Samaritan woman (4.7-26) and with the disciples in the farewell discourses (chs. 14–16).

In other discussions, the meanings of key terms are shared by the participants, but they dispute their application. For example, in ch. 8, the 'Jews' claim that Abraham is their father (8.39) and that God is their father (8.41) but Jesus denies the claims and instead asserts that they are the children of the devil (8.39-47). The 'Jews' reply that Jesus is a Samaritan and has a demon (8.48). In this dialogue the terms are unambiguous. Both parties accept the language used and understand its meaning. The dispute arises over the correct reference of the terms.

Both forms of dialogue serve to enhance the reader's understanding, either by elucidating Jesus' teaching, or by countering opposing views. Both create a unity of discourse and the dominance of a single all-encompassing perspective.

Most of the dialogues present only two interlocutors. Sometimes these are individuals, like Jesus and Nicodemus (3.1-15), or Philip and Nathanael (1.45-46), or Mary and Martha (11.28). Sometimes one or both of the interlocutors is represented by a group, like the brothers of Jesus (7.3), the Pharisees (8.13), the 'Jews' (8.48), the disciples (9.2) or groups within the crowd (7.11-13). This kind of dramatic concretization also occurs in the Synoptics, but where the Fourth Gospel differs from the Synoptics is in its expansion of the drama into a succession of related scenes. For example, in ch. 4, there is the first scene of dialogue between Jesus and the Samaritan woman (4.7-26), then the second between the woman and her fellow citizens (4.28-30), then the third between Jesus and the returned disciples (4.31-38) and then the final scene between the woman and her fellow citizens after they had met Jesus (4.40-42). In ch. 9 there is the first scene of dialogue between Jesus and his disciples (9.2-5), then the second scene of Jesus' instructions to the man born blind (9.6-7), then the third scene of dialogue between the neighbours (9.8-9) whose questions are resolved by the man himself (9.9), then the fourth between the man and his neighbours (9.9-12), the fifth between two groups of Pharisees and the man (9.13-17), the sixth between the 'Jews' and the man's parents (9.18-23), the seventh between the 'Jews' and the man (9.24-34) and the final scene of dialogue between Jesus and the man (9.35-38). This whole series of scenes then leads into further dialogue between Jesus and the Pharisees (9.40–10.21). Although the Synoptics sometimes provide Jesus with relatively long discourses (e.g. Mk 4; Mt. 13 and 5–7; Lk. 8.4-18 and 6.20-49), only in the passion narratives do we find a similar extended series of dramatic scene shifts.

Since the speech of one character is only distinguished from that of another by formal attribution, not by vocabulary and style, it is sometimes difficult to decide whether sections should be read as the words of a character or as a comment by the narrator. For example, in ch. 3 it is unclear whether Jesus' discourse to Nicodemus ends in v. 15 or v. 21. Again, John's speech in the same chapter could end at v. 30 or v. 36. In any case, the statements in vv. 31-36, whether from John or the narrator, develop themes introduced by Jesus in his private conversation with Nicodemus in vv. 3-15.

The absence of descriptive details concentrates attention on the dialogues and monologues. The preponderance of direct speech, especially in dialogues, makes the presentation dramatic, but, because no distinctions are made between the speech patterns of different exponents, each speech or narrator's reflection serves to explore the themes which the Gospel presents. Each develops the message that Jesus is the Christ, the Son of God, a message which those who are attuned to God's purpose are depicted accepting.

1.5. *Filling in Gaps from Other Sources*

I have already noted (§1.3) that the text requires readers to fill in gaps about Jewish feasts from Scripture. We have also seen that the text does not provide descriptions which distract the reader from what is said (§1.1). Descriptions of the characters cannot be filled out from other documents, however, because even when the same characters are mentioned elsewhere in the New Testament, or in other writings of the period, like those of Flavius Josephus, little or nothing is said about appearances. These are blanks which can be filled only by imagination or by our general knowledge of the lives of people in the first century CE. The text itself discourages such concretization. Geographical details can sometimes be supplied, although some of the sites mentioned in the Gospel, like Bethany across the Jordan (1.28) or Aenon (3.23), cannot be identified with certainty. Nevertheless, in general, the geography of Galilee, Samaria and Judaea can be reconstructed from the evidence available, as well as details about Nazareth, Capernaum and especially Jerusalem, which was dominated by the Temple buildings, as a glimpse at a historical atlas will demonstrate. According to the Fourth Gospel, the Temple provides the background to much of Jesus' activity in Jerusalem (2.14; 5.14; 7.14; 10.23), but it is Josephus's descriptions which have to be consulted to gain any sense of its plan, size or splendour, in spite of the fact that the Gospel presupposes its stupendous dimensions in the rhetorical question of the 'Jews': 'It has taken 46 years to build this temple; and will you raise it up in three days?' (2.20). Nor is any explanation given for the presence of animals and money changers in the Temple, even when they afford Jesus the opportunity of demonstrating his zeal (2.14-17). We have to surmise that animals were provided so that pilgrims would not have to take them to Jerusalem when they wanted to offer sacrifices, and that money changers provided a service which made possible the payment of the Temple tax, in a situation in which various currencies of various values were in use. The Fourth Gospel concentrates on impressing readers with a sense of Jesus' dignity, and does not elaborate alternative sources of wonder. Perhaps this helps to explain why the Johannine Jesus, unlike the Matthaean, never gives positive teaching about sacrifice, the Temple tax or tithing. The Fourth Gospel mentions incidentally that 'Jews' going to Jerusalem for Passover purified themselves (11.55) and that they sought to avoid defilement (18.28), but nothing is said about Jesus' purifying himself before entering the Temple, in spite of his close proximity to the dead in the story of Lazarus. Corpse impurity required a seven-day ritual of purification (Num. 19). Jesus' own teaching about purity in the Fourth Gospel seems to use the word in its metaphorical sense (e.g. 13.10-11; 15.3).

There are other gaps in the narrative, too, which are perhaps even more surprising to modern readers. The Fourth Gospel presupposes but rarely explains the political, social and economic circumstances of Palestine at the time when Caiaphas was high priest, and Pilate was present in Jerusalem, his office unspecified, but his power over life and death emphasized (18.31; 19.10). We know, from other references in the New Testament and from Josephus, that Herod Antipas was tetrarch of Galilee and Perea at the time, but the Fourth Gospel does not mention him. For information about the political power structure in Galilee and Perea, and Judaea and Samaria, where Roman rule was imposed through a Herodian puppet or the high priest, who could sometimes mitigate its effects, but who could not entirely remove the heavy burden of taxation to Rome, we have to look to Roman sources or to Josephus once more. The social repercussions, especially the increasing divisions between rich and poor, are unremarked in the Fourth Gospel, although they are often repeated in stories from the Synoptic Gospels (e.g. Mt. 18.23-35; 20.1-16; 25.14-30 and parallels), where warnings about the distracting dangers of riches are common (e.g. Mt. 6.19-21, 24; 19.16-22 and parallels). No clear indication about how Jesus financed his mission is provided by any source, however, in spite of the intriguing statement in Jn 12.6 that Judas 'had the money box' and that 'he used to take what was put into it'. The reference suggests that Jesus and the disciples shared expenses, but only Lk. 8.3 indicates that Jesus' mission was sometimes supported by women who had been healed.

Something of the social tensions between men and women, and between Jews and Samaritans, is indicated in the story of the Samaritan woman (4.9 and 27), but otherwise only the vaguest impression of Jewish social life emerges. Unlike the Synoptics, the Fourth Gospel gives no teaching about divorce or about family relations. Jewish groups like the Essenes, the Zealots, the Sadducees, the Herodians and the scribes, mentioned by Josephus and, in some cases, by the Synoptics, do not appear in the Fourth Gospel. The word 'council' is used in 11.47 to describe a meeting called by chief priests and Pharisees, and these two groups constitute the sole leadership of Jews according to John. Distinctions between various opponents of Jesus have disappeared, and the Fourth Gospel is often content to describe them simply as 'Jews'. This vagueness makes the Gospel an unrewarding source for modern historians who want to reconstruct either the history of the period depicted and Jesus' role in it, or to ascertain the historical circumstances of the author or readers implied by the narrative, as we shall see in Part III.

Moreover, there are even gaps in the narrative about the twin aspects of Jesus' public ministry, healing and teaching. For example, we are told that when Jesus was in Jerusalem 'many believed in his name when they saw the *signs* which he did' (2.23), but at this stage Jesus had performed only one recorded sign, at Cana in Galilee, and none in Jerusalem. The first account of a miracle in Jerusalem is found in ch. 5. Again, in ch. 6, we are told that by the Sea of Tiberias in Galilee 'a multitude followed him because they saw the signs which he did on those who were sick' (6.2), but only one miracle of healing had been recorded in Galilee (4.46-54). In each case, we have to assume that Jesus performed miracles which are not described. Similarly, when Nicodemus first meets Jesus he asserts, 'Rabbi, we know that you are a teacher come form God' (3.2), yet the only public teaching of Jesus so far given is his enigmatic promise, 'Destroy this temple and in three days I will raise it up' (2.19). Again, in response to Annas's question, Jesus claims to have taught openly in *synagogues* (18.20), but only ch. 6 sets any of his teaching in a synagogue (6.59).

These features tie in with others in the Fourth Gospel which suggest that the narrative relates a story already familiar to its readers, who are in a position to fill in these gaps. For example, John is assumed to be a baptizer (1.25) before readers are told that he was baptizing (1.28), and his baptismal ministry is never explained. Later, in 3.24, we are told that 'John had not yet been put in prison', a statement which assumes that the reader knows he will be imprisoned, although when and why is never mentioned. The Fourth Gospel, unlike the Synoptics, does not include an account of his death. Moreover, in 3.26, John is addressed as 'Rabbi', which the Gospel interprets as 'teacher' (1.38), but the only teaching given by John is that which relates to his own and Jesus' identities. Unlike the Synoptics, the Fourth Gospel does not depict John as a preacher of repentance.

Similarly, the disciples Andrew and Simon Peter are introduced as if they are already well known: 'One of the two who heard John speak and followed him [Jesus] was Andrew, Simon Peter's brother' (1.40). And in this verse, Simon is called Peter before Jesus gives him the nickname (1.42). Again, in ch. 11, Mary is introduced as the woman who anointed Jesus (11.2) before that incident is described in 12.1-8.

Once we recognize that the Fourth Gospel *retells* a story already familiar to readers, we are no longer puzzled by the many gaps. The story is retold to emphasize the theological significance of Jesus' life, rather than to provide a full biography. Hence, there is no sense of the historical development of his ministry. We are told nothing about cultural or family influences on the young Jesus which prompted him to define his role in society. Nor are we told about earlier and later conceptions of his ministry. Each of the incidents recorded helps the reader to understand the significance of Jesus' entire life, rather than his psychological or social development. In this the Fourth Gospel conforms to ancient rather than modern depictions of a person's life. Ancient depictions of individuals are descriptions of character types (see Wiedemann 1989: 50). Hence, the order of incidents is determined by the impression they make on the reader rather than by an interest in historical sequence. For example, Jesus' teaching in ch. 7 at the Feast of Tabernacles in the autumn begins by justifying his healing on the Sabbath, recorded in ch. 5, which, according to the chronological order, happened before the Passover in the spring mentioned in 6.4, that is at least six months earlier. Similarly, at the Feast of Renewal in the winter (10.22), Jesus' teaching refers to his 'sheep' (10.26-28), picking up the imagery from his discourse in 10.1-18, which was set at the Feast of Tabernacles in the autumn. Only the reader can easily make these connexions, not the characters within the story. It is the exposition of theological themes for the reader which determines the order. The sense of a plot is created only by the reactions of acceptance or rejection of Jesus, which reach their climax in the passion narrative. The whole Gospel is a preparation for the correct theological understanding of Jesus' crucifixion.

2. *Perspective*

2.1. *The Omniscient Narrator*

A second way in which a narrative is focused is through the narrator. There can be many different kinds of narrators. Some are characters within the story whose perspective is limited, some are reliable, others unreliable. Some, like the narrator of the Fourth Gospel, are both omniscient and reliable. He is not an outside observer of personalities who know more about themselves than he does. On the contrary, he knows more than a character within a story could be expected to know. The Prologue presumes knowledge of God's eternal existence and of his purpose in creation, and the narrator records events in the story in terms of this insight. In illustrating the outcome of the Prologue, the structure of the story exemplifies the narrator's knowledge, and the explanatory intrusions confirm his understanding, as in the comment in 12.43: 'For they loved the honour of people more than the honour of God'.

2.2. *The Omniscient Narrator's Knowledge of Characters*

The narrator has inside information about his characters' beliefs, understanding and emotions. He does not have to infer them merely from their behaviour, nor is he in any doubt about their unexpressed thoughts or perceptions.

a. Of the disciples, he knows when and what they believe:

> And his disciples believed in him (2.11).

> When, therefore, he was raised from the dead, his disciples remembered that he had said this, and they believed the Scripture and the saying which Jesus had spoken (2.22).

> Then the other disciple, who reached the tomb first, also went in, and he saw and believed (20.8).

He is aware of their suppositions: 'Some thought that, because Judas had the money box, Jesus was telling him, "Buy what we need for the feast"; or that he should give something to the poor' (13.29). He knows when and what they remember, so that they come to a new understanding in retrospect, as in 2.22 above, or in 12.16: 'His disciples did not understand this at first; but when Jesus was honoured, then they remembered that this had been written of him and had been done to him', or in 20.9: 'for as yet they did not know the Scripture that he must rise from the dead'. And he recognizes when they are startled: 'Just then his disciples came. They marvelled that he was talking with a woman, but none said, "What do you wish?" or "Why are you talking with her?"' (4.27), and when they are glad: 'Then they were glad to take him into the boat' (6.21) or 'Then the disciples were glad when they saw the Lord' (20.20).

b. Of Jesus, the narrator identifies what he perceives and knows:

> Perceiving then that they were about to come and take him by force to make him king, Jesus withdrew again to the mountain by himself (6.15).

> But Jesus, knowing in himself that the disciples murmured at it, said to them, 'Do you take offence at this?' (6.61).

> For Jesus knew from the first who those were who did not believe, and who it was that would betray him (6.64).

> This he said to test him, for he himself knew what he would do (6.6).

> When Jesus knew that his hour had come to depart out of the world to the Father. . . Jesus, knowing that the Father had given all things into his hand, and that he had come from God and was going to God. . . (13.1, 3).

> After this, Jesus knowing that all was now finished, said, to fulfill Scripture, 'I thirst' (19.28).

He knows whom Jesus loves: 'Now Jesus loved Martha, and her sister, and Lazarus' (11.5), 'Having loved his own who were in the world, he loved them to the end' (13.1), 'One of his disciples, whom Jesus loved' (13.23 and 19.26; 20.2; 21.7, 20). He discerns when Jesus is disturbed or troubled: 'When Jesus saw her weeping, and the Jews who came with her also weeping, he was deeply moved in spirit and troubled' (11.33), 'Then Jesus, deeply moved again, came to the tomb' (11.38).

c. The narrator presents similar interior views of other characters. He knows that neither Jesus' brothers nor the 'Jews' believe in him: 'For even his brothers did not believe in him' (7.5), 'Though he had done so many signs before them, yet they did not believe in him' (12.37). On the other hand, the royal official and some of the authorities do believe in him:

> The man believed the saying which Jesus spoke to him and went his way (4.50).

> And he himself believed and all his household (4.53).

> Nevertheless, many even of the authorities believed in him, but for fear of the Pharisees they did not confess it (12.42).

He understands that Joseph, too, is a secret disciple: 'Joseph of Arimathea, who was a disciple of Jesus, but secretly, for fear of the Jews' (19.38). He is aware of the feeble man's ignorance about Jesus: 'Now the man who had been healed did not know who it was, for Jesus had withdrawn' (5.13). He recognizes that the 'Jews' or the Pharisees often fail to understand what Jesus says: 'They did not understand that he spoke to them of the Father' (8.27), 'This figure Jesus used with them, but they did not understand what he was saying to them' (10.6). And he knows what they suppose: 'When the Jews who were with her in the house, consoling her, saw Mary rise quickly and go out, they followed her, supposing that she was going to the tomb to weep there' (11.31). And as he has knowledge of God, so he has knowledge of the devil's manoeuvres: 'When the devil had already put it into the heart that Judas Iscariot, Simon's son, would betray him' (13.2), 'Then, after the morsel, Satan entered into him' (13.27).

In spite of this access to private information, however, it would be misleading to suggest that this narrator is interested in the psychology of his characters, as most modern narrators are. He is really interested in whether people believe in Jesus or not, and whether they are good or bad.

2.3 *The Omniscient Narrator's Knowledge of Character's Plans, Reasons and Motives*

Because of this interest, however, he does identify characters' plans, reasons and motives. He knows why Jesus remains in Galilee: 'After this, Jesus went about in Galilee; he did not go about in Judaea, because the Jews sought to kill him' (7.1). He recognizes what the disciples dare not ask: 'Now none of the disciples dared ask him "Who are you?" They knew it was the Lord' (21.12). He realizes why the disciples leave Jesus alone at the well: 'For his disciples had gone away into the city to buy food' (4.8). 'Fear of the Jews' he often offers as an explanation of people's behaviour (7.13; 9.22; 12.42; 19.8, 38; 20.19). He makes plain that the 'Jews' seek to kill Jesus and why: 'This is why the Jews were seeking all the more to kill him, because he not only used to break the sabbath but also used to call God his own Father, making himself equal with God' (5.18); why the chief priests and Pharisees send officers to arrest him: 'The Pharisees heard the crowd thus muttering about him, and the chief priests and Pharisees sent officers to arrest him' (7.32 and 44); and that some are motivated by a desire for human honour rather than God's (12.43). He knows what persuaded the 'Jewish' council to destroy Jesus:

> 'If we let him go on thus, everyone will believe in him, and the Romans will come and destroy our holy place and our nation.' But one of them, Caiaphas, who was high priest that year, said to them, 'You know nothing at all; you do not understand that it is expedient that one man should die for the people, and that the whole nation should not perish'. . . So from that day on, they took counsel how to put him to death (11.48-53).

'Jewish' reluctance to go into the praetorium is explained: 'They themselves did not enter the praetorium, so that they might not be defiled, but might eat the Passover' (18.28), as is their request to have the corpses removed from the crosses: 'In order to prevent the bodies from remaining on the cross on the sabbath (for that sabbath was a high day), the Jews asked Pilate that their legs might be broken, and that they might be taken away' (19.31). Even the presence of the fire in the courtyard is accounted for: 'Now the servants and officers had made a charcoal fire, because it was cold' (18.18). He is aware of why the chief priests plan to put Lazarus to death:

> When the great crowd of the Jews learned that he was there, they came not only on account of Jesus, but also to see Lazarus, whom he had raised from the dead. So the chief priests planned to put Lazarus to death too (12.9-10).

He knows that Judas would betray Jesus: 'Judas Iscariot, one of the twelve, he who was to betray him' (12.4), and that his is the work of the devil (13.27). The reason why Joseph and Nicodemus place Jesus' corpse in a nearby tomb is also explained: 'So, because of the Jewish day of preparation, as the tomb was close at hand, they laid Jesus there' (19.42).

All this information could have been given through the direct speech of the characters depicted, and generally the Gospel prefers direct speech. In most of these instances, however, the characters keep their plans and motives private.

2.4. *The Omniscient Narrator's Knowledge of Statements' Significance*

An interesting feature of the narrator's omniscience is the way in which he sees what characters mean by what they say, even when the audience within the story fails to understand.

> Jesus answered them, 'Did I not choose you, the twelve, and one of you is a devil?' He spoke of Judas, the son of Simon Iscariot, for he, one of the twelve, was to betray him (6.71).

> But he spoke of the temple of his body (2.21).

> Now this he said about the Spirit, which those who believed in him were to receive; for as yet the Spirit (had not been given), because Jesus was not yet honoured (7.39).

> Now Jesus had spoken of his [Lazarus's] death, but they thought that he meant taking rest in sleep (11.13).

> He said this to show by what death he was to die (12.33).

> He [Caiaphas] did not say this of his own accord, but being high priest that year he prophesied that Jesus should die for the nation, and not for the nation only, but to gather into one the children of God who are scattered abroad (11.51-52).

> This he [Judas] said, not that he cared for the poor, but because he was a thief, and as he had the money box, he used to take what was put into it (12.6).

> Isaiah said this because he saw his honour and spoke of him (12.41).

Perhaps related to this are those instances in which he indicates when words or actions fulfil scripture or one of Jesus' prophecies:

> This was to fulfil the saying which he had spoken, 'Of those whom you gave me, I lost not one' (18.9; cf. 17.12).

> This was to fulfil the saying Jesus had spoken to show by what death he was to die (18.32; cf. 12.32).

> This was to fulfil the scripture, they parted my garments among them, and for my clothing they cast lots (19.24).

> He said, to fulfil scripture, 'I thirst' (19.28).

> For these things took place that the Scripture might be fulfilled, Not a bone of him shall be broken. And again another scripture says, They shall look upon him whom they have pierced (19.36-37).

> It was that the saying spoken by the prophet Isaiah might be fulfilled, Lord who has believed our report. . . (12.38).

> Therefore they could not believe, for Isaiah again said, He has blinded their eyes. . . (12.39-40).

On one occasion, he interprets Jesus' words about Peter's death, and this is one of the few instances in which, outside of Jesus' direct speech, the narrator shows independent knowledge of a future beyond the story related: 'This he said to show by what death he [Peter] was to honour God' (21.19). Elsewhere, the narrator indicates that the disciples understood the significance of Jesus' actions and teachings after his death (e.g. 2.22; 12.16), at a time which does not come within the compass of the story.

It is because the narrator knows more than most characters that their remarks can carry both a straightforward and an ironical meaning. 'Are you greater than our father Abraham who died? And the prophets died. What do you claim to be?' (8.53-54) is both a question to Jesus in the story and a true indication that Jesus is greater than Abraham and the prophets. Thomas's 'Let us also go that we may die with him' (11.16) and Peter's 'Lord, why can I not follow you now? I will lay down my life for you' (13.37) are both empty promises in the story and characterizations of true discipleship (15.12-14). Caiaphas's advice, 'It is expedient that one man should die for the people and that the whole nation should not perish' (11.50) is both a cynical, political remark in the story and a true elucidation of the significance of Jesus' death, an ironical meaning which is so important in the narrative that it is made explicit (11.51-52) and referred to again later (18.14).

2.5. *Characters' Attitudes to Jesus*

The narrator, then, is separate from and has more knowledge than most of the characters. Through the individual incidents, he depicts the characters' reactions to Jesus, commitment or hostility to him, and in this way guides the reader's response. The 'Jews', and especially their leaders, the Pharisees and chief priests, soon harden into Jesus' opponents set on destroying him. The crowds are usually bemused (chs. 7–10), so that their reactions oscillate between enthusiastic but uncomprehending affirmation of Jesus' messiahship (6.15; 12.12-13) and violent repudiation (8.59; 10.31, 39). The Pharisees, who are portrayed as controlling and therefore excluding from the synagogue (12.42 and perhaps 9.34), are consistently antagonistic to Jesus (chs. 7–10; ch. 18). Together with the chief priests, they seek to arrest him and take counsel to condemn him to death in his absence (11.47-53). The chief priests are even prepared to kill Lazarus (12.10) since the miracle of his resuscitation has increased Jesus' popularity. They play an increasingly important role in the passion narrative, organizing Jesus' arrest (18.3), subjecting him to preliminary questioning (18.13), and handing him over to Pilate (18.28). They are the first to call for Jesus' crucifixion (19.6) and are led by events to confess 'We have no king but Caesar' (19.15). Their final act is to ask Pilate to change his notice over the cross, 'Jesus of Nazareth, the King of the Jews' (19.21).

Nicodemus is the only named character who fails to make a decision, remaining the good but puzzled observer who tries to prevent injustice (7.51) and who joins Joseph at Jesus' burial, paying homage when Jesus is safely dead (19.39). Like the unnamed man healed at the pool (5.1-15), he never recognizes Jesus' true worth. On the other hand, the questions raised by the Samaritan woman (4.29) prompt the Samaritans to respond positively to Jesus, finally acknowledging him as messiah and saviour of the world (4.42). Similarly, the man blind from birth at first recognizes Jesus as a prophet from God and then as the Son of man (9.17, 38).

The disciples, and after 6.67, the twelve, serve the function of defining an adequate response to Jesus. Their first confessions in ch. 1 suggest something of Jesus' importance but show no awareness of his destiny. Gradually, all except Judas come to accept Jesus as the messiah who must suffer (6.66-71). During his ministry they sometimes fail to see the point of his words and actions but understand him in retrospect after his death (2.22; 12.16). They lack courage in the face of danger, in spite of their promises, and leave Jesus to be arrested alone (18.8-12). Peter denies him (18-25-27). But finally, they are commissioned by the risen Jesus in an act of recreation (20.22 cf. Gen. 2.7).

John the Baptist also bears witness to his belief in Jesus but there is no development of his faith (1.31-34). From the beginning he assesses accurately his own role as witness to someone greater who will supercede him (1.19-37), immediately confirming the narrator's estimate of him in the Prologue (1.6-9, 15). Divine inspiration had made John aware of how to recognize his successor, and when the events took place, he was able to describe them as part of his confession that Jesus is both lamb and Son or chosen one of God (1.29, 34). Later, he confesses Jesus' messiahship (3.28).

2.6. *Jesus' Omniscience*

Although the narrative is not focused through any of the characters, it is focused *on* Jesus. This focus is sharpened by the fact that, unlike others in the story, Jesus has unlimited knowledge. He is the only character who shares the narrator's and God's omniscience. Jesus' understanding of other characters is as intrusive as the narrator's. He immediately recognizes the true qualities of everyone (2.25), and this is illustrated in his response to individuals. He nicknames Simon Cephas, the rock (1.42), he calls Nathanael 'a true Israelite in whom is no guile' (1.47), he knows about the Samaritan woman's marital status (4.16-18), and he notices the extreme feebleness of the lame man at the pool (5.6-9). Like the narrator, he knows what others are thinking

(6.61) and who does not believe in him (6.64; 7.6-7), even though he is absent when doubts are expressed (20.24-29). He understands people's desires (16.19). He identifies the puzzlement of the crowds when it is not openly expressed to him (7.28). He is aware of 'Jewish' plans to kill him (7.19). From ch. 7 onwards his own plans are circumscribed by theirs, so that twice he has to withdraw from their territory (10.39-40; 11.54) before finally deciding to go to his death in Jerusalem at Passover time (12.1). He knows that Judas will betray him (13.18-30; 17.12) and sees this as the work of the devil (6.70). Like the narrator's, Jesus' knowledge is confirmed as the story unfolds. His predictions about the manner of his death (12.32) and about the disciples' escape (17.12), Peter's denial (13.38) and Judas' betrayal (13.18-30) are fulfilled in the story.

Even more importantly, he has knowledge of his origin from the Father and refers to himself as one sent by the Father to carry out a particular mission (5.19-47; 7-10), which involves acting as God's agent in bringing life, light and judgment. He sees the necessity of his death from the beginning of his ministry (3.14-16; 10; 12.32-33) and understands that his death completes his mission (19.28).

Jesus' teaching about the future includes not only future events which are related in the story, but also descriptions of discipleship in a future beyond the story. The farewell discourses (chs. 14–16) predict both the horror of persecution and the joy of belief and give assurances about another helper who will guide them, the spirit of truth. Briefly, too, Jesus glimpses the disciples' eschatological resurrection (6.39, 40, 44, 54) and their final dwelling with the Father (14.2).

This agreement between the narrator's omniscient perspective and that of his chief protagonist, Jesus, adds enormously to the didactic power of the narrative. A single vision is doubly reinforced (see Culpepper 1983: 34-43).

2.7. *Omnipresence and Retrospection*

Although the narrator is omniscient and has access to people's thoughts, most of the information he supplies takes the form of observations of the scenes depicted. Yet his position in any scene cannot be pinpointed exactly. He sees everything he needs to see and is not limited to a particular place. For example, in the account of Jesus' trial by Pilate, the narrator can describe what took place between Jesus and Pilate within the praetorium and what happened between

Pilate and the crowds outside the praetorium (18.28–19.16). The narrator is omnipresent. What he tells readers is determined by his own interests and theirs, not by partial observation.

The sense of the narrator's complete control of the story, exemplified by his omniscience and omnipresence, is also intensified by his retrospective view. The events which he describes took place in the past and he relates them in the past tenses of the Greek language. He is therefore in a position to create a coherent narrative which omits less salient features of the story in favour of highlighting what is important for understanding, as he explains to readers:

> Now Jesus did many other signs in the presences of his disciples, which are not written in this book, but these are written that you may believe or continue to believe that Jesus is the Christ, the Son of God, and that continuing to believe you may have life in his name (20.30-31).

2.8. *Omniscience and Omnipotence*

Both the narrator and Jesus are omniscient, but they are not omnipotent. Their power is limited to the art of persuasion. Both Jesus within the story and the narrator in telling the story attempt to bring the audience to a new insight, a new perception of reality which is different from that presupposed by Jewish, Hellenistic, Roman or most other cultures. They try to persuade people to see that God gives insight, superabundance, life, even to the dead, and that his creative purpose is visible in Jesus' life and even in Jesus' death on a cross. The cross is a paradigm of God's love for humanity, as well as of human obedience to God. The cross is also a demonstration of impotence, of Jesus' failure to persuade those who held power in society that his teaching and activity exemplified his messiahship. The narrator seeks to mitigate Jesus' failure by retelling the story persuasively, with the help of hindsight.

Although both Jesus' and the narrator's power is limited, does not the Fourth Gospel picture God as omnipotent? In a sense it does. God is the source of all existence, so that without God's creative power nothing would exist (1.1-5). Nevertheless, the God of the Fourth Gospel does not exercise this power in ways familiar to human beings in their dominance of fellow human beings. God does not force people to live in obedient conformity to his will, since the Gospel makes clear that many reject his offer of life. Logically, the Gospel seems to assert two contradictory views. On the one hand, nothing happens in the world without God allowing it to happen. Indeed, God is even responsible for giving faith in Jesus to his followers: 'No one can come to me unless the Father who sent me draws him' (6.44). On the other hand, only once does the Gospel state, as some Old Testament narratives do, that people's hardness of heart is also an expression of God's power (12.40, quoting Isaiah). Rather, the rejection of God's offer of life is entirely humanity's responsibility and contrary to God's purpose:

> For God so loved the world that he gave his only Son, that whoever believes in him should not perish but have eternal life. For God sent the Son into the world, not to condemn the world, but that the world might be saved through him. . . He who does not believe is condemned already because he has not believed in the name of the only Son of God. And this is the judgment, that the light has come into the world and men loved darkness rather than light, because their deeds were evil (3.16-19).

In the Gospel, God's power is exercised only in one direction, only in bringing life from death, as Jesus' resurrection finally demonstrates. But humanity remains free to decide whether it prefers to safeguard its own life, or to accept the offer of life from God. To accept is to give up its own security now and to face persecution and possibly death, as Jesus did, for the sake of life after death.

It seems, then, that God's power in the world is limited to sending agents like the prophets, John, Jesus and his disciples, which means that, like Jesus and the narrator, God only persuades and does not compel. Nevertheless, the Gospel posits a reality beyond this world, beyond death, over which God has absolute control.

2.9. *Conclusion*

In many ways, the perspective of the Fourth Gospel is like that of Scriptural narratives of prophets and kings in Exodus–Deuteronomy, Joshua–2 Kings and 1 and 2 Chronicles, and like the Synoptic Gospels. Here, too, the narrator is omniscient and gives information about God's purposes and people's secret thoughts. In our culture we are familiar with the role of the omniscient narrator, but we reserve it for fiction or popular biography, and exclude it from history-writing, in which the narrator's perspective is strictly limited by the evidence available. Biblical narratives, however, like their contemporary counterparts, use this convention for history-writing, although just what kind of history the Fourth Gospel relates I shall define in Part III. The role of the omniscient narrator in biblical narrative is to lead the reader to a true perception of reality, by giving information at appropriate moments, and by determining the consistent ideology of the narrative. He can also withhold information until the reader is able to grasp its full significance, as the narrator of the Fourth Gospel does in forming Jesus' predictions of his passion into statements about his future uplifting (e.g. 3.14; 8.28) and only gradually showing that this will involve death on a cross (12.27-33). The narrative is structured aesthetically to bring out the theological significance of history, despite the tension which this causes, in order to create a complete picture of reality for the comprehension of readers.

But Old Testament narratives and the Synoptic Gospels require their readers to work hard at discerning the point of the narrative, because none of the characters share the omniscience of God or the narrator, and their narrators do not always make explicit the point of juxtaposing incidents. The omniscience of Jesus in the Fourth Gospel means that Jesus' discourses provide a running commentary on the significance of his ministry. They explicitly define his relationship with the Father and his fulfilment of the Father's mission. The Fourth Gospel is therefore less elusive than other biblical narratives. Nevertheless, the presence of ambiguous terms and statements, like those about Jesus' honour and exaltation, and the use of irony mean that the narrative can be misunderstood. In particular, the portrait of Jesus, especially in chs. 2–12, has prompted a Docetic reading, according to which Jesus is seen as God merely masquerading as a man. We know that the Gospel was popular among Gnostics, whose Christology was Docetic, and the case for a Docetic reading has been argued recently, most strongly by E. Käsemann (1968, but see the criticisms by Thompson 1988). This book will argue for a different reading. It understands the Jesus of the Fourth Gospel as a vulnerable human being, whose death on a cross is central to its theodicy, but it also recognizes that Jesus' omniscience poses a problem for such a view. It is possible, however, to appreciate this emphasis in the portrait of Jesus in a way which does not lead to Docetism, as an attempt to counter an alternative interpretation of the facts. That Jesus was betrayed by one of his twelve disciples, denied by another, deserted by others and crucified by his enemies, might suggest that he was a poor judge of character and political realities, and that his death was a tragedy. Stressing his insight into peoples' characters and his knowledge of his mission from God makes such an interpretation unthinkable. Alongside these statements, moreover, others unequivocally depict Jesus' vulnerable humanity. He truly dies (19.30) and is buried (19.40). 'The λόγος was flesh', the good shepherd who lays down his life for the sheep (10.11). He is moved to tears by the tears of others mourning Lazarus' death (11.35). He is deeply troubled when he faces martyrdom (12.27-28). Most of the narrative of Jesus' life creates the impression of aloofness, but that is because its interest is theological rather than psychological. Jesus is obedient to the Father's will, so nothing can move him to act otherwise. Hence he takes the initiative in healings and in deciding when to face death in Jerusalem. He identifies himself to the soldiers and officers who come to arrest him, secures the freedom of his disciples and allows himself to be arrested. In spite of this dignified aloofness which theology imposes on characterization, however, Jesus' behaviour is to be understood as the expression of love (11.5 and 13.1), a love which requires him to lay down his life for his friends (11.5 and 16; 15.13). The Gospel does not picture Jesus as God, merely appearing to be a man. It pictures him as a man wholly dedicated to the mission God sent him to fulfil, a mission which leads through death to resurrection.

Chapter 2

STRUCTURING TIME IN THE FOURTH GOSPEL

When we read any narrative, we become involved in at least three different times: the time we spend reading, the time of the narrator and the time of the story. The time spent by the reader will vary from reader to reader and depend on circumstances. The time of the narrator is usually later than that of the story, as in the case of the Fourth Gospel, so that the story is told with hindsight.

I shall discuss first the time of the story, paying attention to the variety of ways in which the narrative presents it, and I shall look briefly at the time of the narrator but shall consider the time of the reader only in the section on tempo (see Genette 1980, 1989).

1. *History and Eternity*

The story of Jesus' ministry is set within a very general presentation of human history from its beginning (1.3-13), but this presentation is structured by a concern not just with history but with eternity. The Gospel begins in eternity (1.1-2) and the reader is repeatedly reminded of the eternal dimension in the discourses within the story. Here 'eternal' does not mean 'everlasting' but a dimension outside of time, God's existence 'apart from' and 'before' the creation of time and space. In Greek, verbal forms express exact time distinctions and they can refer to existence outside of time only metaphorically. In the Prologue the verb 'to be' (εἰμί) is used in the imperfect metaphorically to express eternal existence: 'In the beginning *was* the λόγος and the λόγος *was* with God and the λόγος *was* God'. 'In the beginning' does not mark the beginning of Jesus' ministry, as it does in 15.27 and 16.4, but refers to eternity, before history existed. 'Was' means 'what is eternally the case', but 'was' is chosen rather than 'is' because what is contemplated is eternity without creation, and from the perspective of a creature 'was' seems to capture the meaning most adequately. History is contrasted with eternity by changing the verb 'to be' to the verb 'to become' (γίνομαι) used in the aorist (e.g. 1.3). The eternal dimension is not, however, simply a backdrop but determines and dominates all else: God creates the world, the human world, creating life and giving enlightenment, and history is judged in terms of God's plan for creation, not as an autonomous process. In spite of darkness, ignorance and rejection, light is not extinguished. Moreover, God's determination to enlighten the human world is focused in the life of a particular man, 'the λόγος became or was flesh' (1.14). 'Became' or 'was' (γίνομαι) indicates the existence of the man in history, in his vulnerability and mortality (flesh). The Prologue shows that the story of Jesus' ministry is to be viewed as the revelation of the eternal God's purpose.

Jesus' words and actions are presented in these terms in the story. His miracles are signs of his sonship, and he exemplifies God's love by drawing people into a fuller life in acknowledged dependence on the Creator. The stereotyped view of human history in the Prologue is repeated in the story. A contrast is noted between Jesus' acceptance by Samaritans (4.1-42), Galilaeans (4.45) and, potentially, Greeks (12.20-32), and his rejection by 'Jews' (e.g. chs. 7–8) and especially by 'Jewish' leaders (e.g. 10.8; 11.47-53). Jesus' dialogues with 'Jews', which take up most of the story of his public ministry, also refer to Jewish history, but there are no references to Greek or Roman history. This is because the story focuses on relations between Jesus and his 'own', the 'Jews', as the Prologue focuses on relations between the true light and its 'own' (1.11). Key figures from Jewish history, especially Abraham and Moses, are used in Jesus' attacks on contemporary 'Jews' (e.g. 5.45-46 and 8.39) and Jewish ancestors are used as examples (e.g. 6.31-34). Again, history is taken as typical not particular. How long before the time of the story Abraham or Moses lived is left unclear, but 'Jews' within the story are related to this past as descendants or adherents.

The story which the Fourth Gospel tells, then, is intended to illuminate the eternal dimension of God's creative purpose for his world.

2. *The Time of the Story*

2.1. *Date and Duration*

The Fourth Gospel tells a story of the ministry of Jesus of Nazareth in Galilee, Samaria and Judaea which led to his crucifixion in Jerusalem. It does not provide dates as a modern biography or story would, but historical period and place are simply assumed and mentioned incidentally: Galilee, Samaria, Judaea and Jerusalem at a time when Pilate was in the praetorium, during a year when Caiaphas was high priest. Some of the place names, including Jerusalem before the Temple was destroyed, Bethany, Bethsaida, Nazareth, Cana, Capernaum, the Jordan, the Sea of Tiberias, in so far as we know anything about them, fit into this period.

The progression of years in the story is marked by references to annual Jewish festivals, and since three Passovers are mentioned (2.13, 23; 6.4; 11.55), the ministry related extends over more than two years. The story does not tell of Jesus' going to Jerusalem for every Jewish feast of the year, nor is he always in Jerusalem when a feast is noted (6.4, Passover), but what feasts are mentioned occur in an order which conforms to that of Scripture: Passover in the spring (2.13, 23); an unspecified feast of the Jews (5.1); Passover in the spring (6.4); Tabernacles in the autumn (7.2); Renewal or Hanukkah in the winter (10.22; there is no clear break between 7.2 and 10.22), and Passover in the spring (11.55; 12.1; 13.1; 18.28; 19.14). The feasts which are named provide theological themes which Jesus develops in discourses or which the narrator uses to interpret the crucifixion. Otherwise, two Sabbaths are mentioned, both occurring while Jesus is in Jerusalem (5.10; 9.14). That the Sabbath is a weekly event seems to be assumed, although the fact goes without mention.

Apart from these references to annual and weekly events, time sequence could hardly be less precise. Very often incidents and discourses are linked by 'after this' (2.12; 19.28) or 'after these things' (3.22; 5.1; 6.1; 7.1; 19.38). Within sections a sequence of days is sometimes noted. Three different functions seem to be served by this arrangement: (1) to divide and thereby highlight separate units, (2) to indicate a new beginning, or (3) to make typological connexions of theological importance.

1. At the beginning of the story, for example, incidents centring on John, then Jesus, take place over a series of days (1.29, 35, 39, 43) which separate different testimonies to Jesus. Similarly, 2.12 mentions the stay of Jesus, his mother, brothers and disciples in Capernaum for 'not many days' to underline the break between the Cana and the Jerusalem stories, whereas 6.22 'the next day' links the discourse with the feeding miracle and the walking on the water at night.

2. In ch. 2, a new section begins with the expression 'on the third day' (2.1), which cannot refer back to the sequence in ch. 1 because that involves at least five days, but it is used as an idiom, common in Scripture, to indicate a new beginning (e.g. Hos. 6.1-2; Gen. 42.18). Again, in ch. 4, Jesus spends two days with the Samaritans (4.40), which means that the second miracle at Cana, like the first, takes place 'after two days', that is on the third day (4.43). Both these references hint proleptically at the new beginning effected at the resurrection which takes place on the third day (20.1).

3. The reference to 'the last day of the feast' of Tabernacles (7.37) introduces the themes of water, spirit and light, just as the concluding incidents in the story (chs. 18–19) take place in relation to Passover to show that Jesus died at the time when the Passover lamb was sacrificed (12.1, 12; 13.1; 18.3, 28; 19.14, 31, 42).

The presentation seems strange to modern readers because historical precision is replaced by what is typical not particular.

2.2. *Ellipsis*

Since the events described in the Fourth Gospel could not have filled all the time which the story allows, that is, more than two years, it is immediately clear that there are temporal ellipses. We have to assume, for example, that Jesus and his disciples regularly ate, drank and slept, though these everyday occurrences are only occasionally or never mentioned. Moreover, we noticed in Chapter 1 that the text sometimes assumes or refers to events which are not described. In relation to Jesus' signs, the conclusion in 20.30 formally acknowledges that others were performed which are not recorded, and at the end of ch. 21, a more general statement recognizes ellipses: 'But there are many things which Jesus did; were every one of them to be written, I suppose that the world itself could not contain the books that would be written' (21.25). Occasionally, the narrative makes us aware of the fact that time is passing in which nothing of what Jesus said or did is related. For example, we are told nothing of what passed between John's two disciples and Jesus when they stayed with him (1.39) or between Jesus, his mother, his brothers and his disciples when they stayed together in Capernaum (2.12). Again, at the end of ch. 10, we learn that Jesus withdrew across the Jordan to the place where John at first baptized, but only the remarks and belief of those who met him there are noted. When Jesus next withdrew to Ephraim with his disciples (11.54), what they did is left blank. These references provide pauses between Jesus' otherwise busy life-style. In ch. 11, Jesus' absence allows the authorities time in which to encourage the Passover pilgrims in Jerusalem to let them know his whereabouts, so that they could arrest him (11.55-57).

Another ellipsis becomes apparent in the introduction to Jesus' arrest (18.1-2). We are told that the garden across the Kidron Valley, which Jesus and his disciples entered when they left the supper, was known to Judas, 'for Jesus often met there with his disciples'. This fact had neither been mentioned earlier nor had such meetings been described. By referring to it at this point, the narrative seems to indicate the way in which Judas betrayed Jesus, namely that he guided the soldiers and officers to a place where Jesus could be arrested, conveniently away from the crowds.

If these occasional references make us aware of ellipses, most of the references to time passing obscure them. 'After this' and 'After these things' give a sense of progression which is general rather than specific.

2.3. *Retrospection*

It is not uncommon for narratives to begin stories in the middle and to fill in earlier parts of the story through retrospection. The Fourth Gospel begins the story of Jesus' ministry when Jesus is an adult, but does not fill in details from his earlier life to any great extent. We gather only that he is a Jew, untrained in Jewish learning (7.15), that he came from Nazareth in Galilee (1.45-46), that he was not yet 50 years old (8.57), that his origins were known (7.27), that his father was Joseph (1.45) and that his parents and his brothers were still alive (2.1; 6.42; 7.3). Perhaps his origins were thought to be illegitimate, if 8.41 is intended as a jibe against him in this sense.

Very occasionally, gaps left in the earlier part of the story are filled in later (e.g. 1.48; 4.20; 6.26; 6.70; 7.25; 9.22) but retrospection is used most frequently in the story not for a biographical but for a theological purpose.

2.3.1. Time and again, Jesus speaks of himself as the one sent by God the Father, 'I came forth from God and have come, for I did not come on my own initiative but he sent me' (8.42 and see, e.g., 7.28-29; 11.42; 12.49; 13.3, 16; 17.3, 21), and of God as the Father who sent him (e.g. 7.16, 18, 28, 33; 8.16, 26; 12.44; 14.24). The highest authority is thereby claimed for Jesus' teaching and behaviour: commissioned by God, he acts as God's agent, revealing God's purpose, and in relation to the disciples he provides the example of what the Gospel regards as genuine human life in obedience to God (13.34; 15.10-12). His fate is therefore to be shared by the disciples (e.g. 15.18 and throughout the discourses in chs. 13–16), and in this way his authority is passed on to them. When Jesus calls them by name (1.42; 10.3; 20.16), he chooses them (15.16) to follow his example (13.34; 15.10-12), to encounter the same hatred (15.18; 17.14), and to experience the same death (12.25-26). Their commission by Jesus (17.18; 20.21-22) defines their role.

2.3.2. The past is also related to the present of the story through the fulfilment of prophecies. Statements made in the distant and unspecified past by prophets and narrators in Scripture are said to be fulfilled in Jesus' life, while other Jewish religious expectations are not fulfilled. In these instances, the narrative reaches beyond the scope of the story for statements and beliefs, but in other instances, prophecies made within the story are fulfilled.

1. The story presupposes that the Jewish Scriptures are authoritative for Jesus, his adherents and opponents. Each accepts them as intimations of God's purpose and looks for their fulfilment. Occasionally, references are used polemically without specifically mentioning acceptance by Jesus: 'It stands written in *your* law, I say you are gods' (10.34 and see also 15.25), but more often, prophecies are assumed to be oracles of God, quoted by Jesus (e.g. 6.45; 7.38; 13.18) and fulfilled in his ministry. Twice the disciples see the fulfilment of prophecy in an incident in Jesus' life (2.17; 12.16), but in these instances the time is not that of the story but that of the disciples after the end of the story (see below, §3). Similarly, the narrator later interprets events in the light of Scripture (e.g. 12.14-15, 38-40; 19.24, 28, 36-37).

2. Although Scripture is accepted as authoritative and although Jesus is pictured as the messiah predicted in Scripture, messianic expectations among the 'Jews' in the story are treated circumspectly. To the Samaritan woman, Jesus reveals that he is indeed the messiah (4.25-26), and he admits as much to the 'Jewish' crowds (10.24; see also the speculation in 7.25-26), but triumphalist expectations are rejected. In 6.15 the narrative depicts Jesus as having to withdraw in order to avoid being made king. In 12.14 Zechariah's prophecy about humility is quoted against the crowd, which is rejoicing at the advent of their king, and Jesus chooses to ride into Jerusalem in humility. At the end of Jesus' public ministry the crowds are confused because their expectations remain unfulfilled: 'We heard from the law that the Christ remains forever. How can you say that the Son of man must be lifted up? Who is this Son of man?' (12.34). At his trial before Pilate Jesus explains that his kingdom is not 'of this world' (18.36). In general, the 'Jews' who allude to Scripture and who look for or assume its fulfilment (e.g. 6.31; 7.12, 40-44; 12.13, 34) misconceive its significance.

3. Of prophecies fulfilled within the story, that of Caiaphas to the 'Jewish' council which condemned Jesus to death provides the best example (11.49-53). The narrative both interprets it (11.51) and refers back to it at the point of fulfilment (18.14).

4. A number of Jesus' statements are understood as prophetic and their fulfilment is mentioned, for example 5.38 is fulfilled in 6.36, 11.4 in 11.40-44, 13.18 in 18.2, 13.38 in 18.25-27, 17.12 in 18.9, 21.6 is fulfilled immediately. These fulfilments within the story both give it an aesthetic unity and provide a basis for taking seriously prophecies in the story which point to a fulfilment in the indefinite future (e.g. 13.7 and see below §2.5.2).

2.4. *Repetition*

One way of emphasizing the significance of an incident is to refer to it repeatedly. Genette makes the following distinctions in clarifying narrative repetitions:

> A narrative may relate once an event which happens in the story once.
>
> A narrative may relate a number of times events which happen in the story the same number of times.
>
> A narrative may relate a number of times an event which happens in the story once.
>
> A narrative may relate once events which happen in the story a number of times (1980: 14-16).

In addition, a narrative may recall events already depicted. Where applicable, I shall use these categories in what follows, together with another type of repetition: an event in the story may be presented as a repetition of one outside the story.

2.4.1. A narrative may present a number of times events which happen in the story the same number of times. Most of the examples or repetition in the Fourth gospel come under this heading.

1. Stories about individuals who are called to follow Jesus provide a series with a similar pattern: people are called to follow and to give testimony (1.35-51; 6.66-71; 20.27; 21.1-14).

2. The accounts of what happened at the three Passovers (2.21; 6.51; 12.1) present, both in the story and in the narrative, various ways of understanding Jesus' death and resurrection.

3. In the description of Jesus' arrest, his self-identification, which strikes terror into his adversaries, is given three times (18.5, 6, 7, 8).

4. The story of Jesus' trial before Pilate recounts Pilate's three attempts to release Jesus (19.4, 6, 12). Repetition is necessary so that the emphasis on innocence can obscure the fact that Pilate handed Jesus over to death by crucifixion (19.13-14).

5. Repetition with variations characterizes the appearance stories in chs. 20–21. (a) The two angels in the tomb address Mary Magdalene with the same words as the resurrected Jesus, and Mary's replies are similar (20.13 and 15). The conversations hold back the climax, that Jesus is raised from the dead. Angelic messengers hint at what has happened but allow Jesus himself to convince Mary. (b) The parallel accounts of the appearances of Jesus to the disciples in the absence and presence of Thomas (20.19-23 and 20.26-29) emphasize the reality of Jesus' resurrection both to the disciples and to those not involved in the story, to other disciples and to the readers (20.29). The timing of each appearance on the first day of the week, with a week between, may hint at a eucharistic reference if it is supposed that very early the eucharist was celebrated weekly on Sundays. (c) Peter's threefold declaration of love for Jesus (21.15-17) rehabilitates him after his threefold denial (18.25-27).

6. The vocabulary of the characters in the story is repetitive. Ideas introduced in the narrative of the Prologue—life, light, darkness, world, its own, truth, honour, believing—are picked up and developed, especially in the discourses. As Schnackenburg remarks:

> The technique of the discourses uses a number of effects. . . antithesis, verbal links through key-words, concatenation of ideas by means of recourse to earlier ones, inclusion whereby the thought is brought back to its starting-point, parallelism and variation (1968: I, 115-16).

2.4.2. A narrative may relate once events which happen in the story a number of times, the iterative imperfect.

In the Fourth Gospel events are generally described in the past tense, mostly with aorists and sometimes with historic presents. Occasionally the imperfect tense is used. In many cases a section in the imperfect either describes what had been happening in the background while another incident took place in the foreground (e.g. 4.31-38; 6.16-18; 7.11-13; 8.8-10; 9.16; 10.39; 18.15; 19.29; 20.3-4; 21.12) or allows the narrator to explain to the reader the significance of something just said (e.g. 2.21; 6.6, 71; 7.5; 12.33), but in some cases, the imperfect is iterative, indicating what used to happen, what was typically said and done. For example, in 3.22-23 Jesus' and John's typical activity as baptists is described. The imperfects are italicized:

> After these things, Jesus and his disciples came [aorist] into Judea, and there he *remained* with them and *was baptizing* [repeatedly]. John too *was baptizing* [repeatedly] in Aenon near Salim because there was much water there, and people *used to come* and *be baptized.*

Again, Jesus' action in healing the feeble man on the Sabbath and the 'Jewish' reaction are taken as typical: 'This is why the Jews *used to persecute* Jesus, because he *used to do* these things on the Sabbath' (5.16). Moreover, the rejection of Jesus' teaching (6.60) has a continuing effect on Jesus' behaviour: 'After these things, he *used to go about* in Galilee; he *would not go about* in Judaea, because the Jews *were seeking* to kill him' (7.1 and see also 7.12, 15, 31, 40). In 10.20-21, typical reactions of the 'Jewish' crowds to Jesus' ministry are described:

> Many of them *were saying* [repeatedly], He has a demon, and he is mad. Why listen to him? Others *were saying* [repeatedly], These are not the sayings of a man possessed by a demon.

This use of the imperfect to indicate what was typical helps to fill in the gaps in the story of Jesus' ministry, because an incident described once represents what happened repeatedly.

2.4.3. The narrative may recall its own past. The Fourth Gospel does not relate several times an event which happens in the story once, but it does refer back to events already described.

Many of the accounts of miracles are referred to again in new contexts. In ch. 5 the story of the healing of the feeble man is told (5.2-9), referred to in conversation with the 'Jews' (5.9-13), in conversation with Jesus (5.14), and once more in conversation with the 'Jews' (5.15). Jesus mentions it again in 7.21. Similarly, in ch. 9 the account of the healing of the man blind from birth (9.2-7), is referred to in conversation with neighbours (9.8-12) and with Pharisees (9.13-17), in questioning the man's parents (9.18-23), and again in the man's statement (9.24-34). Later the 'Jews' who mourn with Mary and Martha at Bethany mention the miracle again (11.37). The miraculous feeding (6.2-14) is mentioned in 6.23 and 26. The raising of Lazarus (ch. 11) becomes one of the narrative themes of ch. 12 (12.1, 9, 17).

2.4.4. An event in the story repeats one outside the story.

Events which happened to others in the distant past, in Scripture, correlate with events in Jesus' life according to statements made by Jesus in the story.

1. Moses' lifting up the serpent in the wilderness (3.14-15) is said to prefigure the uplifting of the Son of man.
2. God's provision of manna in the wilderness prefigures his sending of the Son (6.26). Moreover, in the narrative, the crowds murmur against Jesus (6.41, 43, 61) as they murmured against Moses (Exod. 16.7; 17.3; Num. 11.1).

This kind of correspondence if found in other narrative sections, for example Jesus' meeting with the Samaritan woman at the well (4.7) and their discussion about marriage transposes a 'type-scene' from Scripture (Gen. 24 and 29; Exod. 2.15-22). On another level Jesus' walking on the water mirrors not a historical event but the story of creation itself: Gen. 1.2 pictures the Spirit of God moving in the darkness over the waters as Jesus moved in the darkness over the waters (6.16-21).

Although I am listing these features as 'repetitions', each of them repeats what had happened before only in very general ways, since there are also marked differences between the prototype and its imitation. This is true of all repetitions, since the presentation of even exactly the same statement in a new context alters the force of the statement. The differences are even more obvious, therefore, when the imitation varies from the prototype, as it does in the examples cited above. In the next chapter, on genre, I shall explore in more detail the variety of ways in which the Fourth Gospel imitates its Scripture, focusing particularly on its identification of Jesus both with the messiah and with the prophet like Moses.

I have listed examples of repetition which refer back to an incident previously mentioned or familiar from Scripture, or which tell a similar story or make a similar statement on more than one occasion, and have suggested that this is an aspect of retrospection. As will become clear in a moment, repetition is also a feature of anticipation.

2.5. *Anticipation*

Anticipation is less widely used in modern popular storytelling, in which suspense is a major element, than it was in some ancient literature, in which the interest lay in seeing how an inexorable fate would effect the denouement. In the Fourth Gospel the reader is gradually led to understand that God's purpose will be accomplished through Jesus' death.

2.5.1. Jesus' death, described towards the end of the story (chs. 18–19), is anticipated from the beginning in a variety of ways, some of them enigmatic.

1. The 'Jewish' plan to kill Jesus, which is a recurring feature of chs. 7–12, explains the puzzling reference to rejection in the Prologue: 'He came to his own home and his own people did not receive him' (1.11). The decision of the 'Jewish' council (11.47-53) is carried out through Pilate.

2. Judas' betrayal is mentioned at the first crisis in Jesus' ministry (6.64, 71), at the end of his public ministry (12.4) and at the supper table (13.2, 21). Just how he will betray Jesus is left unclear until he leads soldiers to the garden to arrest him (18.2), but the fact of betrayal already hints that Jesus' death will be no accident.

3. The commonplace about working during the day (9.4; see 11.9-10) becomes an enigmatic prediction of the final events and exemplifies the antithesis of light and darkness first introduced in the Prologue (1.4) and developed throughout the discourses, especially in 8.12–9.41 (see 13.30). A parallel way of expressing the same idea is

the statement: 'The ruler of this world is coming' (14.30).

4. The prediction of Peter's denial is connected with an anticipation of dangers that may lead to death, although the only death directly mentioned is Peter's (13.36-38 and see 11.16).

5. Jesus' identification with the Good Shepherd and the definition of a good shepherd as one who lays down his life for the sheep (10.11, 15, 17-18) is repeated too often and explained in too much detail to leave any doubt that Jesus will die voluntarily, but not naturally.

6. Mary's anointing of Jesus' feet (12.1-8) is linked by Jesus to his burial, and later in the same narrative the images of death crowd in (12.24, 33, 35).

7. Allusive statements about Jesus' 'hour' are introduced at the first miracle (2.4) and recur (4.21, 23; 5.25-29; 7.30; 8.20; 12.23, 27; 13.1; 17.1-2). The tenses are sometimes peculiar. Jn 2.4, 7.30 and 8.20 make clear that the 'hour' had not yet arrived at that point in the ministry. Jn 4.23 and 5.25 use the odd expression: 'The hour comes and now is'; 12.23, 13.1 and 17.1 state that 'the hour has come; (see Mk 14.41) and 12.27 refers twice to 'this hour'. The hour is the hour of Jesus' death and what follows from his death. The only way of making sense of 4.23 and 5.25 is to see the first half of the statement 'the hour comes' as relevant to the time of the story, and the second half 'and now is' as relevant to the time of the narrative.

8. References to the uplifting of the Son of man (e.g. 3.14-15) also turn out to be references to Jesus' death by uplifting on a cross (12.33).

9. That Jesus will give his flesh for the life of the world (6.51) is an enigmatic prediction of his death.

10. Jesus often talks of his imminent departure, both to the crowds (7.33; 8.21) and to his disciples (13.33; 14.2, 28; 16.5. See also the narrative statement 13.3). These statements focus on the importance of Jesus' presence which provides opportunities and support that will not always be there in the same way.

2.5.2. Much of the teaching about the future in the story describes what disciples can expect to happen to them in a future beyond that of the story. Two themes are developed: (1) persecution and (2) salvation.

1. In general terms, Jesus declares that disciples will encounter the same kind of hatred from the world (of people) as he encountered (15.18; 16.1-4; 17.14). Indeed, persecution is a mark of true discipleship, an indication that the disciple is not 'of the world' but is 'of

God'. Since bearing witness to Jesus involves persecution, prophecies are meant to forewarn disciples so that when they suffer they do not misunderstand their experience and lose faith (16.4). Peter is a particular example (21.18-19). His martyrdom is predicted by Jesus in the story, interpreted by the narrator, but not described. The characterization of discipleship in terms of persecution is so strong that an apology has to be offered for those, like the Beloved Disciple, who may not experience it (21.20-21). All these statements point forward to a time beyond the scope of the story.

2. The Farewell Discourses (chs. 14–17) draw together hints from the public ministry to depict expectations the disciples may enjoy. Jn 14.2-3 introduces this theme:

> In my Father's house are many rooms; if it were not so, would I have told you that I go to prepare a place for you? And when I go and prepare a place for you, I will come again and will take you to myself that where I am you may be also.

The saying gives assurance of a permanent dwelling with God in the future. Later in the chapter Jesus speaks of dwelling in the believer (14.23), which is a partial but not complete fulfilment of 14.2-3. Beyond history the disciples can look forward to an eschatological fulfilment (5.28-29; 6.39, 40, 44, 54; 12.48).

Nevertheless, 14.12 suggests that before the eschaton disciples will perform the kinds of works Jesus performed. Moreover, after Jesus' death, disciples will be able to carry out works of salvation in a wider context than Jesus was able to do during his ministry: their mission will be to Greeks as well as to Jews (10.16; 12.20-32; 21.1-14). All this will be possible, because the disciples will recognize Jesus' significance in bringing salvation to humanity (17.7-8). The Paraclete or Helper, who is called the Spirit of Truth, will continue Jesus' work through the disciples, helping them both to understand and to stand against the world in bearing witness to Jesus (14.16-17, 25-27; 15.26-27; 16.7-15). In effect the Paraclete seems to be the presence of Jesus with his disciples after his death (14.18-19), which means that the disciples reliance on Jesus will continue (15.1-11). Adherence to Jesus, understood as indwelling (14.20), creates unity among the disciples' (10.16; 17.20-21), expressed as the mutual love of friends (15.12-13). In spite of persecution, then, the disciples can look forward to rejoicing, to asking and receiving from God (16.23), because, although they suffer in the world, the world is not the final reality:

'I have said this that in me you may have peace. In the world you have tribulation; but be of good cheer, I have overcome the world' (16.33).

These twin aspects of the disciples' expectation before the eschaton, persecution and salvation are a mirror image of the ministry of Jesus described in the story. Jesus is an example to the disciples of what they can expect in lives dedicated to the God whose purpose Jesus reveals.

2.5.3. *The use of the perfect tense.* A link is made between the life of Jesus and the future life of the disciples by the use of the perfect tense to describe God's activity in Jesus' mission. This perfect expresses the continuing effect of a past action into the present. It is used very much more frequently in the Fourth Gospel than in the Synoptics. Turner (1963: 83) provides the following numbers for comparison: Matthew 7, Mark 8, Luke 14, but John 77 times. Its frequency in John highlights the enduring significance of Jesus' life. Moreover, key verbs are repeatedly used in the perfect, as in Jesus' declarations: 'And this is the will of him who sent me, that I should lose nothing of all that he [the Father] *has given* me, but raise it up at the last day' (6.39), or 'For *I have given* them [the disciples] the words which you [the Father] gave me, and they received them and know the truth' (17.8). 'To see' is used 17 times in the perfect, as in Jesus' assurance to the disciples, 'If you had known me, you would have known my Father also; henceforth you know him and *have seen* him... He who *has seen* me *has seen* the Father' (14.7-9). 'To speak' is used 10 times in the perfect, as in Jesus' explanation to the disciples, 'The words that *I have spoken* to you are spirit and life' (6.63). The Fourth Gospel, then, makes explicit the continuing relevance of the story it tells.

2.6. *Proleptic Statements*

One of the more surprising features of the story is that some of the statements are proleptic; the future is described as if it is present.

2.6.1. *Gnomic teaching.* Some of Jesus' teaching in the story adopts the proverbial form of wisdom to express a general truth without implication of time. This gives the story an anti-historical quality. Since the general truth expressed is often dependent upon Jesus' complete ministry, however, it is an aspect of prolepsis (e.g. 3.16; 6.35, 53; 8.12; 10.1; 12.44; 13.16-17; 15.1-2, 12-13). What follows are particular examples of this general tendency.

2.6.2. *Eternal life*. 'Truly, truly, I say to you, he who hears my speech and believes him who sent me has eternal life. He does not come into judgment, but has passed from death to life' (5.24 and see 6.47). A literal and straightforward interpretation of this statement taken alone would suggest that believers will not die physically in the future. This, however, is not at all what Jesus teaches elsewhere in the story. Rather, the path to eternal life lies through death (12.24-25). 'Eternal' in 'eternal life' (ζωή αἰώνιος) means 'unending time', and 'eternal life' is the resurrected life after the death of the believer, when he or she will no longer experience 'aging' because that life will not move towards another death. The term is taken over from Dan. 12.2. The 'eternal life' of the believer is therefore different from the eternity of God which has no beginning in space. Since belief in Jesus determines whether a person will be resurrected to eternal life or not (11.25-26), the story gives gnomic statements about the relationship between belief and eternal life which are expressed in the present tense (e.g. 6.54; 10.10, 28). In another passage the future dimension is clearer (6.27 and compare 6.39, 40, 44).

2.6.3. *Judgment*. 'For judgment I came into this world, that those who did not see may see, and that those who see may become blind' (9.39. See also 12.31, 47-48). Because the final judgment on the last day will be carried out according to criteria already present in the world in Jesus' ministry, the outcome of judgment is determined in advance by a person's acceptance or rejection of Jesus, and hence the judgment has, in a sense, already taken place (3.17-18). While a person is still alive, however, he or she may gain or lose faith and so change in relation to the final judgment on the last day (e.g. 5.25-29; 6.39, 40, 44).

2.6.4. *Jesus' departure*. The imminence of Jesus' departure is stressed throughout the Farewell Discourses, but in ch. 17 it is viewed as an accomplished fact: 'Now I am no longer in the world' (17.11 and see 16.33). Jesus, in his final prayer with the disciples before his death, is pictured as already departing to his Father, and caring for his disciples whom he has left behind.

The themes of these proleptic statements: belief, eternal life, judgment, departure, reflect once more God's effective purpose.

2.7. *Conclusion: Cause and Effect*

A narrative like the Fourth Gospel, which places events in a temporal sequence, implies a system of cause and effect. Modern historians are self-conscious about this impression and often recognize it as fundamental to their argument. But when they provide evidence in support of their system of causal relations, they cite social, economic and political power structures, cultural traditions, geographical and temporal constraints, individual characteristics, and the interplay of all of these. They may include references to a belief in a transcendent Creator God, should that belief form part of the cultural tradition, but only from the perspective of its effect on believers. The Fourth Gospel differs from modern histories in one major respect. By beginning with the Creator God's plan for creation, and telling the story of Jesus as the most significant contribution to that plan, it not only notices the effect of this belief on people within the story, but asserts that God is the first cause of all things. The Creator God causes the world and history to come into existence and gives eternal life to those people who conform to the divine conception of human life. Compared to this primary cause, the social, economic and political power structures play a less significant role.

Moreover, this Creator God is continually active, not only keeping the world in being but making his plan known to human beings through prophetic oracles, including the law of Moses, and through the wisdom tradition, all of which was written in Scripture. Finally, his plan is made known through the life, death and resurrection of Jesus, God's human agent, the subject of the story related in the narrative. More than this, however, God actively draws people to Jesus (6.44), and, through his agent, determines the post-mortem future of each individual (5.21; 6.39). God, therefore, is ultimately the cause of everything that exists.

But this is not the whole of the Johannine picture. The Gospel suggest that God's plan is to save the world (3.17). This world, which is created and sustained by God, is also alienated from God and needs to be saved. Moreover, the alienation is of a radical nature, as radical as the opposition between light and darkness (1.4, 9-13; 8.12–10.39), or between sonship and slavery (8.34-38), or between obedience and sin (8.34-35). The story, nevertheless, pictures God's agent, Jesus, effecting God's plan to save the world by overcoming this darkness, slavery and sin. This is especially clear in the Johannine healing stories, which encompass more extreme changes than most of the Synoptic stories: the royal official's son is brought back to life from the verge of death (4.47), the man at the pool is healed in spite of his complete feebleness (5.6), the man born blind sees for the very first time in his life (9.1, 7), and Lazarus lives after being buried for four days (11.17, 44). Moreover, many of those healed do not even believe in Jesus before the miracle. Rather, Jesus acts on his own initiative.

But if God is the first cause of existence, how is this alienation explained? And if God heals people through his agent's activity, why are all people not saved? Actually, the Gospel does suggest that all people will be saved (12.32), but alongside that statement offers others which propose a contrary view (e.g. 8.21; 9.39-41). And at the end of Jesus' public ministry an explanation of unbelief is offered. The narrator paraphrases Isaiah: 'Therefore, they could not believe. For Isaiah said, He [presumably God] has blinded their eyes and hardened their heart' (12.40; see also Isa. 29.10; 42.18-19; 56.10; Deut. 29.2-4). The statement adopts a scriptural view that since God is the cause of all things, even unbelief is caused by God (e.g. Exod. 11.10).

There is, of course, a contradiction in this account of cause and effect, since it makes God the cause of unbelief and yet insists that God's plan is to foster belief (3.16; 6.28-29). Moreover, we would expect such a view to absolve human beings from all responsibility since they are mere puppets of an all-powerful God. But, on the contrary, as in Scripture, human beings are not depicted as puppets but as fully responsible agents, whose disobedience is culpable (e.g. 7.19; 9.41). It is their evil deeds which prevent them from responding to Jesus (e.g. 3.19-21).

Once again, however, this is not the whole of the Johannine picture. Those people who do evil deeds and refuse to believe in God's agent are agents of another power at work in the world, the devil (8.44-47). It is the devil or Satan who entered into Judas at the supper table before he left to betray Jesus (13.27 and 13.2). Should we interpret 13.27 in terms of cause and effect? Certainly Judas, in choosing to betray Jesus, has become an agent of this evil power. But Satan is not a second creator. Rather he is a 'murderer' (8.44). People who perform his evil work do not gain eternal life but 'die in their sin' (8.21). Hence, it would be true to say that for the Fourth Gospel, Satan is not the cause of life, but he is the cause of evil and unbelief, just as God is the cause of belief and good works when people become his agents (6.44; 3.21; 17.11, 15).

These causal connexions naturally determine the ways in which Jesus' death is explained. On the human level, his death is caused by the failure of the 'Jews' and especially their leaders to perceive that he is truly God's messiah. Instead, they perceive him as someone who leads the people astray and whose activity could lead to the destruction of Jewish life and institutions. On the theological level the Gospel interprets the 'Jewish' perception as a deception, as a lie. 'Jewish' leaders are therefore the agents of the devil, seeking Jesus' death instead of accepting the life God offers through him. Nevertheless, the transcendent God who creates life incorporates even this dark element into her plan to save the world. Jesus, God's agent, willingly gives his life in obedience to his Father and is resurrected. The life which God gives, not death, has the last word.

Several layers of causality, therefore, seem to be set side by side in this presentation, without any attempt at coordinating them into a coherent system. On the human plane people responsibly choose to believe in Jesus or not, and to do good works or bad. On the theological level, however, their choice is the effect of their allegiance, to God or the devil. Alternatively, on this level, their unbelief is caused by God's hardening their heart. But ultimately, God is sole Creator and giver of life, and he acts to save people from their sins, from unbelief, from bad actions and their consequences. Nevertheless, only those who respond to God's action can look forward to eternal life. The extremest rhetorical form of the Gospel's statements includes blatant contradictions (e.g. between 1.5 and 1.10-12, or between 3.17 and 3.18, or between 12.39-40 and 12.42), but even when allowance is made for this extremism, and one rhetorical assertion is balanced against another, contradictions remain because the various layers are not linked together into a complete causal pattern. The Fourth Gospel, however, is not alone in its failure to resolve the tension between God's providence and human free will. Other first-century writings, like Paul's and Josephus's, and like the Synoptic Gospels, depended on the same theological traditions in Scripture and repeated the same tensions. It was only much later in the history of the church that a system was proposed by theologians like Augustine in his *City of God* (see Hick: 1966).

I have now examined the time of the story presented by the Fourth

Gospel, but before turning to the time of the narrator, I must mention another time between these two, the time of the disciples after the resurrection.

3. *The Time of the Disciples*

Jesus' statement in 2.19 is interpreted in a number of ways. Within the story, the 'Jews' misunderstand it, and the narrator corrects the misunderstanding: 'But he spoke of the Temple of his body' (2.20-21). It is further interpreted through the disciples: 'When therefore he was raised from the dead, his disciples remembered that he had said this; and they believed the Scripture and the statement which Jesus had spoken' (2.22). Similarly, in 12.16, Jesus' decision to ride into Jerusalem in humility is said to have been understood by the disciples only afterwards. Finally, as already noted, in Jesus' prayer at the end of the Farewell Discourses, the perspective shifts to the time when Jesus is no longer with his disciples:

> And now I am no longer in the world, but they are in the world, and I am coming to you. Holy Father, keep them in your name, which you have given me, that they may be one even as we are one (17.11 and see 17.14-18 and 16.33).

The fidelity of the disciples after Jesus' departure is essential for the success of the mission from God.

The narrative, then, relates two past times, that of the story and that of the disciples who knew and reacted to the story before it became part of the present narrative. Reference to them serves to encourage belief in the reader.

4. *The Time of the Narrator*

In §2 I have included some references to the narrator's time alongside story time when similar perspectives are found in both. The amount of time assumed to have elapsed between the time of the story and the time of the narrator is unspecified, in spite of some apparent hints. It is unclear whether most of the characters are assumed to be still alive in the time of the narrator, although 21.20-23 could be interpreted to mean either that the Beloved Disciple is still alive or that he died a natural death. But his case is special, since it seems likely that he represents Gentile or ideal discipleship (see Chapter 14). More useful is the statement about Peter's martyrdom (21.19), which presupposes knowledge about the manner of his death. This presumably means that it is already a past event.

Another reference, 19.35-36, is very difficult to interpret:

> And he who has seen has borne witness, and his witness is true and he knows that he speaks the truth that you may believe. For these things happened so that the Scripture might be fulfilled, Not a bone of him shall be broken.

Who is the witness mentioned in this passage? One obvious answer is that this witness is the Father, to whose witness Jesus had repeatedly referred during his ministry (e.g. 5.37; 8.18). In other words, 19.35 is an introduction to the quotation from Scripture as an oracle of God. This interpretation is possible, but the expression 'he knows that he speaks the truth' is an odd way of referring to God. Alternatively, the passage could refer to an unnamed human witness. If so, the present tense 'he knows' suggests that the witness is still alive at the time of the narrator.

But to what is he bearing witness? The verses immediately preceding those just quoted read:

> But when they [the soldiers] came to Jesus and saw that he was already dead, they did not break his legs. But one of the soldiers pierced his side with a spear, and at once there came out blood and water.

If this is a straightforward statement about the reality of Jesus' death, the unnamed witness must be confirming that reality. In other words, he must have been present at the crucifixion. Were this interpretation convincing, it would imply that the narrative was written within the lifetime of an eyewitness of the crucifixion.

But this interpretation is unlikely to be correct. The reality of Jesus' death is expressed unequivocally in an earlier verse: 'When Jesus had received the vinegar, he said, "It is finished", and he bowed his head and gave up his spirit' (19.30). If the unnamed witness were confirming this reality, the reference to him should have been placed after v. 30 not after v. 34. Moreover, the description of blood and water flowing from the dead Jesus' side can be taken symbolically, as a depiction of the fulfilment of promises about the efficacy of Jesus' death, made earlier in the text—for example, the promise that when he was honoured out of his belly would flow rivers of living water (7.38, if this ambiguous statement is taken to refer to Jesus and not to the believer), or that he would give 'living water' (4.14), or that he is the lamb who takes away the sin of the world (1.29), or that he would give his flesh for food and his blood for drink (6.53-58). In this case the unnamed witness would be testifying to the efficacy of Jesus' death. He need not have been an eyewitness of Jesus' crucifixion, but a believer for whom Jesus' death had brought the promised new life. The passage is therefore most easily understood to refer to the witness which the narrator himself is giving (cf. 20.31). This means that the time between the story and the narrator need not be limited to the probable life span of an adult eyewitness of the crucifixion.

The time of the narrator, therefore, cannot be exactly ascertained. It is sufficiently long after the story for reflection to have taken place. The narrator interrupts the story at various places to correct errors (21.21; 4.2; 7.22), to discover the significance of something just said (6.6, 71; 7.5; 12.33), to indicate fulfilment of prophecies (e.g. 12.14, 38-41; 18.9; 19.24, 28, 36-37), and, most importantly, to testify to the reality of the salvation depicted in the story (20.31 and 19.35). The narrator directly addresses the reader in 19.35 and 20.30-31, the original ending of the work which is imitated in 21.24. But the Gospel does not include a precise portrait of its implied readers from which the time of narration might be ascertained.

It would be interesting to know, for example, whether unfulfilled prophecies within the story, especially those about persecution, were understood to be fulfilled in the time of the narrator and of those he addresses. If so, it would afford a link between them and Jesus in the story, and would suggest one of the times in which Christians were persecuted. But alternative interpretations of the references to persecution are possible. For example, they could encourage the community to sympathize with those whose witness included a martyr's death, or they could warn the community against a complacency that has come to terms with 'the world'.

It seems reasonable to suppose, therefore, that the narrator's time at least postdates Peter's martyrdom, and perhaps postdates the death of other disciples depicted in the story. But we cannot date the narrator's time more exactly, because we do not know how long a period is required for the kind of mature reflection on a familiar story which the narration encapsulates.

5. *The Time of the Reader*

5.1. *Tempo*

The way in which the length of the narrative is related to the time an incident would have taken to happen in the story provides its tempo. In the Fourth Gospel there is great variation. Events described in chs. 12–20 take place in the final week, and the rest of the ministry of over two years is related in chs. 1–11. In the first section no attempt is made to give a full account of Jesus' ministry. A year passes between Jesus' visit to Jerusalem where he meets Nicodemus (2.13) and the feeding miracle by the Sea of Tiberias (6.1), during which he or his disciples exercised a baptizing ministry (3.22; 4.2), and he went about preaching (4.7-42; 5-6) and healing (2.23; 4.46; 5.2) in Galilee, Samaria and Jerusalem. Another year elapses between the feeding miracle and the meal at Bethany (12.1), during which a series of disputes and two miracles are placed in and around Jerusalem and the council's condemnation of Jesus is noted. Twice Jesus withdraws from Jerusalem to avoid arrest, but, as we noted earlier, nothing is told of his activity (10.40-41; 11.54).

The incidents themselves are explained in the discourses and dialogues. Only one quarter of the narrative is description without dialogue, more than half is dialogue and the rest Jesus' monologue, but proportions vary in different sections. In chs. 1–12 they roughly conform to the average, but in chs. 13-17 only a very small part is narrative and most is Jesus' monologue. In chs. 18–19, on the other hand, Jesus makes no long speeches, and otherwise there is only slightly more narrative with dialogue than without. In chs. 20–21 a quarter of the narrative is without and the rest is with dialogue. Since in reading direct speech, the time taken to read approximates most closely the time taken within the story, speech inevitably slows down the tempo of the narrative. As the story approaches its climax, the tempo slows more and more, providing time for reflection (chs. 13–17) before events crowd in to fill the day of Jesus' death.

6. *Conclusion*

In structuring time, the Fourth Gospel describes the eternal in language which is fashioned to capture distinctions of time, and it makes the eternal fundamental to its presentation of the story. No part of the story can be understood without reference to the Creator God and her salvific purpose. Moreover, in depicting the significance of Jesus' life for believers, the narrative sometimes includes nonsensical statements: 'Now I am no longer in the world' (17.11). Its rhetoric of extreme oppositions involves both obvious contradictions and unresolved tensions. It drew on the theological reflections of Jews in their Scripture and on Christian traditions, but these did not provide a complete and systematic analysis of causality. When we read the Gospel, we become aware of the need for such an analysis, but it seems that the original writer and reader did not feel that need.

Chapter 3

THE GENRE OF THE FOURTH GOSPEL

> Interpretation proceeds by steps, and the first step on which everything else depends, is the decision to which genre a given work is to be assigned (Gombrich 1972: 121).

A genre is a species of literature such as tragedy, comedy, history or biography. It defines the organizing principle which gives coherence to its parts. It is therefore concerned both with details of content like motifs and style, and with the way in which these details contribute to the whole. For example,

> a comedy is a work in which materials are selected and managed primarily in order to interest and amuse us: the characters and their discomfitures engage our delighted attention rather than our profound concern, we feel confident that no great disaster will occur, and usually the action turns out happily for the chief characters (Abrams 1971: 25).

It is immediately obvious that the Fourth Gospel is not a comedy, but what is it, and how can its genre be defined?

No matter how creative an individual author, he or she is not a completely free agent in creating a literary work, if the work is to be read and understood by others. The sense of a text must be shared by author and readers for meaning to be communicated, and just as language cannot be used arbitrarily if it is to make sense, so the literary form must be comprehensible. This does not mean, however, that the traits and motifs of the new work must be identical to those of previous texts, but enough must be shared so that family likenesses can be discerned. Nor is genre a static entity. Motifs and vocabulary can be borrowed from an old genre to create a new genre, as when history is transformed into a novel. In order to define the genre of a given work, it is necessary to examine its relationship to other texts which existed at the time of its composition. This will be done in the case of the Fourth Gospel.

Unfortunately, we do not know with certainty when, where and by whom the Fourth Gospel was written. No reliable external information exists, and the Gospel itself does not tell us. We are left to infer what we can from the text itself. We shall examine this question in detail in Part III. It is safe to suppose, however, that it is a Christian work, written in the Graeco-Roman world, towards the end of the first century CE.

The Fourth Gospel is written in Hellenistic Greek. It is therefore reasonable to compare it with other Greek works from the period which seem to bear some resemblance to it. Moreover, the text itself cites passages from a particular collection of literature, to which it assigns supreme authority, its Scripture. It uses these passages to bolster its argument (e.g. 6.45; 12.38-42; 19.24, 37). I shall therefore begin by noting similarities and differences between the vocabulary, motifs and arrangement of the Fourth Gospel and its Scripture, and will then go on to explore relationships with other contemporary literature.

1. *The Fourth Gospel and its Scripture*

Freed's careful study (1965) of the scriptural quotations in the Fourth Gospel shows that it is generally impossible to decide whether they are based on the Hebrew Masoretic text as it has survived, or on the Greek version, the Septuagint, as it has come down to us. Some Hebrew manuscripts of Zech. 12.10 have the same reading as Jn 19.37, and Jn 13.18 may also depend on the Hebrew rather than the Greek. The difficulty in deciding which version is presupposed arises from the fact that, as Freed remarks, 'In every instance his quoted text appears to be adapted to its immediate context, to his literary style, and to the whole plan of the composition of his Gospel' (p. 129). This is true whether the quotation is placed on the lips of Jesus or not.

The Fourth Gospel refers to 'the Scripture' or 'the Scriptures' formally when introducing quotations. In 7.38, 10.35, 13.18 and 17.12 Jesus is the speaker and in 19.24, 28 and vv. 36-37 the references are from the narrator. Jn 7.42 is a remark of the people about Scripture's mentioning Christ's descent from David. Alternatively, the expression 'it is written' is used by both Jesus and the narrator: 2.17; 6.31, 45 (in the prophets); 10.34 (in your law); 12.14, 16 (it had been written of him); 15.25 (to fulfil the word that is written in their law). There are also three references to the fulfilment of Isaiah's prophecies, one from John the Baptist (1.23) and two from the narrator's reflection on Jesus' public ministry in 12.38-40. In addition, Scripture or 'what is written' is mentioned without quotations by the narrator in 2.22 and 20.9, and by Jesus in 5.39, 7.38 and 8.17. In 5.46 Jesus twice appeals to what Moses wrote, which he takes to be testimony to his own mission.

The margin of the Nestle–Kilpatrick edition of the Greek New Testament (1957) notes relevant passages from Scripture to which the Fourth Gospel is alluding or referring. These include references or allusions to Genesis, Exodus, Leviticus, Numbers, Deuteronomy, Joshua, 1 and 2 Samuel, 1 and 2 Kings, 2 Chronicles, Nehemiah, Tobit, 1 Maccabees, *4 Maccabees*, Psalms, Proverbs, Ecclesiastes, Job, the Wisdom of Solomon, Ecclesiasticus, *Psalms of Solomon*, Micah, Zechariah, Isaiah, Jeremiah, Baruch, Ezekiel and Daniel. A.C. Sundberg (1964: Table I, 54-55) also links *4 Ezra* 4.8 with Jn 3.13. It is clear from this list that reliance on the Septuagint is involved, since some of these book are not found in the Hebrew Scriptures. Most frequent reference or allusion is made to books which appear in both the Hebrew and the Greek versions, however, to the Pentateuch, Psalms, Isaiah, Jeremiah and Ezekiel.

A.C. Sundberg (1964) and James Barr (1983) have shown that at the end of the first century and the beginning of the second century CE, there was neither a Jewish nor a Christian canon, in the sense of an accepted list of the books to be reckoned as Scripture, so it is difficult to decide whether all of the books that later formed the Christian Old Testament canon were known to the community in which the Fourth Gospel was written. Moreover, it is hard to imagine what kind of access to manuscripts the writer of the Fourth Gospel had. Were scrolls kept by the community for use in the liturgy? Were the Scriptures learnt by heart so that they could be quoted without reference to the written word? Unfortunately, we have no external evidence to settle these questions. Nevertheless, that large parts of Scripture were familiar is suggested by the Fourth Gospel's direct quotations and by the vocabulary and theological perspective of the whole work.

No one can read the first verses of the Fourth Gospel without being reminded of the first verses of Genesis (see below), and in general the

Johannine text shares with its Scripture the presupposition that the world is the creation of a loving God who holds everything in being and whose purpose is to encourage humanity to live a full life in conformity with his creative will. Most important, without the scriptural conception of humanity made in the image and likeness of the transcendent God and its emphasis on humanity's imitation of God's justice and mercy, it would have been impossible for the Fourth Gospel to present the story of Jesus as a revelation of God's love for the world. Moreover, the arrangement of material, juxtaposing narratives of events, including miracles, with dialogues and discourses is shared by the Fourth Gospel with those parts of its Scripture which describe the lives of prophets, especially Exodus–Deuteronomy and 1 and 2 Kings. We shall look at these parallels in more detail.

1.1. *Moses and the Exodus*

The Fourth Gospel often refers to scriptural stories about Moses (e.g. 5.45; 6.25-51; 7.19), and there are obvious similarities between the form, content and vocabulary of the story in Exodus, Leviticus, Numbers and Deuteronomy and that in the Gospel according to John (see Teeple 1957, Glasson 1963, Meeks 1967). Moses, like Jesus, is God's spokesman sent to Israel with a particular mission (Exod. 3–4; Jn 7.16) which is not undertaken on his authority but on God's (LXX Num. 16.28; Jn 5.19, 30; 8.42). Empowered by the Spirit (Num. 11.17; Jn 1.32), Moses is the shepherd who performs the signs and works of God to bring his enemies to acknowledge God and to encourage belief among the Israelites, although lack of faith is mentioned more frequently (shepherd: Num. 27.17; Jn 10.11; signs: Exod. 3.12; 7.3; Deut. 13.1; Jn 2.11; 20.30-31; works: Exod. 34.10; Num. 16.28; Jn 5.36; acknowledgement; Exod. 7.5; 14.4; Jn 10.32; belief: Exod. 4.1; 14.31; Num. 14.11; Jn 10.38; unbelief in spite of signs: Deut. 29.2-4; Jn 12.37-40). Not that most of Moses' signs in Egypt have anything in common with the Johannine signs, but the provision of water (Exod. 15.22-23; 17; Num. 20) and bread (Exod. 16; Num. 11) for the Israelites in the wilderness, which exemplifies God's active support of his people, is taken up in the Gospel (Jn 4.7-15; 6.1-4; 7.37-39). Also, Jesus' first sign, changing the water in the stone vessels into wine (Jn 2.1-11), may echo Moses' first sign of changing water into blood, including the water in stone vessels (Exod. 7.19). Further, both Moses and Jesus understand that their 'food is to do the will' of God and 'to accomplish his work' (Exod. 34.28; Deut. 8.3; Jn 4.34). Again in both texts the signs lead up to the deliverance God effects through the sacrifice of the Passover Lamb (Exod. 12; Jn 19), so that they make known God's honour (Exod. 15.1-21; Jn 1.14), and the terms δοξάζω (honour) and ὑψόω (exalt) are associated (Exod. 15.2; Jn 3.14; 12.28) to praise the God who brings salvation. Moses and Jesus share the identical mission of making God's name known and honoured (Exod. 3.13; Jn 17.1-8), as a God who is faithful to his people (ἀλήθος, Exod. 33.16; Jn 1.47; 8.31; ἀληθινός Exod. 34.6; Num. 14.18; Jn 7.18). The Pentateuch uses ἀλήθως in the sense of 'really' and ἀληθινός in the sense of 'faithful', and the Fourth Gospel both mirrors this usage and greatly develops the potential that the Greek words for 'truth', 'true', 'truly' possessed for its soteriology.

Like the story of Jesus in the Fourth Gospel, the story of Moses and the Exodus is presented in a narrative which is dominated by dialogue and monologue, but there is a difference between the two. In Exodus–Deuteronomy God speaks directly to Moses, and Moses delivers the message to Pharaoh or Israel. In the Fourth Gospel there is only one verbatim speech from God (12.28). Instead, it is repeatedly stated that Jesus does and says only what he has seen and heard the Father doing (e.g. 5.19; 8.28; 17.8). Nevertheless, the Johannine emphasis on Jesus' direct and immediate access to the Father does have much in common with the portrait of Moses. Exod. 33.11 declares that 'Yahweh used to speak to Moses face to face, as a man speaks to his friend' (see also Deut. 34.10), an idea expressed in different terms in Num. 12.8 (LXX), 'With him [Moses], I [Yahweh] speak mouth to mouth, clearly and not in dark speech, and he beholds the glory of Yahweh'. Because the Septuagint describes Moses' vision of God as a vision of glory, Moses' transfiguration in Exod. 34.29-35 can be understood to develop the same language: 'the appearance of the colour of his face was glorified'. Jesus, too, shares God's honour (17.5, 22), his followers perceive his honour (1.14; 17.24), and his mission demonstrates that God honours him (7.39; 8.54; 17.1).

There are also similarities and differences in the use of the key terms 'to ascend' and 'to descend' (ἀναβαίνω and καταβαίνω). In the Exodus story Moses ascends the mountain on which Yahweh descends, and descends from the mountain to instruct and lead the people (Exod. 19 and 24). In the Fourth Gospel Jesus is depicted, in a sense to be explored later, as the one who has descended from heaven and who will ascend to the Father at the end of his ministry (e.g. 3.13; 6.51; 20.17). In other words, both Moses and Jesus descend to the people to make God known. We should note, by the way, that in general the Johannine depiction of creation as the heavens above (ἄνω) and the earth beneath (κάτω) is derived from its Scripture (e.g. Exod. 20.4; Deut. 5.8), and not, as is sometimes suggested, from Greek speculations. Non-Jewish Greek literature uses ἄνω to mean 'on the earth' and κάτω to mean 'under the earth'.

A large proportion of the Pentateuch details God's commandments which the Israelites are advised to hear and obey. Jesus' words are also to be heard and obeyed, although there is only one command: to love as Jesus loved. The summary of the law of Lev. 19.18, 'You shall love your neighbour as yourself', is interpreted by the example of Jesus, who laid down his life for his friends (Jn 15.12-14). But the Gospel does not indicate how the command would work itself out in the social life of the community. Nothing is said about sex, marriage, divorce, the family or relations with the state. By contrast, the Synoptic Gospels contain teaching about sex, marriage, divorce and relations with the state (Mt. 5.27-32; 19.3-9; 22.15-22 and parallels), and the First Gospel advocates celibacy for the sake of the kingdom of heaven (19.10-12). Paul's epistles also discuss divorce and celibacy (1 Cor. 7), as well as considering slavery (1 Cor. 7.21-24; Philemon) and relations with the state (Rom. 13). Moreover, polemic against the sexual mores of Hellenistic society is common in the Pauline epistles (e.g. Rom. 1.24-27; 1 Cor. 5–6) and reflects the tensions which existed between the new Christian ethos and the old order from which pagan converts came. Obedience to parents or to husbands is particularly stressed in the deutero-Pauline epistles (e.g. Eph. 5.21–6.4; Col. 3.18-21). The former is taken for granted in the Synoptics (e.g. Mt. 21.28-31; 19.19 and parallels; 15.4-5 and parallels), although it is sometimes set aside (e.g. Mt. 8.22 and parallels; 10.34-37 and parallels). Johannine silence about such questions could be explained in a number of different ways. Perhaps they had already been settled and the Gospel is to be understood as a second-generation Christian document. Perhaps no traditional teaching had been handed down from Jesus to the community. In either case, since Scripture provided detailed teaching, it may have been felt that the Gospel should supply no more than a summary in the light of Jesus' example.

Both the Pentateuch and the Gospel encourage readers by asserting that obedience will bring 'peace' which is contrasted with fear (Exod. 18.23; Lev. 26.6; Jn 14.27; 16.33). Again as the Law, God's λόγοι, expresses God's will, so Jesus, the λόγος become man, makes God's purpose known (Exod. 20.1; Jn 17.8). The Prologue describes the λόγος 'tabernacling' among people (1.14 ἐσκήνωσεν) as the Tabernacle of witness (ἡ σκηνὴ τοῦ μαρτυρίου) was the place where God met with Moses and made known his honour (Exod. 33.7). 'Witness' is a central theme of the Fourth Gospel, too, in that Jesus bears witness to God (Jn 3.11, 32) and God bears witness to Jesus through the signs, Scripture, John the Baptist and the Paraclete (Jn 5.31-47; 15.26). Jesus' crucifixion is decisively important to Jesus' role as God's witness, and again a link is made with the Moses story in 3.14, although Jesus plays the part assigned to the serpent rather than to Moses.

In view of these similarities, it is surprising that the Fourth Gospel never uses the word 'covenant' to describe God's relationship with his people. Nevertheless, vocabulary associated with the covenant concept in Scripture is found in the Gospel. Malatesta's study (1978) of εἶναι ἐν (to be in) and μένειν ἐν (to remain in) in the First Epistle of John argues that the epistle takes up covenant language from Scripture, and this has obvious implications for the Gospel, where the same words are used:

εἶναι ἐν:	1.4, 10; 9.5; 11.10; 12.35; 14.10, 17; 15.11; 17.11
μένειν ἐν:	6.56; 8.31, 35; 12.46; 14.10; 15.4, 5, 6, 7
μένειν εἰς:	6.27; 8.35; 12.34
μένειν ἐπί:	1.32, 33; 3.36
μένειν παρά:	14.17, 25
μένειν:	9.41; 12.24; 15.16

Malatesta draws special attention to the importance of Jer. 31.33, Ezek. 36.26-27, Exod. 17.7, 2 Kgs 1.3, 6, Isa. 45.14; Jer. 8.19, Ezek. 39.7, Psalm 61, Isa. 30.18, especially in the Septuagint version, in providing Johannine vocabulary (see also Pss. 9.7; 33.11; 89.36; 102.12; 111.3; 117.2; Wis. 7.27; Isa. 40.6; 66.22). In addition, the intimacy of the covenant is expressed in terms of God's knowledge of Israel (Amos 3.2), language which is used of the intimacy of Father and Son in the Gospel (10.15). Moreover, the Johannine picture of Israel as God's own people, albeit a rejecting people, as in the Prologue's 'He came to his own home and his own people received him not' (1.11) or in Jesus' testimony 'that a prophet has no honour in his own country' (4.44) assumes the Scriptural covenant, as, for example, in Exod. 19.5: 'Now, therefore, if you will obey my voice and keep my covenant, you shall be my own possession among all the nations'. According to the Gospel, however, the majority of Jews are disobedient. Only a few respond to Jesus and become his own people (10.14), forming a new community endowed with the Spirit and keeping the love command in fulfilment of Ezekiel's prophecy about the new covenant.

> A new heart I will give you, and a new spirit I will put within you; and I will take out of your flesh the heart of stone and give you a heart of flesh. And I will put my spirit within you and cause you to walk in my statutes and be careful to observe my ordinances (36.26-27).

This means that, although the Fourth Gospel does not use the word 'covenant', it does develop the idea of the covenant community in receipt of God's blessings and faithfulness to him.

The Pentateuch describes Moses' mission achieving its end: the rescue of the Israelites from Egypt to a land where they could live in a community obeying God's will, but the venture involves failures which threaten and finally cost Moses' life. Not only does Pharaoh seek to kill him (Exod. 10.28) but he is in danger of being stoned by desperately disillusioned Israelites (e.g. Exod. 17.4; Num. 14.10). His followers often murmur against him (Exod. 16.2; Num. 11.1). He offers his life to save the people from the consequences of their idolatry (Exod. 32.32) and finally his life is forfeit before the promised land is entered (Deut. 32.50). The book of Deuteronomy gives his farewell discourses, looking back on his experiences and forward to the new community life in the promised land. Parallels with the Johannine portrait of Jesus are clear. The 'Jews' murmur against him (6.41). Pilate finally hands him over to be crucified (19.16) after he had escaped from stoning on two occasions (8.59; 10.31) but his life is given willingly so that his disciples may become a new and loving community, as he explains in his Farewell Discourses (chs. 13–17).

It is possible, then, to see the Fourth Gospel as a transposition of the theological story of Moses and the Exodus. Other terms are common to both texts. The idiom 'on the third day' indicates the decisive day (Exod. 19.16; Jn 2.1; 20.1); in Exodus, the Israelites are an ἔθνος, a λαός and a συναγωγή, as they are in John, but the Gospel does not refer to them as 'sons of Israel'. Rather the Gospel refers to Jesus as a true Israelite (vine: 15.1) and as God's son, as Israel was God's first-born son (Exod. 4.22). ἀγαπάω ('to love'), ζάω ('to live') and ζωή ('life') are themes of Deuteronomy and of the Fourth Gospel, but ζωή αἰώνιος ('eternal life' Jn 6.40, 47) is taken from Dan. 12.2, where a notion of post-mortem resurrection is shared with the Gospel but not with the Pentateuch. Hence Deut. 13.1 can speak of a prophet arising (ἀνίστημι, cf. Num. 24.17 LXX) but not mean resurrection. Since both the Pentateuch and the Fourth Gospel are soteriological, they use σωτηρία ('salvation'—e.g. Exod. 14.13; 15.2; Jn 4.22 cf. 42) and depict God's 'way' (e.g. Exod. 32.8; Jn 14.6), but whereas Exodus often mentions χάρις ('grace'—e.g. Exod. 33.12, 17; 34.9), it is found only in the Prologue of the Fourth Gospel (Jn 1.16-17).

I have so far drawn attention to the similarities and have mentioned differences largely in terms of 'transposition', but it is striking that John does not make use of the image of God's presence as a pillar of fire, preferring instead the more benevolent theme of light, mentioned only in connexion with the plague in Exod. 10.21. The Fourth Gospel's belief in the resurrection of Jesus and, in the future, of those who believe in him, is clearly not derived from the story of Moses, which is much more interested in the prosperity of descendents than in individual survival. Moreover, there is a marked difference in scale: Moses leads multitudes, the twelve tribes, towards the promised land, but Jesus leads only twelve disciples, for whom verbal battles have replaced military ones, and individual baptism has replaced the crossing of the Red Sea and the Jordan.

Perhaps the most surprising difference between the two accounts, however, is the omission by the Fourth Gospel of any reference to or warning against idolatry. Such warnings pepper the Pentateuch (e.g. Exod. 20.4, 23; 23.24; Lev. 20.1-9; 26.1-2; Deut. 4.3, 15-40), and the story of Israel making the Golden Calf and suffering punishment (Exod. 32–34) stands at the centre of the Exodus account as a paradigm of God's hatred of idolatry. This dominant pentateuchal motif is absent from the Fourth Gospel and the omission is difficult to explain. Outside Palestine before 70 CE, and increasingly within Palestine after that date, pagan temples and shrines dominated the landscape. There can be no doubt that the Fourth Gospel's theological perspective would have conceived these institutions as idolatrous (4.21-24). The epistles of Paul do not ignore these realities (e.g.

Rom. 1.23-25; 1 Cor. 8–10; 2 Cor. 6.14-18; Gal. 5.19-20). Why does the Fourth Gospel? Two possible answers spring to mind. The first is that the Fourth Gospel confines the career of Jesus within Galilee, Samaria and Judaea before the destruction of the Temple, and depicts him engaged in a mission to these peoples. No polemic against idolatry would be necessary in this context. Nevertheless, since, in his Farewell Discourses (chs. 14–17), the Johannine Jesus does give warnings to disciples about their future, the dangers of idolatry in the Graeco-Roman world could have been mentioned, just as Moses mentions them in his farewell discourses. The second is that the Gospel is addressed not to new Christian converts from paganism, as Paul's letters are, but to second-generation Christians for whom idolatry is no longer a living option. Moreover, the 'Jews' of the Fourth Gospel are accused of being children of the devil (8.44-45), that is, devotees of a false god. It is in opposition to them that devotion to the one true God is stressed, but the lesson could easily be applied to worshippers of pagan deities.

In Deut. 18.15-18 Moses recounts God's promise that in the future he would raise up a prophet like Moses:

> I [the Lord] will raise up for them a prophet like you [Moses] from among their brethren; and I will put my words in his mouth, and he shall speak to them all that I command him. And whoever will not give heed to my words which he shall speak in my name, I myself will require it of him.

The passage is never explicitly quoted in the Fourth Gospel, but it seems to have influenced the Gospel's portrayal of Jesus. Jesus is rightly acknowledged as 'the prophet who is to come into the world' (6.14; cf. 4.19; 7.40; 9.17), whereas John is not that prophet (1.21, 23, 25). Jesus himself accepts the designation when he testifies 'that a prophet has no honour in his own country' (4.44). Moreover, Jesus speaks the words which the Father has given him (17.8; 7.16; 8.26-38). That the Gospel sees Jesus as the prophet like Moses explains the many connexions which can be made between the stories of each of them.

2.2 *Elijah and Elisha*

Both Buchanan (1968) and Brown (1971) have drawn attention to parallels between the Johannine story of Jesus and the scriptural stories of Elijah and Elisha. In outline, Elijah's life is similar to Jesus' in that he suffers persecution but is vindicated by God. Buchanan makes much of the fact that Jesus performs seven signs, Elijah seven and Elisha fourteen, and he details similarities in accounts of particular miracles. Most commentators accept that the Johannine story of the multiplication of the loaves (Jn 6.1-14) reflects a similar one about Elisha (2 Kgs 4.42-44) in its use of κρίθινος ('barley loaves') and παιδάρίον ('young lad'—2 Kgs 4.12, 14, 25; 5.20), but no other parallels are quite so convincing. Buchanan cites: Jn 6.16-21 and 2 Kgs 2.8, 14; 6.1-7; Jn 9.1-7 and 2 Kgs 6.15-19; Jn 11.1-44 and 1 Kgs 17.17-24; 2 Kgs 4.18-37; 13.21; Jn 2.1-11 and 1 Kgs 17.8-16; 2 Kgs 2.19-22; 3.13-20; 4.1-7 and 38-41. To this list he might have added Jn 4.7-15 and 1 Kgs 17.8-16. Moreover, the contents of Jesus' prayer in 11.41-42 are the same as Elijah's (1 Kgs 18.37). It seems unlikely that the Fourth Gospel intended a close parallel between Jesus and Elisha, however, since it explicitly denies that John is Elijah (Jn 1.21), and in fact the similarities between the stories of Elijah and Elisha and those of Moses are much closer than between 1 and 2 Kings and the Fourth Gospel. Like Moses, Elijah is fed in the desert, supplies food in a famine, divides the water, calls on heavenly fire and is victorious in war. Like Moses, Elisha provides wholesome food and water, cures leprosy and uses it as a punishment, turns water into blood, divides the water and is victorious in battle. Apart from the vocabulary in 2 Kings 4, there is no exact correspondence in terminology between 1 and 2 Kings and the Fourth Gospel. Nevertheless, the pattern of persecution and divine vindication is found not only with Moses, Elijah, and to a lesser extent Elisha, but with Jeremiah too. In general, then, the Fourth Gospel presents Jesus as a prophetic 'type' who conforms most closely to Moses.

1.3. *Israel and the King*

'Thus says the Lord: "Israel is my first-born son"' (Exod. 4.22). So Moses is instructed by God to address Pharaoh. The relationship of father to son, especially the dependence of the son on the father, the father's care for the son, and the son's obedience to the father, is used metaphorically in the Pentateuch to explain Israel's relationship with God (e.g. Deut. 1.31; 8.5). In the same way, Israel's representative, the king or messiah, is called God's son:

> I [Yahweh] will be his [Solomon's] father and he shall be my son. When he commits iniquity, I will chasten him with the rod of men, with the stripes of the sons of men, but I will not take my steadfast love from him (2 Sam. 7.14-15, cf. Ps. 2.7-9).

And Israel's sonship brings with it obligations to make God known to all peoples (e.g. Exod. 19.6: a kingdom of priests. It is the priestly function to make God known). It is not surprising, therefore, that in the Fourth Gospel, Jesus, Israel's messianic representative, is called God's son (e.g. 1.49; 5.18-47; 8.34-36; 17.1-5). Jesus, unlike Israel, is obedient to God, even when that obedience requires death on a cross (e.g. 5.19-20; 12.27-28), and hence Jesus is the true vine (15.1-11), in contrast to Israel, described as choice vines which produced only wild grapes (Isa. 5.2) or as a vine plucked up in fury, cast down, dried up, its fruit stripped off, its strong stem (the king) withered, and consumed by fire (Ezek. 19.12). According to the Fourth Gospel, the scriptural hopes for and expectations of God's son, Israel, are now fulfilled in the obedient life of the true representative of Israel, his messiah, Jesus (12.13; 19.19), who will draw all people to himself (12.32). Like the messiah described in Deut. 17.14-20, Isaiah 9 and 11, and Micah 5.4, Jesus is chosen by God (1.34) to fulfil his purpose. Whether the Fourth Gospel uses the title 'Son of God' in other ways will be discussed later. Here attention is drawn to the fact that the designation is taken from and used in some ways determined by Johannine Scripture.

1.4. *The Son of Man and the Man*

Pilate presents Jesus to the Jewish crowds in these words, 'Behold the man' (19.5). It will be argued in detail later that not only is Jesus' humanity central to the drama of the Fourth gospel, but that his humanity, his way of living a human existence in obedience to God, is presented as *the* way for people to live (e.g. 14.6). Jesus is not just simply a man, but the epitome of what God intended in creating the human race. This is why some of Jesus' sayings in the Fourth Gospel take over from its Scripture a Hebrew or Aramaic idiom, 'Son of man' (e.g. Ps. 8.4; Dan. 7.13), in its generic sense, and it is why the sayings generally use the definite article, *the* Son of man (e.g. 12.23-26). The full significance of the idiom 'the Son of man' is controversial, and the issues will be set out later. What is less controversial is that the Fourth Gospel portrays Jesus both as the true Israel and as *the* human being, who exemplifies the kind of existence which those who believe in him are encouraged to adopt. Believers are both to remain in Jesus the true vine (15.2-8), and to conform their lives to his (12.23-26; 13.12-17). In the Fourth Gospel, therefore, Jesus plays not only the prophetic role of making God known, but also that of the perfect human being whose life is a model for his followers.

1.5. *Key Terms from Other Parts of Scripture*

At the end of §1.1 I noted some key terms in the Moses story which the Fourth Gospel fails to develop, and also differences which I explained as 'transposition'. In addition, important Johannine concepts like 'light' and 'truth' seem to receive little attention in the Exodus story. Creation images of the opposition of light and darkness are, however, developed in the poetic sections of Scripture, in Psalms and frequently in Isaiah and Job. In the ethical sphere light and darkness symbolize good and evil (e.g. Job 22.11; 24.14, 15, 16; Ps. 35.6; Isa. 58.10), and darkness means death and destruction (e.g. Job 10.21-22; 15.22; 18.6; Ps. 105.28 in an account of Moses as God's servant; Isa. 5.30; 8.22) while light is associated with God's honour and salvation (e.g. Job 19.8; 37.15; Ps. 112.4; Isa. 9.2; 29.15, 18; 42.7, 16; 49.9; 60.1-2; Wis. 5.6; 7.25-26; 17.20-21; 18.1, 4).

Like the Pentateuch, the Fourth Gospel uses ἀληθινός in the sense of 'faithful' (7.28). In the rest of the Septuagint, as in the Pentateuch, ἀλήθεια (truth) and cognates generally mean 'fidelity' and 'faithful', but the following examples express the meaning 'genuiness' and 'genuine': Isa. 27.18, Jer. 2.21, Prov. 8.7 and Tob. 8.7; or 'accurate': Job 19.4, Ps. 5.9, Prov. 22.20-21, 26.28, 1 Esd. 4.33-40, Wis. 2.17, Sir. 37.15, Tob. 5.11, 13, 7.10. Nowhere in the Septuagint, however, is there quite the concentration on these terms found in the Fourth Gospel.

1.6. *Wisdom Literature*

There is something of a consensus among scholars that the Fourth Gospel is influenced by Wisdom literature. This is sometimes misleadingly described as the influence of 'Judaism' or of 'Hellenistic Philosophy' in distinction from that of Scripture, presumably because Protestants accept only the Hebrew Scriptures as the 'Old Testament', but the Greek Scriptures with which John seems to be familiar included not only Job and Proverbs but the Wisdom of Solomon, Ecclesiasticus and Baruch as well. This, then, is another aspect of scriptural influence on the Johannine text. Brown (1966) provides a very useful list of 'wisdom motifs' in the Fourth Gospel, citing especially Job 28, Proverbs 1–9, Sirach 1, 4.11-19, 6.18-31, 14.20,

15.10; 24; Wisdom of Solomon 6–10; Bar. 3.9–4.4, and concluding:

> This short treatment should help to support our contention that Wisdom literature offers better parallels for the Johannine picture of Jesus than do the later Gnostic, Mandaean, or Hermetic passages sometimes suggested. However, John has noticeably modified details of the presentation of Wisdom by introducing a much sharper historical perspective than is found in the O.T. poems. If Jesus is incarnate Wisdom, this incarnation has taken place at a particular place and time, once and for all (pp. cxxii-ccxxiii).

1.6.1. *Resurrection.* One way in which Wisdom literature has contributed to Johannine theology has already been mentioned: the belief in post-mortem resurrection draws most obviously on Dan. 12.2, but Nickelsburg's study (1972) demonstrates the way in which prophetic and wisdom motifs contributed to its development. Wisdom stories about the persecution and vindication of the righteous in this life (e.g Joseph in Gen. 37–50; Esther; Dan. 3 and 6; Susanna) and the poem depicting the fate of the servant in Isaiah 52–53 furnish the structure and the language for expressing belief in post-mortem vindication in the Wisdom of Solomon 1–6 and in Daniel 12, and hence provide the Fourth Gospel with a developed tradition for explaining the significance of the suffering of Jesus and his disciples. In this instance, the Fourth Gospel is closer to Daniel since it uses 'resurrection', whereas the Wisdom of Solomon prefers the terms 'immortality' (ἀθανασία) and 'incorruptibility' (ἀφθαρσία).

1.6.2. *Gnomic statements.* Another feature which the Fourth Gospel shares with Wisdom literature is its liking for gnomic statements which describe a truth without implication of time: 'He who believes in the Son has eternal life' (Jn 3.36) is similar to 'He who finds me finds life' (Prov. 8.35 and see Jn 5.24 and Prov. 4.13; Wis. 1.12). Perhaps C.F.D. Moule (1962) in his essay on the individualism of the Fourth Gospel puts too much stress on the 'individualism' of this Wisdom form. The Gospel prefers personal address in the singular (e.g. 3.15, 16, 18, 33, 36; 5.24; 6.47, 54; 7.37) but it often juxtaposes singular and plural (e.g. 1.14, 16; 3.11, 19; 4.23, 24, 42, 48; 5.25; 6.53, 69; 7.13; 8.34; 17.3, 6, 20; 20.23) as Proverbs does (e.g. 8.17 = plural; 8.35-36 = singular). These similarities exist, but in comparison with Proverbs and the Wisdom of Solomon, the Fourth Gospel is repetitive, developing only a few themes from chapter to chapter. In this respect, it is much more like exhortatory sections of Exodus, Leviticus and Deuteronomy.

1.6.3. *Key concepts from Wisdom literature.* The best way of illustrating similarities and differences between Wisdom writings and the Fourth Gospel is to elucidate the meaning of the term λόγος in the Prologue (Jn 1.1-18). Whether the Gospel adapts a poem which existed separately or itself supplies a semi-poetic prologue, these verses provide an appropriate theological and christological introduction to the work. Within the Prologue what does ὁ λόγος mean and why was it used? Like the beginning of Genesis, the Prologue begins with ἐν ἀρχῇ ('in the beginning') and there are many other echoes of Genesis 1: the creation of light and life, the creation of human beings in God's image and likeness, and, as far as λόγος is concerned, the description of creation through God's speech. Instead of using the term λόγος, however, the Genesis account makes a series of statements: 'God *said*, Let there be light, and there was light...God *said*...', but taking up this imagery, Ps. 33.6 LXX does use λόγος: 'By the λόγος of the Lord, the heavens were made, and all their host by the breath of his mouth'.

Mention of God's λόγος is found in other parts of Scripture too. Prophetic inspiration is expressed as the reception or perception of the λόγος of the Lord' (Isa. 2.1; Hos. 1.1; Joel 1.1), and the Law is described as 'the statements (λόγοι) of the Lord' (e.g. Exod. 20.1; Deut. 32.46). In some passages λόγος is even given a quasi-independent existence: 'He sends forth his command to the earth; his λόγος runs smoothly... He sends forth his λόγος and melts them' (Ps. 147.15 and 18) and in the Septuagint of Hab. 3.5, λόγος goes forth before God's face. Even this personification, however, although it undoubtedly influenced the choice of λόγος in the Prologue, is still not quite identical with Johannine usage. The Prologue asserts that θεός and λόγος exist eternally in distinction: the λόγος is πρὸς τὸν θεόν ('with God') and θεὸς ἦν ὁ λόγος ('the λόγος was God'). The second clause cannot be interpreted as a declaration of complete identity, equivalent to ὁ λόγος ἦν ὁ θέος because this would involve a direct contradiction of the previous clause. On the other hand, the statement does not mean that ὁ λόγος was 'a god' or 'divine'. As Harner (1973) has shown, θεὸς ἦν ὁ λόγος, with an anarthrous predicate *before* the verb, means something between these two extremes: ὁ λόγος has the nature of θέος but the terms are not synonymous, not exactly equivalent or interchangable.

Many commentators have pointed to similarities between statements in the Prologue about λόγος and statements in Wisdom literature about σοφία ('wisdom'). Like λόγος, σοφία is said to exist at the beginning (e.g. Prov. 8.22), although Wisdom is the first of creation, whereas the Johannine λόγος exists apart from creation. Wisdom is also 'with God' (e.g. Prov. 8.30 παρ' αὐτῷ not πρός αυτόν, and Wis. 9.4), God's agent in creation (e.g. Prov. 3.19; Wis. 7.22). In Wis. 9.2 λόγος and σοφία are used in parallel: 'Merciful Lord, who has made all things by your λόγος, and in your wisdom has fashioned man'. Further, Wisdom is associated with life (e.g. Prov. 8.35) and light (e.g. Wis. 7.26), and like the light of the Prologue, Wisdom is in the world (e.g. Sir. 24.6) but rejected by people (e.g. Prov. 1.29), although some accept it (e.g. Wis. 7.27). In Sir. 24.8 Wisdom is instructed to 'make your home in Jacob; find your heritage in Israel'. Moreover, Wisdom is unique (μονογενής) and reflects God's glory (δόξα) (e.g. Wis. 7.22-25). These resemblances to the λόγος of the Prologue are certainly arresting, although none exactly corresponds to the Johannine statement that the λόγος became or was flesh (1.14). They also raise the problem: Why does the Prologue use λόγος and not σοφία? Three factors may have played their part. Firstly, the links which λόγος affords with speculation about creation, the Law and prophetic inspiration, already noted, are important. Secondly, σοφία is a feminine noun and when personified 'wisdom' is always a woman. The Prologue reaches a climax with the λόγος becoming a man, Jesus, and perhaps the masculine λόγος was felt to be more appropriate. Thirdly, λόγος plays an important role in Stoic philosophy, expressing divine immanence, which is akin to part, though not the whole, of the Johannine meaning, and such a connexion with popular philosophy would be advantageous.

It is fair to conclude that the Wisdom writings which formed part of the Gospel's Scripture have influenced Johannine speculation, especially about creation and enlightenment.

1.6.4. *'I am'*. One of the sharpest differences between the Fourth Gospel and the first three Gospels is its depiction of Jesus' declaring truths about himself. Not only are there no messianic secrets in John, but Jesus tells opponents and enemies who he is as openly as he tells disciples (e.g. 5.19-47; 8.12-30; 18.20, 36-38). One of the ways in which he does so is to make statements beginning 'I am', as in 'I am the Good Shepherd' (10.11) or 'I am the true Vine' (15.1). In

Scripture prophets do not use this form, but, on the contrary, point away from themselves by introducing their oracles, 'Thus says the Lord'. The form 'I am...' is found in Scripture, however, in the Wisdom writings, where personified Wisdom speaks of her attributes. For example,

> I, Wisdom, dwell in prudence, and I find knowledge and discretion... I have counsel, and sound wisdom, I have insight. I have strength. By me kings reign, and rulers decree what is just... I love those who love me, and those who seek me diligently find me... I walk in the way of righteousness, in the paths of justice, endowing with wealth those who love me, and filling their treasuries (Prov. 8.12-21).

Or again, in Sir. 24.3-31:

> I came forth from the mouth of the Most High; it is I who covered the earth like a mist... Before time began, he created me and I shall remain for ever... I took root among the people whom the Lord had honoured... There I grew like a cedar of Lebanon... I grew like a fair olive-tree... Like cassia and camel-thorn, I was redolent of spices; I spread my fragrance like choice myrrh... I was like the smoke of incense in the sacred tent... I put forth lovely shoots like the vine... Whoever feeds on me will be hungry for more, and whoever drinks from me will thirst for more... As for me, I was like a canal leading from a river, a watercourse into a pleasure garden. I said, I will water my garden, drenching its flower beds.

So, Jesus declares who he is in the manner of personified Wisdom, using the same 'I am' formula, and combining it with images and concepts from other parts of Scripture—the vine, the shepherd, the door, bread, light, the way, life, truth, resurrection—to declare who he is. The differences between Proverbs 8 and Sirach 24 on the one hand, and the Johannine Jesus on the other, are the differences between personification and a person, as Brown has made clear (1966: cxxii).

Occasionally, the Johannine Jesus says 'I am' without adding a predicate, and scholars have disagreed about the meaning of some instances of this 'absolute' use. Some examples are uncontroversial, however. When the soldiers arrive to arrest Jesus, he identifies himself as the one they seek by declaring ἐγώ εἰμι, that is, 'I am (he)' (18.5, 8). The same meaning, self identification, is to be found in Jesus' statement to his disciples, frightened at the sight of his walking on the water: 'It is I' (ἐγώ εἰμι, 6.20). Moreover, Jesus is not the only person in the Gospel to identify himself with those words. The man born blind, when questioned about his identity, declares ἐγώ εἰμι, 'I am he/It is I' (9.9).

Jesus' statements in 8.28 and 13.19 are best understood in the same way. In each case Jesus identifies himself as the person whom he had introduced earlier in the discourse. In 8.28 he identifies himself as the one who declares to the world what he has heard from the Father, mentioned in 8.26, 'When you have lifted up the Son of man, then you will know that I am he/it is I, and that I do nothing on my own authority but speak this as the Father taught me'. Again, in connexion with Jesus' prediction about the betrayer, Jesus goes on to say, 'I tell you this now, before it takes place, that when it does take place, you may believe that I am he' (13.19), that is, that Jesus is their teacher and Lord, who knows whom he has chosen (13.14 and 18).

The peculiarity of one reference, however, 'Truly, truly, I say to you, before Abraham was, I am he' (8.58) has prompted many commentators to look for another meaning. The saying forms the climax to a discussion about the relative importance of Abraham and Jesus. Jesus claims that anyone who keeps his teaching will not die (8.51), to which the 'Jews' reply that Abraham and the prophets had died and ask rhetorically whether Jesus is greater than Abraham. Jesus, as usual, replies indirectly. He claims to know God and mentions that Abraham rejoiced to see his day, interpreting Abraham's laugh positively (Gen. 17.17) and God's promise as fulfilled in his own mission. The 'Jews' misunderstand his interpretation of Scripture as a ridiculous claim to have seen Abraham. Jesus' final reply, the obscure saying of 8.58, must in some sense answer the 'Jewish' question and, at the same time, make clear the Jesus is superior even to Abraham. The 'Jews' understand that he claims some kind of superiority since they try to stone him (8.59). But why is Jesus' reply so elusive? What possible meanings does it convey? πρίν ('before') is a temporal conjunction. Taken literally, the first clause refers to a time before Abraham existed. Does the whole statement mean something like this: 'Yes, I have seen Abraham, because I existed before Abraham, and have existed ever since. In fact, I am God, and this is what makes me superior to Abraham?'

Brown (1966: Appendix IV) argues that it does, because he understands Jesus' ἐγώ εἰμι as a pronunciation of the name of God, and hence, as a claim to be God. What is the evidence for such a use of ἐγώ εἰμι? Exodus 3 tells the story of the revelation of God's name to

Moses. In 3.14 the Septuagint translation renders the Hebrew: ἐγώ εἰμι ὁ ὤν, 'I am he who is'. The passage hardly warrants the suggestion that ἐγώ εἰμι functions alone as the divine name, since here it is not alone (cf. Exod. 6.7; 7.5; 20.1). Nevertheless, in prophetic oracles, in which God's uniqueness is stressed, the Septuagint does translate the Hebrew for 'I (am) he' by the Greek ἐγώ εἰμι (e.g. Isa. 43.10; Joel 2.27). But we should notice that here ἐγώ εἰμι does not function as a divine name, but as a self-identification. God identifies himself as the unique Creator. In other words, the expression functions in these Scriptural examples in exactly the way it functions in Jn 18.5, 8, 6.20 and 9.9, namely, to allow the speaker to identity himself. Of course, the 'self' identified in each instance is different. In the prophetic oracles God identifies himself as God, and in the Fourth Gospel the man born blind identifies himself as the man born blind (9.9).

Nevertheless, Brown insists that the doubling of the 'I am' in the Septuagint translation of Isa. 43.25, 'I, I am he who blots out your transgressions': ἐγώ εἰμι ἐγώ εἰμι ὁ ἐξαλείφων...' means that the second 'I am' is a declaration of the divine name. In other words, God declares, 'I am "I am" (= divine name), who blots out your transgressions'. Were there evidence that elsewhere 'I am' is the divine name, this would be a possible, but not a necessary reading of the Septuagint of Isa. 43.25 (and cf. Isa. 51.12). Without such evidence, however, Brown's suggestion is merely fanciful, an attempt to find later Catholic christological doctrine in the Fourth Gospel. The only evidence from Scripture which he cites in support of his case is the Septuagint of Isa. 52.6, 'Therefore my people should know *my name*, because I am he, who speaks (ἐγώ εἰμι αὐτὸς ὁ λαλῶν); I am here (πάρειμι)'. Brown interprets 'my name' and 'I am' as parallel expressions which should be identified, but if 'I am' is a name in the second clause, it is impossible to translate, since a verb not a name is required. Lindars rightly rejects Brown's argument as unconvincing (1972: 336). He points out that if Jesus' ἐγώ εἰμι in 8.58 is to be understood as a name, the statement should read 'Before Abraham was, I am "I am"'. It is better, as in the case of Isa. 52.6, to allow ἐγώ εἰμι its verbal force, but how are we to understand it?

If we construe it in the light of the other examples of its use in John, namely as a self-identification, does this make sense in the context? The statement would be translated, 'Before Abraham was, I am he'. We noticed that in 13.19 Jesus' 'I am he' refers back to claims made about himself a few verses earlier (13.14 and 18), that is, to the claim that he is teacher and Lord. In 8.28, too, Jesus' 'I am he' refers back to his earlier assertion that he teaches only what he hears from the Father (8.26). So here in 8.58 Jesus' statement appropriately refers back to the opening words of the discourse, to the statement which provides its theme, 'I am the light of the world' (8.12). As the light of the world, Jesus fulfils God's promise to Abraham, that 'in him all the nations of the earth would be blessed' (Gen. 12.3). He is therefore superior to Abraham.

But are Lindars (1972) and others correct in referring 8.58 back not to 8.12, but to 1.5? According to the Prologue light shone in the world even before Abraham. Long after Abraham was dead, however, the light was focused through one man, Jesus (1.14; 8.12). Is Jesus' remark, 'Before Abraham was, I am he' a reminder that he is the eternal λόγος? This is neither an obvious nor a necessary reading. If a connexion was intended between 8.58 and 1.4-5, surely the imperfect tense of the verb 'to be' would have been used, as it is in the Prologue. The use of the present tense, 'I am', connects with its use in 8.12.

How, then, are we to construe, 'Before Abraham (was)'? The verb γενέσθαι is omitted by codex D and the old Latin versions and may be an addition occasioned by later christological developments. The literal meaning refers to the time before Abraham was born. On a literal level it answers the question put by the 'Jews', 'Have you seen Abraham?' (8.57) with, in effect, 'Yes'. The 'Jews' react to the absurdity of the answer, that a man not yet 50 lived before Abraham did, by trying to stone him. All this suggests, however, that the 'Jewish' interpretation is to be rejected, just as Nicodemus's literal interpretation of Jesus' advice to be born again (3.4) is a misunderstanding which has to be rejected. But if the statement is not to be taken literally, how else can it be taken? It can be taken metaphorically to refer not literally to time, but metaphorically to precedence. This movement between literal time and metaphorical precedence had already been explored in relation to John (1.15, 27, 30). Just as John came before Jesus in time, so did Abraham. Nevertheless, Jesus is superior to both of them. The brief statement 'Before Abraham, I am he' asserts that, in spite of Abraham's temporal priority, Jesus, as the light of the world, who fulfils God's promise, is superior to Abraham.

We should conclude, therefore, that the Johannine Jesus' use of the 'I am' form draws on Wisdom declarations from its Scripture, and does not assert Jesus' divinity.

1.7. *Satan*

One important term, not yet mentioned, which the Fourth Gospel derives from parts of its Scripture, from sections produced in the Persian and Hellenistic periods, is that of Satan (13.27—a transliteration of the Hebrew), or the devil (6.70; 8.44; 13.2—a Greek translation of Satan), or the ruler of this world (12.31; 14.30; 16.11). Satan or the devil is referred to in the opening chapters of Job, where he is pictured as Job's tempter, but he does nothing which has not received God's sanction. He is rather God's agent and angelic messenger than God's opponent. In 1 Chron. 21.1, however, he incites David to number Israel, a matter which displeases God. Here the devil plays the role of God's adversary, as in the Fourth Gospel. In Wis. 2.24 the devil is made the source of death. The Fourth Gospel calls him a murderer (8.44). The expression 'the ruler of this world' seems to be a Johannine invention—there are no instances outside the Fourth Gospel—and it derives from the Johannine picture of the world alienated from God.

The devil in the Fourth Gospel succeeds in preventing people from believing in Jesus. He, not God nor Abraham, is the father of unbelieving 'Jews' (8.44). As the ruler of the world, he is active in bringing about Jesus' death (14.30), yet that death is the means by which he is overcome (12.31; 16.11). He inspires Judas to betray Jesus (13.2), and enters into him at the supper table (13.27), language which suggests possession. Indeed, in 6.70 Judas is simply identified with the devil.

We should notice that, particularly in comparison with the Synoptic Gospels, references to the devil are infrequent, and his role generally conforms to that in Scripture, without much indication of developments in demonology which can be seen in writings like *1 Enoch* and *Jubilees*, developments reflected in the Synoptic Gospels. In the Fourth Gospel the devil does not tempt Jesus (*contra* Mt. 4/Lk. 4), is not called 'Beelzebul, the prince of demons' (e.g. Mt. 12.24-32 and parallels), and does not use demons to possess human beings in order to cause illness or madness. At least, the notion that demons cause madness is found only in 'Jewish' accusations against Jesus, 'Are we not right in saying that you are a Samaritan and have a demon?' (8.48; 7.20; 10.20-21), and these references do not make it clear whether the 'Jewish' taunts are both wrong and superstitious, or just wrong. The Fourth Gospel never depicts Jesus' casting out demons to effect cures. The Johannine Jesus is much more like the miracle-working prophets Moses, Elijah and Elisha, than the magicians of the first-century CE Graeco-Roman world.

1.8. *Summary*

It may be useful at this point to notice how far the motifs, vocabulary, arrangement and genre of the Fourth Gospel are explained by reference to Scripture, and how far the Fourth Gospel differs from its Scripture. The Fourth Gospel depicts Jesus as a prophet like Moses who makes God known to his people. Many of the motifs and much of the vocabulary used in the two are common, as is the juxtaposition of dialogue, monologue, miracle and accounts of opposition. Nevertheless, the Fourth Gospel usually does not follow Exodus–Deuteronomy in reporting God's direct speech within the dialogues, and only two of the Johannine miracles echo Moses' (the changing of water into wine, the feeding of the five thousand). The number of Jesus' miracles is the same as that of Elijah's: seven; Elijah, Elisha and Jesus raise the dead, although the procedures are different in each case (1 Kgs 17.17-24; 2 Kgs 4.18-37; Jn 11.1-44), and they feed the hungry (1 Kgs 17.8-16; 2 Kgs 4.42-44; Jn 6.1-14). Unlike the Synoptic Jesus, the Johannine Jesus does not follow Elisha in curing leprosy (2 Kgs 5; Mt. 8.1-4 and parallels). In general, moreover, Jesus does not share with these prophets the miracles of destruction, like Moses' signs in Egypt which force Pharaoh to let Israel go (Exod. 1–12), Elijah's calling down fire from heaven (2 Kgs 1), or Elisha's cursing the boys which results in their destruction by bears (2 Kgs 2.23-25). The Johannine Jesus' miracle of changing water into wine may echo that of Moses' changing water into blood in the Egyptian vessels of stone (Exod. 7.19) and it fulfils the scriptural promises of the superabundance of wine which God will provide in the future (e.g. Amos 9.13; Jer. 31.12), but it is also like the miracles of Dionysus (e.g. Pliny, *Natural History* 2.231; 31.16; Diodorus Siculus 3.66; Pausanias 6.26.1-2; Plutarch, *Lives*; Lysander 28.4; Ovid, *Metamorphoses* 13.650; Euripides, *Bacchae* 706-11; Achilles Tatius 2.1-6). The healings of the lame man and of the man born blind, however, can be seen as the fulfilment of prophetic expectations like those in Isa. 35.5-6: 'Then shall the eyes of the blind be opened...then shall the lame man leap like a hart'. Furthermore, the Johannine portrayal of Jesus as the Christ, the expected King, has transformed scriptural expectations by identifying Jesus, the Christ, with the prophet who suffers and is vindicated by God.

Nevertheless, there is a fundamental difference between the scriptural prophets and the Johannine Jesus. While both prophets and Jesus are inspired by God's Spirit to become agents of God's words and works, Jesus alone is God's λόγος become man. The scriptural prophets make God known only in their words and deeds, and in spite of suffering rejection and persecution, whereas Jesus makes God known in his words, deeds *and* in his death, which is both his honouring of God and God's honouring of him (13.31-32). The difference lies therefore at the theological level. The God of the Fourth Gospel, unlike the God of the prophets, is revealed in Jesus' death on the cross, not just in mighty works of power. Both old and new narratives seek to justify and explain God's ways to people, and do so by using similar vocabulary, motifs and arrangement, but the ways of God are slightly different in each. Jesus' vindication by God comes only after his death on a cross.

Not only does the Johannine Jesus make God known to humanity, he also exemplifies what God intends a human being to be. As the Son of man, as the true Israelite or Son of God, as the messiah or kingly representative of Israel, Jesus says not 'Thus says the Lord' but 'I am the Bread of Life, the Light of the World, the Door, the Good Shepherd, the Resurrection and the Life, the Way, the Truth and the Life, the true Vine'. He provides his disciples with a model to follow, and, once again, his death is centrally important to the depiction of human destiny: 'Greater love has no one than this, that he lay down his life for his friends' (15.13 cf. 13.34; 12.24-26).

The genre of the Fourth Gospel, therefore, like that of scriptural narratives, is a theodicy, a vindication of divine providence in view of the existence of evil, but the theology is focused in the portrait of one man, Jesus, whose death, as well as his teachings and miracles, provides knowledge of God and of human destiny. Like its Scripture, it tells a story about the past to persuade readers of the validity of its conception, combining theology and history in a narrative structured through the vision of an omniscient narrator.

I shall consider later in this chapter how far the Fourth Gospel has been influenced by non-Jewish Hellenistic portraits of religious leaders in its depiction of Jesus. For the moment, we should recall that some details may point to Hellenistic influence: the connexion, but with differences, between λόγος and Stoic teaching about the λόγος immanent in the world, and the mirroring of Dionysian stories in that of Jesus' changing water into wine. In addition, the Johannine preference for the Stoic term, κόσμος ('world'), instead of the Hebrew idiom 'the heavens and the earth' (e.g. Gen. 1.1), may be explained as polemic against what the Gospel regards as a false understanding of human order, but it was probably derived from Greek portions of its Scripture (e.g. the Wisdom of Solomon).

2. *Judaism*

That the Fourth Gospel interprets the life of Jesus in terms taken from its Scripture has been sufficiently demonstrated, although differences have also been noted. Some commentators have suggested further that the Gospel exhibits influence from contemporary Judaism which cannot be explained by the fact of a shared Scripture. In particular, links with the Dead Sea Scrolls, rabbinic writings and Alexandrian writings have been proposed.

2.1. *The Dead Sea Scrolls*

The dualism of light and darkness and of the Two Ways, and the eschatological perspective found in the Dead Sea Scrolls and in the Fourth Gospel have prompted scholars to speculate about relations between these documents. The vision of life as a choice between one way and another, between light and darkness, is typically scriptural in its polarization of extremes, so that it is certainly the case that the Fourth Gospel and the Dead Sea Scrolls develop insights from Scripture with regard to their own experiences, the Dead Sea Scrolls emphasizing priestly interests and the Fourth Gospel prophetic and Wisdom. These major differences in emphasis, which affect both tone and outlook, make it unlikely that direct influence is involved, but do the Dead Sea Scrolls fill in any of the gaps left between Scripture and Gospel?

Charlesworth (1972) asserts that the Fourth Gospel and 1QS 3.13–4.26 share the following terminology.

2.1.1. *(The) Spirit of Truth: Jn 14.17; 15.26; 16.13 and 1QS 3.18-19; 4.21, 23.* The phrase may be significant because it is found nowhere in the Septuagint, although the 'way of truth' (e.g. Gen. 24.48; Ps. 25.4-5, 10 LXX; Ps. 119.30) is common, and 'God of truth' (e.g. Ps. 31.5 LXX; Est. 4.40) and 'λόγος of truth' (e.g. Ps. 119.43, 160 LXX) are used. Num. 24.2-3 and Isa. 42.1-3 associate spirit and truth: 'And the Spirit of God came upon him... The oracle of Balaam...the oracle of the faithful man (ὁ ἄνθρωπος ὁ ἀληθινῶς) who sees...' and 'I have put my Spirit upon him, he will bring forth justice to the nations...he will bring forth justice in truth'. The role of bringing justice to the nations helps to explain the function of the Spirit of Truth in John 16. Again in the Septuagint, Spirit of God (e.g. Gen. 1.2; 8.1; 41.38; Num. 23.6; 24.2; 1 Kgs 10.10), the Spirit of the Lord (e.g. Judg. 3.10; 6.34; 11.29; Wis. 1.7; Mic. 3.8), the divine Spirit of Wisdom (e.g. Exod. 31.3; 35.31; Wis. 1.6; 7.7), the Spirit of life (e.g. Gen. 6.17; 7.15; Ezek. 10.17) are frequently used.

If the parallel in wording is equivalent, τὸ πνεῦμα τῆς ἀληθέιας in the Fourth Gospel and *rwḥ 'mt* in the Dead Sea Scrolls, is the meaning the same? In the Dead Sea Scrolls, the Spirit of Truth is an Angel of Truth inspiring people to live righteous and holy lives according to the Law as sons of light and sons of truth. God had also established another Spirit, of Falsehood and Darkness, which inspires people in equal measure to live in sin as sons of falsehood and of darkness (see also *T. Jud.* 20.1). Here 'truth' has the connotation 'fidelity', as in Scripture, which is one of its meanings in the Fourth Gospel. Could Johannine usage have developed out of Scripture through postulating Jesus as the revealer of the true way for people to live, as someone who can be identified with Truth (14.6), so that his Spirit, another Paraclete, is described as the Spirit of Truth? This is the most likely explanation. The War Scroll from Qumran looks forward to a final battle between the sons of light and the sons of darkness, when, with God's help, political victory will be gained by the sons of light. The Johannine story expects no such political victory (see Barrett 1975: 57).

2.1.2. *The Holy Spirit/Spirit of Holiness: Jn 14.26; 20.22; 1QS 4.21.* There are abundant examples of 'Holy Spirit' in the Septuagint, for example Ps. 51.11; Wis. 1.5, 6, 7; Isa. 63.10.

2.1.3. *Sons of light: Jn 12.36; 1QS 3.13, 24, 25.* 'Sons of light' is certainly a Semitic expression, but I can find no example of the phrase in the Septuagint. In the Fourth Gospel, it seems to be equivalent to τέκνα θεοῦ (children of God) from the Prologue (1.9-13). In the New Testament, the expression occurs in Lk. 16.8 and 1 Thess. 5.5 (and see Eph. 5.8, τέκνα φωτός). It is found frequently in the Dead Sea Scrolls, but only once in the Fourth Gospel, where υἱός ('Son') is usually reserved for Jesus. In this case it seems more likely that the Gospel is dependent on Christian tradition than on the Dead Sea Scrolls.

2.1.4. *Eternal life/in perpetual life: Jn 3.15, 16, 36 etc.; 1QS 4.7.* Here the Fourth Gospel is dependent upon Dan. 12.2, and, unlike the Dead Sea Scrolls, uses the language of resurrection.

Of the four examples, only 2.1.1 and 2.1.3 carry any force and are hardly sufficient to indicate influence. Brown's conclusion (1966) seems reasonable:

> In our judgment the parallels are not close enough to suggest a direct literary dependence of John upon the Qumran literature, but they do suggest familiarity with the type of thought exhibited in the scrolls (p. lxiii).

2.2. *The Rabbinic Writings*

Barrett (1978) proposes that the Fourth Gospel reveals numerous contacts with rabbinic Judaism, and, of the examples he cites, the following could have a bearing on the genre of the Gospel.

2.2.1. Elementary processes of criminal law are assumed: that the accused be allowed to speak before his judges (7.51) and that two witnesses who agree are necessary to establish any fact (8.17). In both instances, however, the stipulations are from the Law irrespective of rabbinic tradition: Exod. 23.1; Deut. 1.16; 17.4-6; 19.15.

2.2.2. Like rabbinic discussions, the Gospel assumes that to carry a mattress on the Sabbath is illegal (5.10). This instance is not compelling, however, because carrying burdens on the Sabbath is forbidden in Jer. 17.21 and Neh. 13.19, and because a similar story was handed down in Christian tradition (Mk 2.1-12 and parallels).

2.2.3. Barrett is rightly only tentative in suggesting that 7.37 and 8.12 may indicate knowledge of ritual practice in Jerusalem at the Feast of Tabernacles. Jesus' teaching is more obviously based on Zechariah 14 and Ezekiel 47, and on the scriptural references to the light perpetually burning in the sanctuary (Exod. 27.20; Lev. 24.2; Num. 4.16; 2 Chron. 4.20). (See the section on Jesus and the Temple in Chapter 10.)

2.2.4. Jn 1.51 is said to show knowledge of rabbinic exegesis. The Hebrew *bô* (upon it or him) in Gen. 28.12 is ambiguous and could mean that the angels ascended and descended either upon the ladder (which is the Septuagint interpretation) or upon Jacob. The Fourth Gospel pictures the angels ascending and descending upon the Son of man, who plays the role of the ladder, while Nathanael, the true Israelite, plays the role of Jacob who saw the vision. It appears that the Fourth Gospel is following the Septuagint.

2.2.5. Again Barrett suggests that Jn 8.56 assumes knowledge of the rabbinic tradition that Abraham went into all the days of history and therefore saw in advance that day of the messiah, citing *Gen. R.* 44.25 which interprets Gen. 24.1. But he fails to note that 2 Esd. 3.14 refers to God showing Abraham how the world would end. Moreover, in Jn 8.56 the reference to Abraham's 'rejoicing' may be a positive rather than a negative interpretation of Gen. 17.17 (cf. Gen. 21.6). This, then, is a difficult case, because the source may be scriptural.

Barrett concludes:

> No part of the rabbinic literature was written down until a date later than the composition of John. Direct literary relationship is out of the question, and some apparent parallels may be merely fortuitous. But when all such allowances have been made it remains very probable that John himself (or perhaps the authors of some of his sources) was familiar with the oral teaching which at a later date was crystallised in the Mishnah, the Talmud and the Midrashim (1978: 27-28).

In addition, Lindars (1972) adds two further points.

2.2.6. He contends that ch. 6 turns on the rabbinic equation of manna with the Law given at Sinai and that it includes a specific rabbinic argument (6.45). The first part of this statement may be doubted. Chapter 6 is straightforwardly understandable on the basis of scriptural references, especially Exodus 16, Ps. 78.20, Numbers 11, Deut. 8.3, Neh. 9.20, Wis. 16.20, Amos 8.11 and Isa. 55.10-11. On p. 251 Lindars develops the second part of his statement with some caution. He agrees with Borgen that the quotation in v. 31 is expounded word by word, as in rabbinic homilies, and suggests that the structure of John 6 follows rabbinic models like that described by Bowker, with a quotation taken neither from the Seder nor the Haphtarah at the beginning but which bridges the two (Jn 6.31 is therefore assumed to come from Ps. 78.24 not from Exod. 16), and later a quotation from the Haphtarah (Jn 6.45 quoting Isa. 54.13 is assumed to be the Haphtarah to the Exod. 16 Seder although this is denied on the same page), and finally a concluding quotation from the Seder (Jn 6.58 is considered an allusion to Exod. 16). The argument is a little forced, and Lindars has to admit that

> If it were a Christian homily composed on Jewish models, it is now adapted to its present position as a typically Johannine discourse. He has punctuated it with dialogue. Even the proemial text in v. 31 is placed on the lips of the Jews (1972: 253).

2.2.7. Finally, Lindars claims that the idea of the hidden messiah (7.27) is known from rabbinic sources but is not found in the Old Testament. Here he admits that surviving rabbinic evidence is late. On the other hand, he refers to a significant text from Scripture, 2 Esd. 13.52: 'No one on earth can see my son and his company until the appointed day' which may have given rise to the belief (see also *Pss. Sol.* 17.42). Nevertheless, the meaning of 7.27 may be different (see below, Part III, Chapter 13, §2, *Jewish Beliefs).*

These examples, rather than indicating the Gospel's dependence on rabbinic sources, reinforce the conclusion reached earlier, that the Gospel is dependent on the Scripture it took over from Judaism.

2.3. *Hellenistic Judaism*

There are some striking parallels between the language of the Fourth Gospel and that of *Joseph and Aseneth* and some of the writings of Philo. No scholar has supposed John's direct dependence on these sources, but noting similarities and differences helps to situate the Fourth Gospel in its first-century cultural milieu.

2.3.1. *Joseph and Aseneth.* The story of *Joseph and Aseneth*, which takes its cue from the reference in Gen. 41.45, 'Pharaoh gave to Joseph Asenath, the daughter of Potiphera, priest of On, for his wife', to give an account of Aseneth's conversion from idolatry to Judaism before her marriage to Joseph, and of the dangers she faced afterwards, is a Hellenistic Jewish tale, drawing on its Scripture but also on Hellenistic romance to present a lively entertainment as well as a lesson for Jewish readers and listeners. Its genre, therefore, has little in common with the Fourth Gospel, but one of its motifs, conversion, and some of its language offer parallels (see Schnackenburg 1984). C. Burchard (1985) dates it in the period between the first century BCE and the beginning of the second century CE, and argues that Greek was the original language of composition.

The Fourth Gospel shows no interest in polemicizing against idolatry, and its concern for conversion applies to 'Jews' as to others (e.g. 3.1-5), but, as in the Fourth Gospel so in *Joseph and Aseneth*, conversion is God's call from darkness to light, from error to truth and from death to life (*Jos. Asen.* 8.10; Jn 8.12, 32; 11.25-26). Through renewal by God's Spirit, a new human life is enlivened by God (*Jos. Asen.* 8.11; Jn 3.1-15; 7.38-39). This involves eating bread of life, drinking God's cup of blessing and living in God's eternal life for ever (*Jos. Asen.* 8.5, 9, 11; 15.5; 16.8, 14-16; 19.5; 21.21; Jn 6, especially 6.35, 38, 48-51). Aseneth's angelic visitor tells her that the honeycomb which he miraculously supplies is 'a comb of life, and everyone who eats of it will not die for ever (and) ever' (*Jos. Asen.* 16.14; 27.10; Jn 6.58), and he assures her of a place of rest in the heavens (*Jos. Asen.* 15.7; Jn 14.2-3). By kissing Aseneth, Joseph imparts to her 'Spirit of life', 'Spirit of wisdom' and 'Spirit of truth' (*Jos. Asen.* 19.11; Jn 20.22; 15.26).

There is no reason to suppose that the Fourth Gospel has drawn directly from *Joseph and Aseneth* for some of its vocabulary. Rather, both are influenced by the same Scripture, especially by its manna and Wisdom traditions, and hence similar ideas are coincidentally expressed in the same language. Moreover, *Joseph and Aseneth* is more at home in the Hellenistic world than is the Fourth Gospel. *Joseph and Aseneth* looks forward to life, immortality and incorruptibility (e.g. 8.5) while the Fourth Gospel's believers look forward to resurrection (e.g. 6.39; 20.1-29); *Joseph and Aseneth* portrays Joseph as a semi-divine being (6.3-8) whereas the Fourth Gospel portrays Jesus as a vulnerable human being (1.14).

2.3.2. *Philo*. Philo, who lived in Alexandria in the first half of the first century CE, was a Jewish scholar whose education gave him a commanding knowledge of both his Jewish and his Greek heritage. His works take the form of homilies on verses from the Jewish Law (Genesis, Exodus, Leviticus, Numbers and Deuteronomy) and use an allegorical method to discover meanings beyond the literal. These meanings are often expressed in terms borrowed form a variety of Greek philosophical schools, in particular Platonic, Stoic and Aristotelian. Any interpreter of Philo, therefore, is faced with material which is never ordered in a systematic manner. As H.A. Wolfson (1948) sums up the problem:

> The fact that so many philosophers belonging to opposite schools of thought are drawn on by him without any evident discrimination, the fact also that philosophic problems are not treated by him systematically but are dragged in, as it were, upon the casual suggestion of scriptural texts, and moreover the fact that he never seems to have any difficulty in connecting any philosophic thought with any scriptural verse create the impression that Philo was a preacher with a flair for philosophy rather than primarily a philosopher (I, 97-98).

But it is this false impression that Wolfson's study counters, by showing where and how Philo is indebted to his Scripture and to philosophical insights in working out a theological scheme which was to engage Jewish, Christian and Muslim theologians for many centuries to come. Wolfson demonstrates that Philo's fundamental beliefs were derived from Jewish Scripture and that his philosophical expositions were designed to commend the truth of Scripture to philosophers. Hence, in spite of a frequent borrowing of terms, Philo attempts to refute the teachings of those Greek schools whose views were incompatible with the revelations of Scripture, in particular Aristotelianism, Epicureanism and Stoicism. Philo's relationship to Platonism was, however, different. He adopted the essential principles of Platonism and revised and adapted it to conform to the teachings of Scripture, except in his discussions of the nature of the human beings, in which he adopted Platonism and abandoned Scriptural teachings.

One of the key terms in Philo's exposition of Scripture he shares with the Prologue of the Fourth Gospel, the term λόγος. Wolfson suggests that this term recommended itself to Philo in much the same way as it did to the Fourth Evangelist, as a word which was used in Scripture in connexion with creation, Wisdom, the Law and prophecy. But Philo's much more extensive writings and much greater interest in philosophical theology prompted him to explore the significance of the concept in ways far beyond the scope of the Fourth Gospel.

Wolfson shows that Philo uses λόγος with three quite distinct references (chapters 4 and 6). Firstly, λόγος is the mind of God in which the intelligible world is conceived as a thought:

> As, then, the city which was fashioned beforehand within the mind of the architect held no place in the outer world, but had been engraved in the soul of the artificer as by a seal; even so the universe that consisted of ideas would have no other location but the divine λόγος, which was the author of this ordered frame (*Op. Mund.* 5.20).

Secondly, λόγος is created by God before the creation of the world. In this sense, λόγος unites the ideas which are the archetypes of individual things in the world, and is the pattern and cause of the world as a whole, as well as the archetype of the human mind. Hence, in some texts the λόγος is described as God's creation, not as an aspect of God's essence.

> The λόγος of God, the first principle, the archetypal idea, the first measure of the universe (*Quaest. in Gen.* 1.4).

And the λόγος as the archetype of the human mind is often mentioned:

> For it is the mind (νοῦς) of man which has the form of God, being shaped in conformity with the ideal archetype, the λόγος which is above all (*Spec. Leg.* 3.207).

Again:

> But it is the lot of man, as we see, to occupy the place of highest excellence among living creatures because his stock is near akin to God, sprung from the same source in virtue of his participation in reason (λόγος) which gives him immortality, mortal though he seems to be (*Spec. Leg.* 4.4).

Thirdly, λόγος is immanent in the world. In this sense λόγος represents the immutable laws of nature as in Stoicism. Yet there is a distinction between Philo's view and the Stoic conception. In Stoicism λόγος is an active material principle, whereas in Philo λόγος is immaterial, the extension into the world of the incorporeal λόγος:

> The garments which the supreme λόγος of Him that is puts on as a raiment are the world, for he arrays himself in earth and air and water and fire and all that comes forth from these (*Fug*. 110).

But these disparate elements in the world are harmonized by the λόγος:

> All the earth shall not be dissolved by all the water which has gathered within its hollows, nor fire be quenched by air, nor, on the other hand, air be ignited by fire, since the divine λόγος stations himself between the elements, like a vocal between the voiceless elements of speech, so that the universe may send forth a harmony like that of a masterpiece of literature, for he mediates between the opponents amid their threatenings and reconciles them by winning ways to peace and concord (*Plant*. 10).

Hence, human beings who live in harmony live according to the divine λογός:

> And therefore when I hear those who say, 'We are all sons of one man, we are peaceful' (Gen. 42.11), I am filled with admiration for the harmonious concert which their words reveal. 'Ah my friends', I would say, 'how should you not hate war and love peace, you who have enrolled yourselves as children of one and the same father who is not mortal but immortal, God's Man (ἄνθρωπον θεοῦ) who being the λόγος of the Eternal must needs himself be imperishable?' (*Conf. Ling*. 41).

It will be clear that the genre of Philo's writings, the allegorical interpretation of scriptural verses in Greek philosophical terms, differs from the genre of the Fourth Gospel. Yet the Prologue of the Fourth Gospel is a reinterpretation of the Genesis creation story in the light of Wisdom speculation and the story of Jesus, and so has something in common with Philo's expositions. How far do their conceptions of λόγος correspond? The first verses of the Prologue conceive the λόγος as an aspect of God's eternal existence and as God's plan in creation. Unlike Philo, however, the Prologue does not state that the λόγος as God's plan was created. Moreover, as the plan through which all material existence was made, λόγος is also immanent in the world, and specifically as the light of humanity. Again, like Philo and unlike Stoicism, λόγος is immaterial. Yet in all this, the Prologue of the Fourth Gospel gives the impression that it is a development of scriptural insights without direct reference to Greek philosophers. None of the technical terms of Platonism are used and there is no awareness, as there is in Philo, of the erudite discussions of these issues by the Greek philosophical schools.

Moreover, the relationship of the λόγος to humanity in the Johannine Prologue and in the rest of the Gospel is conceived differently from the way it is in Philo. The Fourth Gospel does not suggest that human beings are immortal because they participate in the divine λόγος through their reason. Rather, human beings perceive the λόγος and are enlightened in recognizing the world as the creation of God. They are to live in accordance with God's will made known by his λόγος in creation, in the Law and the prophets, and finally in the obedient life of Jesus of Nazareth. Jesus' life is lived in accordance with God's plan for humanity, in complete dependence upon and obedience to God, and hence, the Prologue states that the λόγος became flesh in him. But it is Jesus' fulfilment of God's mission which makes him exemplary for other human beings and which leads God to raise him from the dead. In the Johannine conception human beings, including Jesus, are mortal. Life beyond death is understood not in terms of the immortality of a soul which is akin to God, but in terms of the resurrection of the body (*contra* Philo).

Something of this difference between the Fourth Gospel's and Philo's understandings can be grasped by comparing the Gospel's portrait of Jesus and his followers with Philo's portrait of Moses and the Israelites (*Vit. Mos.* 1). Philo has transformed Moses from a prophet into an ideal philosopher king and the Israelites into obedient and courageous followers who not only deserve God's mercy but also discern that humanity is endowed with a divine seed which ensures their future immortality. Here the influence of Plato upon Philo is marked and the absence of that influence on the Fourth Gospel can easily be recognized.

In sharing the term λόγος with Philo, the Johannine Prologue shares some of Philo's perceptions, but those result not from mutual influence but from profound meditations on the same Scripture in the service of quite different understandings of human destiny.

3. *Non-Jewish Greek Literature*

I began this study by noting that the Fourth Gospel itself points to Scripture as its antecedent and I have now examined various aspects of that dependence. The Gospel, however, is written in Greek and the language may be supposed to provide contact with the concepts and traditions which are non-biblical. Is it necessary to assume literary dependence on non-biblical writings? I have already suggested that the choice of λόγος in the Prologue may have been influenced to some small extent by its use in popular Stoic philosophy, although this is hardly a matter of literary dependence. Some commentators have suggested that the most important contact with Greek philosophy is made by the Johannine concentration on ἀλήθεια (truth) and cognates, which will be discussed below. Dionysian analogies to Jn 2.1-11 give the account a wide appeal. Again, Jesus as the 'light of the world' (Jn 8.12) may gain resonance from non-biblical beliefs about the sun as the divine source of light. In addition, the use of κόσμος for 'world' may polemicize against Stoic conceptions of a self-sustaining ordered universe.

3.1. *The* Corpus Hermeticum

C.H. Dodd (1968) has claimed that the *Corpus Hermeticum*, and especially the *Tractate Poimandres*, with its combination of Platonic, Stoic and oriental concerns, offers impressive analogies to the Fourth Gospel in form, language and religious belief, although no literary dependence is suggested. 'It seems clear that they [the tractates of the *Corpus Hermeticum*] represent a type of religious thought akin to one side of Johannine thought, without any substantial borrowing on the one part or the other' (p. 53). Comparison is complicated by the fact that the *Corpus Hermeticum* has been influenced to some extent by the Scripture which the Fourth Gospel accepted, and this will have to be taken into account.

The *Tractate Poimandres* is a response to a request to learn about the nature of existent things and to know God. Drawing on the imagery of Genesis 1–3 and on Greek philosophical tradition about creation and the four elements, fire, air, water and earth, a vision of light, representing Mind or God, and of the holy λόγος, the Son of God, who separates the four elements, show how Mind/God, being light and life, gave birth to another mind, the Demiurge, who created the seven planets and the lower sphere of life, while Mind himself created Man in his image. When Man descended and was united with the lower sphere his nature became twofold, mortal and immortal. Hence, what rational man needs to recognize is that he is immortal and that the cause of death is love of the body. Recognition brings entry into life again, an ascent which reverses the primal fall, rids man of his passions and restores his divinity.

On pp. 34-35 Dodd provides a list of parallel expressions in *Poimandres* and in the Fourth Gospel. In the Gospel some of these expression refer to Christ but in the Poimandres Tractate they refer to the Son of God, or Poimandres, or the prophet, or the heavenly Man. The most obvious similarity is the use of the combined terms 'life and light' to describe God's being (e.g. Jn 1.9; 8.12; *Corp. Herm.* 1.32, 6), although in the Poimandres Tractate this light and life forces order onto an alien nature, and hence presupposes an ultimate dualism, akin to Platonism but foreign to the Fourth Gospel. From this there follows a second difference: 'all things' are created through the λόγος in Jn 1.3, but only the separation of the elements is brought about in Poimandres. Again, Poimandres identifies λόγος and Son of God, whereas the Fourth Gospel reserves Son of God to refer to the man Jesus. This suggests that each text has taken the term λόγος from Scripture and used it in its own system.

The anthropology of Poimandres shows affinities with Genesis 1–3, creation in God's image and the subsequent fall. Dodd suggests that the Tractate views this archetypal man as the Platonic 'idea' of man, and thinks that such notions have influenced the Fourth Gospel's use of the term 'the Son of man', but this is a contentious issue. On the other hand, the emphasis on knowledge of God as necessary to humankind's salvation is common to both, although dependence on the Septuagint may underlie each, because once again there is similarity and difference. The knowledge that interests the Fourth Gospel is that revealed in Jesus, in whom readers are encouraged to believe (e.g. 17.3), knowledge that God loves the world and acts to save humanity (e.g. 3.16-17). In Poimandres the knowledge that saves people is recognition of their divine origin and nature (e.g. *Corp. Herm.* 1.17-18).

It is to other sections of the *Corpus Hermeticum* that Dodd refers to throw light on the Johannine use of ἀλήθεια. He traces the primary Johannine source in the Septuagint but thinks that passages like Jn 18.37 and 8.32 are best explained in Greek philosophical terms:

> ἀλήθεια. . . stands here for the realm of pure and eternal reality, as distinct from the world of transient phenomena. Similarly. . . Jesus says that he has come to bear witness to 'the truth' i.e. to the divine reality as now revealed to men. There is the same movement of meaning between 'reality' and 'knowledge of reality' that we find in Greek philosophical language from Plato onwards (1968: 176).

Dodd quotes parallels in *Corp. Herm.* 13.6, 9 and in the fragment *Peri Aletheias*, p. 172. It seems to me, however, that Dodd is here importing into the Fourth Gospel without warrant a Platonic conception of 'truth'. It is correct to recognize that the Fourth Gospel uses 'truth', the two adjectives for 'true' (ἀληθής and ἀληθινός) and the adverb (ἀληθῶς) more frequently than the other New Testament writings but this is not because the Gospel adopts the Platonic conception of immaterial, archetypal ideas of which existent things are mere reflections. This Platonic language and the philosophy which explains it is never found in the Fourth Gospel. Rather, John follows the Septuagint in the range of meanings the words exemplify.

In the following instances 'truth' is the opposite of 'error' or 'lie': 5.33, 8.32, 40, 44, 45, 46, 16.7; in the following instances, it means 'fidelity': 1.14, 17; and in the following it combines the previous two meanings, 'truth' as the opposite of 'error' with the connotation of 'fidelity': 14.17, 15.26, 16.13, 17.17, 19, 18.37-38. On the other hand, in 3.21 it means 'right' rather than 'wrong', while in 4.23-24 it means 'the genuine' as opposed to 'the sham'. Jn 14.6 is probably best understood as 'the genuine' with the connotation 'fidelity'. The adverb usually means 'genuinely' or 'properly' (1.47; 4.42; 6.14, 55; 7.40; 8.31) but in 17.8 the English 'really' (without Platonic connotations) expresses the meaning. The adjective ἀληθινός means 'genuine' (1.9; 4.23; 6.32; 15.1), or 'faithful' (7.28), perhaps in 17.3 combining both these meanings, or 'true' as the opposite of 'false' (8.16; 19.35). In 4.37 'for here the saying holds true' seems to mean 'properly applies'. The adjective ἀληθής also means 'genuine' (6.55), or 'faithful' (7.18; 8.26) but is used most frequently for 'true', the opposite of 'false' (3.33; 4.18 = 'accurate'; 5.31-32; 8.13-14, 17; 10.41 = 'accurate'; 19.35; 21.24). All these meanings are found in the Septuagint (see Barr 1961: 187-205).

It is precisely because the Fourth Gospel does not share the strictly Platonic view of 'truth' that it does not encourage people to live a life of rational contemplation of the eternal ideas, but instead to live the life of obedience to God's will which Jesus exemplifies, trusting to God's fidelity in saving people from sin.

In general, then, the *Corpus Hermeticum* offers interesting parallels to Johannine language and thought but these stem ultimately from the Septuagint, while differences are to be explained by the fact that the Corpus is also directly determined by some Platonic philosophical conceptions which are alien to the Fourth Gospel. (See Kilpatrick 1957: 36-44; Barrett 1975: 29). The kind of knowledge of Greek philosophy shown by the Fourth Gospel is rather like most modern westerner's knowledge of Marxism or Freudianism. Key terms from these systems, like alienation or the Oedipus complex, have entered common parlance and are used without reference to the full part they play in the original systems. So the Fourth Gospel uses 'truth', λόγος and 'world' without accepting either a Platonic or a Stoic conception of reality. Nor does the Gospel formally refu1te the systems from which the words come, but simply offers an alternative view. Moreover, the Fourth Gospel is uninfluenced by the genres in which these philosophies were explored and expounded. Although it presents dialogues, they are completely unlike Platonic dialogues which rationally and philosophically tease out the meaning of words and the logic of arguments. The Fourth Gospel is homiletical not philosophical, and it supports its argument by appealing to authoritative Scripture, not logic. It does not examine its presupposition that God is the creator of the world, but simply adopts it from Scripture. The form of epigrammatic Wisdom statements, however, is common to much didactic literature, and the Fourth Gospel's use of it would seem familiar to Greeks and Romans as to Jews. These links with Hellenistic culture would help to make the Gospel more comprehensible to non-Jewish and non-Christian people in the Graeco-Roman world.

3.2. *Philostratus's Life of Apollonius of Tyana*

The fact that Jesus is depicted both teaching and performing miracles would also, in general, make the Gospel understandable to Greek readers, as a biography of a religious leader. Unfortunately, the biography which is most like the New Testament Gospels, Philostratus's *Life of Apollonius of Tyana*, is late, published in 217 CE, and may itself have been influenced by the Gospels, although it tells the story of Apollonius, who taught and performed miracles in the second half of the first century CE, and claims to be based on the memoirs of Apollonius's disciple, Damis. When we compare the account of Apollonius's life with that of Jesus in the Fourth Gospel, however, the differences are more apparent than the similarities.

Apollonius is an ascetic who calls people to abandon their dependence on material well-being in order to release their divinity from its material fetters (*VA* 8.7). Hence, at the end of the story, he does not die, as Jesus does, but disappears into the eternal sphere of the immortals. Moreover, his work is influential on the grand scale. He travels throughout the Roman Empire restoring temples, and even goes as far as Egypt, and beyond the Empire to India, so that much of the appeal of the work comes from the descriptions of these journeys. He is also an adviser to emperors. By contrast, Jesus is a provincial from a minor and obscure part of the Roman Empire who confines his activity to that area, and who meets no more eminent a Roman than Pilate, the local governor. The difference in scale affects in each case the kinds of miracles performed and the content of predictions of the future. For example, Apollonius foretells an outbreak of plague in Ephesus (4.4), Nero's attempt to cut a canal through an isthmus (4.24), a thunderbolt hitting Nero's cup (4.43), Nero's downfall (5.10-11), the fates of the next three emperors (5.13), and the deaths of Titus (5.32), Domitian (8.23, 26) and Nerva (8.27-28). Jesus, on the other hand, predicts his own death (Jn 10-11), his return to the Father (17.5, 11, 13), and his parousia (14.3; 21.22, 23), the future joy and suffering of the disciples (16.20; 15.18-20), their resurrection after death (6.40; 12.25), their final dwelling with God (14.2-3) and the success of his completed mission in drawing all people to himself (12.32). Again, Apollonius, like Jesus, performs miracles but only one of them is at all like Jesus'. Apollonius raises a young girl from the dead (*VA* 4.45), but even in this case he uses touch and a secret spell, whereas Jesus simply calls Lazarus out of the tomb (Jn 11.43-44). In other words, the connexion between Jesus' first miracle at Cana and Dionsyian motifs is closer than that between Jesus' healings and Apollonius's.

Nevertheless, these tenuous links between the Fourth Gospel, Greek philosophy and Hellenistic biographies of religious leaders would have opened the Gospel to Greek readers ignorant of Johannine Scriptures. It would probably have seemed a strange and alien example of the genre, however, because its presuppositions, both theological and anthropological, were not shared by most Greeks, and many of its motifs, like Jesus' provincial origin or his resurrection appearances, would offend their expectations.

4. *John and the Synoptic Gospels*

It has been suggested that the Fourth Gospel is a theodicy, justifying God's ways to its readers by depicting a particular view of human life through its story of the life, death and resurrection of Jesus of Nazareth. Are we to suppose that the Fourth Gospel's genre is a new invention, albeit drawing on its Scripture, or should we see the Fourth Gospel as a development of a genre which already existed in texts known to the author and readers, namely the Synoptic Gospels? In the chapter on *Focus* (Chapter 1), we noted that the Fourth Gospel seems to retell a story which is already familiar.

This is an important question when considering genre, because, no matter how close the Fourth Gospel is in structure and vocabulary to the Exodus story and to Wisdom literature, its genre is to some extent different, not least in its single focus on Jesus, its eschatology and its conception of Satan or the devil. Acquaintance with previous examples of the genre would mean that John is not a new literary species. It will be argued in Part III, Chapter 11, that the Fourth Gospel is probably dependent on the Synoptics. But similarities, especially with Mark and Luke, and possible knowledge of them, raises the question: in what respects does the Fourth Gospel differ from the Synoptics, and, in particular, from Mark?

The most obvious difference between Mark and John is that Mark concentrates on what is seen, and John on what is said. The Second Gospel gives readers a series of dramatic incidents, carefully associated, full of lively graphic details, with echoes of or references to scripture, but it leaves the reader to work out implications for themselves. Each incident is fairly self-contained and can be taken out of context and elucidated in preaching, as form critics have often noted, but the Gospel itself rarely draws out what is to be inferred, leaving the reader to reflect and ponder on the meaning. In most instances what dialogue is provided merely serves to explain the action. The Fourth Gospel is just the reverse. Incidents are used to introduce long reflections in dialogues or monologues so that what is said is primary. The reader's inferences are already structured by the text.

In Chapter 1 it was noted that the Fourth Gospel differs from most parts of the Synoptics in presenting a whole series of scenes, rather than a single event. Moreover, even the long sections of Jesus' teaching are dramatized by including the remarks of interlocutors, who misunderstand his statements (e.g. 3.4; 4.11-12, 15; 8.22; 14.8), or who ask for clarification (e.g. 3.9; 4.20; 6.30, 52; 7.15; 8.25; 13.36; 14.5), or who make assertions which Jesus then refutes (e.g. 5.18; 6.40; 8.13, 33, 39, 41, 48; 10.33). This Johannine love of dramatic dialogue which elucidates the significance of Jesus' activity in miracles and preaching may even have led to the invention of episodes to illustrate Jesus' teaching in the Synoptics. For example, Pharisaic rejection of Jesus after his raising of Lazarus (chs. 11 and 12) illustrates Lk. 16.31, 'If they do not hear Moses and the prophets, neither will they be convinced if someone should rise from the dead'; or the story of doubting Thomas (20.24-29) illustrates Mt. 28.17, 'But they [or some] doubted'.

The only discourses in Mark are contained in ch. 4 and ch. 13, and both differ from those in John. In Mark 4 parables draw on imagery from farming and village life to explain opposition to Jesus. The 'failure' of his preaching and healing ministry, which will be increasingly emphasized, is analogous to failure and success in farming and is therefore unsurprising. This form of exhortation in parables is rarely exemplified in the Fourth Gospel, where scriptural images, the shepherd, the light, the vine, are given gnomic expression and expounded. These expositions owe more to Wisdom literature and to the prophecies of Ezekiel than to parables like that of Nathan (2 Sam. 12.1-7). Mark 13 is an 'apocalyptic discourse' depicting final judgment in images familiar from prophetic books like Ezekiel, Zechariah and Daniel. The Fourth Gospel eschews this form, while not abandoning belief in an ultimate judgment and resurrection, and concentrates on the help and support available to a suffering community in the immediate future in this world. Since the discourses in the Fourth Gospel encourage decision for or against Jesus now, depictions of future punishment become superfluous. They are replaced by simple statements (e.g. 3.19-20; 8.34-38; 9.39-41).

One characteristic they share. Neither in Mark nor in John is the reader encouraged to sympathize with Jesus and the two are unlike Luke in this respect. Luke's Jesus is appealing and likeable, John's and Mark's Jesus is austere and strange. On the other hand, Mark's description of the disciples and suppliants does invite the reader's identification, whereas in the Fourth Gospel this is less the case. John's love of dialogue and monologue distances the readers and encourages them to think and decide.

In one respect, the simpler plan of Mark's Gospel—Galilaean ministry, with success followed by increasing opposition, and Jesus' single journey to Jerusalem, there to preach and confront Jewish leaders, to be tried and to die—is complicated by John's. The Fourth

Gospel intersperses Jesus' success in Galilee and Samaria with his failure in Judaea, giving Jesus four visits to Jerusalem. Perhaps this arrangement is dictated by a desire for variety; dialogues leading to success, or at least superficial acceptance, give some relief from the acrimonious debates in Jerusalem. Theological and christological claims also clearly exercise an influence: the light comes to his own (the Judaeans) and is rejected, while promises to Israel, especially those encapsulated in the festivals of Passover, Tabernacles and Renewal, are fulfilled in Jesus.

Historical accuracy may also play a part, but this is debatable. Since many of the disputes in the Gospel traditions are confrontations between Jesus and the Pharisees, they are better set in Jerusalem or Judaea where it is certain these groups would be found. Vermes (1983: 5, 31) doubts whether Pharisees lived or worked in Galilee. The Fourth Gospel's account of Jesus' trial and death also fits better into the historical situation in Jerusalem when Pilate was governor than do the other Gospel accounts. In John Jesus is submitted to preliminary questioning by a chief priest (18.19-24) and then tried by Pilate, whose verdict leads to Jesus' crucifixion as a Jewish messianic pretender. Nevertheless, historical veracity cannot have been a primary motive in the formation of the Fourth Gospel, since historical situation is assumed, not described in detail, and since Jesus' Johannine discourses are much more like Christian reflections on Jesus' significance than verbatim records of Jesus' preaching. (For a much fuller treatment of the relationship of the Fourth Gospel to the first three, see Robinson 1985.)

Another major difference between the Fourth Gospel and the other three, particularly Mark, is the absence of much of the Synoptic teaching about the kingdom of God. The expression occurs only in 3.3 and 5. Whereas the imminence of God's kingdom is central to the Synoptic account of Jesus' teaching, the Fourth Gospel concentrates the reader's attention on defining who Jesus is, and attempts to lead him or her to the confession that Jesus is God's prophet, messiah and Son. These confessions are also present in the Synoptics, but there they are linked to the belief that God is shortly to establish his kingdom. The Gospel according to Matthew even describes this future kingdom as a παλιγγενεσία, a new creation (19.28). Instead, the Fourth Gospel prefers teaching about the eternal life which Jesus promises to believers. Of course, eternal life is the life of the future kingdom of God, a post-mortem eternal existence for those who are resurrected, but the Fourth Gospel emphasizes the need for choices to be made in the present, rather than emphasizing what God is about to do in the future. Perhaps this is why Jesus' gift of the Spirit to his disciples in 20.22 is expressed in terms reminiscent of the creation of Adam in Gen. 2.7. The Gospel envisages the community as already, at least potentially, a new creation, even before the final transformation at the last judgment. Nevertheless, the differences between John and the Synoptics should not be exaggerated. All four justify their belief that God is saving his world by telling the story of Jesus' life, death and resurrection, so that who Jesus is and what happened to him are as important for the Synoptics as they are for the Fourth Gospel.

In spite of the uncertainty about the Fourth Gospel's dependence on or independence of the Synoptics, and in spite of the differences between them, we can conclude that, in general terms, they share the same genre. All four Gospels are theodicies, justifying the Creator God's love of humanity by telling the story of Jesus' life, death and resurrection. His crucifixion is perceived as the inevitable consequence of people's sin, of their selfish arrogance in opposition to God, and at the same time as the revelation of God's generous care for humanity in bringing about the possibility of a life lived from God, the creator and sustainer of the world. Jesus' martyrdom is thus a paradigm both of God's saving purpose and of humanity's unselfish response. It is this view of Jesus' death which the Gospels seek to make comprehensible, by taking up traditions about Jesus and forming them into a coherent whole which both reflects Scripture and gives it new meaning. In spite of the Gospel's tragic elements, therefore, they are not tragedies. Jesus' martyrdom is the unjust humiliation of an innocent man but it is also his final act of obedience to God and it is the way which leads through death to eternal life.

Only what is essential to the central message finds a place in the Gospels. Humanity's sin and its consequences are realized through the opposition of groups to Jesus and through brief biographical sketches of individuals. God's creative love is demonstrated in Jesus' miracles and teaching, and finally in his conscious and willing acceptance of his death. His life and death is also a model for disciples. The resurrection, which is not resuscitation but the beginning of a transformation and redemption of the spoiled creation, does not make death irrelevant, but gives it significance as the expression of love. It transforms a tragedy into a theodicy, a justification of God's purpose in creation through the story of Jesus.

Jesus is portrayed not as a national leader, but as the Lord of a small band of disciples, although the small scale is intended to have large implications, as the commissioning of the disciples, representing the twelve tribes of a new Israel, indicates. Of prime importance is the community, dedicated to the redemption of God's world, rather than individual salvation for its own sake. Of course, belief in resurrection involves individual bodily survival after death, but this means that community becomes an eternal project, not just one related to the world as it is now.

What questions, then, are appropriate to this kind of narrative? Two different sets of questions seem to be proper: historical and theological. Readers are encouraged to accept that Jesus was the messiah, a man who lived the life of a charismatic preacher and healer in Palestine under the High Priest Caiaphas and the Roman administrator, Pilate, and they may justifiably ask whether this is likely and how far the details of the four portraits can be relied upon as being accurate. The paucity of independent information about Jesus makes many of the questions difficult, though no less appropriate or pressing.

The four Gospels seem to take historical data for granted and are not interested in offering the kind of evidence and support that modern historians require. They devote their energy to theology, since they rightly recognize that belief in the revelatory significance of the life of a man who was crucified is not generally acceptable. This is why echoes of Scripture play such a fundamental role in the defence, but the modern reader, for whom Scripture can neither be assumed to offer final proof in argument nor the guarantee that sense rather than nonsense is being advocated, must raise more basic questions: Does it make sense to see the world as the creation of God, and if so, what can be said about God? Does it make sense to believe that a man's life can reveal God's purpose and humanity's? Is there any significance in human suffering and if so what is it? What meaning, if any, can be given to the concept 'sin'? What does 'love' involve and should it be a central human concern? All the Gospels raise these issues, and the Fourth Gospel meditates upon them, but in a seductive rather than an intellectual manner. Modern readers have thrust upon them some very perplexing philosophical tasks.

Part II

KEY CONCEPTS AND METAPHORS

Chapter 4

Introductory Remarks

1. *The Reader's Task*

Literature communicates both by what is written, and by what is implied by what is written. Not everything which a text means is made explicit, nor is what is written always to be understood literally. Like most texts, the Fourth Gospel uses metaphors, and their metaphorical sense is to be discerned. For example, Nicodemus completely misunderstands Jesus' metaphor of rebirth when he asks, 'How can a man be born when he is old?' (3.4). This misunderstanding serves to guide the reader towards a recognition of the metaphor, while also highlighting the difficulty of a radical change of life. Again, like many other pieces of literature, the Fourth Gospel employs a particular form of irony, that in which characters in the story make statements which express a sensible meaning within the story, but which take on a fuller and ironical meaning from the perspective of the narrator. So Caiaphas advises the council that 'one man should die for the people', which makes sense in the context of the story, but the narrator reinterprets the statement as a prophetic acclamation of the significance of Jesus' death (11.47-53). In order to appreciate the irony, the reader has to shift from the perspective of the character to that of the narrator.

Indeed, in reading every sentence of the Fourth Gospel, the reader is required to make connexions with what precedes and follows at the two levels of story and narrative, to answer questions like: what kind of statement is this, literal, ironical, metaphorical, theological, philosophical? To answer such questions, attention has to be paid not only to the grammar and syntax of sentences, but also to the immediate literary context and the place of the statement within the whole work.

But answers to questions about relations between words, phrases, clauses and sentences within a work are not the only ones which affect meaning. Literature refers to things external to itself, and it does so in different ways. First of all it refers to other texts, and, again, this can happen both explicitly and implicitly, as in the Fourth Gospel's explicit references and implicit allusions to its Scripture. Secondly, it refers to a reality which it partly assumes and partly depicts. For example, on the most basic level the Fourth Gospel assumes a physical setting in which human beings are born and die, they are either male or female, they must eat and drink to stay alive, and they are subject to physical and mental pleasure and pain. It largely assumes the particular historical setting of its story, in the Palestine of the first century CE, when it was part of the Roman Empire, although the mention of Caiaphas, Pilate and various places helps us to see that the narrative is a kind of history. But the Fourth Gospel refers to other aspects of reality which it emphasizes: that the world is the creation of God, whose love for humanity is the key to understanding the story (3.16). This prompts readers to ask how the theological and historical references are related, and how far the theological perspective is coherent.

The reader's task is constructive. The text's potential meanings have to be realized by the reader for understanding and communication to be successful. In the case of the Fourth Gospel, this task is not easy, because it is sometimes unclear whether a statement is literal or metaphorical, and a comparison of commentaries will indicate something of the wide range of possible readings. No claim can be made for the complete veracity of the reading which follows, but it is hoped that other readers will find it helpful in provoking their own search for meaning.

Not all the references or metaphors in the Fourth Gospel can be examined in a book of manageable length. A selection must be made of those which are most pertinent for understanding. Fortunately, the text repeats key terms which it explores in narrative and dialogue, so the selection is to a large extent determined by the text itself. Nevertheless, a reader in the twentieth century has always to take into account the fact that the text is not complete in itself. It does not present everything that could be said about the significance of Jesus of Nazareth. In structuring reality, it highlights some aspects to the exclusion of others. This recognition is already implicit in the Christian church's decision to include the Fourth Gospel in its canon alongside many other accounts of Jesus' significance, whose structures and emphases are different. Moreover, the twentieth-century reader is aware of many alternative interpretations of reality which give Jesus no central role.

All literary works, then, foreground some matters and leave others in shadow. What any text ignores, however, is often as important for understanding as what it acknowledges. For example, the Fourth Gospel provides no account of Jesus' birth, childhood or adolescence. It does not consider how influences from his family or society shaped his psychological development, sense of self-awareness or conception of his mission. Nor is any attention paid to the way in which he planned and developed his strategies. Jesus' ministry in the Fourth Gospel is a unified whole, without false starts which require him to reconsider his tactics. Movement towards a climax is determined solely by other people's acceptance or rejection of him. This is because the story is being told to enhance the reader's understanding of Jesus' entire mission, rather than out of biographical interest. Each incident treats an aspect, not an earlier or later conception, of that mission. Every action, dialogue and discourse is therefore a microcosm of the whole. What determines the order of the narrative is not historical development but the reader's understanding of who Jesus is and what he accomplishes. Hence, the reader is constantly encouraged to place the story in the context of the narrator's perspective.

2. *Myth or Metaphor*

In his *Theology of the New Testament*, Bultmann describes the Johannine portrait of Jesus in the following terms:

> In short, then, the figure of Jesus in John is portrayed in the forms offered by the Gnostic Redeemer myth. . . It is true that the cosmological motifs of the myth are missing in John, especially the idea that the redemption which the 'Ambassador' brings is the release of the pre-existent sparks of light which are held captive in this world below by demonic powers. But otherwise Jesus appears as in the Gnostic myth as the pre-existent son of God whom the Father clothed with authority and sent into the world. Here, appearing as a man, he speaks the word the Father gave him and accomplishes the works which the Father commissioned him to do. In doing so, he is not 'cut off' from the Father but stands in solid and abiding unity with him as an ambassador without fault or falsehood. He comes as the 'light', the 'truth', the 'life' by bringing through his words

> and works light, truth and life and calling 'his own' to himself. In his discourses with their 'I am...' he reveals himself as the Ambassador, but only 'his own' understand him... In the world out of which he calls his own to himself he is despised and hated. But he leaves the world; as he 'came' so he 'departs' and takes leave of his own, whom in his prayer he commits to the Father's care. But his departure also belongs to his work of redemption, for by his elevation he has prepared the way for his own to the heavenly dwelling places into which he will fetch his own... Especially the literary devices with which John builds the discussions—the use of ambiguous concepts and statements to elicit misunderstandings—are indicative that he lives within the sphere of Gnostic–dualistic thinking. For those ambiguities and misunderstandings are far from being merely formal technical devices. Rather they are the expression of his underlying dualistic view; the Revealer and 'the world' cannot understand one another (1955: II, 12-14).

In spite of the differences between Johannine theology and Gnosticism which Bultmann freely acknowledges—differences in cosmology and anthropology—he insists that the Johannine Jesus is a mythological heavenly Redeemer who descends to earth and reascends to heaven, that the theology of the Fourth Gospel is presented in the form of a myth:

> It is clear that in the person of Jesus the transcendent divine reality became audible, visible and tangible in the realm of the earthly world... In all that he is, says and does, he is not to be understood as a figure of this world, but his appearing in the world is to be conceived as an embassage from without, an arrival from elsewhere. Jesus is he 'whom the Father consecrated and sent into the world' (10.36)... In more vividly mythological formulation it is also possible to say that he came down from heaven (3.13; 6.33, 38, 41f.)... He is here, so to speak, only as a guest; the hour is coming when he must depart (13.1 cf. 1.14 'he tented among us'). He came and will go again (8.14; 16.28; cf. 13.3; 14.12, 28; 16.5, 10, 17)... As he came down from heaven—mythological language again—he will ascend again thither where he previously was (6.62; cf. 3.13)... His coming and his going belong together as a unit, the unity of his activity as Revealer (1955: II, 33-34).

Bultmann recognizes the mythology of the Fourth Gospel in order to demythologize it into existentialist categories, but his perception of the underlying Gnostic Redeemer myth has influenced not only his pupils (e.g. Käsemann 1968) but many other interpreters (e.g. Dodd 1953, Meeks 1967, Barrett 1978, Moloney 1978, Loader 1989). Not that the meaning of the word 'myth' is defined or its use analysed or argued for. It is simply taken for granted.

'Myth' has a wide range of possible meanings but the following are relevant to the present discussion. It can be defined as a traditional narrative involving supernatural persons and embodying ideas on natural and social phenomena. In this sense we refer to 'Babylonian myth' or 'Greek myth'. It is usual to go on and distinguish those mythologies which refer to a pantheon of gods, from theologies which refer to God who is transcendent. But Bultmann and his followers make no such distinction, since they depict the Fourth Gospel as theological and yet the story of Jesus as a myth. There is a related meaning of 'myth' as a fictitious person or thing or idea. Bultmann both insists that Jesus was a historical not a mythical character in this sense (although some of his followers, like Käsemann, see Jesus as a mythical character) and implies that the myth, as an idea about him, is fictitious, although he treats the myth as an important fiction which expresses a truth in non-literal terms. Hence he can demythologize the New Testament while claiming that his version retains the truth of the gospel.

In order to accept Bultmann's assertion that the Johannine story of Jesus is expressed in mythological language we are required to understand literally Jesus' statements about his descent, his mission from the Father, his coming into the world, his departure and ascension to the Father, and then de-mythologize them. We have to suppose that the Fourth Gospel's view of reality posited a heavenly realm in which God or the λόγος or the Son or the Son of man are literally situated above the world to which the Son literally descends and from which he literally ascends back to heaven. It is not always clear whether we are supposed to envisage the Son in his heavenly abode as a human individual or as a divine individual, but that he is some kind of individual capable of literal movement is required (e.g. Loader 1989: 154).

I find it impossible to discover this myth in the Fourth Gospel. It is notable, for example, that the Prologue never mentions 'the descent' of the λόγος, but states that the λόγος exists in the world as light and became flesh. Moreover, 'the Son of God' is a description of the man Jesus, not of the λόγος or any 'pre-existent' entity. Indeed, the use of the terms 'pre-existence' and 'pre-existent' by so many New Testament scholars is evidence of the kind of theological muddle which results from their presuppositions about myth. To assert 'Christ's pre-existence', or occasionally even 'Jesus' pre-existence' (e.g. Loader 1989: 17, 113) is to say that 'Christ existed before Christ existed' which is obvious nonsense. What they imply by 'Christ's pre-existence', however, is that 'before' (understood metaphorically) Christ appeared in the world of human beings and was recognized by people, he 'lives' eternally as a transcendent being. But who is 'he' who lives eternally? The only answer to this question which the Fourth Gospel provides is its assertion that 'God' and λόγος exist eternally. In identifying Jesus as the 'Son of God', it does not state that this son exists eternally, either as a human or as a divine individual or entity. What it does state is that God's eternal λόγος, his eternal purpose or plan for humanity, was instantiated in the human and vulnerable ('flesh' 1.14) life of Jesus, who lived and died and was resurrected to a transformed and everlasting individual human existence. Further, in ch. 3 Jesus demands that the 'Jew' Nicodemus be born again, born from above, but does not require him to ascend to heaven. At the end of the Gospel Jesus is resurrected from the dead, he does not simply ascend to heaven. And the resurrected Jesus sends Mary Magdalene with this message for the disciples: 'Go to my *brethren*, and say to them, I am ascending to my Father and *your* Father, to my God and *your* God' (20.17), which seems to imply that the disciples are to share Jesus' sonship in lives of obedient dedication to God.

To make sense of the Gospel, it is necessary to understand the language of descent, mission, ascent, arrival and departure not as myth but as metaphors of allegiance (see Chapter 7). A metaphor associates a name or descriptive term or phrase with an object or action to which it is not usually applied, in order to create a single new perception, as in 'the ship ploughs the sea', for example. Although it is sometimes supposed that metaphors are confined to florid prose or poetry, in fact they are ubiquitous in everyday speech. It is difficult to say anything without them. We even treat 'word' as if it were a 'parcel', possessed or passed from one person to another: 'She hasn't a good word for him' or 'Give me your word'. We are adept at unselfconsciously recognizing metaphors and understanding them, not literally but metaphorically (see Soskice 1985). Should Mr Jones tell me that his wife is a sloth, I should naturally understand the statement metaphorically as a complaint about his wife's indolence. Two matters are clear. The first is that a metaphor cannot be understood if it is taken literally. The second is that a metaphor can be true or false.

Mrs Jones may defend herself from her husband's charge that she is a sloth by pointing to the many obligations she meets and offices she successfully fulfils day by day, of which her husband is apparently unaware, or she can admit the truth of the description. Similarly, when the Fourth Gospel relates Jesus' claim to be the true vine, the truth or falsehood of the metaphor's reference to Jesus is the issue about which readers as well as characters within the story have to make up their minds.

In theological language, metaphor is as indispensable as it is in other discourse. The statement 'God creates' seeks to capture a truth about God but it does so metaphorically. God is like a potter or an artist except that she creates *ex nihilo*. As the ultimate source of human existence, God is like a father or a mother, although God does not reproduce sexually. Moreover, some associations have a greater range of correspondences than others. For example, to state that 'God is a lion' indicates God's power, especially his power for destruction, whereas to say 'God is Israel's husband' indicates that God manages Israel's life for her true benefit, a matter which has very broad implications for understanding both 'God' and 'Israel'.

The Fourth Gospel uses many different metaphors to express its theological understanding of Jesus' life, death and resurrection. Many of the metaphors complement each other and help to elucidate the metaphorical relationship of Father and Son. Some metaphors are in tension with others, like that of abiding in Jesus set alongside that of following his way (Pamment 1985). Chapters 5–10 will explore the key concepts and metaphors of the Gospel, and their interrelationships.

Chapter 5

THE THEOLOGICAL PERSPECTIVE: GOD AND λόγος, FATHER AND SON, LORD, AND THE SPIRIT PARACLETE

The Fourth Gospel is a theological work. This chapter will explore the ways in which a particular theological perspective is expressed in the Prologue and in the story which follows.

1. *God and* λόγος

'God' (θεός) is a word which the Gospel uses in some ways already familiar from its Scripture, although Scripture employs two words, 'God' and 'Lord' (κύριος) to refer to the creator and sustainer of the world (e.g. Gen. 2.15). 'Lord' is the Greek term which the Septuagint places in the text when the Hebrew reads 'YHWH'. It will be necessary to consider whether 'God' and 'Lord' in the Fourth Gospel also refer to the same reality, but first attention will be paid to its use of 'God'.

We should notice that the Fourth Gospel sometimes includes the definite article with 'God' and sometimes omits it. Is there a difference in meaning, or are the two synonymous? It seems that, generally, they are synonymous. For example, when 'from God' is expressed with ἀπό, it is always without the article (3.2; 13.3; 16.30), but when it is expressed with another preposition, ἐκ, it is sometimes with the article and sometimes without (1.13; 7.17; 8.42, 47), and, similarly, when it is expressed with παρά (with, by the side of), it is sometimes with and sometimes without the article (1.6; 5.44; 6.46; 8.40; 9.16; in 16.27 only some manuscripts omit the article). Nevertheless, Harner (1973) has argued that the omission of the definite article from the expression 'and the λόγος was God' (1.1) is significant since the grammar and syntax ('God' functions as a predicate, and is placed first in the clause, before the verb 'was') show that God and λόγος are not completely identical. In this instance grammar and syntax are not the only considerations, since the position of the clause immediately after the statement 'the λόγος was *with* God' requires that some distinction between λόγος and 'God' be retained to avoid contradiction.

Statements about 'God' in the Fourth Gospel indicate his transcendence and distance from the material world. Although the Prologue introduces the λόγος first to readers, his transcendence is indicated by declaring that the λόγος was with God 'in the beginning'. The statement assumes that God is transcendent, existing before and independently of the world. The 'otherness' of God is also suggested by statements later in the Gospel. Jesus tells the Samaritan woman that 'God is spirit' (4.24, cf. Isa. 31.3) in order to explain what kind of worship is appropriate to such a being. The narrator states boldly at the end of the Prologue that 'No one has ever seen God' (1.18). These remarks propose that God in himself is beyond the powers of human comprehension, because he is mysteriously different from anything encountered in the world.

But is not the plain assertion 'No one has ever seen God' contradicted by the story which follows? Does not the story insist that Jesus has seen God, and that the disciples, in seeing Jesus, have seen God (e.g. 5.19 and 14.8-9)? Not quite, since the passages read:

> The Son can do nothing of his own accord, but only what he *sees* the *Father* doing (5.19).
>
> Philip said to him, 'Lord, show us *the Father,* and we shall be satisfied'. And Jesus said to him, 'Have I been with you so long and yet you do not know me Philip? He who has *seen* me has *seen the Father*' (14.8-9).

Two matters must be decided in relating 1.18 to 5.19 and 14.8-9 (cf. also 5.37; 6.46; 8.38). First, is 'Father' to be identified with 'God' in the sense defined above? 'Father' is a term which expresses relation. It does not define what an existent is in himself, but only in relation to other things, in these cases in relation to Jesus. Secondly, does 'see' have the same meaning in each sentence? In Greek, as in English, 'see' can refer to either physical or mental perception. So 1.18 denies that anyone has physically seen the transcendent God. Jn 5.19 affirms that Jesus has seen the Father physically or that he has perceived him mentally, and the latter is the more likely meaning. In 14.8-9 Philip asks to be shown the Father physically, and Jesus replies that he has seen Jesus physically, and in so doing has perceived the Father mentally. Jesus therefore goes on to ask Philip whether he *believes* that Jesus is in the Father and the Father is in him (14.10).

Let us return to considering other examples of statements about God, since most of them serve to explain how this transcendent God affects the world which he created. According to the Prologue, divinity is to be understood not simply as mysterious 'otherness' but also as λόγος. λόγος was with God 'in the beginning', 'before creation'. An eternal distinction is posited between the mysteriousness of God in herself and λόγος as God. What then does λόγος mean? The term has a range of possible meanings: speech, statement, prophecy, command, matter (under discussion), reason, plan. In English Bibles λόγος is usually translated 'Word', but this is the translation of the Latin Vulgate *verbum*. It is inappropriate as a rendering of the Greek λόγος. The Greek for 'word' is ῥῆμα or ὄνομα, not λόγος. Goodenough explains the various uses of λόγος.

> Logos means primarily the formulation and expression of thought in speech, but from this it took on a variety of associated meanings. For example, it could mean the formula by which a thing is constituted, like a formula in chemistry; so Aristotle most commonly used it. It could mean a phrase or speech of almost any kind of length, even an oration, but never a single word. And it could be turned back upon the process by which utterance was formulated in thought, and so come to mean reason. . . The Stoics distinguished two types of logos, that within the mind, or reason, and that projected in speech. . . The term logos had many other special meanings: it should often be translated 'ratio' or 'proportion' in the mathematical sense; the *orthos logos*, the 'right logos', was reason producing proper formulations with special reference to legal thought, so that the right logos of Nature was Natural law; the *idios logos*, the 'private logos', was a private account in the sense of a privy purse; the *hieros logos*, the 'sacred logos', was the secret revelation given to an initiate in the Mystery Religions. Logos, then, is almost anything except the English 'word' (Goodenough 1962: 103-104).

The Prologue states that 'all things were made *through*' the λόγος which suggests that the term connotes God's plan in creation. And λόγος is identified with all that is creative: life and light. In relation to the world, then, λόγος is the expression of God's purpose, both in creating a good and comprehensible world and in enlightening people to recognize that purpose. According to Scripture and to the Fourth Gospel, God had revealed his purpose, his λόγος, to prophets like Moses and through Wisdom (see Chapter 3, §1.6.3). In other words, λόγος is not God in himself but God's expression of his purpose in creating and sustaining the world. But if this is the case, why is a distinction made 'before' creation, 'before' there was a world to receive God's life and light? Scriptural Wisdom writings had pictured God's bringing his plan or Wisdom into existence as the first stage in creation (e.g. Prov. 8.22), but the Prologue implies that there never was a 'time' when λόγος was not distinct from God, since λόγος existed 'in the beginning'. In this way, the Prologue avoids the error of writing about eternal, transcendent reality as if that reality has a history. In fact the problem cannot be avoided altogether, since our ordinary language has to be stretched to discuss eternity at all. So the Prologue uses time expressions metaphorically, 'in the beginning', 'was'. Nevertheless, it eschews treating eternity as if it has a history, as if God changed at a particular time. It does not imply that God decided at a particular time to make the world according to a plan which he then formulated for the purpose. Rather, God's plan is an eternal expression of his being. Time is a category of the world, and people have a history. From the perspective of the Prologue, human history is to be understood in terms of the creator's purpose.

The Prologue relates that the λόγος became flesh, that in an individual man, Jesus, God's plan is instantiated (1.14). And the λόγος is not mentioned again in the Prologue after this point. Rather, it is God who is the instigator of Jesus' mission and of a believing response to it (see below). By not mentioning the λόγος again, after the statement 'the λόγος became [or was] flesh', the Prologue indicates that, from the reader's perspective, God has finally and fully communicated her purpose in the life, death and resurrection of Jesus, and that the reader has no need to look elsewhere to find it.

In the rest of the Gospel λόγος usually refers to Jesus' statement or teaching (e.g. 2.22; 5.24; 6.60; 7.36, 40; 8.31, 37, 43, 51, 52, etc.) or to the disciples' preaching (17.20), but also to the teaching of Scripture (10.35; 12.38; 15.25). It is not surprising to discover, then, that Jesus' λόγος is not his own but the Father's (8.55; 14.24), which he has given to the disciples (17.14, 17), and which they keep (17.6). Those who oppose Jesus do so because they do not have the Father's λόγος abiding in them (5.38). God's λόγος is appropriately referred to in these contexts because Jesus' teaching explains who he is and how he fulfils God's purpose.

'God' is mentioned in the story of Jesus which follows the Prologue, and there she brings about her purpose through the activities of human agents. It is God who 'sends' John and reveals to him how to identify Jesus (1.6, 29-34). He 'sends' Jesus (3.16, 34), who is his son, his messiah (e.g. 1.41), his lamb (1.29, 34), his bread (6.33), his holy one (6.69). Those who respond positively to Jesus are people who have the love of God in them (5.42, and conversely 8.42), and who are children of God (11.52; cf. 1.12, and conversely 8.41-42). They perform their works in God (3.21; 6.28-29), recognize God's gift (4.10), and hear his words (8.47). It is through the martyrdom of his agents, Jesus and Peter, that God is honoured (13.31-32; 21.19). Twice in the Gospel 'the angels of God' are mentioned, ascending and descending on the Son of Man, an allusion to Jacob's dream (1.51 cf. Gen. 28.12), or speaking to Jesus (12.29). Here they play the role of messengers linking heaven and earth.

In three places in the Fourth Gospel the word 'God' is used in surprising contexts and we need to examine the passages in detail to determine their meanings. The first instance appears in many manuscripts of the Prologue, after the assertion, 'No one has ever seen God' (1.18): 'the only *God*, who is in the bosom of the Father, he has made him known (or has brought news of him)' (1.18). Other manuscripts, many of them later in date, read 'the only Son' instead of 'the only God', but commentators usually explain this reading as assimilation to 3.16 and 18 where 'the only Son' is mentioned. There is, however, a third reading in which 'the only one' is defined neither as 'God' nor as 'Son'. This reading occurs in one of the Vulgate manuscripts, in the Diatessaron, in Origen, and in the writings of some other Church Fathers. The reason why it is not printed as the original reading in the Aland critical edition is because the other readings are more widely attested in the manuscript tradition. But the Prologue of the Fourth Gospel became an important resource for theologians engaged in christological disputes in the early centuries of the Common Era and the temptation to bolster certain interpretations by making them explicit in the Prologue was sometimes overwhelming. The three readings of the phrase in 1.18 evidence the verse's importance in these disputes. The shorter reading, without either 'God' and 'Son', has the best claim to be regarded as the original reading for two reasons. First, it explains the variation between 'God' and 'Son' in the majority of manuscripts as attempts at further definition. It is impossible to explain why either 'God' or 'Son' was dropped from the text by Origen and others if either was original. Secondly, it makes better sense in the Johannine context, picking up the earlier reference to 'the only one with the Father' from 1.14. Nowhere else in the Gospel is 'God' contrasted with 'Father', as it would be if the reading 'the only God' was accepted. Taking the shorter reading as the original, the final statement of the Prologue, 'No one has ever seen God; the only one, who is in the bosom of the Father, he has made him known', appropriately sums up the earlier teaching as an introduction to the story of Jesus which follows. No one has ever seen God, but there is a person, the only one, whose life fully instantiates God's plan for humanity, and in that way makes God known to others. He *is* in the bosom of the Father, since the story will relate that, after his death, he was resurrected from the dead to 'ascend' and live for ever with the Father.

The second instance is the only place in the Fourth Gospel where 'gods' in the plural occurs instead of the singular 'God':

> Jesus answered them, 'Is it not written in the [your] law, I said you are *gods*? If he called them *gods* to whom the λόγος of God came (and Scripture cannot be broken), do you say of him whom the Father consecrated and sent into the world, you are blaspheming, because I said I am the Son of God?' (10.34-35).

The context of the saying in the Gospel is a discussion between Jesus and the 'Jews' in the Temple at the Feast of Renewal, and the theme of Jesus' remarks is his consecration by and dedication to the Father. The 'Jews' ask him why he keeps them in suspense and does not tell them whether he is the Christ (10.24). Jesus replies that he has told them and that, moreover, the works which he does in the Father's name bear witness to him (picking up an argument from 5.36). 'Jewish' unbelief, he then explains, is due to the fact that they do not belong to his sheep, developing negatively the positive teaching given earlier in the chapter (10.14). Those who believe in him are described as gifts to him from the Father (10.29), a frequent assertion in the Gospel (e.g. 6.37-39, 44; 17.2, 6). Believer's safety is assured by this fact and by the unity of purpose between Father and Son. But the statement 'I and the Father are one' (10.33) is ambiguous and leads to misunderstanding. It is taken by the 'Jews' to be a claim to divinity made by a man (10.33), and they attempt to stone him for blasphemy. He defends himself by quoting Ps. 8.26, in the saying at the beginning of this paragraph.

The psalm is understood by modern commentators to depict God establishing justice in his heavenly council, against the 'gods' or 'Sons of the Most High' who have shown partiality to the wicked and ignored the weak and needy. These 'gods' are, then, either foreign gods over whom the God of Israel demonstrates his authority, or angelic beings in God's court who have been acting unjustly. Their destruction is envisaged. Jesus' use of the psalm, however, suggests that the criticism of these 'gods' was read as criticism of unjust decisions in earthly not heavenly courts, an appropriate enough application of the psalm's insights. Moreover, labelling the psalm 'law' seems reasonable in view of its content. Read as a description of the way in which courts should establish God's justice, God's law or λόγος, the psalm implies that those who do so are 'gods' but those who do not will die. In other words, just human judges are 'gods' in the sense that they establish God's justice. 'Gods' has become a metaphor for 'just judges' (see the discussion of Jewish midrashic interpretations of the psalm by Neyrey 1989).

Jesus' reply, therefore, uses the quotation to show that those to whom the λόγος of God came are appropriately called 'gods' in a metaphorical sense. Hence there is no blasphemy in Jesus' claim to be God's son. Jesus can be seen to be God's son because he does his Father's works (10.37). Jesus' argument fails to convince his hearers in the story, but stands as a sufficient justification of his claim in the narrative.

The final instance occurs in Thomas's response to meeting the resurrected Jesus. Jesus encourages Thomas to change from an unbeliever into a believer, and Thomas's 'My Lord and my God' (20.28) is his expression of belief (see 20.29). Naturally, the interpretation of Thomas's words was hotly debated by early church theologians who wanted to use it in support of their own christological definitions. Those who understood 'my Lord' to refer to Jesus, and 'my God' to refer to God were suspected of christological heresy in the fifth century CE. Many modern commentators have also rejected that interpretation and instead they understand the confession as an assertion that Jesus is both Lord and God. In doing so they are forced to interpret 'God' as a reference to λόγος. But it is perfectly appropriate for Thomas to respond to Jesus' resurrection with a confession of faith both in Jesus as his Lord and in God who sent and raised Jesus. Interpreting the confession in this way actually makes much better sense in the context of the Fourth Gospel. In 14.1 belief both in God and in Jesus is encouraged, in a context in which Thomas is particularly singled out. Moreover, nowhere else in the Gospel is Jesus called God. Rather, he is called God's son, and this is the confession that the Gospel urges its readers to make at the end of ch. 20: 'These things are written that you may believe or continue to believe that Jesus is the Christ, the Son of God, and that continuing to believe you may have life in his name' (20.31). If we understand Thomas's confession as an assertion that Jesus is God, this confession in 20.31 becomes an anti-climax. Moreover, if the Gospel really teaches that Jesus is God in 20.28, why does it not make that assertion in the Prologue or in 10.35 or in 20.31, where it could have been most appropriately placed? On the other hand, if we understand Thomas's confession as an expression of belief both in Jesus' messiahship and in the God whose agent he is, it fits perfectly well with the Prologue, with 10.35 and with all the other references to Jesus as God's son, and it does not require us to read 20.31 as an anticlimax.

1.1. *The Prologue*

Since the Prologue is a theological introduction to the rest of the Gospel, it will be convenient to spend some time elucidating its teaching before examining the Gospel's references to Father and Son.

The Prologue begins with a distant perspective and gradually moves towards the reader's present situation. It begins in eternity, with God and λόγος (1.1-2), moves on to creation through the λόγος (1.3), and then mentions the λόγος's role in the lives of human creatures, as their source of life and light (1.4). At this point it introduces a note of opposition, but in a reassuring manner: 'And the light shines in the darkness, but the darkness did not overcome it' (1.5). Now that the reader is aware of an opposition to the light, a historical person, John, can be characterized as someone sent by God to testify to the light (1.6-8). The reference stresses, however, that John was a witness to the light, not someone who could be identified with the light itself.

The next section of the Prologue (1.9-13) can be interpreted in one of two ways, either as a reference to Jesus' advent, or as a reference to the light enlightening people before Jesus' advent. Jn 1.9 is ambiguous and can be translated either: 'The true light, which enlightens every person, was coming into the world' (taking ἦν and ἐρχόμενον as a periphrastic imperfect), or: 'He [i.e. the λόγος] was the true light which enlightens every person coming into the world' (taking ἐρχόμενον as a participle agreeing with ἄνθρωπον). The former translation refers to the light's arrival in the world and would have to be construed as an alternative way of describing Jesus' advent, parallel to 1.14. Jn 1.10-13 would then be understood as a depiction of reactions to Jesus. The difficulty with this interpretation is that it ruins what would otherwise be a startling climax in 1.14. Moreover, the Gospel teaches that even before Jesus' ministry, the light enlightened human beings. The Prologue has already mentioned John (1.6-8), and the Gospel will go on to mention others, especially Moses (e.g. 5.46), Abraham (e.g. 8.56) and Isaiah (e.g. 12.41). It is also appropriate for 1.9-13 to explain more clearly the fate of the light in human history before Jesus' ministry. All that has been indicated previously is that light was not overcome by darkness (1.5). Jn. 1.10-13 goes on to show that darkness symbolizes ignorance and rejection, but that some people nevertheless receive the light and so become children of God, believing in his name, being born from him. Once readers understand that God's light can be ignored or accepted, they are better able to appreciate the fate which awaits Jesus.

There is, of course, a formal contradiction between 1.9, 'the light enlightens every person', and the statements 'the world did not know him' (1.10) and 'his own people did not receive him' (1.11), but the Gospel is fond of expressing its teaching in extreme forms, which then have to be modified. So there is another contradiction between 1.11 and 1.12, between 'he came to his own place and his own people did not receive him' and 'but as many as received him'. Hence, v. 9 is overly optimistic, vv. 10-11 are overly pessimistic, and v. 12 expresses what lies between the two extremes. A similar contradiction is found between 3.32 'no one receives his testimony' and 3.33 'he who receives his testimony'.

In spite of the intimations contained in 1.9-13, the reader can still be surprised by the opening statement of 1.14: 'And the λόγος became or was flesh'. The λόγος, the expression of God's eternal purpose for humanity, is now instantiated not just in prophetic, legal and wise insights but in a vulnerable human life. 'Flesh' rather than 'man' is used to draw attention to the person's susceptibility to injury, decay and death. This first reference to the person who will be the subject of the subsequent story hints at his destiny.

The Prologue continues in the form of a community confession like those in the psalms (e.g. Pss. 21.13; 44.1; 46.7, 11; 48.9; 75.1; 114.18). 'And he dwelt among us, and we saw his renown, renown as the only one from the Father, full of grace and truth' (1.14). The form, confession, is determined by the content. As the rest of the Gospel will show, most people failed to accord Jesus the honour he deserved as God's agent. Only those who believed in him recognized his worth. It is appropriate that in the confession, God is referred to for the first time as Father.

The Prologue then returns to John (1.15) in order to specify in what way he testifies concerning God's light. Now we are told that his witness concerns the person who had been described in 1.14, and what he says about him is quoted: 'This was he of whom I said, He who comes after me [in time] ranks before me because he was before me [in dignity]'. The quotation is repeated in the story of John which follows the Prologue (1.30). The testimony makes it clear that, although the beginning of Jesus' ministry is later than that of John's, Jesus is superior to John. John's witness takes the form of an oracle inspired by God (1.31-34), in which he identifies Jesus as the person upon whom God's spirit descends and remains. Hence Jesus' whole life, as well as his teaching, expresses God's purpose for human beings. John's witness is fundamentally important because he is an outsider, not a member of the Johannine or any other Christian community.

The Prologue concludes with references to the gift which members of the community confess they have received from Jesus. 'Grace instead of grace' (1.16) is explained in the following verse: 'The law was given through Moses, grace and truth came through Jesus Christ'. The passive 'was given' implies that the law was God's gift and the clause corresponds to the first reference to grace in 1.16. 'Grace and truth through Jesus Christ' corresponds to the second reference to grace in 1.16. Are we to suppose that God's law is denigrated by this statement and that the grace given through Jesus replaces his previous gift? Since the law is characterized as God's grace, and since, later in the Gospel, teaching in the law is taken to be authoritative, no denigration can be intended. Rather, Jesus' life, death and resurrection are understood to encapsulate the law's insights. In this conclusion to the Prologue, 1.17 identifies at long last the person described in 1.14 as Jesus Christ. Finally, in v. 18, the importance of Jesus' mission is summarized: 'No one has ever seen God; the only one who is in the bosom of the Father, he has made him known'. Jesus' mission is to make known the invisible, transcendent God. The rest of the Gospel will describe how Jesus, God's human agent, fulfils his mission by remaining obedient to his Father. At the time of this confession Jesus is already 'in the bosom of the Father'. The Gospel will relate how Jesus suffers a martyr's death but is resurrected and ascends to the Father. The Prologue hints at this destiny by referring to 'flesh' in 1.14 and by concluding with Jesus' presence in the bosom of the Father.

2. *Father and Son*

Referring to God as Father is a commonplace in the Gospel's Scripture. God is transcendent creator, but Scripture does not imagine that God set creation in motion like a watchmaker winding a watch and letting it go on unaided. The transcendent God of Scripture, on the contrary, is involved not only in keeping the world in existence, but in influencing people to apprehend her sovereignty (e.g. Gen. 6–9; Neh. 9.6). Scripture therefore depicts the relationship between God and Israel in terms of the relationship between father and first-born son, in order to emphasize both God's loving care for his people and his people's obedient response (e.g. Exod. 4.22; Deut. 32.6, 8; 1 Chron. 29.10; Ps. 103.13). Moreover, as a child is dependent on its father for its existence, people are ultimately dependent on God for their existence (e.g. Gen. 1.26). From the Johannine perspective, however, Israel's history had been the history of a disobedient son. By contrast, the Gospel is the history of the Father's obedient Son.

In modern western society the relationships of sons to fathers are different from those in the first century CE, and the differences need to be borne in mind if the biblical metaphor is to be appreciated. The power and authority of a father in Roman society, for example, is described by Balsdon and Ferguson (1974: 6):

> A father had the same legal power over a son as he had over a slave; he could put him to death (with the approval of a specially summoned family council); he could sell him into slavery. Except with his consent, his son could hold no property; his money was like a slave's, something which this father, like the slave's master, could annex at will. The exercise of the most horrendous of these powers was illustrated in Roman legend and in early Roman history; they were obsolete by (the first century CE). But the unquestioned authority of the *pater familias* continued; a man might be a consul, married with children, but he was still in the power of his father.

The mother's power was legally subordinate to the father's, and, after the father's death, to the son's.

Greeks shared with Romans the same conception of a son's relationship to his father, as the following quotation illustrates. It comes from the dissertations of the first-century Stoic philosopher, Epictetus:

> Bear in mind that you are a son. A son's profession is to treat everything that is his as belonging to his father, to be obedient to him in all things, never to speak ill of him to anyone else, nor to say or do anything that will harm him, to give way to him in everything and yield him precedence, helping him to the utmost of his power (*Dissertations* 2.7).

In Jewish society the picture is much the same. The stories about the patriarchs in Genesis, and especially Abraham's resolve to sacrifice his son Isaac (Gen. 22), illustrate the father's power in Israelite tradition, and although there is some evidence that rabbis tried to set limits to that power (*TDNT*: 974), honouring the father remained fundamental (Exod. 20.12; Deut. 5.16; see Falk 1974). As the first-century Jewish historian Josephus explains:

> Honour to parents the law ranks second only to honour to God, and if a son does not respond to the benefits received from them—for the slightest failure in his duty towards them—it hands him over to be stoned. It requires respect to be paid by the young to all their elders, because God is the most Ancient of all (*Apion* 2.206. See also Philo, *Dec.* 165-67).

> The mere intention of doing wrong to one's parents or of impiety against God is followed by instant death (*Apion* 2.217).

Sirach offers a more positive incentive for honouring parents: 'Remember that your parents brought you into the world; how can you repay what they have done for you?' (Sir. 7.23).

Moreover, in first-century societies, a son was dependent on his father for his education. It would generally be taken for granted that the son's occupation would be the same as the father's. Of course, if the father were rich, he could entrust parts of this education to paid teachers or slaves, but if he were poor, the son would learn directly from the father how to become a competent farmer, fisherman or carpenter. And education was thought to involve hard discipline, as Sirach makes clear: 'Do you have sons? Discipline them and break them in from their earliest years' (Sir. 7.23). The father would also be responsible for teaching his son the cultural and religious family traditions, with the help of religious institutions, like the Temple and the synagogue in Palestine.

This complete dependence of the son on the father, socially, culturally and economically, means that a son was the most useful agent in conducting the father's business. The son's interests were identical with those of his father (see Harvey 1987; Borgen 1968: Part II).

When the Fourth Gospel uses the father–son metaphor to depict the relationship between God and a human being, it is clear that first-century social conventions are taken for granted. The Son of God is entirely dependent on his Father. He lives only for the Father (6.57). He does nothing on his own authority but only what he sees or hears the Father doing (8.38; 10.18; 12.49-50; 14.24; 15.15). The Father is his teacher (8.28). The Son is his Father's apprentice:

> The Son can do nothing of his own accord, but only what he sees the Father doing; for whatever he does, that the Son does likewise. For the Father loves the Son, and shows him all that he himself is doing; and greater works than these will he show him, that you may marvel (5.19-20).

The Father's love for the Son is mentioned in other passages too (3.35; 10.17; 15.9), as well as the Son's love for the Father (14.31). Because of this love, the Father has given everything to the Son (6.37; 13.3; 16.15) and yet the Father demands complete obedience from the Son, and obedience which will lead to the Son's death (3.16; 10.17; 12.27).

The Gospel depicts the Son's activity as that of a human agent, acting on the Father's behalf. The Father 'sent' the Son into the world to achieve his purpose (5.36-37; 8.16; 10.36; 12.49). Hence the Son has come 'in the Father's name' (5.43; 10.25), and the Father has set his seal on his mission (6.27). He does the Father's works (5.17; 10.25, 37; 14.10), fulfils his commands (15.10), speaks his words (8.38; 12.50; 14.24), does what the Father wills (6.40), looks after his interests (2.16), and drinks from the cup he has given him (18.11). It is therefore appropriate that the Son should be accorded the same honour as the Father (1.14; 5.23; 12.28). Those who hate the Son hate the Father (15.23-24), those who love the Son are loved by the Father (14.21-23; 16.27). To see the Son doing the Father's work is therefore tantamount to seeing the Father (14.9), since the Father dwells in the Son, his agent, as the Son dwells in the Father (10.38; 14.10-11; 17.21). In this sense the Father and the Son are one (10.30) in spite of the fact that the Son acknowledges the Father's superiority (14.28).

The Son can rely on the Father's support (16.32). It is the Father who bears witness to him (5.37; 8.18) because the Son is making the Father known (8.19; 10.15; 14.7, 10-11; 16.3). The Father honours him (8.54; 12.26; 17.5) and is honoured by him (8.49; 14.13; 15.8). Since the Son is the Father's representative in the world, no one comes to the Father except through him (14.6).

2.1. *Honour and Honouring*

It will have been noticed that in translating the Greek noun δόξα and the Greek verb δοξάζω, I have chosen the English word 'honour' rather than the ambiguous words 'glory' and 'glorify'. δόξα has a range of possible meanings, depending on the context. It can mean 'fame, renown, honour' and that is the meaning required by the Fourth Gospel's usage. It can mean 'brightness, splendour, radiance' (Acts 22.11; 1 Cor. 15.40-41) and hence can be used metaphorically of God's majesty (Rom. 1.23) but this meaning fails to make sense in the Johannine context. When Jesus' first miracle at Cana (2.1-11) serves to make Jesus' honour (δόξα) known and to evoke the belief of the disciples, it is not the case that the miracle is an open manifestation of God's glory and majesty. Had it been so, it would have been impossible for any human being to resist, yet the miracle remains insignificant for most onlookers and only Jesus' disciples believe in him. Jesus is not pictured as God himself striding the earth and occasionally displaying God's majesty. The honour due to Jesus as God's human agent has to be discerned, and it is discerned by only a few of his followers. Most people seek honour (δόξα) from other human beings instead of from God (12.43; see also 5.41, 44; 7.18; 8.50, 54) and it is this orientation which makes it difficult for them to recognize the honour Jesus gives to and receives from God.

The Johannine use of δοξάζω also requires the meaning 'honour' rather than the meaning 'clothe in splendour, glorify'. Jesus honours the Father and is honoured by him not in a splendid enthronement or a dazzling display of power but in a criminal's death on a cross (12.23-36; 13.31). The Johannine use of δοξάζω is synonomous with τιμάω (honour) with which it is sometimes juxtaposed (8.48-55 and 12.23-36, and see the juxtaposition of δόξα and τιμάω in 5.23-44. The noun τιμή 'honour', is used once at 4.44). This is another example of the Johannine fondness for synonyms to create variety (compare 'send'—ἀποστέλλω and πέμπω; 'love'—ἀγαπάω and φιλέω).

In Jesus' final prayer (ch. 17), when he meditates on the significance of his imminent death and intercedes for his community of followers, he sums up his relationship with the Father and with his disciples in these terms: 'The honour which you [the Father] have given to me, I have given to them [the disciples], so that they may be one as we are one' (17.22). The disciples will not receive honour from human beings. On the contrary, they can expect persecution (15.18–16.4). But the honour which Jesus received from the Father because of his obedience to the Father's will is to be theirs as well, insofar as they serve the same purpose. And ch. 21 refers to the fact that one of the disciples, Peter, honoured God in a martyr's death like Jesus' (21.18-19).

But why, in the prayer, does Jesus refer to the Father's giving him honour before the creation of the world? There are two references. Jn 17.5 states, 'And now honour me with yourself, Father, with the honour which I had with you before the world was'. That Jesus' honour and the Father's should coincide is a request already made in 17.2-4. But 17.5 is ambiguous. It is usually understood to imply that Jesus existed before the creation of the world, and that he requests to be honoured on earth or in heaven with the honour he enjoyed then. But the Gospel never states that the human being, Jesus, the 'I' of the request in 17.5, existed anywhere at any time before he was born and lived in Palestine. What it does state, in the Prologue, is that God's plan, his λόγος, existed 'in the beginning'. It is this plan that the Father eternally honours, and since Jesus embodies this plan in his obedient life, his honour is an instantiation of the honour accorded by the eternal Father to his plan. In other words, it is 'honour' which exists 'before the world was', not Jesus, and this is because whatever the Father does, whether honouring or loving, he does eternally. In 17.24 Jesus requests that the disciples may be with him to observe or perceive the honour which the Father has given him because he loved him before the foundation of the world:

> Father, I desire that they also, whom you have given to me, may be with me where I am, so that they may observe or perceive my honour which you have given to me because you loved me before the foundation of the world.

It is the Father's love which is an eternal reality. It is the eternal Father who loved before the foundation of the world, and whose love finds expression in honouring the man Jesus because of his obedience, an obedience which does not recoil even in the face of a death by torture, a death which is dishonourable from a worldly perspective. Hence Jesus' desire that the disciples will see his death not as a disgrace but as the honour accorded him by the Father.

In expressing the relationship of God's son to God in terms of the son–father metaphor, the Fourth Gospel exploits aspects of the relationship which involve the Father's love, concern and support, the Son's commission, obedience, even in laying down his life, and dependence, and the honour which they share. To know one is therefore to know the other. But like all metaphors, its usefulness is limited. God is not a human father. He cannot show a human being what he is doing as a human father would. The Son cannot see and hear him as he could a human father. As creator of the world, the works which God performs are giving life in a more ultimate sense than would be true of a human father, just as his exercise of judgment is more final than a human father's. So this son, Jesus, in doing the works of this Father, is commissioned to make God's light, life and love humanly recognizable (5.21-29; 9.1-41). Those who reject him are not just rejecting the agent of a human father, but are rejecting God (8.34-59).

Nevertheless, the Gospel insists that the transcendent God can be known through the human being Jesus. The way had been prepared for such an unlikely suggestion by the Gospel's Scripture. The idea that humanity is made in the image and likeness of God (Gen. 1.26) was explored in Scripture in largely moral terms. Israelites owed God their obedience and allegiance because God created them, redeemed them from slavery, made his will know to them, and gave them an inheritance. They imitated God in living just and merciful lives. The law codes and prophetic oracles indicate what obedience, justice and mercy mean for human existence. In the Fourth Gospel Jesus, God's Son, exemplifies both human dependence on God and this moral union. By living from the Father, he demonstrates what it is to be a genuine human being at the service of other people.

In spite of the many assertions to the contrary in ancient and modern commentaries, I can find no convincing evidence in the Fourth Gospel for interpreting 'the Son of God' as an attribution of divinity. Certainly the Gospel claims that God's λόγος, God's purpose for humanity, is fully exemplified in Jesus' life, death and resurrection, but that is by no means the same as stating that Jesus is divine.

One of the arguments used by commentators (e.g. Barrett) to support their view that the Fourth Gospel expresses belief in Christ's divinity depends on an interpretation of the narrative statement in 5.18:

> This is why the Jews were seeking rather to kill him [Jesus], because he not only used to break the sabbath but also used to call God his own Father, making himself equal to God.

Although this is a narrative account of 'Jewish' accusations against Jesus, commentators propose that it is to be understood ironically, as an accusation within the story, but as a true statement on the narrative level. It can hardly function in that way, however, because Jesus' discourse in 5.19-46 refutes this accusation. Jesus is the Son of God, but he is not equal to God. He can do nothing of his own accord (5.19, 30). The Son's dual mission, to give life to the dead and to exercise judgment (5.21-24), is the expression of the Father's love for the Son (5.20), a gift from the Father (5.26-27, 36). The whole discourse emphasizes Jesus' dependence on God. He is a human being carrying out the mission assigned to him by the Father. Moreover, God is not exclusively his own Father. He is the Father of all obedient sons and Jesus seeks to call others into that filial relationship (e.g. 11.52; 12.36; 17.10, 14, 16-19, 21, 23, 26; 20.17, 22-23).

A second passage which has sometimes been construed as an expression of belief in Christ's divinity (e.g. Barrett) is Jesus' claim, 'The Father and I are one' (10.30). It is certainly interpreted by the 'Jewish' audience in that way: 'It is not for a good work that we stone you but for blasphemy, because you, being a man, make yourself God' (10.33). But, again, this is a 'Jewish' misunderstanding. Jesus' declaration in 10.30 had been immediately preceded by his acknowledgement of the Father's superior greatness: 'My Father, in regard to what [the sheep] he has given to me, is greater than all, and no one is able to snatch them out of his hand' (10.29; this translation represents a reading which explains the other variants in the manuscription tradition). Moreover, the first half of this chapter (10.1-18) had described Jesus as the Good or Model Shepherd who lays down his life for the sheep. This is the command he received from the Father (10.18). Are we to suppose that the problem of associating the diametrically opposed concepts of divinity and death had not occurred to the author of the Fourth Gospel? To do so would force us to overlook the sophisticated theological reflection of the Prologue and the rest of the Gospel. The Gospel describes God as 'spirit' (4.24) and Jesus as 'flesh' (1.14), and it contrasts flesh and spirit (3.5-8). Nevertheless, it explains that human beings like Jesus (1.32) and the disciples (20.22) are inspired by God's Spirit. Had the Gospel taught that Christ is divine, an alternative way of relating divinity and humanity would have been required. But none is offered.

Furthermore, there is no compelling reason for interpreting 'son of God' as an attribution of divinity. It is used in that way in Hellenistic Greek literature, for example, in Philostratus' *Life of Apollonius of Tyana*, but such works exhibit fundamentally different theological, philosophical and anthropological belief systems. The belief system which the Fourth Gospel exhibits is derived from its Scripture, and in that Scripture 'son of God' is used metaphorically to refer to Israel's relationship with God. The Fourth Gospel teaches that Jesus is the True Vine (15.1), the True Israelite, and calls him 'the Son of God' in that sense.

According to the Fourth Gospel, Jesus' life of exemplary obedience is lived in a world in which most people ignore God. So his teaching and activity meet with opposition which eventually leads to his unjust execution. The Gospel has not abandoned its Scripture's view that the world is God's creation, beloved by God (3.16), but it reckons with a human world which has turned from God, in ignorance and imagined independence.

Not that worldly existence before Jesus' advent is viewed in entirely negative terms. In spite of the Gospel's love of extremes—light and darkness, love and hate—its rhetoric does in fact leave room for something in between. This is why Jesus is not the only person the Gospel reckons God inspired to make his will known. Figures from Scripture, especially Abraham (8.56), Moses (5.46) and Isaiah (12.38-41), are given the role of looking forward and bearing witness to Jesus. John, too, is sent by God and inspired to recognize Jesus and bear witness to him (1.6-8, 15, 19-36; 3.27-30). According to the Prologue, the light and life which issue through the λόγος into the world were not completely overcome by darkness before Jesus came into the world (1.5, 9-13). Moreover, Jesus testifies to John: 'He was a burning and shining lamp, and you were willing to rejoice for a while in his light' (5.35).

Nevertheless, the Fourth Gospel centres attention on Jesus. His life is described to show that worldly existence is not what God wills, and to demonstrate that a human life lived from God is richer and more enjoyable than alternatives, in spite of the inevitable human rejection and suffering encountered. Jesus' life, then, makes the Father known in the sense that it exemplifies the fulfilment of his will and demonstrates his love for humanity.

This is why, in the Fourth Gospel, Jesus does nothing except in obedience to God. He does not live from the world but from God. He does not pursue worldly interests but God's. The language is not 'subordinationist' in the sense that some commentators have supposed (e.g. Haenchen 1980, 1984) since it is language about a human being, Jesus, not about an eternal, transcendent relationship.

In the Fourth Gospel Jesus is described as God's only-begotten Son (e.g. 3.16; see Pss. 22.20; 25.16; 35.17). Jesus is uniquely able to make God's purpose known because he embodies God's λόγος (1.14). For this reason, throughout the story, only he justly claims to be the Son of God (10.38; see 8.41-47). Nevertheless, his life is exemplary, and insofar as others follow his example, they too become sons of God and 'sons of light' (12.36), obedient to his will, agents who make him known to the world. This is the sonship which the 'Jews', according to the Gospel, should not have rejected (8.12-59). It is the sonship which the disciples accept by following Jesus (e.g. 14.21; 16.23-27). Like Jesus, they are not 'of the world' (17.14, 16). They too will act in the Father's name (17.11), they too are sent on the same mission as Jesus was (17.18; 20.21). Jesus is sanctified that they may be sanctified (17.19). When Jesus' mission is complete, he tells Mary Magdalene to 'Go to my *brothers* and say to them, I am ascending to my Father and *your* Father, to my God and *your* God' (20.17). Jesus' life is unique in that it provides an example which is final and complete, but it does not divide him from other human beings. Inasmuch as they hear and obey his words, follow his example, they too embody God's λόγος (17.6-8). By dwelling in Jesus they participate in the indwelling of Father and Son (15.1-11; 17). They are to be taught by God (6.45). Their love is to mirror Jesus' (15.12-13). Jesus is uniquely important in first making God's purpose known completely, but he is not otherwise a unique person, except in the prosaic sense that all individuals are unique. Rather, his kind of life is to be lived by everyone. The intention of God, to relate to human beings as to children (1.12), and to gather the scattered children into one community (11.52), is fulfilled in Jesus and those who follow him (10.11-16; 17.20-21). And that relationship does not end with death. In the Farewell Discourses Jesus promises the disciples that he goes away to prepare their dwelling place with the Father (14.2-3). Jesus' seven signs demonstrate the revivifying effects of God's creative activity through his agent and son. Dependence on God brings light (ch. 9), life (4.46-54; 11) and fullness of life (chs. 2; 5; 6.1-21). The signs signify that in spite of people's blindness, feebleness and inadequacy, the Father draws them to himself through the Son (12.32).

It is because Jesus' sonship is exemplary that much of his teaching about the Son is expressed not in the first person but in the third person. Only once, in response to a question from the 'Jews', does he say, 'I am the Son of God' (10.36). Naturally, the reader is made aware that Jesus is God's son, through the confessions of others (Jn 1.34, although here the original reading is probably 'chosen one' not 'son'; Nathanael, 1.49), and it is belief in this Son of God, Jesus, that the Gospel encourages (3.16-18, 36; 6.40; 11.4, 27; 17.1; 20.31). But all the other references to 'the son' are general (3.35), even when Jesus is the speaker (5.19-26; 8.35-36). Indeed, the light which Jesus gives to the world (8.12) is intended to transform others into 'sons of light' (12.36).

3. *Lord* (κύριος)

In the Greek translation of the Hebrew Scriptures, 'Lord' was used when 'YHWH' appeared in the Hebrew. 'YHWH', God's name, was not pronounced, so 'Lord' replaced it. Three of the scriptural quotations in the Fourth Gospel include the word 'Lord'. In 1.23 Isa. 40.3 is slightly amended to 'Make straight the way of the Lord' as a depiction by John of his own mission. In 12.13 'Blessed is he who comes in the name of the Lord' is a quotation from Ps. 118.26 with which the crowds greet Jesus on his way to Jerusalem. In 12.38 the apparent failure of Jesus' public ministry is interpreted as a fulfilment of Isa. 53.1, 'Lord, who has believed our report, and to whom has the arm of the Lord been revealed?' In all these quotations, 'Lord' refers to the Lord God.

'Lord' is a term of commitment and dependence. In the social environment of the first century it expressed the slaves' acknowledgment of their master's authority, and the Fourth Gospel uses it in that sense in 13.16, 15.15 and 20. According to 15.15, however, the relationship of disciples to Jesus is not to be conceived in those terms. Rather, the disciples are Jesus' friends, because they share Jesus' knowledge of the Father. Later, as we have already noticed, the text seems to imply that they are not just friends, but brothers of Jesus (20.17).

More generally, in the first century, 'Lord' was used as a term of respect, when the speaker addressed a human being to whom allegiance was felt. One human being to whom allegiance was required was the king. In Scripture David, for example, is habitually addressed as 'Lord' (e.g. 1 Sam. 25.24-27; 2 Sam. 13.32; 14.12, 20; 15.21; 19.19). Most of the Johannine instances are examples of this usage, addressed to Jesus by the disciples (e.g. 11.3, 12; 13.37) or by others (4.15, 49; 5.7; 11.21, 27). Once someone other than Jesus is called 'Lord' (12.21, Philip by the Greeks), and once Jesus is called 'Lord' unknowingly by Mary Magdalene, when she mistakes him for a gardener (20.15).

Because it is often used in addressing Jesus, 'Lord' with the definite article functions as a reference to Jesus by the narrator (4.1; 6.23; 11.2; 20.20; 21.12), by the disciples (20.25; 21.7), or by Mary (20.2, 18). As a term of commitment, it is sometimes qualified by the personal pronoun, '*my* Lord' (20.13, 28).

But since the Fourth Gospel also calls God 'Lord' in the scriptural quotations, could the references to Jesus also imply connotations of divinity? The only reference which would lend support to such a view is Thomas's confession, when he recognizes the risen Jesus, 'My Lord and my God' (20.28). But we have already seen reason to interpret this statement as an expression of belief both in Jesus as Lord, and in God. In the Fourth Gospel, therefore, 'Lord' appropriately expresses commitment to the man Jesus, the messiah. The quotations from Scripture make it clear that this messianic Lord, Jesus, comes in the name of the Lord God.

4. *Spirit and Paraclete*

One of the ways in which Scripture envisages God influencing people is by inspiring them with his Spirit. The success of kings (e.g. 1 Sam. 10.6, 10; 16.13), prophetic insight (e.g. Num. 11.26; 24.2; Isa. 61.1) and Wisdom (Gen. 41.38-39; Sir. 39.6; Wis. 1.5, 7; 9.17) are all attributed to the work of God's Spirit. Moreover, some prophetic oracles look forward to a time when God's Spirit would inspire the whole people (e.g. Isa. 44.3; Ezek. 36.36; Joel 2.28).

But both Scripture (e.g. 1 Kgs 21.5; Pss. 31.5; 77.3, 6) and the Fourth Gospel also use 'spirit' in an anthropological sense to characterize an aspect of human existence. So, for example, Jesus' spirit is disturbed by Mary's weeping at her brother's death, and Jesus weeps too (11.33-35). Again, his spirit is upset over the disciple who will betray him (13.21). Finally, in the account of his death, the fact of death is noted by the expression, 'he bowed his head and gave up [his] spirit' (19.30). These references to anthropological spirit have no bearing on the subject of inspiration by God.

In presenting Jesus as both prophet and messiah, the Fourth Gospel declares that he is endowed with God's spirit. The subject is first introduced into the story by John. In distinction from the Synoptics, however, the narrator does not describe Jesus' baptism, but John reflects on what happened when he met Jesus, in order to bear witness to him. Perhaps this shift in perspective is devised to avoid a contradiction. The Prologue describes Jesus as the λόγος become flesh. It is reasonable to infer from this that he was always inspired by God's Spirit, not subsequently endowed with the spirit. What happens when John meets Jesus, according to the Fourth Gospel, is simply that Jesus' inspiration becomes known to others through John's witness. The story is presented in the following way. John had been led by God to testify that a man would come after him who ranked before him (1.15, 30), and had also been told by God how to recognize this person. So John asserts:

> I myself did not know him; but for this I came baptizing with water, that he might be revealed to Israel. . . I saw the Spirit descend as a dove from heaven, and it remained on him. I myself did not know him; but he who sent me to baptize with water said to me, 'He on whom you see the Spirit descend and remain, this is he who baptizes with the Holy Spirit.' And I have seen and have borne witness that this is the Son [or Chosen One] of God (1.30-34).

There is a particular emphasis in John's testimony to Jesus' endowment with God's Spirit. God's inspiration of Jesus is not to be viewed as sporadic but permanent, because the Spirit descended and *remained* upon him. This means that everything related of Jesus in the story should be taken as evidence of his inspiration, not simply his wisdom or signs. He is the obedient Son of God, permanently inspired by God. And this is why Jesus' baptism of others will be unlike John's water baptism. It will be baptism in the Holy Spirit.

But when is such a Spirit baptism to be expected? The Gospel mentions that Jesus baptized at 3.22 and at the beginning of ch. 4, but there it also immediately contradicts the previous statements by saying that only Jesus' disciples baptized (4.2). What are we to make of this contradiction? Later in the Gospel, in 7.37-39, the narrator explains that the Spirit will not be given until Jesus' mission is complete (see below). Is 4.2 an attempt to avoid the impression either that the Spirit was given when Jesus baptized others during his ministry, which would contradict 7.37-39, or that Jesus baptized during his ministry but that this baptism did not endow people with the Spirit, which would contradict 1.33? If 4.2 is an attempt to make the Gospel's presentation more coherent, it must be a secondary gloss, since the best way of avoiding a contradiction between 1.33 and 7.37-39 on the one hand, and 3.22 and 4.1 on the other, is to cut out 3.22 and 4.1. But if 4.2 is a secondary gloss, and 3.22, 4.1, 1.33 and 7.37-39 are to be reconciled, the only way of doing so is to suppose that Jesus baptized as John did during his ministry (3.22 and 4.1), and that John's prophecy about Jesus' baptism in the Spirit is fulfilled only after his death (7.37-39 fulfilled in 20.22), and not through baptism in this instance but through recreation (see below).

Some of Jesus' teaching about God's Spirit is given in his public ministry. The first instance occurs in his private discussion with Nicodemus, a ruler of the Jews, who comes to Jesus at night but receives no enlightenment (3.1-15). As in other Johannine dialogues, Nicodemus takes Jesus' statement literally, and misunderstands it. Jesus suggests that people need to be born ἄνωθεν ('again' or 'from above') but Nicodemus thinks this means he must enter his mother's womb a second time (3.3-4). Nicodemus's misunderstanding serves the useful function of indicating how difficult any kind of rebirth would be. Jesus therefore explains that the birth to which he refers is from water and the Spirit (3.5). Many commentators (e.g. Barrett 1950, who argues that teaching about the Spirit presupposes a context of Christian worship) take this to be a reference to Christian water baptism which also bestows the Spirit on believers, but an alternative understanding of the reference to water makes better sense. A double contrast is made in Jesus' reply to Nicodemus, that between water and Spirit, and that between flesh and Spirit (3.5-6). Water probably refers, therefore, to the water of natural birth. Jesus insists that it is not enough for human beings to be born in an ordinary way, of water or of flesh, but that they must be reborn 'from above', from the Spirit. In other words, their lives should become vehicles of God's Spirit. The mysteriousness of God's inspiration is then highlighted by a play on the double meaning of the word πνεῦμα, which can be translated as 'wind' or 'Spirit' (3.8). Just as the origin of the wind is mysterious, so the origin of the Spirit, in God, is mysterious, but its effects can be recognized, like ths noise of the wind. The teaching holds out the possibility that a person's life can be transformed by God's Spirit. What such a transformation means we can see by reading the story of Jesus, upon whom the Spirit has already been bestowed.

The reader is therefore reminded of this in a further statement about Jesus, either from John or from the narrator: 'He whom God has sent speaks the words of God, for it is not by measure that he gives the Spirit' (3.34). Although the focus of this saying is upon Jesus' teaching ('the words of God'), the denial that God gives the Spirit by measure suggests once again that the whole of Jesus' life evidences his permanent inspiration.

The second instance occurs in the discussion between Jesus and the Samaritan woman about the relative merits of Jewish and Samaritan worship of God. Jesus both acknowledges Jewish superiority (4.22) and goes on to define the kind of worship God requires.

> But the hour is coming, and now is, when the true worshippers will worship the Father in spirit and truth, for such the Father seeks to worship him. God is spirit, and those who worship him must worship in spirit and truth (4.23-24).

The first reference to time is the time of the story, 'the hour is coming', and refers to the time when Jesus' mission will be finished. The second reference to time, 'and now is', refers to the time of the narrator, when believers worship God in spirit and truth. Here 'truth' seems to mean 'loyalty' or 'sincerity', or perhaps a mixture of both. The statement makes it clear that since God is spirit, the only worship appropriate to him is that inspired by his Spirit. Presumably, the references to 'living water' (4.10, 14), which Jesus offers the woman earlier in the narrative, are metaphors for the Spirit (see 7.38-39 below). In the case of 4.23-24, Barrett is right to point out that the subject is worship, but the teaching is concerned with the inspiration of worship, not its forms.

The next reference to the Spirit occurs after the discourse on the

Bread of Life, in 6.63. The discourse refers to the story of God's giving manna in the wilderness, in Exodus 16 and Numbers 11, where God is understood to test the people: 'that I may prove them, whether they will walk by my law or not' (Exod. 16.4). The people's murmurings against Moses and Aaron are interpreted as murmurings against God (Exod. 16.6-8). The people are therefore to see the glory of the Lord, and to eat flesh at twilight and bread in the morning (Exod. 16.9-12). Similarly, in John 6, the people's murmurings against Jesus are in effect murmurings against the Father who sent him (e.g. 6.29). He is the Bread of Life (6.48), whose flesh is to be eaten (6.52-56). On hearing the discourse, however, most of Jesus' followers withdraw, so that, at the end of his Galilaean ministry, he is left with only the twelve disciples (6.60-71). In other words, most of the people fail God's test, as they did in the wilderness. What is it in Jesus' discourse that followers find so difficult to accept? It teaches that people should eat true nourishment for eternal life, the bread from heaven, which is Jesus (6.51-59). The food which Jesus makes available, however, is his flesh and blood, and followers are to find nourishment in those. 'Eating' is obviously metaphorical rather than literal, and the teaching seems to mean that followers are to make Jesus' life their own, they are to embody his life. But to do so involves accepting the kind of suffering and death which he accepts. As a turning point in Jesus' ministry in the Fourth Gospel, the section is parallel to that set at Caesaraea-Philippi in the Synoptics, where Jesus first predicts his death and tells his disciples that they too are to lose their lives (Mt. 16.21-26, and parallels).

In this context, what does 6.63 mean by 'spirit'? 'The spirit is that which creates life, the flesh is of no profit; the words which I have spoken to you are spirit and life'. The saying begins by making the same contrast between spirit and flesh which had already been used in Jesus' remarks to Nicodemus (3.6), and suggests that ordinary human existence in the flesh is not what matters most. It is God's Spirit which gives fullness to human life, even when death has to be accepted. Jesus' teaching in the discourse, the words that he had spoken to them, are 'spirit and life' in that they indicate what fulness of life entails for human beings.

Most commentators suggest that 6.51-58 bears some relation to the Christian eucharist, and this is probably so, if we accept that all Christian churches of the first century celebrated the eucharist as a memorial of Jesus' death in the way that Corinthian Christians did (1 Cor. 11). But the Fourth Gospel shows no interest in eucharistic practice as such. Instead, it focuses on Jesus' death and its significance. In other words, it is concerned with the theology which underlies Christian eucharistic practice.

Jesus' next saying about the Spirit, 7.37-39, set at the Feast of Tabernacles, has caused three different difficulties for interpreters. The first arises from the fact that 7.37-38 can be read in two distinct ways: (1) 'If someone thirsts, let him come to me and drink. He who believes in me, as Scripture says, out of his heart shall flow rivers of living water', or (2) 'If someone thirsts, let him come to me and let him who believes in me drink. As Scripture says, out of his heart shall flow rivers of living water.' It has to be remembered that the earliest manuscripts contain no punctuation, and punctuating the verses one way suggests that the rivers flow from the believer (1), while punctuating them in another suggests that the rivers flow from Jesus (2).

A second difficulty comes from trying to identify the particular place in Scripture to which reference is made. There is no exact parallel to Jn 7.37-38 in Scripture, although Isa. 44.3, 55.1, 58.11, Ezek. 47.1, 12, Zech. 14.8, Prov. 18.4, Sir. 24.30-34 and Ps. 78.16 use similar imagery and vocabulary.

The third difficulty, in 7.39, is evidenced by a variety of readings in different manuscripts:

> For as yet the Spirit had not been given (Latin, Syriac).
> For as yet the Holy Spirit had not been given (B and some versions).
> For the Spirit was not yet ($\mathfrak{P}^{66}$ ℵ Q others).
> For the Holy Spirit was not yet (W f^1 f^{13} others).
> For the Holy Spirit was not yet upon them (D and some versions).

The reading 'For the Spirit was not yet' is probably original, and the other versions of the saying are attempts to prevent its contradicting what had been said earlier in the Gospel about Jesus' endowment with the Spirit. The saying makes sense in the context of the whole Gospel only if it refers to the Spirit's bestowal on believers after Jesus has been honoured at the completion of his mission.

The second of the two possible translations of 7.37-38 makes better sense in the context. If Jesus is taken to be the source of the Spirit, a link is made both with his earlier teaching about providing 'living water' (4.10), and with his later teaching about sending the Spirit to his disciples after his departure (see below), a prediction which is fulfilled in 20.22. The alternative, which posits the believer as the source of the Spirit, seems to require a reference to Spirit-baptism which the believer will give after Jesus' mission is complete, something which is not mentioned in the text, even when the future life of the disciples is outlined in the Farewell Discourses. We should have to infer it from Jesus' commission to forgive or retain sins (20.23), but this is more likely to refer to the disciples' responsibility to arouse faith in Jesus than to their responsibility to baptize.

The perspective of 7.37-39, that the Spirit would be given later, explains why most of Jesus' teaching about the Spirit is reserved for his disciples. In the Farewell Discourses (chs. 13–16) he looks beyond his earthly existence in order to prepare disciples to continue his ministry after his death and resurrection. It is at this point in the Gospel that a completely new term is introduced to define the future role of the Spirit in the lives of the disciples: παράκλητος:

> And I will pray the Father, and he will give you another Paraclete [or possibly, another, a Paraclete], to be with you forever, the Spirit of truth whom the world cannot receive because it neither sees him nor knows him (14.16-17).

The suggestion made by Windisch (1968), that the Paraclete passages are interpolated from a pre-Christian source, has been rightly rejected by modern commentators (e.g. Johnston 1970; Barrett 1978; Brown 1971; Schnackenburg 1979, 1982). But what does 'Paraclete' mean? Grayston (1981) has examined relevant Greek sources between the fourth century BCE and the third century CE, and rightly concludes:

> Philo provides the most ample usage of the term and makes it possible to discern two distinguishable meanings. When *Parakletos*. . . is used as a noun it indicates someone called in to help another person, either (a) by giving advice about a difficult decision or (b) by giving support to someone making a claim, or settling a dispute, or rebutting a charge (p. 72).

Although the term is sometimes used in legal contexts, it does not derive its meaning from legal practice, but has a more general sense, like 'supporter' or 'sponsor'. Those commentators and translators who have tried to force a legal interpretation onto the Fourth Gospel, translating παράκλητος by 'advocate', are therefore doubly wrong, because they distort the meaning of the Gospel on the basis of a false definition.

That the disciples should be promised the gift of God's Spirit by Jesus, and that this Spirit is connected with 'truth', in 14.16-17, simply focuses and develops hints given earlier in the Gospel. But why is the new term, Paraclete, introduced? If the translation 'another Paraclete' (rather than 'another, a Paraclete') is accepted, it implies that during Jesus' ministry, Jesus himself is the disciples' Paraclete or supporter, but that, at his departure, they receive support from 'another Paraclete'. The parallel roles of Jesus and the Spirit Paraclete, listed by Brown (1971: Appendix V) give substance to this reading. For example, both the Paraclete and Jesus come into the world from the Father (15.26; 5.43), whose gift they are (14.16; 3.16), since both are sent by the Father (14.26; 3.17). Jesus is the Truth, the Paraclete is the Spirit of Truth (14.6, 17). Jesus is the Holy One of God, the Paraclete is the Holy Spirit (6.69; 14.26). The disciples recognize Jesus and will recognize the Paraclete (14.7, 9; 17). Both Jesus and the Paraclete will remain in and with the disciples (14.17, 20, 23; 15.4, 5; 17.23, 26). Both are teachers (6.59; 7.14, 18; 8.20; 14.26) who bear witness (8.14; 15.26), although Jesus bears witness to and honours the Father (12.28), whereas the Paraclete bears witness to and honours Jesus (16.14). The world rejects both Jesus and the Paraclete (5.43; 12.48; 14.17) because it does not know them (16.3; cf. 7.28; 8.19; 14.7, 17).

The Gospel portrays Jesus as a man permanently inspired by God's Spirit. The Farewell Discourses look beyond the time of Jesus' departure to that in which the disciples will receive the Spirit too, so that their lives can become exemplary like Jesus' (15.12-27). In 14.17 it is the Spirit of Truth that will inspire and help the disciples to keep Jesus' commandments. In other words, the Spirit will enable the disciples to remain faithful, as Jesus remained faithful (6.32-33).

Similar teaching is found in 14.26: 'But the Helper, the Holy Spirit, whom the Father will send in my name, he will teach you all things, and bring to your remembrance all that I have said to you'. With the aid of the Holy Spirit, the disciples will be taught to remember and understand Jesus' teaching. Once again, the Spirit enables them to be faithful disciples. The Spirit is sent from the Father, as Jesus was, and is sent in Jesus' name, as Jesus was sent in the Father's name (e.g. 5.43; 10.25). The Spirit, then, is Jesus' agent as Jesus is the Father's agent.

It is possible that chs. 15–17 were added to the Farewell Discourses at a second stage, and that originally ch. 18 followed immediately after ch. 14. At the end of ch. 14 Jesus instructs his disciples to leave the supper table, 'Rise, let us go hence' (14.31), and 18.1 describes this happening, 'when Jesus had spoken these words, he went out with his disciples across the Kidron Valley'. Moreover, chs. 15–17 seem to explore teaching already given in chs. 13–14, and may represent an alternative, expanded presentation of the same themes. A similar expansion happened when ch. 21 was added to ch. 20. Indeed, ch. 14 and chs. 15–16 can be understood as alternative developments of 13.31-35 (e.g. Brown 1966: II, 589-91; Johnston 1970).

In ch. 14 the promise of another Paraclete is made in response to the disciples' sorrow and fear at the prospect of Jesus' departure. In 15.26 it is made in the context of remarks about the world's hatred and persecution of both Jesus and the disciples (15.18-25),

> But when the Helper comes, whom I shall send to you from the Father, even the Spirit of Truth, who proceeds from the Father, he will bear witness to me; and you are my witnesses because you have been with me from the beginning.

In spite of Jesus' suffering and death, and a similar fate which awaits the disciples, the Spirit of Truth will bear witness to Jesus. As in 14.26, the Spirit's role is to help disciples understand Jesus' life. Moreover, the juxtaposition of 'he will bear witness to me' and 'you are my witnesses' may imply that the Spirit bears witness through the disciples, enabling them to remain faithful to Jesus (cf. 14.17). Loving one another as Jesus loved is essential to their witness (15.12-14 cf. 13.14-15, 34-35). Fidelity to Jesus is a dominant motif of the discourses (e.g. 14.11, 18, 29; 16.1). But we should notice that, in distinction from 14.16 and 26 according to which the Father sends the Paraclete, in 15.26 Jesus sends him, although he is said to proceed from the Father. The Father who sends the Paraclete in Jesus' name (14.26) and Jesus who sends him from the Father (15.26) are therefore treated as alternative expressions of the same mission. This is the case because Jesus always acts as the Father's agent.

The final statements about the Paraclete are set in the context both of Jesus' departure, as in 14.16-17, 26, and of persecution, as in 15.26. Jesus reassures his disciples,

> It is to your advantage that I go away, for if I do not go away, the Helper will not come to you; but if I go, I will send him to you. And when he comes, he will expose [or convict] the world concerning sin and justice and judgment: concerning sin, because they do not believe in me;

> concerning justice, because I go to the Father, and you will see me no more; concerning judgment, because the ruler of this world is judged (16.7-11).

Since the Spirit can arrive only after Jesus' mission is accomplished (cf. 7.37-39), it is appropriate that the departed Jesus is pictured sending him to the disciples (cf. 15.26). In this saying the Paraclete's role is defined in relation to the world. He will expose the world for what it is. The verb ἐλέγχει means either to 'convince/expose' or to 'convict'. In 8.46 it means 'to convict' and in 3.20 it means 'to be exposed'. The RSV, in an attempt to use one word in conjunction with sin, justice and judgment, translates the verb 'convince', but this is inappropriate, because the world is not to be convinced, but exposed and convicted. The world will be convicted of sin because it does not believe in Jesus. According to the Fourth Gospel, it is sin which prevents belief in Jesus (e.g. 3.17-21; 9.35-41). Justice will be exposed because Jesus' departure, after a trial which is a travesty of justice (the betrayal of an innocent man) establishes justice. And this will involve the condemnation of the 'ruler of this world', the deceiver and father of lies (8.44) who fosters the world's rejection of the Father and the Son (12.31-32; 13.27).

The most obvious way in which to interpret the narrative's account of Jesus' trial and crucifixion is to see them as the triumph of injustice, the victory of 'the ruler of this world' who destroys Jesus. The role of the Paraclete is to reverse this common-sense understanding, to expose its limitation and misperception. The Gospel interprets Jesus' death not as a tragic defeat, although it happens as a result of worldly sin and unbelief, but as his free self-surrender to God, his final act of service to his disciples and the revelation of God's love for the world (3.16). And it is the disciples who need assurance of this if they are to follow Jesus' example. Hence the Spirit of Truth will lead them into all truth, that is, into complete understanding of and fidelity to Jesus. So the passage continues:

> I have many things to say to you, but you cannot bear them now. When the Spirit of Truth comes, he will lead you into all truth; for he will not speak on his own authority, but whatever he hears, he will speak, and he will declare to you the things that are to come. He will honour me, for he will take what is mine and declare it to you. All that the Father has is mine; therefore I said that he will take what is mine and declare it to you (16.12-15).

The saying does not imply that 'new', in the sense of 'different', teaching will be given by the Spirit. 'The things that are to come' are the passion events which will soon be related. The Spirit will take 'what is Jesus'', his passion, and clarify its meaning for the disciples, according Jesus the honour he deserves. The final statement corrects any possible misconception by insisting that what is Jesus' is also the Father's, and has been given by the Father to Jesus. The Paraclete, then, will preserve the disciples' fidelity in providing insight into Jesus' significance. The Spirit, like Jesus, does nothing on his own authority. He reminds disciples of Jesus' teaching (14.26), speaks what he hears (16.13), and honours Jesus by declaring what his life signifies (16.15).

Within the Farewell Discourses, however, there are other passages which describe Jesus' future presence with the disciples, rather than the Spirit's. For example, immediately after the first promise of the Spirit's advent (14.16-17) Jesus says, 'I will not leave you desolate; *I* will come to you' (14.18). The saying cannot be interpreted as a reference to Jesus' return at the end of the world, because Jesus goes on to say, 'the world will see me no more, but you will see me' (14.19). Moreover, Jesus promises to dwell in disciples as the Father dwells in Jesus (14.20), a mutual indwelling which is characterized by love (14.21-23). Since the world loves neither Jesus nor the Father, it cannot 'see' Jesus (14.24) just as it cannot receive the Spirit (14.17). This teaching then leads into the second promise of the Spirit's future mission 'in Jesus' name' (14.26). We would probably be right, therefore, to understand the statements about the Spirit's future advent and Jesus' as synonymous. Jesus, upon whom God's Spirit remains, so that his life shows what living from God means, passes on his/God's Spirit to his disciples, whose lives are to conform to his.

Finally, Jesus' promises are fulfilled in the resurrection narrative: 'He breathed (ἐνεφύσησεν) on them and said to them, "Receive the Holy Spirit. If you forgive the sins of any, they are forgiven; if you retain the sins of any, they are retained"' (20.22-23). Jesus' action recalls the account of the creation of Adam in Gen. 2.7, 'God breathed (ἐνεφύσησεν) into his nostrils the breath of life; and man became a living being'. The Fourth Gospel replaces the Septuagint πνοή (breath) with 'the Holy Spirit' because it depicts not creation, but re-creation. Jesus' departure has brought about the possibility of the disciples' re-creation or rebirth, and they receive the Spirit for their mission of forgiving and retaining sins, that is, their mission of persuading others to believe in Jesus and to live lives characterized by a love like his. Their responsibility is nothing less than continuing Jesus' work.

Scholars have often noted a slight difference in emphasis between the teaching about the Spirit in chs. 1–12 and 20.22-23 on the one hand, and, on the other hand, the teaching about the Paraclete in the Farewell Discourses. The teaching about the Spirit outside the Farewell Discourses focuses on its role in regeneration, whereas the teaching about the Paraclete focuses on its role in ensuring the disciples' fidelity. The difference is explained, however, by the change in perspective. The Farewell Discourses look forward to the time in the future, after the death and resurrection of Jesus, when the disciples will already have been regenerated by God's Spirit, but will need spiritual support to remain faithful to the mission entrusted to them.

Barrett's suggestion, mentioned earlier, that teaching about the Spirit in the Fourth Gospel is presented in the context of worship, cannot be sustained. The Gospel's teaching about the Spirit is theological and christological, and since such teaching affects worship, it is as relevant to worship as everything else in the Gospel is. But, apart from 4.23, the subject is not worship, but Jesus' relationship to the Father and to the disciples. The Gospel uses Spirit language to make comprehensible its claim that Jesus' life is a manifestation of God's love for the world (3.16), and that the disciples, by following him, also make God known. God's Spirit overwhelms people to bring about a transformation of life, orientating them away from the world of common sense that dictates self-preservation and towards God who gives eternal life.

It may seem appropriate, therefore, to accept the definition of the Spirit as divine *power*, offered by Johnston (1970) and Isaacs (1976). It is true that the Spirit is sometimes connected with power in Scripture and in Philo's writings, as they show, but 'power' hardly captures the nature of divine inspiration in the Fourth Gospel. The powerful are not tried unjustly and executed. Perhaps, if the miracles of Jesus were to be viewed in isolation, apart from their context in the Gospel, they could be seen as acts of 'divine power', but the Fourth Gospel does not isolate them. On the contrary, from the first, hints about Jesus' crucifixion play their part in the elucidation of the signs' significance (e.g. 2.4, 11; 6.1-59). The miracles do not force belief in

Jesus' power. They are better understood as paradigms of God's love for humanity, just as Jesus' death is. They make known the honour due to Jesus, not to any by-stander who happens to see them, and who would certainly be impressed by powerful acts, but to believers who recognize Jesus as God's Son, sent to save the world.

What prompted this particular Johannine development of teaching about the Spirit? Most commentators agree with Brown in supposing that two matters determined the Fourth Gospel's emphases. The first is the 'delay' in the Parousia. Since Jesus' imminent return had not happened as quickly as Christians like Paul seem to have expected it, teaching about 'another Paraclete' is thought to fill the 'gap'. It is true that the Paraclete Spirit is to help disciples in their day to day life in the continuing world. 'Delay' is no longer felt to be a problem, as it is in the Pauline epistles. Rather, the focus is on how to continue to live in a hostile world for the indefinite future. In Jesus' absence, 'another Paraclete' supports disciples in their opposition to the world. This is a possible explanation of the Johannine perspective.

Brown's second suggestion is that the Paraclete should be understood to take over the role of eyewitnesses. It is assumed that, by the time the Fourth Gospel was written, eyewitnesses of Jesus' ministry had died. The fact that we are dealing with a Gospel about Jesus' historical life, and not just with a sermon, suggests a concern with history. But we should notice that it is those who followed Jesus from the beginning to the end of his ministry, that is the twelve (except Judas who betrayed him) who are to be inspired by the Paraclete. At the end of the Gospel the success of Jesus' mission depends on these disciples making him known to others. Implicitly, then, the Gospel assumes dependence on their witness.

Nevertheless, the twelve are not named at the end of ch. 6 (contrast the lists of twelve disciples in the Synoptics, Mt. 10.2-4 and parallels). It is left unclear whether all those mentioned in ch. 1 are to be counted among the twelve. Only three of the four, Peter, Andrew and Philip (not Nathanael), are mentioned by name in chs. 6–20, together with Judas Iscariot, Thomas and another Judas. Moreover, the 'beloved disciple' to some extent overshadows even Peter from ch. 13 onwards, although he is not named. Brown assumes that he is a historical disciple, one of the twelve, and that the Johannine text looks back to him as an authority. But Bultmann's suggestion (1971), that he is not a historical character but rather a portrait of an 'ideal disciple', makes better sense (see ch. 14). The fact that the Gospel fails both to provide a full list of the twelve disciples, and that it does not trace the handing down of the tradition through their successors to the author of the Gospel, suggests that the later church's concern to justify its fidelity to the tradition by providing lists of apostolic succession is alien to the Fourth Gospel.

Moreover, in the Fourth Gospel the form in which people are depicted bearing witness to Jesus is far removed from modern recitals of eye-witness accounts. We are not provided with the kind of details about time and place, nor about the people who bore witness, which would be required, for example, in courts of law today. Most of the witnesses, whether for or against Jesus, are merely described, not named: the twelve, the Samaritan woman, the Samaritans, the man born blind, the Pharisees, the chief priests. And the witness they bear is couched in the language of the narrator, not in the verbatim, idiosyncratic language of individuals, even when they are named. In other words, the Gospel does not provide the kind of testimony which would convince outsiders looking for historical veracity. Rather, the Gospel allures readers into accepting its witnesses on its own terms. The witness which is supposed to impress outsiders is that of the community united in love (e.g. 13.34-35; 14.18-24; 15.12-13; 17.20-21). The role of the Paraclete is to help disciples understand Jesus' significance and remain faithful to him through all vicissitudes. Hence, the Paraclete enables them to live a united, loving existence.

Rather than replacing eyewitnesses, then, as Brown suggests, the Paraclete ensures that some of the eyewitnesses of Jesus' ministry, the original disciples, remain faithful, so that they can continue his mission of making God known. But the Gospel itself seeks to perform the task of making God known too. This implies that the author is also inspired by the Paraclete, in spite of the fact that the Gospel includes no claim that the author was an eyewitness of Jesus' historical ministry, only that he, with others, came to believe in Jesus as the messiah, the Son of God. Perhaps Brown's suggestion, then, can be accepted in this modified sense: the Paraclete ensures the fidelity of believers to Jesus, whether they were eyewitnesses of his historical ministry or not. Those who were not eyewitnesses, however, depend on the testimony of those who were, for fundamental knowledge of Jesus' teaching and healing, of his crucifixion and resurrection. The Paraclete inspires believers to recognize the significance of these events and to live in conformity with Jesus' example. The death of eyewitnesses, therefore, may have prompted the Johannine emphasis on and definition of the Spirit-Paraclete's role as a way of explaining and safeguarding the conformity of belief and life through generations of Christians.

Chapter 6

Opposition to God: The World, the Ruler of this World, the 'Jews' and Eschatology

Although the Fourth Gospel asserts that God, through the λόγος, creates all things (1.3), it recognizes that opposition to God exists in his creation.

1. *The World*

The world as κόσμος refers not only to all that exists, but to everything in an ordered system. In Stoicism there is no contrast between κόσμος and God, but κόσμος is ordered in a rational way by its immanent God, λόγος, or by God as craftsman. The only contrast in Stoicism is between this ordered interaction of cosmic sympathy, by which all parts of existence hold together, and fire, the cyclical conflagration which brings κόσμος to an end, only to begin all over again. Ordering and conflagration go on forever. Human choice is a decision to recognize, or not to recognize, the necessity which orders cosmic existence. In Stoic terms, then, κόσμος is self-sufficient.

The Hebrew Scriptures, and their Greek translation, do not refer to the world as κόσμος but as the heavens (above) and the earth (beneath) (e.g. Gen. 1.1; Exod. 20.4). The Fourth Gospel does not use this Hebrew idiom for creation because, as we shall see later, it treats heavenly and earthly, above and below, metaphorically. It asserts, however, that God made everything that exists through the λόγος: 'All things were made through him and without him was not anything made' (1.3), but it takes from the Greek works of its Scripture the word κόσμος to refer to the world as God's creation (see Cassem 1973). In the Wisdom of Solomon κόσμος means 'creation' (1.14; 2.24; 5.20; 7.17; 9.3, 9; 11.17, 22; 13.2; 14.14; 16.17; 17.20; 18.24), or 'life' (7.6), or 'the human world' (6.24; 10.1;

14.6). When κόσμος is used in a system which posits the transcendent Creator God, the Stoic conception is clearly modified. In particular, the κόσμος is no longer seen as self-sufficient, but as dependent upon the Creator God.

In the Fourth Gospel, as in the Wisdom of Solomon, the world as God's creation encompasses not only human life, but all physical existence (e.g. Jn 1.1-3; 17.5, 24; 21.25), and, because the world is God's creation, nature itself intimates something of God. The nature of the wind (πνεῦμα) intimates the nature of the Spirit (πνεῦμα) (3.8), human dependence on light intimates dependence on God for enlightenment (1.4-5; 11.9), human need of water and bread for life intimates human need of God (4.10; 6.31-34), birth intimates rebirth (3.3, 5), and creation re-creation (20.22). Nevertheless, in the Fourth Gospel it is the human world which is the main focus of attention. κόσμος in John most often refers to the human world, and the word takes on negative connotations because this world sees itself as independent instead of acknowledging its reliance on God. In taking up a Stoic word, then, the Fourth Gospel polemicizes against the Stoic conception by asserting that the world is not to be reckoned in its own terms, but is to be seen in terms of the Creator God who brought it into existence through her λόγος or plan. Jesus, as the λόγος become flesh, demonstrates what the human world should be like, living from God.

Hence, in the Fourth Gospel, 'to be of the world' is contrasted with 'to be of God' (15.18-19), 'to be of the world' is to seek honour from fellow human beings instead of from God (7.18; 12.42-43). The human world which ignores God (1.9; 17.25) cuts itself off from the life God gives and stands in opposition to God. Jesus, therefore, calls disciples 'out of the world' (15.19; 17.6) not in the sense of removing them to an esoteric sphere (13.1; 17.15-16) but in the sense of recalling them to a life which comes from God (3.16-21; 17.2-3). The world, alienated from God, is in a state of sin or unbelief from which it must be saved by God's lamb (1.29), God's Son (3.16), the Saviour of the world (4.42), the bread of life (6.51), the light of the world (8.12; 12.46-47). Jesus' kingdom is 'not of this world' (18.36). The world therefore hates him (7.7; 15.18) and will hate his disciples (15.18-19). The disciple has to hate his life in this world (12.25) and to rejoice because Jesus has overcome the world (16.33).

The Fourth Gospel opposes to this human world, this false sympathetic order, a different community, honoured not by people but by God (12.26), conforming its life to Jesus' (12.24-26; 13.34-35; 15.13), and remaining in Jesus, the true vine (15.1-11).

2. *The Ruler of this World*

The opposition of the human world to God is represented by the ruler of this world (12.31; 14.30; 16.11), Satan (13.27) or the devil (6.70; 8.44; 13.2).

> He was a murderer from the beginning, and has nothing to do with the truth, because there is no truth in him. When he lies, he speaks according to his own nature, for he is a liar and the father of lies (8.44, cf. Wis. 2.24).

The Gospel depicts Jesus as the truth, that is, as the true way to live (14.6) in fidelity to God, and the devil as the father of lies, that is, as the originator of infidelity and falsehood. He is a murderer because he is held responsible for unbelief which leads both to Jesus' death and to the death of unbelievers (cf. Gen. 3). Looking to his imminent death, therefore, Jesus remarks, 'The ruler of this world is coming' (14.30). Nevertheless, he goes on to explain that 'he has no power over me; but I do as the Father has commanded me, so that the world may know that I love the Father' (14.30-31). Jesus' death is therefore 'the judgment of this world' (12.31; 16.8-11), the means by which the ruler of this world is judged (16.11) and cast out (12.31).

As the father of lies, the devil has many children, all those who do not believe in Jesus (8.45) and who do evil deeds (3.19; 8.40; 10.31, 39). In particular, the devil is responsible for taking possession of one of Jesus' disciples, Judas Iscariot, so that he betrays Jesus. At the supper 'the devil had already put it into the heart that Judas Iscariot, Simon's son, would betray him' (13.2). Later, 'after the morsel, Satan entered into him [Judas]. . . So, after receiving the morsel, he immediately went out; and it was night' (13.27-30). Judas, inspired and possessed by Satan, is a child of darkness who betrays Jesus, the light of the world (see Chapter 2, §2.7).

These are the only references in the Fourth Gospel to a person possessed by the devil. In contrast to the Synoptics, the Fourth Gospel never attributes illness to demon possession and never represents

Jesus' healings as exorcisms. Rather, unbelief and betrayal are the work of the devil. Perhaps the difference is to be accounted for by the fact that the Johannine perspective on the world is so narrowly focused on the human world. As the ruler of this world, Satan rules the human world rather than material existence. So illness is related to sin or unbelief (5.14; 9.2-5) but not to demon possession.

3. *The 'Jews'*

Those who do not believe in Jesus are 'of the world', like Jesus' brothers (7.3-7), or, more often, in the Fourth Gospel, the 'Jews' and their leaders, the Pharisees and the chief priests. Like their representative, the devil, whose children they are, they do not believe Jesus when he tells the truth (8.46). They are 'of the world' because they depend on the worldly honour they receive from fellow human beings, instead of seeking honour from God (12.43), or they rely on their privileged position as children of Abraham (8.39) and ignore the witness he and Moses give to Jesus (8.56; 5.45-46). They will therefore die in their sins (8.24), blind in their rejection of the light Jesus brings (9.41). Their leaders are more interested in safeguarding the continuing worldly existence of the nation than in justice, although, ironically, in advising that 'it is expedient for you that one man should die for the people' (11.50), Caiaphas, the high priest, prophesies the efficacy of Jesus' death. They do the devil's work in helping to arrest Jesus (7.32, 45-52; 10.39; 18.3) so that he can be questioned and then handed over to Pilate for execution (18.19-24, 28). They persuade Pilate to have him crucified (18.28–19.16). They are murderers like their father, the devil.

The ignorance and self-sufficiency of the human world, alienated from God, is, in this way, captured in the portrait of the 'Jews' and their leaders. These 'Jews' are one-dimensional characters, with a single trait, unbelief in Jesus because of their immorality. Other 'Jews' are slightly more rounded characters. Nicodemus, who goes to Jesus at night (3.1-2) but who hesitates to commit himself, nevertheless ineffectually defends him (7.50-52) and pays him homage when he is dead, together with Joseph of Arimathea, who is a disciple (19.38-40). Moreover, occasionally the Gospel notes that some 'Jews' (8.31) and even some of the authorities (12.42) believe in him. Often, too, the crowds are impressed by Jesus, without coming to the full belief the

Gospel expects (e.g. 2.23; 6.15; 12.12-15). Mary and Martha, on the other hand, become believers (11.5-44), and Lazarus puts at risk his own life, given back to him by Jesus' miracle, by his association with Jesus (12.10-11). Eleven of his twelve disciples, through the vicissitudes of misunderstanding and cowardice, finally receive their commission to become his emissaries (17.18; 20.22-23). In doing so, they show themselves to be no longer 'of the world' (17.16).

Why the 'Jews' are singled out and caricatured as unbelievers who embody the world's opposition to God I shall have to consider later, when I examine questions of reference in the final section of the book. For the moment, we should notice that the Gospel presents Jesus' appeal as universal, directed to the whole of humanity, although the ministry of the historical Jesus is confined to Jews. Only after his death will the mission encompass non-Jews (10.16; 12.20-26).

4. *Eschatology**

Since Rudolf Bultmann published his commentary on the Fourth Gospel, attributing the passages about future eschatology to the work of an ecclesiastical redactor, scholars have been forced to examine closely the logic of Johannine eschatology: does the teaching about the present experience of eternal life force us to see the teaching about future eschatology as a secondary intrusion? Perhaps the most searching of recent expositions is provided by R. Schnackenburg (1979, EXCURSUS 14, pp. 426-437). He sees the passages about future eschatology (5.28-29; 6.39, 40, 44, 54, 57; 12.48) as 'clearly suspect' and thinks they come from the Johannine circle (cf. 21.22; 1 Jn 2.28; 3.2; 4.17). The Evangelist, he claims, had no interest either in the future of the world or in the earthly journey of the church, since the things of the future were unimportant to him. Although Schnackenburg finds no evidence of Johannine polemic against the kind of traditional future eschatology represented in the Synoptics, he does find evidence of a radical reorientation which uses different intellectual categories: the vertical perspective replaces the horizontal–temporal perspective. And this reorientation expresses a concern with 'the existential situation and ultimate fate of the individual' (p. 435). Johannine eschatology is dominated by Christology: the present union

* An earlier version of this section appeared in *JSNT* 15 (1982): 81-85.

of believers with their Lord is the primary and controlling idea.

Schnackenburg mentions arguments that have been cited to show that Johannine theology is open to a future eschatology: (1) an anthropology which believes in the resurrection of the body rather than the immortality of the soul; (2) a vision of future glory for the disciples (12.26; 13.36; 14.2-3; 17.24); (3) the horizontal, historical perspective from creation (1.3; 17.5 and 24) through the history of Israel (Abraham, Moses, the prophets and John the Baptist), which cannot be dissolved into an endless continuum at Jesus' return to the Father. But he dismisses these arguments by pointing to (1) the presence of resurrection now (11.23-25) in the enduring fellowship of disciples with Jesus (16.22); (2) the view that 12.26, 13.36, 14.2-3 and 17.24 represent not so much future eschatology as the vertical perspective of the heavenly world; (3) the contention that John does not distinguish periods of time, but concentrates all salvation in the person of Jesus. I characterize Schnackenburg's replies as a dismissal because they do not seem to amount to a refutation.

Schnackenburg is clearly correct in stressing that Christology is central for John and in pointing to the dominating influence of the vertical perspective over the horizontal, although he admits that these two perspectives are not irreconcilable. But, because a central contention of Johannine Christology, that the Father sent the Son to save the *world* (1.29; 3.16-17; 6.33, 51; 8.12; 9.5; 12.19), is not dealt with at this point, justice is not done to the Johannine picture as a whole.

Moreover, in the Fourth Gospel the absence of an apocalyptic discourse which foresees the transformation of the whole physical creation (contrast the Synoptics, Mt. 24–25 and parallels, and Paul, e.g. Rom. 8.19-25) may be explained because the Fourth Gospel conceives the world essentially in human terms. It is interested in the fate of this human world, which is why the vertical perspective dominates the horizontal, but without excluding it. Since God is always and forever the source of people's life, the Gospel depicts humanity as open or closed to the life God gives now and always. Since Jesus performs signs which demonstrate God's gift of life, people are forced to decide between belief and unbelief. Belief in Jesus opens the way to God's gift, unbelief cuts people off and brings judgment upon themselves (3.16-21).

The gnomic statement: 'He who believes in the Son has eternal life' (3.36) indicates the relationship between belief in Jesus and eternal life, but does it imply that eternal life is somehow a present possession? One may reason that since belief in Jesus is possible now, eternal life can be a present possession. But what does 'eternal' mean? Jn 5.24 interprets: 'He does not come into judgment but has passed from death to life'. Jn 6.51 interprets: 'If anyone eats of this bread, he will live for ever'. The most important reference is 11.23-27. I am unhappy about Schnackenburg's interpretation of this passage. He claims that John is polemicizing against the Jewish expectation placed on Martha's lips (11.24) and that it replaces it with belief in resurrection now. If this is the case, it is difficult to see why John uses two words, life and resurrection, and what meaning is attached to the word 'resurrection'. Rather, Jesus' claim, 'I am the resurrection and the life' (11.25) is interpreted through two gnomic statements: 'He who believes in me, though he die yet shall he live', and 'whoever lives and believes in me shall never die' (11.25-26). The first statement interprets the word 'resurrection' and means that whoever believes in Jesus and dies a normal physical death will be resurrected. The second statement interprets 'life' and explains that the life which comes from God and enlivens people's present existence makes physical death irrelevant. Here we have a double perspective. The life which God gives enlivens believers now, determining their relationship to God and the human world, and it will effect their post-mortem resurrection. By 'resurrection' it means post-mortem bodily life, the personal survival of the individual as is clear from ch. 20. This is the kind of teaching we would expect from a Gospel which begins with creation: resurrection is not a rejection of the world but a transformation of the world. Since belief in Jesus is crucial, the Gospel encourages people to believe in Jesus now and to continue believing in him.

What difference does it make to the Johannine perspective that the resurrection of Jesus is not an event awaited at the end of time, but is a reality now? Thc disappearance of Jesus' body is a past event (20.1-10). Paul, Mark and Matthew integrated belief in Jesus' resurrection into their horizontal, temporal scheme by making it the first of the eschatological events (1 Cor. 15; Mk 13; Mt. 24). John's vertical scheme offers an alternative account: Jesus has ascended to the Father (chs. 14–17; 20.17-18). The disciples' post-mortem future is to be with Jesus (13.36; 14.2-3; 21.22; see Lk. 23.43; 24.51) or to behold and share his honour (17.24; 12.26). Jesus ascends to the Father and the disciples are to follow and to be with him.

Nevertheless, this vertical perspective is not irreconcilable with a horizontal perspective. Indeed, the horizontal perspective is necessary to make sense of resurrection language. Johannine emphasis on the eternal creative activity of God is illustrated by reference to Abraham, Moses, the prophets and John the Baptist in the past. Similarly, the references to the disciples' beholding Jesus' honour in the future are set alongside passages about future resurrection and judgment (5.28-29; 6.39, 40, 44, 54, 57; 12.48) which complete this horizontal schema. Moreover, twice in the Gospel Jesus speaks of coming again to take his followers to be where he is (14.3; 21.22).

Bultmann and Schnackenburg are correct, however, in drawing attention to the incidental nature of references to the kingdom of God (3.3, 5), the future resurrection of believers (5.28-29; 6.39, 40, 44, 54) and the parousia of Jesus (14.3; 21.22). These eschatological beliefs are simply mentioned, without illustration in the parables found in the Synoptic Gospels. I have already noted in Chapter 1, however, that the Fourth Gospel seems to assume prior knowledge of the story it tells, and it will be argued in Chapter 11 that it probably assumes knowledge of the Synoptic Gospels, or, at least, of a story very much like that told in the Synoptics. Since the Synoptics focus attention on God's imminent kingdom, illustrating the teaching in similes and parables, the Fourth Gospel is free to take such illustration for granted. This then leaves room for an expansion of the Synoptics' teaching about Christology and about the need for belief in Jesus at the present time, in a world alienated from God.

Chapter 7

METAPHORS OF ASSOCIATION

> Scripture may offer glimpses of the nature of God and his plans for the universe, but the reality of God's existence, the explanation of life's perplexities and the precise delineation of the future hope were not easily resolved on the basis of Scripture alone... Indirect means could not provide the assurance and conviction which were necessary for those who were particularly perplexed by the circumstances which confronted them. What was required was a direct and authoritative answer to man's most pressing questions, not a variety of conflicting human opinions about the meaning of a particular passage in Scripture... The unveiling of the counsels of God directly to the apocalyptic seer and thence to his readers meant that the latter were being offered an answer directly from the mouth of God himself... God reveals his mysteries directly to man and thereby gives them knowledge of the true nature of reality so that they may organize their lives accordingly (Rowland 1982: 10-11).

In these words, Christopher Rowland introduces his study of apocalyptic literature, produced in the centuries before and after the Fourth Gospel. Apocalyptic presented its unveilings of reality mainly through visions of or journeys to a heavenly world. The revelations placed present earthly experience in perspective and looked forward to God establishing justice in the future.

The Fourth Gospel contains no accounts of apocalyptic visions or journeys. It does not even contain extended predictions about Jesus' future return to earth, in contrast to the so-called apocalyptic discourses of the Synoptic Gospels (Mt. 24–25, parallels). Yet it shares with apocalyptic the belief that 'God reveals his mysteries directly', giving people 'knowledge of the true nature of reality so that they may organize their lives accordingly'. In a sense, the Fourth Gospel turns the language and imagery of apocalyptic on its head, in order to achieve the same ends. God's nature and his plan are to be perceived not through a heavenly journey but in Jesus' earthly journey. The language is not that of ascent and descent, but of descent and ascent. The narrator does not relate fantastic dreams but the life and death of a human being. According to the Fourth Gospel people need not journey to heaven to see God, but should perceive God's purpose in the man whose story shows them the true nature of reality—God's love for the world (3.16)—and exemplifies the way to live, not only in the difficult circumstances of first-century Palestine, but whenever or wherever people find themselves.

1. *Sending* (ἀποστέλλω, πέμπω)

The crucial significance of characters' lives, recounted in the Fourth Gospel, is often indicated by the language of God's commissioning. The expression 'God sent' stresses God's initiative, and suggests that the activity of the person sent can be understood only in terms of God's purpose (see Miranda).

The Fourth Gospel uses two Greek verbs for sending, ἀποστέλλω and πέμπω. ἀποστέλλω is used in the ordinary literal sense of one person sending others to perform particular tasks (1.19, 24; 5.33; 7.32; 11.3; 18.24; cf. 9.7) but most occurrences posit God or the Father as the subject and are metaphorical. πέμπω functions literally on only one occasion (1.22) and is found most frequently in a formula referring to God as Jesus' 'Father who sent me' (4.34; 5.23, 24, 30, 37 and many others). John the Baptist also refers to God as 'He who sent (πέμπω) me to baptize in water' (1.33). Also, like Jesus, John is 'a man sent (ἀποστέλλω) from God' (1.6). The parallel between John and Jesus is limited, however, in that John is sent solely to bear witness to Jesus. His ability to do so comes from God's revelation to him about the one who would come after him (1.33).

The formula, 'the Father who *sent* (πέμπω) me' is often found in contexts in which Jesus is disclaiming any authority of his own. He tells his disciples: 'My bread is to do the will of him who *sent* me and to accomplish his work' (4.34). When professing that he imitates the Father in working on the Sabbath, he tells the 'Jews': 'I can do nothing on my own authority; as I hear I judge; and my judgment is just because I seek not my own will but the will of him who *sent* me' (5.30). The people impressed by the miraculous feeding are told:

> I have come down from heaven not to do my own will, but the will of him who *sent* me; and this is the will of him who *sent* me, that I should lose nothing of all that he has given me, but raise it up at the last day (6.38-39).

Jesus' work is not his own, and it has to be accomplished in a limited time: 'It is necessary for us to work the works of him who *sent* me while it is day' (9.4). Neither are Jesus' words his own: 'My teaching is not mine but that of him who *sent* me' (7.16) or 'The Father who *sent* me himself has given as a commandment what I say and speak' (12.49) or 'The λόγος which you hear is not mine but the Father's who *sent* me' (14.24).

Many of these references are found in the context of Jesus' disputes with 'Jewish' groups in chs. 5–12. There Jesus demonstrates the reality of his commission by restoring the feeble (5.1-9), giving sight to the blind (9.1-7) and life to the dead (11.1-44). Those who know the Father who sent Jesus are attracted to him: 'No one is able to come to me unless the Father who *sent* me draws him' (6.44) because 'He who believes in me does not believe in me but in him who *sent* me' (12.44) or 'He who receives me receives him who *sent* me' (13.20). Conversely, those who reject Jesus 'do not know him who *sent* me' (15.21). Similarly, 'He who does not honour the Son does not honour the Father who *sent* him' (5.23 cf. 17.18).

The Father who sent Jesus is seen not only to determine what he says and does, but also to enable him to carry out his mission. The refrain 'He who *sent* me is true' (7.28 ἀληθινός, 8.26 αληθής) expresses God's fidelity and is parallel to 'He who *sent* me is with me' (8.29) or 'I am not alone, but I and he who *sent* me' (8.16). In these disputes with 'Jewish' groups in chs. 5–12, then, the Father is Jesus' chief witness, through human spokesmen or Scripture or Jesus' works (5.30-47, especially v. 37): 'The Father who *sent* me bears witness to me' (8.18). So close is the association between the sender and the one sent that it can be asserted: 'He who sees me sees him who *sent* me' (12.45 cf. 13.16). Hence, 'He who hears my λόγος and believes him who *sent* me has eternal life' (5.24) because God's purpose in sending the Son is to give life (3.16-21).

The same vocabulary describes the advent of the Paraclete, except that the tense is future: 'The Paraclete, the Holy Spirit, whom the Father *will send* in my name, he will teach you all things, and bring to your remembrance all that I have said to you' (14.26). Since Jesus was sent from the Father, the relationship between Jesus and the Paraclete has to be clarified with the idiom 'in my name', and the Paraclete's role defined as bringing to rememberance Jesus' teachings (cf. 14.24). In 15.26 it is Jesus who does the sending: 'When the Paraclete, whom I *shall send* to you from the Father, comes', but he sends the Paraclete 'from the Father' (cf. 16.7).

Since the Paraclete effects his witness through the disciples (14.26; 15.26; 16.7-15), the commissioning of the disciples fulfils these promises: 'As the Father *sent* (ἀποστέλλω) me, so I *send* (πέμπω) you. And when he said this, he breathed on them and said to them, Receive the Holy Spirit' (20.22). Therefore, the disciple is conceived as representing Jesus in his own person: 'He who receives anyone whom I *send* receives me' (13.20).

Many of the occurrences of ἀποστέλλω in the Fourth Gospel also refer to Jesus as the one sent by the Father (3.34; 5.36, 38; 6.29, 57; 10.36), but πέμπω stresses God's activity, ἀποστέλλω Jesus' status. Jesus' claims to knowledge are buttressed, and accusations of presumption are countered, with the assertion 'He *sent* me' (7.29; 8.42). Belief in Jesus is belief in him whom the Father sent (11.42; 17.8, 21, 23), knowledge of Jesus is knowledge that God sent him (17.3, 25). Again, the context of most of these sayings is polemical. What opponents fail to recognize is that Jesus is the one sent by the Father for a particular purpose: 'For God *sent* the Son into the world, not to condemn the world, but that the world might be saved through him' (3.17).

Similarly, the disciples are those sent by Jesus to represent all that he represents. Hence the warning: 'A servant is not greater than his master nor *he who is sent* [ἀπόστολος, the only example of this word in the Fourth Gospel] greater than he who *sent* (πέμπω) him' (13.16). This means that their mission, like Jesus', will include suffering. Jesus' prayer to the Father repeats the same idea: 'As you [the Father] *sent* me into the world so I *sent* them [the disciples] into the world' (17.18). Earlier, Jesus had summed up the disciples' mission: 'I *sent* you to reap what you did not sow; others have laboured and you have entered into their labour' (4.30). Clearly, the Fourth Gospel envisages the mission of others besides the disciples, of the Samaritan woman (4.39), of those who were not companions of Jesus (20.29), and of the narrator of the Gospel.

This language about mission, borrowed from the everyday speech of administration, had already been used metaphorically about relations between God and people both in pagan Greek literature and in the Septuagint. Rengstorf (1964) cites Epictetus's reference to Cynics, for example, who were conscious of being commissioned by Zeus (Epictetus, *Dissertations* 3.22, 69). In the Septuagint Johannine language is found in the context of the commissioning of prophets, especially Moses in Exodus 3–4 (ἀποστέλλω is the verb used in all the following references. πέμπω is used infrequently in the Septuagint, but significantly in connexion with God's sending Wisdom and the Holy Spirit from heaven, Wis. 9.10, 17). God commissions Moses with the words: 'Come, I *will send* you to Pharaoh that you may bring forth my people, the sons of Israel, out of Egypt' (Exod. 3.10. See also 3.13, 14, 15; 4.13, 28; 5.22; 7.16). In performing his task, Moses, like Jesus, is not alone: 'God said, But I will be with you' (3.12), and Moses is assured of God's presence in a sign: 'And this shall be the sign for you, that I have *sent* you: when you have brought forth the people out of Egypt, you shall serve God upon this mountain' (3.12). B.S. Childs (1974) has suggested a feasible history of tradition to throw light on the meaning of this statement. He outlines two patterns of sign giving in connexion with prophetic oracles of promise or threat in the early tradition of the Old Testament. According to the first, 'A threat is made by a prophet. The sign is given to confirm the threat. It precedes the fulfilment, but participates already in the reality' (p. 58, e.g. 1 Sam. 2.34; Jer. 44.29). According to the second, 'In the call narrative, the sign follows the appointing to an office. It serves to confirm the appointment by means of an extraordinary event which legitimizes the authority of the one doing the appointing (p. 58, e.g. 1 Sam. 10.1; Judg. 6.14). The narrative in Exodus 3–4 shares features from each of these forms. It conforms to the second pattern, the call narrative, except that the extraordinary event, the bush that burns without being consumed, precedes rather than follows the commissioning. On the other hand, as in the first pattern, Israel's future worship on the same mountain is foreshadowed by Moses' worship, and the burning bush as a symbol of God's presence prefigures that of fire (Exod. 3; 19).

There is, of course, no straightforward call narrative about Jesus in the Fourth Gospel, but the testimony of John about the Spirit descending and remaining on him (1.32) recalls 'The Spirit of the Lord is upon me because the Lord has anointed me to bring good tidings to the afflicted' (Isa. 61.1; if ἐκλεκτός is the original reading of 1.34, this also encourages a connexion with Isa. 42.1). After the Prologue's statement that the λόγος became flesh, a call narrative would seem superfluous, but in contexts of argument or encouragement, references to the Father's sending Jesus, or to Jesus as the one sent by the Father, gives to Jesus' teaching and actions both purpose and authority. As in Exodus, this commissioning is accompanied by signs which both legitimize Jesus' claims (5.19-47) and precede and participate in the reality of salvation Jesus' life affords (see also Brown 1966: I, Appendix III). And as Moses was succeeded by other prophets like himself (Deut. 18.15, 18, e.g. Elijah), Jesus is succeeded by the Paraclete working through the disciples.

This suggests that the Fourth Gospel is portraying Jesus and his disciples as prophets like Moses, and, indeed, Jesus is called a prophet or the prophet by several characters in the Gospel (see Teeple 1957; Glasson 1963; Meeks 1967; Miranda 1972; Boring 1982). The Samaritan woman, impressed by Jesus' knowledge, exclaims: 'Sir, I see that you are a prophet' (4.19); the people who saw the feeding sign declare: 'This is indeed the prophet who is to come into the world' (6.14); in the Temple some who hear Jesus' preaching conclude: 'This is really the prophet' (7.40), although the chief priests and Pharisees decide the issue differently: 'Search and you will see that no prophet is to arise from Galilee' (7.52). Nevertheless, the man cured of blindness is sure that Jesus 'is a prophet' (9.17). Once even Jesus likens his mission to that of a prophet, in a proverbial saying: 'A prophet has no honour in his own country' (4.44), which explains his rejection in Judaea. Jesus, then, is a prophet like Moses, commissioned by God to save his people, but this is part of a broader picture, according to which Jesus is the Son of his Father, his Father's agent who represents him on a mission to perform a crucial task.

2. *Giving* δίδωμι

A second important metaphor which explores Jesus' significance uses the verb 'to give' (δίδωμι) with 'God' as subject. Programmatic for the Fourth Gospel is the saying in 3.16: 'For God so loved the world that he *gave* his only Son, that whoever believes in him should not perish but have eternal life'. (There may be an echo of the story about Abraham's sacrificing his beloved son Isaac, but the vocabulary of Jn 3.16 is not the same as that of Gen. 22.) The life of Jesus is construed as the Creator's gift which brings the possibility of eternal life to everyone. God's whole creative endeavour, moreover, is an act of generosity. From the beginning those who received 'the light' were given power to become 'children of God' (1.12). All earthly authority is, in fact, delegated by God, even Pilate's (19.11). In the past God had demonstrated his generosity, particularly to Israel, giving the Law and the Scriptures which already spoke of Jesus (1.17; 5.39). He had given the manna from heaven to feed the Israelites in the wilderness, and now gives them the true bread from heaven, Jesus, the Son of man (6.31-59). This bread gives life to the world.

Here the Fourth Gospel is picking up from the Septuagint the language of God's generosity. In the Greek classical tradition the gods are said to give κῦδος or victory, but more often evils (e.g. Homer). In Sophocles and Euripides good fortune is seen as a divine gift, but even this idea is remote from the world of the Fourth Gospel. The notion that everything that happens depends on God's bounty is expressed in Job's blessing: 'The Lord *gave* and the Lord has taken away; blessed be the name of the Lord' (Job 1.21). Land and progeny are God's gifts to the patriarchs and their descendents (Gen. 17.8, 16, 20; 24.7; Josh. 24.3-4). Moses and the prophets are given the ability to work signs (Exod. 4.21; Isa. 7.14) and to speak (Exod. 4.11; Jer. 1.9; 5.14). God gives the people bread (Exod. 16; Ps. 78) and meat (Num. 11.18) to eat in the wilderness, and the Sabbath rest (Exod. 16.29). These gifts are all intimations of the salvation he gives (Ps. 18.35), especially through the renewal of his covenant with Israel:

> A new heart I *will give* you, and a new spirit I will put within you; and I will take out of your flesh the heart of stone and *give* you a heart of flesh. And I will put my spirit within you and cause you to walk in my statutes and be careful to observe my ordinances. You shall dwell in the land which I *gave* to your fathers; and you shall be my people, and I will be your God (Ezek. 36.26-28).

Hence, the Wisdom of Solomon sees wisdom, prudence and understanding as God's gifts (Wis. 9.4; 7.7, 9). Moreover, in Deutero-Isaiah, the servant is given as a covenant to the people, a light to the nations (Isa. 42.6; 49.6).

Taking over this tradition, the Fourth Gospel declares that the Father gave the Son (3.16). The idea is developed so that everything Jesus achieves is understood as the Father's gift: 'No one can receive anything except what is *given* him from heaven' (3.27), but 'the

Father loves the Son and *has given* all things into his hand' (3.35; 13.3). In his ministry Jesus does the 'works which the Father *has granted* me to accomplish' (5.36; 17.4) and he is given God's λόγος or 'the commandment what to say' (17.8, 14; 12.49; and 14.31 in some manuscripts). The Gospel gradually unfolds the way in which God's loving gift of the Son is mirrored in the Son's giving of himself: 'The Bread that I *shall give* for the life of the world is my flesh' (6.51). Generosity begets generosity. This is 'the cup which the Father *has given*' Jesus to drink (18.11).

Any success in the ministry is also reckoned as God's gift: 'All that the Father *gives* me will come to me' (6.37; cf. 10.29; 17.6-7, 9) or 'No one can come to me unless it *is granted* him by the Father' (6.65), and Jesus loses none of those given to him (18.9). Moreover, Jesus fulfils the Father's purpose in giving to these believers eternal life (17.2). He gives 'living water' so that it 'will become in him [the believer] a spring of water welling up to eternal life' (4.10, 14), or 'bread from heaven', 'the food which endures to eternal life which the Son of man *will give*' (6.27). As the good shepherd, he '*gives* them [the sheep] eternal life and they shall never perish' (10.28).

So the gifts received by Jesus from the Father are passed on to believers. As Jesus received a commandment from the Father, he gives the disciples 'a new commandment', to love as Jesus loved (13.34). He gives them an example to follow (13.15; see Sir. 44.16 where Enoch is described as 'an example of repentance to future generations' and where the same word for 'example', ὑπόδειγμα, is used). The honour which Jesus was given by the Father is also to be given to disciples (17.22, 24). Nevertheless, the disciples are not to be left to follow his example merely from their own resources. Like Jesus, they are to receive the Spirit from the Father (14.16; 7.38-39). Then, anything they ask of the Father in Jesus' name they are sure to receive (15.16; 16.23).

This metaphor pictures the whole of human life and potential as God's gift. The world is not self-sufficient. Rather, recognition of dependence upon God is what gives humanity its real dignity. The Fourth Gospel manages to convey this message without presenting believers as puppets or taking responsibility from them. On the contrary, they are seen as God's emissaries and delegates. God's generosity inspires Jesus' generosity, and Jesus' generosity inspires the disciples'.

3. *Coming and Going*

When we ask strangers where they come from, the question usually means 'Where were you born?' or 'Where were you brought up?' rather than 'Where were you five minutes ago?' We sometimes ask such questions because we suppose their answers provide information about people's characters and predilections. Similarly, asking someone where she is going can refer either to her immediate itinerary or to her long-term ambitions. In the Fourth Gospel Jesus himself often talks about his arrival and departure, and this language gives to his life a sense of purpose and destiny. And this sense is reinforced by links with the theological structure of the narrative. Ultimately, the purpose Jesus fulfils is God's purpose. Hence, ultimately, he comes from God and goes to God.

3.1. ἔρχομαι *(Come) and* ἐξέρχομαι *(Come Forth)*

In the Fourth Gospel ἔρχομαι is most frequent in its ordinary literal sense, whether Jesus is the subject or someone else (e.g. 1.29; 4.46, 54; 11.20; so also 4.47 with ἥκω, have come). Metaphorically, however, the verb expresses commissioning from God, as an alternative to 'God sent'. In the Prologue we are told that the light comes into the world from God (1.9), or comes to its own (1.11). The metaphor of light coming into the world describes the Son in 3.19. Hence, in 8.14, Jesus asserts that he knows whence he came and can therefore bear witness to himself as the light of the world. He is the light of the world because his entry into the world serves the Father's purpose: 'I *came* that they may have life, and have it abundantly' (10.10 cf. 3.16). This purpose is to be perceived in his death on the cross: 'For this purpose, I *have come* to this hour' (12.27; see also 18.37 where 'I have come' is parallel with 'I have been born'). Jesus' leadership is therefore contrasted with that of the Pharisees: 'All who *came* before me are thieves and robbers... I am the door' (10.8 and 10). But 'all' does not include John the Baptist, who '*came* for testimony, to bear witness to the light' (1.7). Nevertheless, John's testimony asserts Jesus' superiority: 'He who *comes* after me ranks before me' (1.15, 27, 30). In 3.31 again Jesus' importance is stressed by combining horizontal with vertical metaphors: 'He who *comes* from above is above all; he who is of the earth belongs to the earth, and of the earth he speaks; he who *comes* from heaven is above all.'

In the Septuagint ἔρχομαι sometimes serves to distinguish God's activity in the world: 'Behold the Lord *comes* with might' (Isa. 40.10), often through his Spirit: 'The Spirit of the Lord *came* upon me' (Ezek. 2.2; 3.34), or Wisdom: 'There *came* to me a Spirit of wisdom' (Wis. 7.7), or name: 'Behold, the name of the Lord *comes* from afar' (Isa. 30.27), or purpose: 'Let the purpose of the Holy One draw near, and let it *come* that we may know it' (Isa. 5.19), or λόγος: 'Where is the λόγος of the Lord? Let it *come*' (Jer. 17.15), or glory: 'And behold, the glory of the Lord of Israel *came* from the east' (Ezek. 43.2). Possibly, Mal. 3.1 refers to the advent of a human messenger, but, more likely, to God: 'The messenger of the covenant in whom you delight; behold, he *is coming*'. It seems, then, that language from the Septuagint which metaphorically draws attention to God's activity is applied to Jesus, in the Fourth Gospel, because Jesus is God's agent, acting on his Father's behalf.

Some of the Johannine uses of ἔρχομαι are not past or present, but future: 'I will not leave you desolate; I *will come* to you' (14.18, 28), or 'If a man loves me, he will keep my λόγος, and my Father will love him, and we *will come* to him and make our home with him' (14.23). These promises are fulfilled with the coming of the Paraclete (14.26; 15.26; 16.7-16), so it is not surprising that the same verb describes his advent. The reference to Jesus' future advent in 21.22-23, however, is not fulfilled in this way, but points forward to the end of history, as does 14.3: 'And when I go and prepare a place for you, I *will come* again and will take you to myself, that where I am you may be also'.

The appropriate response to Jesus' arrival is described metaphorically as 'coming to' Jesus. It is the language of attraction. 'He who does what is true *comes* to the light, that it may be clearly seen that his deeds have been wrought in God' (3.21), or 'I am the bread of life; he who *comes* to me shall not hunger, and he who believes in me shall never thirst' (6.35, see also 7.37, and conversely 3.20 and 5.40). The attraction, however, is ultimately determined by God: 'No one *comes* to me unless the Father who sent me draws him' (6.44-45, 65, and see 6.47 with ἥκω). Moreover, coming to Jesus is the only route to the Father: 'Jesus said, I am the way, the truth and the life; no one *comes* to the Father but by me' (14.6) ἐξέρχομαι (come forth) functions literally, with various subjects, including Jesus (e.g. 1.43; 4.30, 43; 8.59; 10.39). Curiously, geographical origins are expressed literally not with ἐξέρχομαι, except at 4.7 (ἔρχομαι ἐκ) but with εἰμί ἐκ (to be from) (e.g. 1.46; 4.39; 7.27, 52), εἰμί ἀπό (e.g. 1.44, 45; 11.1; 19.38), or πόθεν εἰμί (e.g. 7.27, 28). These expressions of belonging to a place are also used metaphoricaly (see below).

ἐξέρχομαι or ἔρχομαι ἐκ/ἀπό/παρά in a metaphorical sense always has Jesus as subject: 'If God were your Father, you would love me, for I came forth (ἔρχομαι ἀπο) from God and have come' (8.42; 16.28), or 'Jesus, knowing...that he *had come from* God (ἔρχομαι παρά) and was going to God, rose from supper' (13.3-4; 16.7 cf. 17.8). Once again, the language draws on the Septuagint, where God 'comes forth' to effect his policy in the world, 'the Lord God *comes forth* like a mighty man' (Isa. 42.13; cf. Ps. 61.10), sometimes thorough his Wisdom: 'I [Wisdom] *proceeded* from the mouth of the Most High' (Sir. 24.3), or judgment: 'My judgment *comes forth* as a light' (Hos. 6.5), or λόγος: 'From my mouth has *come forth* in righteousness a λόγος that shall not return' (Isa. 42.25 cf. 55.11), or law: 'For a law *will come forth* from me and my justice for the light of the peoples' (Isa. 51.4). This statement is set in parallel to one about salvation: 'My salvation *has come forth*' (Isa. 51.5). In seeing Jesus as God's agent, effecting his salvation, the Fourth Gospel applies this metaphorical language to him.

3.2. *Going (*ἔρχομαι, μεταβάινω, *Pass Over,* ὑπάγω, *Depart,* πορεύσμαι, *Go,* ἀπέρχομαι, *Depart,* ἀφίημι, *Leave)*

Generally, in the Fourth Gospel, these verbs have a literal sense (e.g. 9.7; 7.3; 4.16; 7.35; 4.3, 8; 10.12). Metaphorically, they indicate the end of Jesus' earthly existence: 'Now, I [Jesus] am no longer in the world, but they [the disciples] are in the world, and I *am coming* to you [the Father]' (17.11, ἔρχομαι), or 'His hour had come to *depart out* of this world to the Father' (13.1, μεταβαίνω), or 'I [Jesus] *go* to him who sent me' (7.33 ὑπάγω), or 'I [Jesus] *go* to prepare a place for you [the disciples]' (14.2, πορεύομαι), or 'It is to your advantage that I *go away*' (16.7, ἀπέρχομαι), or 'I *am leaving* the world' (16.28, ἀφίημι). Nevertheless, 'You [the disciples] know the way where I *am going*' (14.4, ὑπάγω) because Jesus is the way (14.6) that the disciples must follow (13.14-15).

The Septuagint employs πορεύομαι, ἀπέρχομαι and ἀφίημι to indicate a person's death (e.g. Gen. 3.19; 15.15; 35.18), but not ἔρχομαι, μεταβαίνω or ὑπάγω. Mt. 26.24 and Mk 14.21 use ὑπάγω euphemistically of death, and Liddell and Scott cite examples from classical literature of ἀπέρχομαι and ἀφίημι with the same meaning.

The metaphors of Jesus' coming and going in the Fourth Gospel give a sense of purpose to Jesus' life, and that purpose is to carry out God's plan, to live in obedience to God from whom all life ultimately comes.

4. *Belonging to a Place or Person*

It has already been noticed (under ἐξέρχομαι) that geographical association is expressed literally with εἰμί ἐκ, ἀπό or πόθεν. ποθέν εἰμί is used ironically with metaphorical overtones only once, in 7.28:

> So Jesus proclaimed as he taught in the temple, You know me, and you know *whence I come*. But I have not come of my own accord; he who sent me is true, and him you do not know. I know him, for I come from him and he sent me.

εἰμί ἐκ, used metaphorically, means 'belonging to a sphere of influence'. 'He who *is of* the earth *belongs to* the earth and of the earth he speaks' is contrasted with 'He who comes from heaven is above all' (3.31). Similarly, 'You [the "Jews"] are from below, I *am from* above; you *are of* this world, I *am* not *of* this world' (8.23). Hence, Jesus declares to Pilate: 'My kingdom *is* not *of* this world. If my kingdom *were of* this world, my servants would fight, that I might not be handed over to the Jews' (18.36). In the Farewell Discourses the disciples are warned that they will incur hatred because they do not belong to the world: 'If you *were of* the world, the world would love its own; but because you *are* not *of* the world, therefore the world hates you' (15.19, cf. 17.14, 16). In these sayings 'earth' and 'world' have the negative connotation of creation at odds with its Creator. The same idea is expressed in terms of belonging to a 'person' rather than a 'place': 'He who *is of* God hears the words of God; the reason why you do not hear them is that you *are* not *of* God' (8.47) or 'You *are of* your father the devil' (8.44). Jesus therefore challenges his 'Jewish' audience: 'If anyone's will is to do his [God's] will, he will know whether the teaching *is of* God or whether I am speaking on my own authority' (7.17). More abstractly, Jesus claims before Pilate: 'Everyone who *is of* truth hears my voice' (18.37). In 10.16 and 26 the figure of the good shepherd caring for his sheep pictures the flock belonging together in the sheepfold: 'And I have other sheep which *are* not *from* this pen' and 'You do not believe because you *are* not *of* my sheep'.

Any idea of movement is absent from these statements, so that they give the impression of a deterministic opposition between those who belong to God and those who do not. But such an impression is corrected by placing them in the context of the rest of the Gospel which makes it plain that everyone comes originally from God, and that it is only failure to acknowledge this which prevents people from accepting the gift of eternal life offered through Jesus. The miracles describing cures of the feeble and blind, and the raising of the dead, show that no individual is completely beyond the scope of God's saving care.

5. *Descending and Ascending*

These metaphors of mission, grace, destiny and belonging are powerfully reinforced by those which are expressed in terms of a metaphorical contrast between 'above' and 'below'. This contrast is exploited in most languages, including English (see Lakoff and Johnson 1980; Wheelwright 1962). Status, for example, is reckoned 'high' or 'low' in expressions like 'he will rise to the top', 'she is at the peak of her career', 'his status has fallen'. 'Good' and 'bad' can also be given a similar vertical orientation in statements like 'things are looking up', 'it's an all-time low', 'he does high quality work'. Lakoff and Johnson argue that both physical experience and social and cultural factors play their part in determining these choices of metaphor. In the Fourth Gospel vertical metaphors are the most immediately arresting of the orientational metaphors, and they are part of a larger metaphorical system of 'above' and 'below' (see Nicholson 1983). These vertical metaphors are not balanced by their opposite, as they are in English, however. In English 'good' and 'bad' can also be contrasted, metaphorically, as 'depth' and 'superficiality'.

5.1. ἄνω *(up, above) and* κάτω *(down, below)*

Used only three times in the Fourth Gospel, ἄνω functions literally in

2.7: 'Fill the jars with water. And they filled them *up*', and in 11.41: 'Jesus lifted *up* his eyes', but in 8.23, the meaning is metaphorical: 'He said to them [the people of Jerusalem], you are *from below* [ἐκ τῶν κάτω, the only instance of κάτω in John], I am *from above* [ἐκ τῶν ἄνω]; you are of this world, I am not of this world'.

In the Septuagint the universe is described either as 'the heavens above' (ἄνω) and 'the earth beneath' (κάτω) (e.g. Deut. 4.39), or with the addition 'and the waters under (ὑποκάτω) the earth' (e.g. Exod. 20.4; Deut. 5.8). Liddell and Scott's lexicon suggests that this use of ἄνω and κάτω is distinctive because in Classical Greek literature ἄνω means 'on the earth' and κάτω 'under the earth'. (In the Fourth Gospel ἀνίστημι, arise, and ἀναστασις, resurrection, follow Classical Greek usage). But in taking over ἄνω and κάτω from the Septuagint, the Fourth Gospel uses them metaphorically: 'the heavens above' represents 'transcendence'. In 8.23, moreover, status is a matter not just of place on a vertical scale, but of belonging: 'You are *from* below, I am *from* above'. The parallel saying repeats the idea with a different metaphor, belonging or not belonging to this world, in which 'world' is creation without the Creator. Jesus' statement claims that he lives solely from God.

5.2. ἄνωθεν *(from above) and* ἐπάνω *(above)*

Because, in the Gospel, status is reckoned in terms of belonging, ἄνωθεν functions metaphorically too. Only one instance is literal, 19.23: 'When the soldiers had crucified Jesus, they took his garments and made four parts, one for each soldier; also his tunic. But the tunic was without seam, woven *from top* to bottom'. All four other references are metaphorical. Two of these occur in the discourse with Nicodemus, 3.3: 'Truly, truly, I say to you, unless someone is born *from above/anew*, he cannot see the Kingdom of God', repeated in 3.7: 'Do not marvel that I say to you, you must be born *from above/anew*'. The statements in 3.31, 19.11 and 23 suggest that the primary Johannine meaning is 'from above', but a deliberate play on the ambiguity of the word allows the correction of Nicodemus' puzzles (see Büchsel 1964). The same metaphorical meaning is found in the Septuagint to refer to 'God above' (e.g. Job 3.4; 31.2). Jesus, however, is not urging Nicodemus to become divine rather than human, but to reorientate his life so that he no longer lives within the confines of a self-satisfied world, but consciously and actually lives from the God who creates the world, and whose purpose is to give people 'eternal life' (3.16).

Jesus' advice to Pilate, in 19.11, places Pilate's claims to power within a similar framework: 'You would have no power over me unless it had been given you *from above*'. This results in Pilate's attempt to act justly, to release Jesus, but in a weak manner which belies his exaggerated claims to authority.

The testimony of John or the narrator in 3.31 makes a similar distinction: 'He who comes *from above* is *above* (ἐπάνω) all; he who is of the earth belongs to the earth and of the earth he speaks; he who comes from heaven is *above* (ἐπάνω) all'. The adverb, ἐπάνω, is normally used of place or number but here has the metaphorical meaning 'pre-eminence'. The distinction between 'from above' and 'from below' in 3.3 and 3.31 is the same, except that in 3.3 Nicodemus is to be born from above, whereas in 3.31 the testimony is to one who comes from above. In both expressions, however, belonging to God is the point of the remark.

5.3. οὐρανός *(Heaven)*, ἐπουράνιος *(Heavenly)*

The quotation from Ps. 78.24 in Jn 6.31: 'He gave them bread *from heaven* to eat', and the introduction to the prayer in 17.1: 'He lifted up his eyes *to heaven*' use οὐρανός ('sky') metaphorically for 'heaven', God's dwelling place. As in the Septuagint (e.g. Ps. 2.4; 10.5; Dan. 2.28; Jdt. 6.19), they indicate that God exists 'apart from' creation. Revelation from God is described as 'heaven opening' (e.g. Ezek. 1.1; Jn 1.51). The other references place 'heaven' after the preposition 'from'. In 3.27 John comments on the information that 'Jesus is baptizing, and all are going to him', 'No one can receive anything except what is given him *from heaven*'. He affirms divine support for Jesus' mission to which he had already borne witness. Although 'heaven' captures the idea of God's transcendence, therefore, his immanent activity in creating a response to his agent can be expressed as 'gift from heaven'.

In the Fourth Gospel, however, Jesus not only receives God's gift, but is himself God's gift 'from heaven'. Most of the references occur in the discourse in ch. 6 (6.31, 32, 33, 38, 41, 42, 50, 51, 58. See Exod. 16). The term 'bread from heaven' is taken from Ps. 78.24 and elaborated. Jesus insists that the Father gave the bread from heaven in the wilderness and that he now gives bread from heaven in the form of Jesus, who came down 'from heaven' to do the Father's will in giving the kind of succour that nourishes eternal life.

Like Jesus, the Bread of Life, the Spirit is also pictured descending *from heaven*: 'And John bore witness: I saw the Spirit descend as a dove from heaven' (1.32). Since, metaphorically, God is envisaged 'above' creation, his Spirit has to descend to inspire people. Nowhere in the Septuagint, however, is καταβαίνω ('descend') used with πνεῦμα ('Spirit'). This is a Johannine elaboration, determined by the other metaphors (see Mk 1.10 and parallels). Likening the Spirit's descent to that of a dove presumably adds connotations of purity (cf. Mt. 10.16).

Jn 12.28 is the only example of a divine oracle in the Fourth Gospel (cf. Mt. 3.17; 17.5 and parallels). The metaphorical use of thunder for the divine voice seems, once again, to be derived from the Septuagint (e.g. 1 Sam. 7.9-10):

> Then a voice came *from heaven*: I have honoured it and I will honour it again. The crowd standing by heard it and said that it had thundered. Others said: An angel has spoken to him. Jesus answered: This voice has come for your sake not for mine.

The point of providing divine assurance in this manner, both here and in the Synoptic story of the transfiguration (Mt. 17.1-8 and parallels), is to dispel the misunderstanding that Jesus' death is a tragic mistake. The Synoptics place it after the first of Jesus' passion predictions, and John places it at the end of his public ministry, just before he is arrested. The form of the story is traditional, but striking in its crudity. Possibly, it was chosen for dramatic effect.

ἐπουράνιος ('heavenly', see Taub 1967) occurs in Jesus' exasperated response to Nicodemus's incomprehension: 'If I have told you earthly things and you do not believe, how can you believe if I tell you *heavenly things*?' The discourse seeks to lead Nicodemus from the literal to the metaphorical level of understanding, modulating 'birth' to suggest 'birth from above', and 'wind' to suggest the mysterious but effective presence of the Spirit. These 'earthly things' are understood to point beyond themselves since they originate from the Creator and provide knowledge of the way in which she works. 'The heavenly things' with which these 'earthly things' are contrasted are delineated in what follows: God's love for the world which is expressed by his giving his only Son to be lifted up (on a cross, as it transpires) so that people may have eternal life (3.12-21). The contrast seems to be this. Whereas natural phenomena, like birth or the activity of the wind, hint at their metaphorical theological significance, and anyone may be expected to ponder them, an event like the crucifixion of Jesus by his enemies cannot so obviously be seen as a gift from God.

5.4. γῆ *(Earth) and* ἐπίγειος *(Earthly)*

γῆ sometimes means 'territory' as in Jn 3.22 (cf. Gen. 13.12; Exod. 20.2), or 'dry land' in distinction from 'sea', as in Jn 6.21, 21.8, 9, 11 (cf. Gen. 1.10), or 'earth' in contrast to 'sky' as in Jn 12.24, 32 (cf. Gen. 1.1). This last usage gives rise to the metaphorical sense 'creation' in contrast to Creator in Jn 17.4: 'I [Jesus] honoured you [the Father] *on earth*, having accomplished the work which you gave me to do'. Here γῆ has no negative connotations, but in 3.31 it is used, like κόσμος ('world'), in conjunction with the idea of 'belonging' to express the sense of the world's limited perspective: 'He who comes from above is above all; he who is *of the earth*, belongs *to the earth* and *of the earth* he speaks'.

ἐπίγειος in 3.12: 'If I have told you *earthly things*, and you do not believe, how can you believe if I tell you heavenly things' is not derived from the Septuagint, although the expression ἐπὶ τῆς γῆς ('on the earth') is common (e.g. Gen. 1.11, 15, 17, 22; Wis. 9.16). The contrast with 'heavenly' is found in Plato's *Republic*, 546a, although there the meaning is literal not metaphorical. In Philo's description of Chaldean astrology, he writes of sympathetic affinity between earthly things (ἐπίγεια) and heavenly (οὐράνια) indicating a kinship between earth and stars which is again literal. Only Phil. 3.19-20 offers a parallel to Jn 3.12, except that 'earthly' has a negative nuance, as in Jn 3.31: 'Their end is destruction, their god is the belly, and they glory in their shame, with minds set on *earthly things* (ἐπίγεια)'. (See Sasse 1964, and 2 Cor. 5.1; Jas 3.15).

This Johannine stress on belonging to one sphere or another, to God or the world, determines the Gospel's use of two verbs of movement, ἀναβαίνω ('go up') and καταβαίνω ('go down').

5.5. ἀναβαίνω *(Go up)*

ἀναβαίνω functions literally in four different contexts in the Fourth Gospel. In Jn 21.22 it means 'going on shipboard', as in Homer and much Classical Greek literature, although the Septuagint prefers ἐμβαίνω or εἰσέρχομαι (e.g. Jon. 1.3, with a variant ἀναβαίνω, 1 Macc. 15.37; Gen. 7.1). Jn 10.1 makes a contrast between normal entry into the sheep pen and that of the thief who 'climbs in (ἀναβαίνω) by another way'. Most frequently (e.g. Jn 2.13; 5.1; 7.8, 10; 11.55; 12.20), ἀναβαίνω describes 'going up to a city', in this case Jerusalem. Since Jerusalem, on a hill like most ancient cities, was physically higher than the coastal and desert regions, the expression is natural, but has already become an idiom, used even when the topographical change is actually from one hilly region (Galilee) to another (Jerusalem) (e.g. 7.8, 10). In the Septuagint 'going up (ἀναβαίνω) to Jerusalem' is a common idiom (e.g. 1 Sam. 8.7; 1 Kgs 12.27).

Within Jerusalem the Temple area was higher than most of the city, so the statement 'Jesus *went up* into the Temple' (7.14) also describes physical movement (cf. the Septuagint of Isa. 37.1). Schneider (1964) calls this idiom 'cultic' because sanctuaries were normally situated on hills.

The Fourth Gospel provides five other instances in which the meaning is not literal or idiomatic, however, but metaphorical. In two cases ἀναβαίνω is linked with οὐρανός, which is also used metaphorically to mean not 'sky' but 'transcendence'. 'Truly, truly, I say to you, you will see heaven opened and the angels of God *ascending* and descending upon the Son of man' (1.51) alludes to Jacob's dream in which angels of God ascend and descend upon the ladder (Gen. 28.12). The metaphor pictures the Son of man as the focus of divine revelation on earth through his constant contact with God. It appropriately extends the 'cultic' sense to express divine transcendence without making the gulf between divine and human unbridgable. With the traditional image of angelic messengers, the narrative encourages readers to perceive the transcendent God's purpose in the Son of man's life. This image reverses that of the angel taking someone on a guided tour of heaven, developed, for example, in the Enochic literature, since it represents the divine making contact with people on earth.

Jn 3.13 also links ἀναβαίνω and οὐρανός: 'No one *has ascended* into heaven but he who descended from heaven, the Son of man'. The general statement, 'No one has ascended into heaven', again seems to stand against the apocalyptic tradition of heavenly journeys. Revelation happens, not when a person ascends to God, but in the life of Jesus, the Son of man, who ascends to heaven only after he has revealed God's plan. The Fourth Gospel depicts this revelation especially in

Jesus' uplifting on the cross, the final mark of his obedience and the exaltation of the Son of man (3.14).

In the two sayings at the end of the Gospel, 'heaven' is replaced by the more personal 'Father':

> Jesus said to her, do not hold me, for I *have not yet ascended* to the Father; but go to my brothers and say to them, I *am ascending* to my Father and your Father, to my God and your God (20.17).

This part of the resurrection narrative, a conversation between Jesus and Mary, draws upon earlier discussions. Mary does not recognize Jesus until he calls her by name (20.16 cf. 10.3), but even then Mary's response is unsatisfactory. She calls Jesus 'Rabbi' as if she expects the old relationship of teacher and disciple to be re-established. In taking hold of Jesus, or trying to do so, she seems to assume that resurrection is resuscitation. On the contrary, however, ascent to the Father marks the distinction between the resuscitation of Lazarus in ch. 11 and the resurrection of Jesus in chs. 20–21. Resurrection is personal survival, but continuity does not exclude change. Jesus' ascension to the Father concludes his earthly mission as it had Elijah's, although Elijah's ascent in a whirlwind is not post-mortem, and is described with the verb ἀναλαμβάνω not ἀναβαίνω (2 Kgs 2.11). After his ascent Jesus' relationship with his disciples no longer takes the form of ordinary human companionship.

Why is this change expressed metaphorically as an 'ascent' instead of, for example, a 'departure'? The parallel with Elijah is instructive. Both prophets, Elijah and Jesus, suffered persecution in carrying out their mission, and both were vindicated not by people but by God. 'Ascending' to God at the end of a life which reached its climax in exaltation on a cross provides this sense of vindication.

In distinction from the Enochic literature, therefore, the Fourth Gospel asserts that revelation occurs in the life of a man, Jesus, who belongs to God, and who is vindicated in his 'ascent' to heaven. Jn 6.62, 'Then what if you were to see the Son of man *ascending* where he was before', is most obviously to be interpreted as a reference to Jesus' literal ascent to Jerusalem, where he was before, but it may also have metaphorical connotations of vindication. It is impossible to express 'transcendence' or 'revelation' or 'divine vindication' without metaphors. In choosing vertical metaphors, the Fourth Gospel is able to employ the sophisticated tradition of the Septuagint.

5.6. καταβαίνω *(Go down)*
Like ἀναβαίνω, καταβαίνω can have a straightforward topographical meaning, for example, in describing the descent to the coastal region of Capernaum (2.12 cf. 4.47, 49, 51; 5.7; 6.16). Again like ἀναβαίνω, with which it is associated in 1.51 and 3.13, it is used in a metaphorical sense to picture the descent of the Spirit (1.32) and of the bread from heaven (ch. 6).

The discourse in ch. 6 provides a christological interpretation of the story of God's raining bread from heaven in Exodus 16 (cf. Num. 11; Ps. 78.21; Wis. 16.20), but καταβαίνω is derived from Num. 11.9. The Johannine teaching makes typological connexions with the manna story, but also suggests distinctions which correspond to those between 'biological life' and 'eternal life'. The Johannine images of the Spirit and the Son descending from heaven use vertical metaphors as an alternative expression of God's graciousness.

6. *Conclusion*

The Fourth Gospel is a theological reflection on the significance of Jesus' life, death and resurrection. It draws on the metaphorical language of the Septuagint to make its message clear. Jesus' life is meaningful for other people because it expresses the Creator God's purpose for humanity. His life is presented, not as an unselfconscious series of accidental effects, not as a tragedy in which injustice triumphs, but as a coherent expression of God's purpose. He belongs to God, does what God requires, lives wholly from God, and hence his life offers a model for imitation by all those who want to live in dedication to this God.

Chapter 8

JESUS, THE SON OF MAN*

'Son of man' (υἱὸς ἀνθρώπου) is a word for word translation into Greek of a Hebrew idiom found frequently in Scripture. Just as 'sons of Israel' is the Hebrew idiom for Israelites, so 'son of man' is the Hebrew idiom for human being. The Greek translates either 'son of Adam' (*ben 'ādām*) or 'son of a human being' (*ben 'ᵉnôš*). For example, Ps. 8.4 asks God, 'What is man that you are mindful of him, and a son of man (*ben 'ādām*/υἱὸς ἀνθρώπου) that you care for him?' The psalm finds it surprising that the transcendent God should concern himself with frail humanity. Similarly, after Ezekiel's extraordinary vision of God, the prophet is addressed as 'son of man': 'Son of man, eat what is offered to you; eat this scroll, and go, speak to the house of Israel' (3.1; see 4.1; 5.1; 6.2; 7.2 etc.) A question parallel to that in Ps. 8.4 is expressed in Ps. 144.3, where the idiom υἱὸς ἀνθρώπου renders *ben 'ᵉnôš*: 'O Lord, what is man that you regard him, or a son of man that you think of him?'

We find the same idiom in Aramaic (*bār 'ᵉnaš*). For example, Daniel 7 recounts a vision of God's judgment. The beasts from the sea, representing world empires and their emperors, are brought to judgment by God and relieved of their destructive power (7.11-12). God replaces their rule by that of a humane king:

> And behold, with the clouds of heaven there came *one like a son of man*, and he came to the Ancient of Days and was presented before him. And to him was given dominion and honour and kingdom, that all peoples and nations and languages should serve him; his dominion is an everlasting dominion which shall not pass away, and his kingdom one that shall not be destroyed (7.13-14).

* An earlier version of parts of this chapter appeared in *JTS* NS 26 (1985): 56-66.

The 'one like a son of man', that is, like a human being in contrast to the beasts, represents a new humane king who rules the community in which the saints of the Most High will share (7.18).

In the period after Daniel 7 was written, the vision influenced other Jewish apocalyptic works. For example, parts of the *Similitudes of Enoch* (*1 En.* 37–71) reinterpret the vision. This section of *1 Enoch* is difficult to date, because no copies have been found among the Dead Sea Scrolls. Other parts of *1 Enoch* formed part of the Qumran community's library, which was hidden in the caves before the community was destroyed by the Roman army in the war from 66–70 CE. In his commentary on *1 Enoch* (1893), R.H. Charles dates the *Similitudes* in the first century BCE, but Isaac (1983) suggests only that *1 Enoch* contained the *Similitudes* by the end of the first century CE. Nevertheless, the *Similitudes* are useful to this study because they provide evidence of Jewish eschatological speculation at about the time when the Fourth Gospel was written.

The *Similitudes* have survived in an Ethiopic version which is a translation of an Aramaic, or, less probably, a Hebrew original. Three different renderings of 'son of man' are found in the Ethiopic version.

1. Son of man: *1 En.* 46.2, 3, 4; 48.2.
2. Son of the Male: *1 En.* 62.5; 69.29; 71.14.
3. Son of the child of the Mother of all the Living: *1 En.* 62.7, 9, 14; 63.11; 69.26, 27; 70.1; 71.17.

Moreover, all these references are with the demonstrative '*that* son of man', never with the definite article and never indefinite.

1 Enoch 46 is most obviously dependent on Daniel 7:

> And there I saw One who had a Head of Days, and his head was white like wool. And with him was another being whose countenance had the appearance of a man, and his face was full of graciousness, like one of the holy angels. And I asked the angel who went with me and who showed me all the hidden things, concerning *that son of man*, who he was and whence he was and why he went with the Head of Days? And he answered and said to me, This is *that son of man* who has righteousness, with whom dwells righteousness, and who reveals all the treasures of that which is hidden, because the Lord of Spirits has chosen him. . . and who is preeminent before the Lord of Spirits in uprightness for ever. And *that son of man* whom you have seen shall put down the kings and the mighty from their seats and shall loosen the reigns of the strong and break the teeth of sinners, because they do not extol or praise him nor humbly

> acknowledge whence the kingdom was bestowed upon them (Quoted from *The Apocryphal Old Testament*, edited by Sparks).

In 62.13-14 'that son of man' is given a role in relation to 'the elect ones' or 'the righteous ones' who seem to correspond to 'the saints of the Most High' in the Daniel vision. The elect ones

> will be saved on that day, and they shall never thenceforward see the faces of the sinners and the unrighteous. And the Lord of Spirits will abide over them, and, with *that son of man*, they shall eat and lie down and rise up for ever and ever.

At the end of the *Similitudes*, the identity of that person, 'that son of man', is revealed to be Enoch himself, who had been taken on his heavenly journeys to see visions of the future which God would establish, for him, and for those who were suffering persecution for their faith (71.14-17). According to the old story in Gen. 5.24, Enoch 'walked with God, and he was not, for God took him'. Taking its cue from this verse, the *Similitudes* offer assurance to faithful Jews through apocalyptic visions which look forward to God's establishing a just and righteous community ruled over by a particular human being, Enoch, 'that son of man'.

We have noticed that, in the visions in Daniel 7 and in the *Similitudes of Enoch*, a human being, a representative kingly figure, will rule over a righteous community established through God's final judgment. The expressions 'one like a son of man', or 'one whose countenance had the appearance of a man' or 'that son of man' draw attention to the humanity of this kingly figure. The expressions are used in the same sense as 'son of man' in the Psalms or in Ezekiel to mean 'a human being'. German scholars were wrong in supposing that 'son of man' meant 'someone who would play a role in the eschatological events'. 'Son of man' means 'human being', and visions like Daniel 7 and *1 Enoch* 62 picture *a man* playing the role of king in the eschatological events (see Lindars 1983: 11-16). 'Son of man', then, is a generic idiom which can be used to refer to humanity in general, or to a particular human being.

Lindars's book also contains a critical assessment of the suggestions put forward by Vermes in his studies of 'the son of man' in the Gospels and in contemporary Aramaic idiom (1973, 1975). In the Gospels 'the son of man' on the lips of Jesus is a self-reference. Vermes has shown that *bār 'enaš* or *bār 'ᵉnaš(a)*, when used generically, may be such a self-reference. For example, when Rab Kahara wishes to return to Babylon because he feels he is not appreciated by his rabbinic teacher in Palestine, Rabbi Yohanan, he asks permission to leave by citing a parable:

> If *bār naš* (a son of man) is despised by his mother but honoured by another of his father's wives, where should he go? Yohanan replied: He should go where he is honoured. Thereupon Kahana left. Then Rabbi Yohanan was told: Kahana has gone to Babylon. He exclaimed: What? Has he gone without asking leave? They said to him: The story he told you was his request to leave (*y*. *Ber*. 5c).

The parable depicts the situation of a man (*bār naš*) and Kahana applies the lesson to himself. Another example uses both the indefinite *bār naš* and the definite *bār naša*:

> It is related that Rabbi (Judah) was buried wrapped in a single sheet, for he said: It is not as *bār naša* goes that he will come again. But the Rabbis say: As *bār naš* goes, so will he come again (*y*. *Ket*. 35a).

The subject discussed is social status in this world and in the world to come after the resurrection. Rabbi Judah was a rich man but was buried in a simple manner. Both *bār naša*, the definite 'the son of man', and *bār naš*, the indefinite 'a son of man', express the generic sense 'every person'. The use of the definite article is appropriate in a proverbial saying.

In a further example, however, *bār naša* is used as an exclusive self-reference:

> Rabbi Simeon ben Yochai said: If I had stood on Mount Sinai when the Torah was given to Israel, I would have asked the Merciful One to create two mouths for *bār naša*, one for the study of the Torah and one for the provision of all his needs (*y*. *Ber*. 3b).

Since such a request is Simeon's alone, *bār naša* is an exclusive self-reference, yet the expression *bār naša* seems to allow that anyone who belonged to the class of human beings to which Simeon belonged, namely those who wished to be able to recite the Torah at all times, would share Simeon's request.

In Aramaic, then, the definite and indefinite *bār naš(a)* can be used when it indicates a man in similar circumstances (*y*. *Ber*. 5c), or when it indicates every human being (*y*. *Ket*. 35a), or when it indicates a particular type of human being (*y*. *Ber*. 3b) (see Casey 1987). The references in the Psalms, quoted at the beginning of the chapter, are also Hebrew examples of the second category. The references in Ezekiel and Daniel and *1 Enoch* are also examples of the third category.

In the Synoptic Gospels, all of Jesus' sayings about 'the Son of man' are definite (ὁ υἱὸς τοῦ ἀνθρώπου) and some of them draw on the imagery of the Son of man coming on the clouds in Daniel 7 (e.g. Mt. 26.64; Mk 14.62). The Fourth Gospel's use of the expression is slightly different in three respects. Although most of the references are definite, one is indefinite (5.27), and on one occasion it is the crowds who speak about the Son of man, not Jesus (12.34). Moreover, the Fourth Gospel never refers to the Son of man coming on the clouds. In the previous chapter I remarked that the Fourth Gospel inverts the apocalyptic imagery of ascent and descent to descent and ascent. Hence it would have been inappropriate for the Gospel to picture the resurrected Jesus' return on the clouds.

Lindars's discussion of the Son of man sayings in the Fourth Gospel largely agrees with the earlier work of F.J. Moloney (1978) in emphasizing that 'the Son of man' designates the agent of revelation. Lindars makes clear that this revelation takes place at Jesus' crucifixion, and in positing Jn 3.14, taken up from the passion tradition, as fundamental to the understanding of all other Son of man sayings in the Gospel, he can argue persuasively about 3.13 that theories involving descending and ascending divine figures throw no light on the meaning of the phrase 'the Son of man' (e.g. Meeks 1972). But he concludes that 'the Son of man' 'is not intended to refer specifically to the humanity of Jesus, though the act of revelation is the climax of his human life' (p. 155). He asserts that Son of man sayings never occur in discussions of the humanness of Jesus so that the term 'may be considered a rather misleading phrase to use' (p. 155). It is sometimes assumed (e.g. Maddox 1974: 189 n. 2) 'that the Church Fathers, from Ignatius and Pseudo-Barnabas on, show a distinct break from the earlier tradition when they take "the Son of man" as referring to the incarnation' but such a supposed break needs explanation, especially as Ignatius and the Fourth Gospel may be close in date and provenance. Further, Lindars dismisses Manson's suggestion of a corporate understanding of 'the Son of man' as 'erroneous' (p. 125 n. 25). I draw attention to these two points because had he abandoned them, he would have been able to show why the Fourth Gospel retains 'the Son of man' in preference to the first person singular pronoun, a question which his present discussion signally fails to answer.

Perhaps Manson's suggestion has fallen on deaf ears because, since C.F.D. Moule (1962) developed R. Bultmann's emphasis on Johannine individualism it has been assumed that the Gospel shows no real interest in community. It is true that it favours the form of direct personal address in the singular (e.g. 3.15, 16, 18, 33, 36; 5.24; 6.47, 54, etc.), but singular and plural are often juxtaposed (e.g. 1.14,16; 3.11, 19; 4.23, 24, 42, 48, etc.) because the Gospel is following the Wisdom form as exemplified in Proverbs (e.g. 8.17 = plural; 8.35-36 = singular). This direct personal appeal should not be isolated, however, from other teaching in the Gospel which takes up the language of covenant or expounds the meaning of 'love'. E. Malatesta (1978) shows that the background to Johannine usage is covenant language in the Septuagint, especially in Isa. 45.14, Jer. 8.19, Ezek. 39.7, Exod. 17.7, 2 Kgs 1.3-6, Deut. 27.26, Isa. 30.18, Psalm 60, Jer. 38.32 and Prov. 15.22. The Fourth Gospel pictures the life of the new community endowed with the Spirit and keeping the love-command in fulfilment of Ezekiel's prophecy about the new covenant (Ezek. 36.26-27).

The images that John uses of the relationship between Jesus and believers (the good shepherd in ch. 10 and the vine in ch. 15) focus attention on Jesus as the source of life. Unlike Paul's teaching about the body of Christ, they allow no development to express believer's mutual dependence. Schnackenburg is right to stress that the Fourth Gospel's interest is christological, because its purpose is to show that unity among believers is dependent, not on human endeavour or organization, but on fidelity to Jesus who is the way, the truth and the life (14.6; 10.16; ch. 17). Yet the Gospel makes it equally clear that believers have a responsibility to fellow human beings. Bearing witness is a major theme of the Gospel (1.19-51; 3.27-36; 4.28-42; 17.20-21; 20.24-29). The new community, re-created by the Spirit (20.22-23), forgives or retains sins, and, by becoming the vehicle of the Spirit's witness (15.26-27), brings to light the world's sin and God's justice and judgment (16.8-11). Its social life expresses the mutual love of believers (13.34; 15.13-14; 17.26) which reflects the love of the Father and the Son (17.23-26). Jesus' laying down his life for his friends is the example of love which disciples are to follow (12.24-26). Far from emphasizing individualism to the exclusion of community, the Gospel uses community as the dominant idea in characterizing the life of the disciples (10.16; ch. 17).

Presupposing only the background that Lindars has shown to be plausible, this chapter will argue that 'the Son of man' in the Fourth Gospel, while referring to Jesus, draws particular attention to his representative humanity, that is, Jesus is pictured as representing not what every person is, but what he or she could and should be. It is therefore misleading to label 'Son of man' a 'christological term' since it does not seek to distinguish Jesus' unique function, but defines the attributes of humanity which all people should exemplify. I shall examine the sayings in the order in which they occur in the Fourth Gospel except that I shall leave the most contentious instance, 3.13-14, for consideration at the end.

The 'Son of man' is first used in the Gospel to provide the climax to stories about the witness of John and that of disciples to Jesus. In response to Nathanael's confession that Jesus is the Son of God and the king of Israel, Jesus promises him that he will see greater things than the knowledge displayed by Jesus at their first meeting (1.50), though as yet what these greater things will be is left unclear. Lindars's suggestion that 'greater things' points forward to the crucifixion as the supremely revelatory act is correct but the ambiguity is deliberate in 1.51 because the reader must gradually be prepared to understand the significance of the crucifixion. Moloney's suggestion (1978: ch. 2), that this section is parallel to the Caesarea-Philippi discussion in the Synoptics is helpful in general, but does not indicate what is specific in the Johannine saying viz. the reflection of the Jacob/Israel story, so that he misleadingly treats 'the Son of man' as a title to point to something greater than 'rabbi' or 'Son of God'. The saying in 1.51 is related, however, not only to the previous verse but to the whole section, as the new introduction 'And he said to him', and the change from second person singular (v. 50) to plural (v. 51) suggest. Jn 1.51 is Jesus' response to all the confessions contained in this chapter: to John's that Jesus is the Lamb of God who takes away the sin of the world (1.29) and that Jesus is he who baptizes with the Holy Spirit (1.33), to Andrew's that Jesus is the messiah (1.41), to Philip's that Jesus is the one about whom Moses and the prophets wrote (1.45) and to Nathanael's confession.

The saying draws on the imagery of the story of Jacob's dream in which he saw 'a ladder set up on the earth, and the top of it reached to heaven, and behold, the angels of God were ascending and descending on it [him]' (Gen. 28.12). Commentators have pointed to the ambiguity of the Hebrew *bô* which led to two interpretations among Jewish scholars: (1) that the angels ascended and descended upon the ladder (= LXX), and (2) that the angels ascended and descended upon Jacob (see Odeberg 1968). John pictures the ascent and descent of angels upon the Son of man. Should 'the Son of man' be understood to correspond to the ladder set up on the earth but reaching to heaven, so that in looking at Jesus, Nathanael, the 'true Israelite', and the other disciples, will see 'heaven opened' as Jacob did in his vision, or should 'Son of man' be identified with Jacob? The former makes sense of more details (the parallelism between the true Israelite and Jacob) than does the latter and should therefore be preferred, especially as it is the Septuagint reading. But why does the Fourth Gospel use the term 'the Son of man' instead of the pronoun 'me'? Perhaps the Prologue offers a parallel. The climax of the Prologue is reached when the λόγος became flesh (1.14), to which John and believers bear witness (1.15-16). After the witness of John and the disciples (1.19-50), the revelation of God in the life of the 'man' is again stressed (1.51) (Cadman 1969: 26-28, 40-42). By referring to Jesus as 'the Son of man', the Gospel once again draws attention to Jesus' humanity.

Since the two Son of man sayings in 3.13-14 have given rise to a variety of disputed interpretations, I shall leave them until last and look next at the saying in 5.27. Chapter 5 concerns Jesus' justification of his healing on the Sabbath by the statement: 'My Father is working still, and I am working' (5.17). The discourse (5.19-47) refutes the 'Jewish' suggestion that Jesus claims equality with God (5.18), avoiding any suggestion that Jesus is a second God but stressing that those who want to see the only God can see him in Jesus' activity, which is summarized as giving life (5.21) and exercising judgment (5.22). The teaching offers encouragement: the restoration of the feeble man to full life manifests God's intention for everyone: 'He who hears my λόγος and believes him who sent me, has eternal life; he does not come into judgment, but has passed from death to life' (5.24). The decision for or against Jesus is crucial. This does not mean that John has abandoned belief in a final judgment at the end of time, but what determines that judgment is a person's decision for or against Jesus and God now. The Gospel makes two statements in tension, which urge the necessity of a right decision now to affect what happens in the future: (v. 25) 'The hour is coming and now is, when the dead will hear the voice of the Son of God and those who hear will live' (metaphorical), and (v. 28) 'The hour is coming when all who are in the tombs will hear his voice and come forth' (literal). Schnackenburg (1979) rejects vv. 27-28 as a secondary insertion but admits that there are no stylistic grounds for doing so.

Jn 5.26 and 27 repeat the summaries of God's activity: giving life and judgment, but why does v. 27 read: 'He [the Father] has given him authority to execute judgment because he is Son of man'? Throughout the discourse Jesus speaks of himself as Son (of God), except in this verse. Does the parallel between v. 22 and v. 27 imply that Son (of God) and Son of man are synonymous in the Fourth Gospel? This cannot be so because such a reading would make a nonsense of v. 27 in which 'he is Son of man' is offered as the reason why the Father gives judgment to the Son of God. In the case of 1.51, the term 'the Son of man' was used to emphasize Jesus' humanity, and such an emphasis would be appropriate in v. 27 too. Perhaps we should detect here an echo of Dan. 7.13 and 22; in v. 22 judgment is given to the saints of the Most High, and in v. 14 authority is given to the one like a son of man. The Johannine text combines the two, the Septuagint of v. 22 supplying κρίσις and that of vv. 13-14 ἐξουσία and υἱὸς ἀνθρώπου, which may explain the unusual anarthrous form of Jn 5.27. Dan. 7.22 seems to imply that the verdict is given in favour of the saints of the Most High, but in combining this text with 7.13, the Fourth Gospel interprets it to mean that the exercise of judgment is given to the Son of man, the representative of the saints of the Most High. And if as 'the Son of man', Jesus' humanity is representative, not only will those who believe in Jesus pass from death to life (v. 24) but in sharing Jesus' humanity, they will exercise judgment. This is in fact the Johannine view, as is clear in Jesus' final commission: 'Receive the Holy Spirit. If you forgive the sins of any, they are forgiven; if you retain the sins of any, they are retained' (20.23).

The discourse on the bread of life in ch. 6 contains three Son of man sayings (6.27, 53, 62). The crowds are pictured following Jesus because of the feeding miracle, understood by them simply in terms of the supply of food. But, as with water in the discourse in ch. 4, so in ch. 6 the provision of bread to sustain life is a sign of the gift of eternal life, and, again as in ch. 4, the discourse points from the provision of food to the provider. At the beginning of the discourse, then, the crowd is encouraged not to labour for food which perishes but for food which endures to eternal life 'which the Son of man will give to you, for on him has God the Father set his seal' (6.27). It is not immediately obvious why this is a Son of man rather than a Son of God statement, since in ch. 5 it is the Son (of God) who gives life, but the reason will become clear when all three sayings are seen in context. The statement that God the Father has set his seal upon the Son of man serves to emphasize the dependence of the Son of man on the Father, and the Son of man's fulfilment of the Father's purpose. In addition, Lindars argues that the statement intends to point to Jesus as the exclusive revelation of God (p. 152). This seems to me misleading because not only does the Gospel present Jesus as the revelation of God but the disciples are called upon to continue his work of making God known to human beings (e.g. 13.12-20; 15.12-17; 17.6-26).

Jn 6.52-59 explains the enigmatic saying at the end of 6.35-51: 'I am the living bread which came down from heaven; if anyone eats of this bread, he will live for ever; and the bread which I shall give for the life of the world is my flesh'. The reference to flesh reminds the reader of the Prologue's statement about the λόγος becoming flesh (1.14). The way in which Jesus will give his flesh (and blood) is by voluntary death, and 6.52-59 explains the meaning of Jesus' death. That the disciples are to eat the flesh of the Son of man and to drink his blood (6.53-54) seems to point to their involvement in voluntary death too (12.23-26). The reason why this is a Son of man saying now becomes clear: it emphasizes Jesus' humanity, a humanity subject to death, and it calls the disciples to share in his voluntary dedication. This is 'the food which endures to eternal life which the Son of man will give' (6.27).

It is not surprising that this teaching is rejected by former followers (6.60-61). They are taunted by Jesus' question: 'Then what if you were to see the Son of man ascending where he was before?' If the followers take offence at teaching about Jesus' death, how much more will they take offence at the actuality: Jesus' ascent, to Jerusalem where he was before (2.13), whence he will ascend to the Father, is a return which begins with the ascent on the cross, hence it is the ascent of 'the Son of man'. Jesus' vulnerability is most obvious in his death, and the fact that this is a Son of man saying hints at what will be made more explicit later, that the disciples must share in Jesus' death:

13.12-20; 13.36; 14.6; 15.13, 20-27 and 16.33.

The play on the literal and metaphorical meanings of ἀναβαίνω (go up)—Jesus goes up to Jerusalem (literal) and he goes up to the Father (metaphorical)—is repeated at the beginning of ch. 7, in Jesus' discussion with his brothers. They urge him to go to the Feast of Tabernacles in Jerusalem in order to display his works there (7.3-4) but Jesus assures them that 'I am not going up (ἀναβαίνω) to this feast, for my time is not yet fulfilled' (7.8). But afterwards Jesus does go to Jerusalem and teaches in the Temple during the feast (7.10, 14-24). Nevertheless, this is not the feast during which Jesus is crucified, rises and ascends to the Father. Hence he does not 'go up' to the Father at this feast.

The next occurrence of the term 'the Son of man' is in 8.28: 'Jesus said: When you have lifted up the Son of man, then you will know that I am he, and that I do nothing on my own authority but speak thus as the Father taught me'. Chapter 8 presents Jesus as the light of the world (8.12) but sets his teaching in a context in which 'people love darkness rather than light (3.19). The dialogue (8.21-30) begins with a misunderstanding by the 'Jews' who think that Jesus' reference to his departure means that he intends to kill himself. Ironically, this is half-true, but 'Jewish' unbelief in Jesus as the one sent by God means that they will die in sin, since their rejection of Jesus is a rejection of light and life. The 'Jewish' question 'Who are you?' provides an opportunity to explore the relationship of Jesus to the Father, as in 5.19-24. Since this teaching is not understood, Jesus again mentions his death, 8.28: 'When *you* have lifted up the Son of man', that is when the 'Jews' have brought about Jesus' crucifixion, 'then you will know that I am he', that is the 'Jews' will be offered for acknowledgement this evidence that he is the light of the world sent by the Father (cf. 12.32). The use of 'the Son of man' in a saying about the crucifixion is understandable in that it stresses Jesus' vulnerable humanity but does it carry overtones of a representative character? The dialogue continues with further exposition of 8.24, the opposition between slavery to sin which leads to death and freedom from sin which leads to eternal life (8.31-38). This section is mainly concerned with the meaning of Jesus' crucifixion as, on one hand, a revelation of the Father's life-giving love and, on the other hand, a demonstration of the lengths to which people (represented by the 'Jews') will go in rejecting God, but the theme of discipleship, touched upon briefly in 8.30, is not explored until ch. 9.

The opposition between Jesus as the light of the world, and 'the Jews' who love darkness rather than light, reaches a climax in the sign: the healing of the man blind from birth (9.1-34). His support of Jesus leads to exclusion from the synagogue (9.34), but Jesus finds him and asks: 'Do you believe in the Son of man?' (9.35). (Many manuscripts read 'Son of God' instead of 'Son of man', but 'Son of man' is undoubtedly the original reading since [a] it has earlier and more diverse manuscript support, and [b] it is the more difficult, giving rise to the variant in later manuscripts.) Why does John pose the question of belief in terms of the Son of man?

The dialogues with the man born blind, the man's parents, and the Pharisees concern Jesus' relationship to God: is Jesus a sinner, or is he a prophet? Had Jesus asked the man if he believed in the Son of God, this would have answered the question. By asking whether the man believes in 'the Son of man', John both provides a suitable introduction for the following statement about judgment and renews the reader's awareness of Jesus' human vulnerability. Further, the Son of man confession seeks the involvement of the disciples—the man excluded from the synagogue community is drawn into Jesus' community—and prepares the reader for the double image of the door and the good shepherd in the discourse to which the incident leads (ch. 10). Not only is Jesus the good shepherd, who lays down his life for the sheep (10.11-14), but he is also the door (10.7-9) through which followers must enter to make his way their own.

The Son of man sayings in 12.23, 34 follow the request by the Greeks to see Jesus (12.20-21), which is not granted immediately; instead Jesus talks of his death. In the parable of the good shepherd the reference to bringing in sheep from another fold (10.16) comes after the reference to the good shepherd's laying down his life for the sheep (10.11-15), which suggests that it is through Jesus' death that all peoples are invited to share in the new humanity. During Jesus' earthly ministry the call is made to Jews, Galilaeans and Samaritans only; after Jesus' death it is made to Gentiles too. Jesus' reply: 'The hour has come for the Son of man to be honoured' refers to his death, which the Gospel calls the hour when Jesus is honoured (e.g. 2.4; 8.20; 12.27-28; 17.1). His death is likened to a grain of wheat which has to fall into the ground to bear fruit (here the Gentile mission is probably included), and the necessity of Jesus' death is linked to the fate of the disciples:

> He who loves his life loses it, and he who hates his life in this world will keep it for eternal life. If anyone serves me, he must follow me; and where I am there shall my servant be also; if anyone serves me, the Father will honour him (12.25-26).

'The Son of man' is used both to emphasize Jesus' humanity in a reference to his free self-sacrifice, and to call disciples to share in it.

Jesus' acceptance of his mission and God's acceptance of Jesus are dramatically portrayed (12.27-30). The rest of the chapter summarizes Jesus' message to the world in an epilogue to the *Book of Signs*. The hour when Jesus is honoured represents not the judgment of men against Jesus, but God's judgment of the world: the conquest of evil ('Now shall the ruler of this world be cast out' 12.31) and the offer of life to all people ('And I, when I am lifted up from the earth, will draw all the people to myself'). The two verbs ὑψόω ('to lift up') and δοξάζω ('to honour') which come at the beginning of the *Servant Song* in Isa. 52.13 (LXX), present Jesus' death on a cross as both his uplifting and his honouring. Jn 12.32 describes Jesus' death as an act that will draw everyone to himself, that is, that will potentially involve all people, and the crowd responds by appropriately introducing the term 'the Son of man' (12.34). Jesus speaks of his own death, but his death exemplifies what is required of his followers. It is therefore fitting that the last words of the 'Jewish' crowds during Jesus' public ministry are: 'Who is this Son of man?' (12.34). Once again the term is used in connection with Jesus' death to stress both the representative and the vulnerable nature of his humanity. Finally, after the footwashing and the prophecy about the betrayer (13.1-30), the Farewell Discourses begin with Jesus' declaration to his disciples: 'Now is the Son of man honoured and in him God is honoured' (13.31), which both sums up previous teaching and provides a heading for the discourses that follow. Jesus' death brings honour both to himself and to God because it is the completion of Jesus' mission (3.16-21 and 12.31-36). The disciples are called to deserve honour by following his example (13.12-17; 15.12-17; 17.22; 21.19).

Although 19.5, Pilate's declaration: 'Behold the man', is not a 'Son of man' saying, it would fit the meaning given for 'Son of man'.

Perhaps the Semitic expression is changed into its Greek equivalent for the lips of a Gentile (Sevenster 1970).

I have now examined every instance of 'the Son of man' in the Fourth Gospel, except those in 3.13 and 14, and have found that a consistent sense emerges which is explicable against the background of the Semitic use: 'the Son of man' indicates Jesus' representative humanity.

Does this meaning hold for the two sayings in 3.13-14? The verses form part of the dialogue with Nicodemus, in which the radical change, the rebirth, that Jesus demands leaves Nicodemus puzzled and Jesus exasperated. Jesus asks him: 'If I have told you earthly things and you do not believe, how can you believe if I tell you heavenly things?' (3.12). The point of the contrast here is that Jesus had tried to help Nicodemus to recognize that earthly experiences like being born and hearing the wind point beyond themselves to God: creation points to the Creator, but Nicodemus remains puzzled in spite of being encouraged to go beyond only the most superficial understanding of life. How then could he believe 'heavenly things', since 'no on has ascended into heaven'? (cf. Prov. 30.4). In other words, no one has personal experience of God, he is dependent on what he can learn about the Creator from his experience of the world. There is an exception to the general rule that 'no one has ascended into heaven' however: it is 'he who descended from heaven, the Son of man. And as Moses lifted up the serpent in the wilderness, so must the Son of man be lifted up, that whoever believes in him may have eternal life' (3.13-14). The saying in v. 14 fits into the pattern we have found in ch. 8: as those Israelites who looked up at the serpent on the standard in the wilderness were directed to God and lived (Num. 21.9), so those who believe in the Son of man lifted up on the cross will have eternal life, if they continue in the way he exemplifies (13.12-20). 'The heavenly things' to which Jesus refers turn out to be his death as both the revelation of God's love to humanity (3.16-21), and the result of people's evil deeds. It is not until these themes are developed in chs. 6, 8, 9 and 10 that the representative nature of Jesus' death is brought out.

But what does v. 13 mean? A contrast is made between the experience of everyone and the experience of *the* Son of man. The Son of man understands 'heavenly things' and manifests God's love in his death. He is not 'from below' but 'from above' (see the earlier teaching to

Nicodemus 3.3, and 8.23 just before the Son of man sayings in 8.28). The language of descent and ascent, of origin 'from above' makes a claim to knowledge of God. The imagery is parallel to 1.51: the Son of man manifests a new revelation of God which people are to make their own. The revelation comes only through Jesus and those who share his humanity, who themselves are born 'from above': hence the use of term 'Son of man'. The story will relate that Jesus, the Son of man, ascends to the Father when his mission is completed (20.17), and Jesus promises his followers that they will join him there (14.3). At the time when the Gospel was written, then, there is one exception to the general rule that no one has ascended to heaven (3.13). It is Jesus who descended from heaven. But the disciples can look forward to dwelling with him in the future, if they share his destiny (14.3).

It is only if 3.13 is read with Gnostic redeemer myths in mind that it appears to say something about the descent of the Primal Man from heaven. Read in the context of the other Son of man sayings in the Fourth Gospel, it makes an exclusive claim for the validity of the revelation in the Son of man's uplifting on the cross. In laying down their lives as Jesus did, the disciples continue his mission of making God known to humanity.

Chapter 9

FURTHER METAPHORS OF JESUS' EXEMPLARY HUMANITY

The Fourth Gospel's portrait of Jesus as Son of God and Son of man elaborates its central theme, Jesus' complete dependence upon God, in order to provide its readers with a perception of human dignity which is to inspire their lives. This central theme is enriched by a series of sayings in which Jesus declares who he is: 'I am the bread of life' (6.35, 48); 'I am the bread which came down from heaven' (6.41 cf. v. 51); 'I am the light of the world' (8.12); 'I am the door of the sheep' (10.7); 'I am the good shepherd' (10.11); 'I am the resurrection and the life' (11.25); 'I am the way, the truth and the life' (14.6); 'I am the true vine' (15.1). With each of these sayings and their explanations, Jesus both proposes a particular way of life which he encapsulates and opposes alternatives. Emphasis falls both on the 'I' and on the predicate.

1. *The Bread of Life*

Hunger and starvation bring people to despair at the callousness of their fellows, to disillusion with life's meaning, and to death. In the first-century world, as in much of the world today, hunger and starvation were often in prospect for the poor. The Johannine Jesus' miracle of the feeding of the five thousand (6.1-14) and the following discourse on the bread of life seeks to dispel despair and disillusion, and to present death as the prelude to resurrection. Jesus, as the prophet (6.14), fulfils the expectations of a second Moses (Exod. 16; Num. 11; Deut. 18.15, 18) or a second Elisha (2 Kgs 4.42-44) in feeding the hungry, multiplying the loaves and fish supplied by the lad (6.9), to satisfy the needs of the people, even exceeding their requirements and leaving the disciples with twelve baskets of fragments (6.12-13). The story illustrates what happens when care replaces callousness. Moreover, the miracle, like all Johannine signs, points beyond the immediate human context to a theological context: Jesus is the vehicle of the Creator God's care for the world. Nevertheless, God does not feed the hungry without the active agency of his prophet. In other words, theological perception is dependent on human obedience. The discourse serves to elucidate this theological dimension.

It therefore opens with the correction of a misunderstanding. The crowds are not 'to labour for the food that perishes' (6.27; see Deut. 8.3; Wis. 16.26; Isa. 55.1-11; Sir. 15.3), that is, they are not to run after Jesus as a miracle worker who has just satisfied their immediate hunger,

> but for the food which endures to eternal life, which the Son of man will give to you; for on him has God the Father set his seal. . . This is the work of God, that you believe in him whom he has sent (6.27-29).

In believing in Jesus as God's agent, the crowds are encouraged to accept Jesus, the Son of man, as the representative of a humanity they are to share. Jesus advocates not passive acceptance of the gift God gives through him, but active participation in the role which he is playing. When Jesus declares 'I am the bread of life; he who comes to me shall not hunger, and he who believes in me shall never thirst' (6.35), he describes who he is in the manner of personified Wisdom (Prov. 8.12-21; Sir 24.3-31). In Prov. 9.5 Wisdom encouraged people to 'come, eat of my bread and drink of the wine I have mixed', and in Sir. 24.21 Wisdom promises 'whoever feeds on me will be hungry for more, and whoever drinks from me will thirst for more'. Jesus' statement transposes these Wisdom sayings in two ways. First of all, it emphasizes the complete nourishment which Jesus supplies, and secondly, it speaks not of Wisdom but of himself, a human being.

The crowd's reluctance to accept their responsibility (6.30-34) leads Jesus to explain his role more fully. 'Coming down from heaven', that is, doing the Father's will (6.39), Jesus is the bread of life, the nourishment that sustains life both within its present mortal limitations and beyond death (6.39-40). 'Eternal life', an expression taken from Dan. 12.2, depicts a quality of life, selfconsciously oriented to doing God's will, and life which does not end in death but leads to resurrection and a continuing existence which is transformed, no longer mortal, no longer confined to history. Believers who make

Jesus' life their own, who eat the true bread which he is, are those drawn by the Father (6.44 cf. LXX Jer. 38[31].3) whose purpose is re-creative (6.41-51).

But 6.51 ends on a surprising note: 'And the bread that I shall give for the life of the world is my flesh'. Up to this point God's purpose had been delineated in purely positive terms: life and eternal life. Jn 6.51-58 modifies this overly optimistic picture by elaborating Jesus' role in a new way. Like bread which is destroyed when it is consumed, Jesus, the bread of life, is destroyed in order to be consumed. The discourse, then, does not envisage life and eternal life as an avoidance of death, but death, in obedience to God, as the route to eternal life. This is the way the Gospel will describe Jesus taking, and believers are encouraged to 'remain in' Jesus (6.56), to continue to follow the path he pioneers. This Passover story in ch. 6 helps to explain the Passover story in ch. 19 when Jesus dies on a cross.

2. *The Light of the World*

Without light we are completely blind, disoriented and unable to find our way. In appropriately setting Jesus' claim to be the light of the world, the human world, at the Feast of Tabernacles in the Temple, the Gospel offers assurance of guidance, as the light burning continually in the Temple reassured worshippers of God's continuing presence to give the light of guidance (2 Chron. 4.20; Pss. 43.3; 119.105; Prov. 6.23). So Jesus is the light of the world in the sense that he illustrates how to live a full and obedient human life: 'He who follows me will not walk in darkness but will have the light of life' (8.12; cf. Job 29.3; 33.30; Wis. 18.4; Sir. 50.29; Isa. 2.5). Acknowledging his dependence on God, knowing whence he came and whither he is going (8.14), recognizing his mission from God (8.18), he opposes those who reject the light his life sheds, especially the Pharisees, whose blindness leads to their death (8.21, 24) and whose perspectives are distorted by their worldliness (8.23, 40-47). They had already planned to arrest Jesus (7.45-52), condemning him without a hearing. Once again, then, the text draws attention to Jesus as one who does what is pleasing to God (8.29), even when it includes allowing his opponents to lift him up (on a cross) (8.28). It is this complete obedience and fidelity to God which brings freedom (8.32), not the freedom of descendents who rely on their privileged birth from the patriarch Abraham (8.33), but freedom from sin, which is disobedience, immorality, infidelity, unbelief. Jesus, like the prophet Ezekiel, warns people that their wickedness will yield death (Ezek. 3.18). True descendents of Abraham would follow their forebear's example in rejoicing at the light Jesus sheds, the fulfilment of Abraham's mission to be a blessing (8.56-58 cf. Gen. 12.2), because death is overcome by life (8.51-52). Jesus therefore signifies something of the meaning of his assertions by performing the sign of giving sight to the man born blind (9.1-7), but even this demonstration serves only to confirm the blindness of his opponents (9.40-41).

These chapters illustrate the paradigmatic description of Jesus' mission in 3.19-20:

> And this is the judgment, that the light has come into the world, and people loved darkness rather than light, because their deeds were evil. For everyone who does evil hates the light, and does not come to the light, lest their deeds should be exposed. But he who does what is true [literally, 'does the truth', a Semitic expression derived from the Septuagint. e.g. Gen. 47.29, Josh. 2.14, 2 Sam. 2.6, where it means 'to deal faithfully'] comes to the light, that it may be clearly seen that his deeds have been wrought in God.

It is God, then, who bears witness with Jesus (8.18), and whose honour Jesus seeks (8.49-50).

3. *The Door*

In the opening verses of ch. 10 Jesus depicts the contrast between the part played by the Pharisees (the thief and robber, v. 1) and by himself (the shepherd, v. 2 cf. Ezek. 34). Jesus is the shepherd whose sheep recognize his voice and follow him (vv. 3-4), as the man born blind had done. The metaphor of seeing is replaced by that of hearing. The sheep do not follow strangers, that is, thieves and robbers (v. 5, cf. the description of the self-serving shepherds, Ezek. 34.1-6).

Since Jesus' cryptic discourse (παροιμία, v. 6) fails to enlighten the Pharisees, however, he is forced to try again. This time he makes a slightly different contrast, between the Pharisees ('all who came before' must refer to the Pharisees, and not, for example, to John the Baptist or to the prophets) as thieves and robbers once more (v. 8) and himself as 'the door of the sheep' (v. 7). The hearing metaphor is replaced by that of access. What he means by 'the door' is explained further: 'I am the door; if anyone enters by me, he will be saved, and will go in and out and find pasture. . . I came that they may have life and have it abundantly' (vv. 9-10 cf. Ezek. 34.23-31). The Fourth Gospel distinguishes two kinds of life. ψυχή stands for ordinary mundane existence which ends in death (e.g. 10.11, 15, 17; 13.37; 15.13), but ζωή, the word used here, stands for that life which is lived from God, and which therefore does not end in death (cf. Gen. 2.7). Thieves and robbers, on the other hand, 'come only to steal and kill and destroy' (v. 10). Jesus therefore claims that his way of life functions as the entrance to eternal life, whereas Pharisaic leadership results in destruction.

4. *The Good Shepherd*

Jn 10.11-18 then returns to the original metaphor of Jesus as the shepherd, now defined with the adjective καλός, which means 'model, ideal or good'. Picking up imagery from its Scripture, especially from Ezekiel 34, Jesus' leadership, as the model shepherd, is again differentiated from that of the Pharisees, who are mere hirelings. At the sight of a wolf, the hirling flees and leaves the sheep to their fate, whereas the good shepherd lays down his life for the sheep. Throughout the discourse, the metaphorical meanings of all the terms, sheep for people, shepherd for Jesus, thieves and hirelings for Pharisees, are obscuring their literal meanings. Shepherds do not normally call their individual sheep by name to lead them out of the pen (v. 3), nor do shepherds normally die when the sheep are threatened by a wolf (v. 11). They drive the wolf away or kill it. But since the Fourth Gospel wants to assert that Jesus is a model leader, a model shepherd, and Jesus did in fact die, the shepherd metaphor has to encompass that feature. So Jesus, the good shepherd, lays down his life for the sheep (vv. 11, 15), and he does so in accordance with what God demands (vv. 15, 18), and to be recognized by his own sheep (v. 14).

The sheep metaphor is then expanded to include those who are not of the original flock (v. 16, cf. the reference to gathering sheep who have been scattered abroad, Ezek. 34.11-16), presumably in John a reference to Gentiles who become followers of Jesus after his death, and whose unity with the first flock (Jews) is ensured by their obedience to the one shepherd (v. 16). Since in laying down his life, Jesus fulfils the Father's will, the Father loves him (v. 17). Jesus freely lays it down and freely takes it again, because this is the command he received from the Father (v. 18).

In this section the teaching is about the nature of leadership, rather than about the nature of every person's relationship with God. Hence, in the appendix to the Gospel, ch. 21, Simon Peter is encouraged to accept the responsibility of leadership, in spite of his three denials (18.25-27), by Jesus' three questions and commands (21.15-17). When Simon affirms that he does love Jesus, Jesus tells him to feed and tend his sheep. And Simon too, as a model shepherd, will have to lay down his life (21.18-19).

5. *The Resurrection and the Life*

When Jesus replies to Martha's confession of faith in the resurrection of her brother, Lazarus, on the last day, at the end of history, with the assertion: 'I am the resurrection and the life (ζωή)' (11.25; most manuscripts, including $\mathfrak{P}^{66}$ and $\mathfrak{P}^{75}$ read 'and the life', although a few, including $\mathfrak{P}^{45}$, omit the phrase), he goes on to explain: 'He who believes in me, though he die, yet shall he live, and whoever lives and believes in me shall never die'. We noted earlier that the Fourth Gospel uses the term ζωή, in distinction from ψυχή, to suggest life lived from God which does not end in death, but a single verb, ζάω, refers to both ordinary physical existence (e.g. 4.50, 51, 53) and the life which extends beyond the grave (e.g. 6.57, 58). Jesus' elucidations correspond to his original double claim. 'I am the resurrection' is explained by 'he who believes in me, though he die, yet shall he live'. He who believes in Jesus, who follows his example, will also follow Jesus in dying physically, but, as he was, will be resurrected to an eternal post-mortem existence. 'I am the life' is explained by 'he who lives and believes in me will never die'. Taken literally, the last clause, 'will never die', contradicts the first statement about dying and living post-mortem (unless it should be translated 'shall not die forever'). If it is correctly translated 'will never die', it has to be taken to mean that belief in Jesus makes death irrelevant. This second statement stresses the importance of faith in Jesus while a person is alive ('lives physically and believes').

Jesus then intimates something of the meaning of his contention by bringing Lazarus back from the dead (11.43-44). Like the feeding miracle which satisfies people's immediate hunger, but points beyond its limited effectiveness to a fuller satisfaction in eternal life, Lazarus's resuscitation, his restoration to ordinary, mortal existence, points beyond its limited effectiveness to resurrection, post-mortem transformation for eternal life.

The narrative of ch. 11 takes trouble to explain that Jesus' miracle is an act of love. Lazarus is described as a man beloved by Jesus (11.3, 5) and even the crowds discern Jesus' love when he weeps at the tomb (11.36). Moreover, this loving miracle brings honour both to God (11.4, 40) and to Jesus (11.4) whose obedient Son he is and whose mission he accomplishes (11.41-42). In this chapter, however, unlike the previous discourses explaining Jesus' self-designations, nothing is said of Jesus' death. Nevertheless, in the next chapter, Jesus' death becomes the theme which links the individual incidents: Mary's anointing is for burial (12.7), Jesus rides into Jerusalem not in triumph but in humility, sitting on an ass's colt (12.12-15), Jesus interprets his imminent death as wheat falling into the ground and dying in order to bear fruit (12.20-25), and he resolutely faces his final hour, the hour of his death (12.27), to bring honour to God and himself, and to draw everybody into his life (12.32). Not only so, but as in earlier more cryptic statements about his death, Jesus' disciples are encouraged to follow him through death to life. Lazarus's existence is now just as perilous as Jesus' (12.10), and, after the simile of the wheat's dying to bear fruit, the disciples are told straightforwardly: 'He who loves his life loses it, and he who hates his life in this world, will keep it for eternal life. If anyone serves me, he must follow me; and where I am there shall my servant be also' (12.25-26).

6. *The Way, the Truth and the Life*

At the supper table, just before the crucifixion, Jesus reassures the disciples by looking beyond the immediate future and beyond the world to a vision of dwelling with God (14.2). Jesus interprets his death in terms of this vision, so that his departure has purpose from the disciples' perspective—he goes to prepare a place for them in his Father's house. The promise in 14.3, that preparation will naturally lead to Jesus' return in order to take them to be with him, prompts the remark: 'And you know the way where I am going' (14.4; alternatively, some manuscripts read: 'Where I am going you know, and the way you know').

To conceive life as a way, a road towards a destination, is common in many linguistic and cultural traditions. In English the metaphor is so habitual that it hardly seems metaphorical in expressions like 'a way of life', 'Did she get her own way?', 'It's out of harm's way'. In Johannine Scripture the metaphor is particularly valued in depicting alternative ways of life, as for example in exhortatory sections of Deuteronomy:

> The Lord will establish you as a holy people to himself, if you keep the commandments of the Lord your God, and walk in his ways (28.9).

If not,

> you shall grope at noonday, as the blind grope in darkness, and you shall not prosper in your ways (28.29).

Again,

> If you will be careful to do all this commandment which I command you to do, loving the Lord your God, walking in all his ways and cleaving to him, then the Lord will drive out all the nations before you. . . Behold, I set before you this day a blessing and a curse, the blessing if you obey the commandments of the Lord your God. . . the curse if you do not obey the commandments of the Lord your God, but turn aside from the way which I command you this day (Deut. 11.22-26 cf. 2 Chron. 6.16, 27, 31; 17.6).

Moreover, one way leads to life and the other to death:

> If you obey the commandments of the Lord your God which I command you this day, by loving the Lord your God, by walking in his ways, and keeping his commandments and his statutes and his ordinances, then you shall live and multiply, and the Lord your God will bless you. . . But if your heart turns away, and you do not hear . . .I declare to you this day that you shall perish. . . I have set before you life and death, blessing and curse; therefore choose life (Deut. 30.16-19).

When the Johannine Jesus declares that he is the way, the truth and the life, he brings together concepts which were already associated in Scripture, the way to life is fidelity to God. Moreover, the way metaphor dominates the whole saying, way, truth and life, as its development shows: 'No one comes to the Father but by me'.

This metaphor of 'the way' is already familiar from earlier parts of the Gospel, too. In fulfilling Isaiah's prophecy, John the Baptist is to 'make straight the way of the Lord' (1.23.), a role which he plays by summarizing Jesus' role as that of 'the lamb of God who takes away the sin of the world' (1.29). And Jesus' way is to be followed by the disciples (1.37; 10.4; 12.19, 26). Jn 8.12 even uses the same imagery as Deut. 28.29: 'He who follows me will not walk in darkness but will have the light of life' (cf. 11.9; 12.35; and Job 33.30; Ps. 56.13). Jesus is the pioneer whose followers must take the same road, no longer, as in Deuteronomy, to a long and prosperous but mortal life, but through death to eternal life. Naturally, Jesus' opponents suppose that he is merely leading people astray (7.12, 47; 12.11).

Since the Fourth Gospel does not present Jesus' life and character in terms of gradual development, however, the way metaphor is not expanded, as it could have been and was, for example, in Bunyan's *Pilgrim's Progress*, to illustrate different vicissitudes on the journey. On the contrary, the Gospel generally prefers a static metaphor which pictures individuals as dwelling places, housing the Spirit (e.g. 'You know him [the Spirit of Truth] for he dwells with you and will be in you', 14.17), or the Father (e.g. 'Do you not know that I am in the Father and the Father in me', 14.10), or Jesus' words (e.g. 'My words abide in you', 15.7) or Jesus himself (e.g. 'He who eats my flesh and drinks my blood abides [μένω] in me and I in him', 6.56). Conversely, 'love' is a dwelling place in which the disciples remain ('You will abide in my love', 15.10) as they abide in Jesus (6.56 above, or 'He who abides in me and I in him', 15.7). Nevertheless, 'the way' and 'the dwelling' metaphors are coordinated by the suggestion that the Father or Jesus draws people to himself (6.44; 12.32), and by the picture of the disciples' final destination in the Father's house (14.2).

'Truth' in Greek has as wide a range of possible meanings as in English, indicating a quality or state of being true, real, genuine, accurate, honest, sincere, or loyal. Hence its opposites are 'lie', 'unreality', 'sham', 'inaccuracy', 'dishonesty' or 'disloyalty'. The Septuagint exhibits this range, but since 'truth' is often combined with 'mercy' or 'grace' to describe people's or God's fidelity (e.g. Josh. 2.14; 2 Sam. 2.6; Ps. 25.10; Est. 2.9, 16, 17; Sir. 7.33; 40.17; cf. the Prologue, 1.14 and 17), some scholars have argued that the idea of fidelity dominates (but see Barr 1961: 187-205). The meaning of 'truth' in Jn 14.6 must therefore be defined by its immediate and general context in the Gospel. Since the Fourth Gospel gives such prominence to the idea of Jesus' obedience to the Father, 'I am the truth' must include the connotation of fidelity, but the combination of 'truth' with 'way' and 'life' also suggests the notion 'genuineness'. Jesus' life is the genuine way to live, not a false way which leads people astray. His example demonstrates what the Creator requires of his creatures, it encapsulates 'the truth' about human existence, that it is to be lived in conscious fidelity to God. De la Potterie (1986) points to the close association of 'truth' and 'wisdom' in Scripture (e.g. Prov. 23.23; Sir. 4.28) and to 'truth' and λόγος in the Fourth Gospel (e.g. 17.17; cf. 8.40 and Prov. 22.21). As the instantiation of God's plan for humanity, Jesus represents the truth in which the disciples are to be sanctified (17.17 cf. 8.31-32).

As elsewhere in the Gospel, ζωή, in contrast to ψυχή, means life lived from God, and hence a life which does not end in death. The combination of the three words in the saying 'I am the way, the truth and the life; no one comes to the Father but by me' encapsulates Jesus' exemplary significance for the disciples and for the whole of humanity.

7. *The True Vine*

Israel's infidelity to God is sometimes criticized in prophetic oracles which represent Israel as a vine or a vineyard. For example, Hos. 10.1 links the prosperity of Israel with its false worship:

> Israel is a luxuriant vine that yields its fruit. The more his fruit increased, the more altars he built; as his country improved, he improved his pillars.

Similarly Isa. 5.1-2 depicts God's frustrated love for Israel:

> Let me sing for my beloved [God] a love song concerning his vineyard [Israel]. My beloved had a vineyard on a very fertile hill. He digged it and cleared it of stones, and planted it with choice vines; he built a watchtower in the midst of it, and hewed out a wine vat in it; and he looked for it to yield grapes, but it yielded wild grapes (see also Ezek. 17.5-10; 19.10-14; and Jer. 2.21).

When, therefore, the Fourth Gospel has Jesus say, 'I am the true vine' (15.1), he professes the fidelity and genuine character of his sonship in contrast to Israel's infidelity and falsity. In the Exodus story Israel had been called God's 'first-born (πρωτότοκος) son' (Exod. 4.22), in the

Fourth Gospel, Jesus is called God's 'only (μονογενής) son' (3.16), that is, the only son who truly fulfils Israel's destiny. It is because he fulfils Israel's destiny that he becomes the light of the whole world (8.12 cf. Isa. 42.6). He is, then, the true vine, whose Father is the vinedresser (15.1). Yet again, Jesus' dependence on the Father is the premiss from which all else follows.

Since the statement is addressed to the disciples in the Farewell Discourses, the figure is developed to explain the relationship of the disciples to Jesus, the true vine. They are its branches (15.2-6). The purpose of the branches is to bear fruit, but the initial exploration of the figure is negative, a warning to those who do not bear fruit: 'Every branch of mine that bears no fruit he [the Father] takes away' (15.2). The statement makes clear that the disciples can have no lasting life apart from that within the vine, tended by the vinedresser. They are not to be disobedient sons, as Israel was. Moreover, even the second development of the image is not wholly positive: 'Every branch that does bear fruit, he [the Father] prunes (καθαίρει) that it may bear more fruit'. καθαίρω means 'to make clean' and is appropriately used of branches of a vine which are stripped of superfluous growths to make them more fruitful. In the context of the world's hatred of Jesus and the disciples (15.18-25), the pruning of branches is a suitable subject. Further, the disciples are made clean by 'the λόγος which I (Jesus) have spoken to you' (15.3), that is, by their keeping Jesus' commandments (15.10).

The elucidation of this teaching in 15.4-11, however, uses language which hardly belongs in discourse about a vine, but which reintroduces a term from Jesus' earlier teaching, the verb μένω which means 'to abide or remain'. (The same verb is used in Isa. 5.2, 4 and 7, but in the sense of God's waiting, rather than abiding or remaining, for the vines to produce grapes.) '*Abide* in me and I in you. As the branch cannot bear fruit by itself, unless it *remains* in the vine, neither can you unless you *remain* in me' (15.4, and see the discussion of μένω earlier in this chapter). Just as one would not normally expect a shepherd to lay down his life for the sheep, so one would not normally draw attention to branches remaining in a vine. The metaphorical meaning of branches as disciples is determining the vocabulary. But this teaching is a necessary development from the earlier statement about the vinedresser (the Father) removing branches (the disciples) which do not bear fruit. The disciples, unlike branches, are consciously to remain 'in Jesus', their lives are to grow out of his life, so that they can bear fruit (15.4-5). Apart from Jesus, they can do nothing worthwhile. So the first teaching about the branch which is cut off is repeated: 'If someone does not remain in me, he is cast forth as a branch and withers; and the branches are gathered, thrown into fire and burned' (15.6). In other words, Jesus' way leads to life, while alternatives lead to destruction.

The implications of abiding in Jesus are then spelt out:

> If you abide in me and my words abide in you, ask whatever you will and it shall be done for you. By this my Father is honoured, that you bear much fruit and so become [or prove to be] my disciples. As the Father has loved me so have I loved you; remain in my love. If you keep my commandments, you will remain in my love, just as I have kept my Father's commandments and remain in his love (15.7-10).

The disciples, then, are to be obedient, in contrast to the Israelites, but in conformity with Jesus. Moreover, the commandment which the disciples are to keep is 'to love one another as I have loved you' (15.12). To some extent this Johannine stress on abiding and remaining offsets another feature of Johannine rhetoric. Since people are continually presented with an either/or choice between two opposites, light or darkness, life or death, believing in Jesus or not, the impression is created that commitment to God is a once-for-all decision. But exhortations to remain in Jesus make it clear that there is really nothing final about an initial commitment, rather that the disciples have consciously to remain faithful, even when to do so will invite persecution.

As so often before, attention is drawn to Jesus' central significance. The unity of the disciples was earlier guaranteed by their belonging to the flock of one shepherd, following him. Here it is guaranteed by their attachment to the vine. These images are not exploited to express the mutual dependence of disciples on one another, as Pauline teaching about the body of Christ is (e.g. 1 Cor. 12). Even when the disciples are told to love one another (15.12), it is Jesus' example they are to follow. Over and over again, the Gospel teaches what is fundamental: conformity to the life of Jesus.

Chapter 10

JESUS THE MESSIAH AND THE SAVIOUR OF THE WORLD

1. *Jesus the Messiah*

A.E. Harvey's book, *Jesus on Trial* (1976), draws attention to the fact that the whole of the Fourth Gospel, not just chs. 18 and 19, presents the trial of Jesus. From the beginning there are witnesses for the defence, John, the disciples, some of the 'Jews', and, most importantly, the Father, and there are witnesses for the prosecution, other 'Jews' and especially their leaders, the Pharisees and the chief priests. The central issue which divides them is whether Jesus is the messiah or someone who leads the people astray. Often, alternative responses to Jesus are presented as a background chorus, groups within the crowd expressing opposing views.

The testimony of John in the Prologue is couched in suitably general terms. He bears witness to the light (1.6) and to the one who comes after him but ranks before him (1.15). The second testimony is repeated in the account of John's ministry which follows the Prologue (1.30). We are probably to infer from John's refusal of the roles, Christ, Elijah and the prophet (1.21), that Jesus will play those roles, since the rest of the Gospel depicts his doing so, and John himself acknowledges Jesus' messiahship (3.28). Moreover, John asserts that he is to prepare the way for someone who is so much greater than himself that he is unworthy to untie the thong of his sandal (1.27). John is to make this person's presence known to Israel (1.31). He identifies Jesus as the lamb of God who takes away the sin of the world (1.29 and 36), as the chosen one (or son) of God (1.34) and as the one on whom the Spirit descends and remains (1.33). Like the kings of Scripture, then, Jesus, God's chosen one, is endowed with God's Spirit (1 Sam. 16.6-13).

Those who are attracted to follow Jesus also recognize him as the messiah. Andrew announces to his brother, Simon Peter, 'We have found the messiah' (1.41). Philip tells Nathanael, 'We have found him of whom Moses in the law and also the prophets wrote, Jesus of Nazareth, the son of Joseph' (1.45). Nathanael is, however, sceptical about someone from Nazareth (1.46), but Jesus' remarkable insight convinces Nathanael that he is 'the Son of God' and 'the king of Israel' (1.49). It has been argued in Chapter 5 that 'Son of God' refers to Jesus' status as the faithful Israelite who fulfils God's purpose for Israel, his first-born son (Exod. 4.22). If this is correct, Nathanael recognizes Jesus as a true Israelite who is Israel's king.

At the end of ch. 1, therefore, the reader is left in no doubt about Jesus' identity, but is urged to accept Jesus as the messiah, chosen by God, endowed with God's spirit, in fulfilment of the promises found in the law and the prophets (Deut. 17.14-20; Isa. 9 and 11; Mic. 5.2-4). The rest of the Gospel explores this role and counters disclaimers.

Chapter 3 returns to the testimony of John. Once again he denies that he is the Christ (3.28) but affirms his own function as the one sent before him (3.28) and as the friend of the bridegroom, rejoicing at his voice (3.29). The voice of the bridegroom illustrates rejoicing in prophesies like Jer. 7.34, 16.9, 25.10, and 33.11. In Isa. 62.10 the people whom the Lord has blessed extol God, 'For he has clothed me with the garments of salvation, he has covered me with the robe of righteousness, as a bridegroom decks himself with a garland'. John's testimony to Jesus as the bridegroom hints at the joy and salvation God bestows through him.

In ch. 4 Jesus himself acknowledges that he is the messiah (4.25-26). His declaration prompts the Samaritan woman to raise, albeit tentatively, with her fellow citizens whether he might be the messiah (4.29). She draws attention to his knowledge of everything she did. This refers back to his knowledge of her marital relations (4.17-18). The passage could be interpreted as a metaphorical reference to Samaritan religion, since Scripture commonly describes fidelity to God in terms of fidelity to a husband (e.g. Hos. 2.12-20; Jer. 2.2-3; 3.1-14). Moreover, this interpretation has the advantage that it appropriately introduces the discussion on genuine worship which follows (4.20-24) and which leads to Jesus' assertion of his messiahship. The primary role of the messiah, according to scriptural prophesies like those in Micah 5 and Isaiah 9 and 11, is to rule Israel justly. But such a mission was naturally thought to affect all the peoples in God's world. For example, Isa. 11.10 prophesies, 'In that day the root of Jesse shall stand as an ensign to the peoples; him shall the nations seek'. Again, Micah predicts that the messiah 'shall stand and feed his flock in the strength of the Lord, in the honour of the name of the Lord his God. And they shall dwell secure, for he shall be great to the ends of the earth' (5.4). The Samaritans who recognize Jesus as 'the Saviour of the world' (4.42), therefore, function as the prototype of the peoples who will be drawn to the messiah, Jesus.

Up to this point in the Gospel, Jesus' messiahship had been acknowledged and accepted. Indeed, in ch. 6 people respond to his feeding miracle by trying to make him king (6.15). Nevertheless, his assertion that he is the bread of life, giving his flesh for the life of the world, divides his audience so that all but the twelve leave him (6.66). In the chapters which follow, his messiahship is questioned and denied by those who do not believe in him.

The scene is set by discussions among groups at the Feast of Tabernacles. Some suggest that Jesus is a good man, others that he is leading the people astray (7.12). Further accusations against Jesus follow. When he mentions that the people are seeking to kill him (7.19), they respond by declaring that he has a demon (7.20), although later his contention is confirmed (7.25, 29, 32, 43, 45-52; 8.59). On the other hand, some of the people from Jerusalem raise the question whether the authorities really know that Jesus is the Christ (7.26). The identification is thought to be difficult because 'we know where this man comes from; and when the Christ appears, no one will know where he comes from' (7.27). Such a belief is expressed in 2 Esd. 13.52: 'Just as no one can know what is in the depths of the sea, so no one on earth can see my son or those who are with him, except in the time of his day'. Jesus, however, refutes the objection by pointing to God as the faithful initiator of his mission (7.28-29). At this point many of the people believe in him and ask the rhetorical question, 'When the Christ appears, will he do more signs than this man has done?' (7.31).

On the last day of the feast, after Jesus' teaching about the Spirit (7.37-39), some of the people accept him as 'the prophet' (7.40) while others acknowledge him to be the Christ (7.41). Still others, however, doubt that someone from Nazareth could be the Christ, since he was expected to come from David's village, Bethlehem (7.42). The Fourth Gospel, unlike those according to Matthew and Luke, never meets this difficulty by setting Jesus' birth in Bethlehem, and never calls Jesus the son of David. In fact, Jesus' life is so unlike that of David, as it is depicted in 1 Samuel 16–1 Kings 2, that the connexion which the Synoptics make could be misleading. Jesus' life is much closer to the descriptions of the messiah in Deuteronomy 17, Micah 5 and Isaiah 9 and 11. And the passage in Deuteronomy does not mention David, but defines the king as 'one whom the Lord your God will choose' (17.15). So, in the Fourth Gospel, Jesus is the messiah because God has chosen him to perform that role.

At the end of ch. 7 the officers who return to the chief priests and Pharisees without Jesus are accused of being led astray because they declare that no one speaks like Jesus (7.45-47). They are told that the authorities do not believe in him and that the crowd is ignorant of the law and therefore accursed (7.48-49). Even Nicodemus, who reminds his fellow leaders that the law requires a man to be given a hearing, is silenced by the retort that no prophet is to arise from Galilee (7.50-52).

Nevertheless, the Pharisees do give Jesus a hearing, and attempt to undermine his claims (8.12-20). Moreover, in spite of some 'Jewish' belief in Jesus (8.31), the discussion becomes more vitriolic. The 'Jews' claim to be descendents of Abraham and children of God (8.37, 39, 41) but Jesus asserts that they are kin neither to Abraham nor to God because they seek to kill him whom God has sent (8.40, 42). Rather, they are children of the devil who is a murderer (8.44-47). The crowd therefore accuses Jesus of being a Samaritan (presumably because Samaritans hold an equally low opinion of Jews) and possessed by a demon (8.48), a charge which Jesus counters by referring to the honour the Father accords him (8.49-50), and to the fact that his followers will not die (8.51). The crowds naturally interpret this statement as tantamount to a declaration of superiority to Abraham and the prophets who had died. This is evidence that he is certainly possessed by a demon (8.52-53). But Jesus simply reiterates that it is the Father who honours him, and that Abraham had rejoiced to see his day (8.54-56). The crowds then misunderstand him, and suppose that he is claiming to have seen Abraham (8.57) whereas he had asserted the reverse, that Abraham had rejoiced to see his day, because he is the light of the world (8.58). The reaction of the crowds is to pick up stones to throw at him, but Jesus escapes by hiding and withdrawing from the Temple (8.59).

After the healing of the man blind from birth, Jesus mounts an attack on his Pharisaic adversaries. He declares, 'For judgment I came into this world, that those who do not see may see [like the man born blind] and that those who see may become blind [like the Pharisees]' (9.39, see vv. 40-41). His discourse about the door and the good shepherd (10.1-18) contrasts his own leadership with that of the Pharisees. They are hirelings and thieves who care nothing for the sheep, whereas Jesus is the good shepherd who lays down his life for the sheep. The imagery is developed from Ezekiel 34. There God promises to gather the sheep into their own land to feed them with good pasture (34.13-14). The lost, the crippled and the weak will be restored and the strong watched over (34.16). The flock will be saved from its prey (34.22). And God 'will set over them one shepherd, my servant David, and he shall feed them. . . and I, the Lord will be their God and my servant David shall be prince among them' (34.23-24). The Fourth Gospel interprets this prophecy by identifying Jesus as the shepherd and by highlighting the way in which he will safeguard the sheep, in laying down his life. Once more, Jesus' audience is divided, some supposing that he has a demon and is mad, others doubting that Jesus' words and actions are those of someone possessed by a demon. As in some previous descriptions of the crowds' responses, those who defend Jesus have the last word. Only the chief priests and Pharisees are more certain in their opposition (10.19-21).

At the Feast of Renewal the 'Jews' demand, 'If you are the Christ, tell us plainly' (10.24). Only to the Samaritan woman had Jesus made such a specific declaration, although with the 'Jews' he had argued repeatedly that he was saying his Father's words and doing his Father's works, from which they could have inferred the answer to their question. In reply, therefore, Jesus repeats the argument (10.25-30). He explains their refusal to believe in terms of the metaphor explored in the first part of the chapter: 'You do not belong to my sheep' (10.26-27, see 10.14), and defines his own sheep as those given him by the Father (10.29-30). But Jesus' statement, 'I and the Father are one' (10.30) provokes his opponents to threaten him with stoning because they think he blasphemes (10.31-33), a charge Jesus refutes (10.34-36). Finally, Jesus appeals to them to recognize his works as those of the Father (10.37-38). He is unsuccessful, however, and escapes arrest by withdrawing across the Jordan to the place where John had baptized (10.39-40). There people confirm John's witness to

Jesus: 'John did no sign, but everything that John said about this man was true' (10.41-42).

Chapter 11 emphasizes that Jesus' return to Judaea jeopardizes his life (11.8, 16). But Jesus had explained in his discourse about the good shepherd that he would voluntarily lay down his life; it would not be taken from him (10.10-17). Moreover, the miracle he performs at Bethany brings a dead man back to life. Even before the miracle, however, his declaration, 'I am the resurrection and the life' (11.25-26) convinces Martha that he is 'the Christ, the Son of God, he who is coming into the world' (11.27). And the 'Jews' who were consoling the sisters, agree with them in supposing that one who had opened the eyes of the blind man could have kept Lazarus from dying (11.37). The prelude to the miracle, however, makes clear that Lazarus had already died and been buried in the tomb for four days (11.17 and 39), and that Jesus is dependent on his Father (11.41-42). In this context he calls Lazarus back to life, and evokes belief in many of the witnesses (11.45). Some nevertheless report to the Pharisees, who, together with the chief priests, call a council to decide what can be done with Jesus, since he performs such signs (11.46-47). They recognize the danger that if they allow him to continue everyone will believe in him. Then the Romans will see the threat to their power and will destroy both place and people (11.48). The high priest, Caiaphas, counsels that it is expedient for one man to die for the people so that the whole nation should not perish (11.50), advice which makes good sense in the political context of the story (compare Josephus, *War* 2.237), but which also takes on a theological meaning in the context of the narrative. This is spelt out by characterizing the advice as inspired prophecy (11.51-52) and by extending its significance to include all peoples. Jesus' withdrawal to the wilderness, however, implies that he is free to choose when to die (11.54).

The final events in Jerusalem at Passover are introduced once again with the crowd's question about Jesus. This time they wonder whether he will attend the feast since the Pharisees and chief priests had ordered people to report his whereabouts so that they could arrest him (11.56-57). But Jesus returns to Judaea quite openly. At Bethany Martha serves his supper with Lazarus, and Mary anoints him 'for the day of his burial' (12.1-8). This is an anointing of the messiah or shepherd who would lay down his life. Crowds are immediately attracted not only to Jesus but also to Lazarus. The chief priests then have to plan Lazarus's death too (12.9-11). Nevertheless, Jesus goes to Jerusalem where more crowds greet him with palm branches as if he is a victorious king: 'Hosanna, blessed is he who comes in the name of the Lord, even the king of Israel' (12.12-13). It is in response to this enthusiasm that Jesus rides an ass into Jerusalem, not in triumph, but in fulfilment of Zechariah's prophecy (Zech. 9.9, alluded to rather than quoted). Even the disciples, however, do not understand the significance of his action until later, after the crucifixion (12.16). And the crowds could bear witness only to the deed, not to its meaning. They had been impressed by Jesus' raising of Lazarus (12.17-18; see 2.23-25). Nevertheless, the Pharisees remark their powerlessness in the face of his popularity, 'You see you can do nothing; look, the world has gone after him' (12.19). Once again the reader is reminded that Jesus will lay down his life; it will not be taken from him.

The Pharisaic reference to 'the world' appropriately introduces a short section in which Greeks, that is non-Jews, are attracted to Jesus, although they do not succeed in meeting him (12.20-22). Instead, Jesus meditates on the significance of his death for his followers (12.23-26). The Fourth Gospel, unlike the Synoptics, tells no stories about Jesus' meetings with Gentiles, but insists that the mission to the Gentiles is the disciples' responsibility after his death (17.20-21). Only the conversion of the Samaritans suggests a wider mission.

Jesus' resolve to fulfill the Father's purpose by laying down his life is confirmed by a voice from heaven (12.27-28). As always, the crowds are divided in their interpretation of the event, some thinking it had thundered, others that an angel had spoken to him (12.29-30). Jesus then explains that his death signifies the judgment of the world by which the ruler of this world will be cast out. His death will draw all people to himself (12.31-33). The crowds understand that he refers to his death but infer from this that he cannot be the messiah since 'the Christ remains for ever' (12.34 cf. Dan. 7.13-14; *1 En.* 62.13-14). Their final statement before his arrest is therefore a question: 'Who is this Son of man?' (12.34). Jesus' final appeal is to urge them to believe in the light so that they may become sons of light (12.36). At the end of Jesus' healing and teaching ministry, therefore, he has failed to convince either his opponents or the crowds that he is the messiah. Even the authorities who do believe are too concerned with the reputation they have amongst their fellows (12.41-43). Moreover, the disciples do not fully understand him until later (12.16). Nevertheless, unbelief is interpreted in terms of God's purpose by paraphrasing Isaiah's oracles (12.36-41). Furthermore, Jesus' ministry is still not complete. His final act, laying down his life, is what will draw all people to him (12.32).

In the Johannine account of Jesus' arrest (18.1-11) the Roman soldiers and Jewish officers are led to the garden by Judas the betrayer. But they have no power over Jesus. He is fully aware of Judas' betrayal (13.21-30), and he gives himself into custody while securing the freedom of his followers. He it is who is determined to 'drink the cup which the Father has given me' (18.11).

When Jesus is taken to Annas, Caiaphas's father-in-law, the reader is reminded of Caiaphas's prophecy that it is expedient for one man to die for the people (18.12-14; see 11.49-52). As in the Synoptics, Jesus' steadfastness in the face of his opponents is juxtaposed with Peter's unfaithfulness (18.15-27). But even Peter's denial had been foretold by Jesus (13.36-38). Annas's question about Jesus' disciples and his teaching prompts him to appeal to those who had heard him speak, but, in contrast to the Synoptics, no witnesses are produced. Rather, Jesus' fate is to be decided by Pilate, since only he can pronounce the death penalty and so bring about what Jesus had predicted (18.31-32; see 12.32-33).

The trial before Pilate is constructed as a series of scenes between Pilate and the 'Jews' outside the praetorium, where they remain to avoid defilement (18.28), and between Pilate and Jesus within the praetorium. The first scene opens with Pilate's question: 'What accusation do you bring against this man?' (18.29). It is remarkable that the question is not answered by stating that Jesus is a messianic pretender who leads the people astray and threatens Roman security, since Pilate's first question to Jesus is about his kingship (18.33), and the crowds state later that 'everyone who makes himself a king sets himself against Caesar' (19.12). The narrative here and elsewhere in the Fourth Gospel gives the impression that it *re*tells a familiar story. The more general opening accusation, that Jesus is an evil-doer (18.10), however, allows the narrator to explore the theme of kingship in a more oblique way. In response to Pilate's first question, therefore, Jesus replies that his kingdom is 'not of this world'. To substantiate the point, he explains that had he been establishing a worldly kingdom, his servants would have fought to prevent his being handed to the 'Jews' (18.36). Nevertheless, as Pilate notices, he does not deny that he is a king. Indeed, that is the truth to which he has borne witness (18.37). Pilate, however, is not concerned with an other-wordly truth (18.38). Instead, he attempts to release Jesus by pronouncing his innocence and by referring to a 'Jewish' custom at Passover time (18.38-40; contrast Mt. 27.15, the governor's custom; Mk 15.8, Pilate's custom; Lk. 23.18 merely records the crowd's demand for Barabbas). Nevertheless, Pilate describes Jesus to the crowd as 'king of the Jews' (18.38) before submitting to their demand for Barabbas (18.40).

Pilate's decision to have Jesus scourged is not explained (19.1-3). Perhaps we should infer that this was punishment for claiming to be a king of any kind, since he is mockingly dressed and hailed as 'king of the Jews'. Nevertheless, for a second time, Pilate tells the crowd he is innocent, in spite of presenting him to them dressed as a king. This time, however, Pilate refers to him only as 'the man' (19.4-5). It is the chief priests and officers who respond with a demand for Jesus' crucifixion (19.6). This allowed Pilate to pronounce his innocence a third time (19.6), but the 'Jews' argue, 'We have a law, and by that law he ought to die, because he makes himself a son of God' (19.7). The wording is significant. These 'Jews" do not believe that God has chosen Jesus. Rather they think he has made himself a son of God. The law about the king in Deuteronomy 17 emphasizes that only an Israelite chosen by God can become Israel's king (Deut. 17.14-15).

Once more Pilate questions Jesus alone, this time asking about his origin (19.8-9). When Jesus makes no reply, Pilate threatens him with the governor's power over life and death, but Jesus places that claim in a broader context. Pilate has no power except that delegated to him 'from above', from God, and, in any case, he is the mere tool of those who delivered Jesus to him, as the rest of the narrative shows (19.10-11). Throughout the story Pilate seeks but fails to release Jesus.

His final attempt is thwarted by the 'Jewish' threat, 'If you release this man, you are no friend of Caesar; everyone who makes himself a king sets himself against Caesar' (19.12). Again, the 'Jews' see Jesus as someone who makes himself king. Nevertheless, when Pilate sits in judgment, his taunt, 'Behold your king' provokes the 'Jews' to deny their faith in God and confess instead 'we have no king but Caesar' (19.15).

The skilful use of dialogue in this narrative directs readers to accept Jesus as the messiah and to condemn Pilate for his ineptitude and the 'Jews' for their blindness. Finally, Jesus is crucified with a public acknowledgment of his messiahship written over the cross: 'Jesus of Nazareth, the king of the Jews' (19.19-20). The chief priests ask that the inscription be changed to 'This man said, I am the king of the Jews' but their request is denied and the acclamation stands (19.21-22).

The whole Gospel attempts to convince the reader that 'Jesus is the Christ, the Son of God' (20.31). It does so by repeatedly raising the question of his messiahship and by allowing Jesus to defend his claim against opposing views. And the opposition itself often wavers, now for, now against Jesus. Nevertheless, Jesus is not a king as David was. He is not a warrior who defeats Israel's enemies in war and founds a dynasty. Rather, in obedience to his Father, he is the Christ of a kingdom which is 'not of this world'. The community of disciples who follow his way does not seek honour from fellow human beings but from God. This community is to be bound together by a love like Jesus'. In fidelity to God it can expect dishonour, hatred and persecution in this world, but can look forward both to joy in this world and to life beyond death. Jesus is the messiah described in Deut. 17.14-20. He is chosen by God. He does not enslave people by multiplying horses, wives, silver or gold. He fears God by keeping all his words, and his heart is not lifted up above his brethren. Like the messiah of Isaiah's visions (Isa. 9 and 11), he brings joy because he is a wonderful counsellor, inspired by God's wisdom and understanding. He is the prince of peace, upholding his kingdom with justice because he does not judge by what he sees and hears, but helps the poor and meek, slaying the wicked 'with the rod of his mouth'. His life expresses his righteousness and fidelity. Like the shepherd of Micah's prophecy (Mic. 5.4), he feeds his flock 'in the honour of the name of the Lord his God' and gives them security.

But the Fourth Gospel has filled out this depiction of Jesus the messiah with elements from scriptural portraits of other figures. He is not only messiah but also the prophet like Moses, whose miraculous signs intimate his significance. Moreover, his life, death and resurrection fulfil all those expectations which people associated with Israel's central sanctuary, the Temple; that is, salvation.

2.1. *The Saviour of the World*

'For God sent the Son into the world, not to condemn the world, but that the world might be saved through him' (3.17). This is how Jesus' mission is summarized at the beginning of his public ministry, and a similar statement is made at the end: 'I did not come to judge the world but to save the world' (12.47). In spite of the rancour of the disputes between Jesus and the 'Jews' in Jerusalem, in spite of the climax of the story in which Jesus is sentenced to crucifixion by Pilate, the perspective of the Gospel is that Jesus' ministry is wholly positive, undertaken not to condemn but to save. The effect of the mission is to save many who seem beyond salvation, the Samaritans, the royal official's child near to death, the feeble man, the hungry crowds, the man blind from birth, the dead Lazarus, the cowardly disciples, but also to confirm the blindness of the worldly. So the positive purpose also defines the nature of opposition as a refusal of God's gifts.

The central importance to salvation of belief in Jesus is brought out by the story of the Samaritan woman and her fellow Samaritans in 4.3-42. When discussing with her the relative merits of Jewish and Samaritan worship, Jesus at first seems to speak as a Jew: 'You worship what you do not know; we worship what we know, for salvation is from the Jews' (4.22), but the dialogue goes on to explain how it is that salvation comes from the Jews: Jesus is a Jew and the woman tentatively accepts Jesus' assertion that he is the messiah (4.25-26). She then raises with others in the Samaritan city whether he could really be the Christ, arousing their interest in him, some even sharing her wonder at his extraordinary knowledge (4.39). Finally, after hearing Jesus themselves, they tell the woman: 'It is no longer because of your words that we believe, for we have heard for ourselves, and we know that this is indeed the Saviour of the world' (4.42). The story shows the gradual awakening of full belief in Jesus as the world's saviour, that is, as saviour not simply of Jews, but, proleptically here, of all humanity.

What is it, then, from which people need to be saved? Some instances of the verb suggest that people are to be saved from death. In 11.12 the verb is used of Lazarus's natural recovery from an illness which would otherwise kill him. Also, at the end of Jesus' public career, he asks ironically whether he should say, 'Father, save me from the hour', that is, from the hour of his death, but he decides that such a request would destroy the very point of his mission: 'No, for this purpose I have come to this hour' (12.27). Nevertheless, the Gospel certainly supposes that people are to be saved from death, but that this is to happen by their re-orientating their lives in order to live from the Creator God who gives eternal life (e.g. 3.1-15). Jesus tells Nicodemus that unless a person is born anew or from above (ἄνωθεν), he or she cannot see or enter the kingdom of God (3.3, 5). Like the ruler in Lk. 18.18, Nicodemus, the ruler of the 'Jews', had come to learn from a teacher he respected, but he receives teaching which highlights the radical nature of the change required even more than that of the Jesus of the Synoptics Gospels. The Synoptic Jesus says, 'Truly I say to you, whoever does not receive the kingdom of God like a child shall not enter it' (Mk 10.15; Lk. 18.17) or 'Unless you turn and become like children, you will never enter the kingdom of heaven' (Mt. 18.3). Each of Jesus' statements suggests that only those who experience their vulnerable dependence can accept God's gift of the kingdom, but the form of the Johannine presentation, in which Nicodemus's misunderstanding emphasizes the common-sense impossibility of the demand (3.4), draws attention to the fact that only God's Spirit can bring it about (3.6-9). The Fourth Gospel has taken up prophetic expectations about the new life which God's Spirit would create (Isa. 32.15; Ezek. 36.26-27) and has expressed the teaching in terms of its metaphorical contrast between above and below. It eschews the language of rebirth which Christianity was to borrow from the mystery religions (παλιγγενεσία in Tit. 3.5 or ἀναγεγεννημένοι in 1 Pet. 2.23) but, like the psalmist (Ps. 2.7), it sees the Creator God as the begetter of this new relationship.

This way of life actually leads through death to resurrection, as the story of Jesus illustrates. The connexion between Jesus' way and salvation is clarified by the discourse on 'the door': 'I am the door; if anyone enters by me, he will be saved, and will go in and out and find pasture' (10.9). To be saved, people are to believe in Jesus, to take him as a model for their lives. Hence Jesus points them to the testimony of John the Baptist in order to convince them: 'You sent to John and he has borne witness to the truth. Not that the testimony which I receive is from a human being; but I say this that you may be saved' (5.34). Ultimately, as the discourse in ch. 5 explains, it is God who bears witness to Jesus, but he does so through John, through Moses and through the signs, the three testimonies whose authority the people were inclined to accept.

This salvation which Jesus brings also has a moral content. It is sin, human rejection of God and his demands, which brings death (e.g. 8.21-24, 34-47; 9.41). It is evil deeds which prevent people from loving the light (3.19). Those who reject Jesus are murderers, seeking to put him to death, agents of their father, the Devil, who is a murderer (8.44-47). The salvation which Jesus brings is freedom from sin (8.36) and new life in a loving community (15.12-17).

2.2. *The Signs*

The miracles in the Fourth Gospel are called signs: 'This, the first of the signs, he did in Cana of Galilee, and made known his honour; and his disciples believed in him' (2.11; cf. 4.54; 6.26; 9.16; 11.47; and see Brown 1971: I, Appendix III). Alternatively, the healing of the feeble man is called work, since it was performed on the Sabbath, and Jesus justifies his action by saying, 'My Father is working still, and I am working' (5.17). Also, the cure of the man blind from birth, another Sabbath healing, is understood to manifest 'the works of God' (9.3). Jesus' brothers, too, encourage Jesus to go to Jerusalem at the Feast of Tabernacles so 'that your disciples may see the works you are doing' (7.3). Here and elsewhere, however, 'works' has a wider meaning than miracles alone. 'Work' includes miracle, but also Jesus' teaching and his death and resurrection, as the work God sent him to perform: 'My food is to do the will of him who sent me, and to accomplish his work' (4.34; cf. 5.20, 36; 7.21; 10.25, 32, 33, 37, 38; 14.10-12; 15.24; 17.4). Moreover, the crowds too are urged to do the work of God: 'This is the work of God, that you believe in him whom he has sent' (6.29). In other words, the crowds are to do God's work by recognizing that God is working through Jesus, and by following him.

In the Septuagint 'the work of God' refers to his acts of salvation, for example, in making a covenant with Israel (Exod. 34.10) or in demonstrating control of nature (Ps. 66.5), especially at the Exodus from Egypt (Ps. 77.12; Deut. 3.24; 11.3). Here the overlap of 'work' and 'sign' is most obvious, since these miracles and others associated with the Exodus are also called 'signs' (e.g. Deut. 7.19; 11.3; 34.11; Num. 14.11, 22). The signs are supposed to evoke belief in the God who saves his people, just as Jesus' signs are intended to evoke belief in him, the Son of God, through whom God saves his people:

> Jesus did many other signs in the presence of his disciples, which are not written in this book, but these are written that you may believe (or continue to believe) that Jesus is the Christ, the Son of God, and that believing you may have life in his name (20.30-31).

But conceiving Jesus' miracles as signs seems to distinguish the Johannine presentation from that of the Synoptics, where Jesus refuses to perform a sign to justify his mission (e.g. Mt. 12.38-42 and parallels). The distinction is, however, no more than semantic. Both in the Synoptics and in the Fourth Gospel (2.18; 6.30), Jesus refuses to perform the kind of sign his opponents require. Nevertheless, in all four Gospels Jesus effects miracles, which the Fourth Gospel presents not as unambiguous demonstrations of his power which convince everyone that his mission is God's but as 'signs' to those whom God draws to himself (6.44-45). In other words, the Johannine signs are not exhibitions of God's overwhelming power, but intimations of what God is accomplishing through Jesus.

We have already noted that none of the Johannine miracles is represented as an exorcism, but that their connexion with overcoming sin is acknowledged. Since sin is understood as opposition to the God whose work Jesus performs, it is summed up as failure to believe in Jesus. This failure is also a moral failure in its origin and consequences (3.19-20; 7.19-30; 8.34-38). The signs both arouse and encapsulate the effects of belief in Jesus, the acceptance of God's re-creative activity through him. So the feeble man is warned to 'sin no more, that nothing worse befall you' (5.14). But when the disciples ask Jesus whether the man born blind suffered such an affliction because of his own sin or that of his parents, are we to construe Jesus' reply as a denial of a connexion between sin and blindness? Jn 5.14 suggests the answer 'No'. Rather, Jesus insists on looking not to the cause of the complaint but to the significance of the miraculous cure he is about to accomplish: 'It is not that this man sinned or his parents [that is, deciding this particular issue is not important] but that the works of God might be manifest in him' (9.3). The sign demonstrates God's effective re-creation (notice the use of clay as in Gen. 2.6-7, and the reference in 9.32, 'Never since the world began'). And the seven signs described by the Gospel partake of the extremism of its rhetoric. The man is not just blind, but blind from birth, and yet his sight is given to him through Jesus; the feeble man is so ineffective that he is unable to help himself, either in getting into the pool at the appropriate time (5.7) or in noticing the identity of the person through whom he is cured (5.13), yet Jesus both heals him and makes himself known to him; the water of Jewish purification at the Cana wedding party is not just turned into a superabundance of wine, but into good wine (2.10); the royal official's son is not just healed of a fever which threatens death, but is cured from a distance at exactly the time Jesus assures his father that he will live (4.50-53); the five thousand are not simply fed by the multiplication of the loaves and fish, but enough is left over to fill twelve baskets of fragments (6.8-13); Jesus does not walk on the water just to impress his disciples, but, like God's Spirit of creation (Gen. 1.2), moves across the water in the darkness and the wind to identify himself as the person through whom God is re-creating his world (6.18-21); finally, Lazarus is well and truly dead before Jesus calls him from the tomb back to life (11.6, 39). Since the Gospel's teaching encourages people to choose between two mutually exclusive ways of living, one leading to death and the other to life, these miracles effectively demonstrate the possibility of the change from death to life which Jesus accomplishes.

But in what sense are they signs? To be signs, the miracles have to exhibit something of the reality they signify, but in a sufficiently partial or ambiguous way to point beyond themselves to what is more fundamental than each individual instance. So, the turning of water into wine (2.1-11) encapsulates something of the reality of Jesus' mission from God: what he brings is even better than purification (2.6), it is positively celebratory, as much more enjoyable as wine is than water. Yet to understand this is but to see in outline what the Gospel will have to fill in with more detail. Not that what is intimated here is ever denied. Joy is precisely what the disciples are to share with Jesus (15.11). But in Jesus' remark: 'My hour has not yet come' (2.4), the text itself warns the reader that the time is not yet ripe to see the full significance of the sign. In other words, the sign hints proleptically at a reality which can only be appreciated with hindsight, when Jesus' mission is complete. Nevertheless, the sign signifies enough to the disciples to awaken their faith in Jesus. We should notice, however, that its effect on other people is not even mentioned. The reactions of Jesus' mother, who requested his help, of the steward who noticed the unusually good quality of the wine served late in the celebrations, of the bridegroom whose attention the steward drew to the wine, even of the servants who filled the jars with water and drew out wine, find no place in the story. Only in so far as their actions confirm the miracle for the reader are they noticed. We can presume their astonishment, but this is not something we are led to dwell upon, because the Gospel makes a distinction between seeing a miracle as a mere wonder, and seeing it as a sign. To understand Jesus as a wonder worker is to misperceive him, a mistake that could have unfortunate consequences, like the attempt to make him king (6.15). The narrator, therefore, specifies the danger at the beginning of Jesus' public career: 'Now when he was in Jerusalem at the Passover feast, many believed in his name when they saw the signs which he did; but Jesus did not trust himself to them' (2.23-24). The narrative of this miracle at Cana, then, focuses the reader's attention on what is important, the reaction of the disciples, who follow Jesus.

The signs, therefore, intimate the fulfilment of God's purpose through Jesus by satisfying people's needs, by exemplifying God's love for the world, and by pointing beyond themselves to God's salvation which finally overcomes death with life. Although these signs hint at a fuller reality, however, we should avoid a distinction which is natural to our culture but alien to that of the Fourth Gospel, namely, a distinction between 'physical' and 'spiritual' We are the inheritors of a dualistic philosophy, developed in the seventeenth century by Descartes and Locke, which separates mind and physical body, and which accords to human thinking an anthropological importance which diminishes that of human materiality. In the light of this philosophy, we are inclined to assume that human memory and perception is what is crucial to human existence and hence we conceive immortality as immaterial. Our desire is for a future disembodied life. The Fourth Gospel shares neither this dualistic anthropology nor the hope it engenders. It tells the story of the disappearance of Jesus' corpse and of his bodily resurrection. Not that his resurrection is a resuscitation like Lazarus's, since it would be inappropriate to ask of the resurrected Jesus 'What was his address?' or 'When did he die a second time?', but it is the resurrection of an individual human being, and human beings are individuated by their materiality. Jesus' resurrection is a material transformation, not just the survival of Jesus' mind or soul.

Hence the physicality of the signs, which provide wine and bread, which heal fever, feebleness, blindness, which bring the dead back to life, is not merely a picturesque way of depicting 'spiritual' realities. Rather, material welfare gives true information about God's care for the world because God creates the material world, including material people, and desires that they fulfil the potential of their material lives by living fully from him in a loving community, both in the present distorted world, and beyond death.

2.3. *The Fourth Gospel's Seven Signs and the Miracles of the Synoptics*

The Fourth Gospel explains in its conclusion to ch. 20 that a selection of signs has been recorded from a larger number of miracles performed by Jesus (20.30). No information is given about these other miracles, but we are in a position to compare the Johannine seven with those in the Synoptics, although we cannot be certain whether any or all of the Synoptics were known to the writer or readers of the Fourth Gospel.

We may begin by noticing the kinds of miracles which are present in the Synoptics but absent from John. There are no exorcisms, which, in the Synoptics, are cures of madness (e.g. Mt. 8.28-34 and parallels) or of epilepsy (e.g. Mt. 17.14-21). Perhaps the cure of epilepsy finds no place in the Johannine scheme because nothing is related of the disciple's mission during Jesus' ministry, as it is in the Synoptics, and this story illustrates the disciples' failure to perform a miracle without Jesus' help. Nevertheless, it is curious that the Fourth Gospel has nothing to say about madness and its cure. The omission highlights the rational character of the Gospel which seeks to lure its readers into a reasoned comprehension of Jesus' significance. The atmosphere it creates is unlike that of the Second Gospel, in which Jesus' frenetic activity can be interpreted negatively by his opponents and relatives as a sign of madness (3.21) or of his possession by Beelzebul (3.22-27 and parallels), or positively as victory over demons (e.g. 3.27; 5.20). By contrast, in the Fourth Gospel 'evil' finds expression in argument, not in crazy behaviour (e.g. 9.1–10.39). So when Jesus is accused by the 'Jews' of having a demon and being mad (10.20), it is because of his teaching. His miracles prove he is not mad (10.21).

Again, leprosy, which made a person unclean and cut him or her off from the community, is cleansed by Jesus according to the Synoptics (e.g. Mt. 8.1-4 and parallels). Is the Johannine omission to be explained by the supposition that the distinction between clean and unclean played no part in the Johannine world, in spite of its presence in Scripture? In the Jewish world leprosy uncleanness was removed by sacrifice in the Temple and washing (Lev. 14.1-32; cf. Mt. 8.4). The sacrifice of a lamb and hyssop are mentioned as part of the Levitical ceremony. According to the Fourth Gospel, Jesus is 'the lamb of God who takes away the sin of the world' (1.29), and hyssop is used when he dies on the cross (19.29). Could it be that Jesus' death is understood as the final fulfilment of this and other Temple sacrifices, a fulfilment which obviates the need for animal sacrifice in the future? This thesis will be argued in section 3, but, if it is correct, would not such a perception lead to the inclusion of a cleansing miracle, rather than to its exclusion?

The reason for the omission seems to lie elsewhere. The Fourth Gospel tells only seven miracle stories, each of them significant at that particular point in the narrative. The first Cana miracle (2.1-11) creates a general impression of the character of Jesus' ministry and is appropriately placed at the beginning of the story. The second Cana miracle (4.46-53, the cure of the royal official's son from a distance) serves to illustrate the initial success of Jesus' Galilaean ministry, in contrast to his rejection in Judaea (4.44; 5.1-47). The third sign, in Jerusalem (5.2-9, the healing of the feeble man), is set on the Sabbath. Jesus tells the man to take up his bed and walk, thereby encouraging him to break the Sabbath law against work. Although Jesus himself does not work, since curing by word does not involve work, a generalizing statement, 'This is why the Jews used to persecute Jesus, because he used to do these things on the Sabbath' (5.16), provides the lead into the discussion of Jesus' relationship to the Father. The fourth miracle again takes place in Galilee (6.1-14, the feeding of the five thousand), but this time it introduces the discourse on the bread of life, after which even most of the Galilaeans withdraw their support, and Jesus is left with the twelve (6.66-71). The fifth sign (6.16-21, walking on the water) is given only to the disciples and helps to explain their fidelity when others depart. The sixth sign (9.1-7, the cure of blindness), in which Jesus does break the Sabbath by making clay (9.6), justifies Jesus' contention to be the light of the world (8.12). The seventh and final sign (11.43-44, calling Lazarus out of the tomb) warrants his claim to be the resurrection and the life, bringing his public ministry to a climax which directs the reader to the end of the book and Jesus' own resurrection. A leprosy cure could have prompted a discussion on the nature of the community Jesus tells his disciples to form, but that takes place in private, at the supper table (chs. 13–17) where no leper is present. It is, then, the structure of the Gospel which excludes a leprosy cleansing.

The Synoptics also contain a number of miracles performed to cure Gentiles (Mt. 8.5-13, 28-34; 15.21-28 and parallels). In the Fourth Gospel all those healed are Jews. Again, such Gentile healings are excluded by the Gospel's structure. The Greeks' attempt to see Jesus

(12.20-22) is unsuccessful. Jesus' reply is a meditation on the significance of his death for the disciples (12.23-26). In this manner the Gospel indicates that the mission to Gentiles is to happen after his death. The 'sheep who are not of this fold' (10.16) are Gentiles whom the disciples will admit (17.20). Perhaps this is why there is only one feeding miracle of the five thousand in John. The feeding of the four thousand in Matthew and Mark (Mt. 15.32-39 and parallel) is normally construed as a Gentile feeding.

Another feature which distinguishes the Johannine account of miracles from that of the Synoptics is the absence of women amongst those healed (contrast, e.g., Mt. 8.14-15; 9.18-26; 15.21-28 and parallels). It is not that the Synoptics are particularly sensitive to the fates of women in the patriarchal societies they reflect (there are no women among the twelve disciples), but women appear more frequently both in the narratives and in the parables, and issues which were important to women, like divorce, are discussed in the ethical teaching. John has the story of the Samaritan woman, who is a half-hearted missionary, although even she shares the fate of most women in being judged on the basis of her marital status (4.16-18). Mary and Martha are beloved by Jesus (11.5) and ch. 11 tells of their awakening belief in him. The same Mary anoints Jesus' feet for burial (12.1-8). At the supper Martha serves (12.2). Jesus' mother alerts him to the lack of wine at the Cana wedding (2.3) but otherwise plays no active part in the narrative. Jesus stays with her in Capernaum (2.12) and makes arrangements for her welfare from the cross (19.26-27). She is accompanied by other women at the crucifixion (19.25), including Mary Magdalene, who witnesses the crucifixion, discovers the empty tomb (20.1-2) and to whom the resurrected Jesus first appears (20.16); but the role she is given is simply that of messenger to the disciples (20.2, 17-18). We have to conclude that the Fourth Gospel recognizes the usefulness of women, but only in their subsidiary function of waiting upon men.

Other miracles found in the Synoptics are not so much excluded from the Johannine account as subsumed within those related. For example, the cure of the paralytic, effected through Jesus' command to take up his bed and walk (Mt. 9.1-8 and parallels) is subsumed in the story of the feeble man (5.2-9), the healings from a distance (Mt. 8.5-13; Lk. 7.1-10; Mk 7.24-30; Mt. 15.21-28) in the cure of the official's son (Jn 4.46-54), the Sabbath healing of the man with the withered hand (Mt. 12.9-14 and parallels) in the two Sabbath miracles (Jn 5.2-9; 9.2-41), the stilling of the storm (Mt. 8.23-27 and parallels) in the story of the walking on the water during a storm (Jn 6.16-21), the cures of dumbness or deafness (e.g. Mt.9.32-33 and parallels) in the story of the healing of the blind man which leads into the discourse about the shepherd whose sheep hear his voice (Jn 10.3), the raising of Jairus's daughter and the widow of Nain's son (Mt. 9.18-26 and parallels; Lk. 7.11-17) in the raising of Lazarus (Jn 11.1-45). Finally, Jesus' cursing of the fruitless fig tree, which is used in the Synoptics to represent God's judgment on an Israel which rejects its messiah (Mt. 21.18-22 and parallels), finds no place in the Fourth Gospel because the same point is made at such length in Jesus' disputes in Jerusalem (chs. 5; 7–12) and in the depiction of the true vine (15.1-11).

3. *Jesus and Scriptural Institutions*

3.1. *The Sabbath*

Two of Jesus' healings take place on the Sabbath and give rise to the accusation that he breaks the Sabbath (5.18 and 9.16). But the debate which follows in each case does not focus on the issue: What is work? but on the issue: Who is Jesus? Is he a sinner or is he God's agent? Both in ch. 5 and in ch. 9, the reader is encouraged to recognize Jesus as God's agent. In ch. 5 what is stressed is that Jesus does nothing on his own authority but only what he sees the Father doing—giving eternal life and exercising judgment. Hence the healing of the feeble man on the Sabbath exemplifies the life God gives in forgiving sinners (5.14). In ch. 9 it is the man healed of blindness who bears witness to Jesus by asking, 'How can a man who is a sinner do such signs?' (9.16) and by asserting, 'We know that God does not listen to sinners, but if anyone is a worshipper of God and does his will, God listens to him... If this man were not from God, he could do nothing' (9.31-33). Hence, the healed man recognizes Jesus as a prophet (9.17), and later, after his exclusion from his community (9.34), Jesus convinces him of his own identity as the Son of man (9.35-38). The healing of the blind man on the Sabbath exemplifies the sight and insight which God gives to those who are drawn into Jesus' new community.

But why are these Sabbath healings? Are they simply set on the Sabbath so that criticism can allow a fuller explanation of Jesus' significance or is there some more substantial connexion with the Sabbath? Keeping the Sabbath holy by resting from everyday work is commanded in the Decalogue (Exod. 20.8-11; Deut. 5.12-15). This command precedes Moses' giving the law on Sinai, however, and goes back ultimately to creation (Exod. 16; Gen. 2.2). Those who break the Sabbath are liable to death by stoning (Exod. 31.12-17; 35.3; Lev. 4.27-35; Num. 15.32-36). The Johannine Jesus' behaviour can be construed as breaking the Sabbath command because he works by making clay (9.6) and he causes someone else to work by carrying a burden (5.8-11; cf. Jer. 17.22).

Stories in the Pentateuch (e.g. Exod. 16; Num. 15.32-36) and many prophetic oracles (e.g. Ezek. 20 and 22; Jer. 17.19-27) give the impression that Israel failed to keep the Sabbath (cf. Neh. 13.15-22). Ezekiel accuses Israel of profaning God's Sabbath, given as a sign that God sanctifies them:

> I gave them my sabbaths, as a sign between me and them, that they might know that I the Lord sanctify them. But the house of Israel rebelled against me in the wilderness; they did not walk in my statutes but rejected my ordinances, by whose observance man shall live; and my sabbaths they greatly profaned (20.12-13; cf. 20.18-44).

Even in celebrating the Sabbath, however, Isaiah accuses them of affronting God because of their injustice:

> When you come to appear before me, who requires of you this trampling of my courts?. . . New moon and sabbath and the calling of assemblies— I cannot endure iniquity and solemn assembly. Your new moon and your appointed feasts my soul hates; they have become a burden to me, and I am weary of bearing them. When you spread forth your hands, I will hide my face from you; even though you make many prayers, I will not listen; your hands are full of blood (1.12-15 cf. Hos. 2.11; Amos 5.21-24).

Clearly, God's statutes and ordinances, including the Sabbath command, are intended to bring the life that God promises to Israel. Keeping commands like the Sabbath is meant to enhance community life and becomes empty when that life is destroyed in other ways. While Jesus' behaviour on the Sabbath can be construed as breaking it, therefore, the Fourth Gospel seems to imply that this is a superficial judgment. Rather, since Jesus' healings restore people to fullness of life, they demonstrate the fulfilment of promises for keeping the Sabbath. The healings intimate that fullness of life which fidelity to

God ensures. Hence, 'Jewish' repudiation of the man to whom Jesus gives sight frees him to become an adherent of Jesus (9.35-38; cf. 10.9-10; Isa. 56.3-8; 58.13-14). It seems that Jesus' healings on the Sabbath have become, in the Fourth Gospel, paradigms for understanding God's purpose. Those who oppose Jesus are pictured as opposing God's purpose like the people criticized by Isaiah. They are murderers, seeking to kill Jesus.

3.2. *The Temple and its Festivals*

One of Jesus' miracles also fulfils the expectations fostered by the celebrations of the festival at which it occurs. Jesus' feeding miracle at Passover time (6.1-14) recalls and exceeds the miracle of the manna in the wilderness after the exodus from Egypt (Exod. 16). The correspondence of expectation and fulfilment is found, however, not only in relation to festivals and miracles, but also in relation to the Temple itself where the festivals were celebrated.

The Temple was the central sanctuary of first-century Judaism, the place where God's name dwelt and where the sacrifices ordained by God in Scripture were carried out. It was supported by the Jews in Palestine through tithing and the Temple tax, and by Jews in the diaspora through the Temple tax and gifts. The three great pilgrim festivals, Tabernacles, Passover and Unleavened Bread, and Weeks (e.g. Exod. 23.14-17), drew thousands of Jews from all over the Roman and Middle Eastern world. The Temple was a holy shrine, and those who wished to enter its courts had to go through the prescribed rituals which removed uncleanness before they could tread the holy ground. Uncleanness was not synonymous with sin. Blessings from God, like the birth of a child, or compassionate acts demanded by Scripture, like burying the dead, would result in uncleanness, the latter requiring a seven-day ritual for its removal (Lev. 12; Num. 19). But the Temple sacrifices were also concerned with the people's sins and with the ways in which God ordained in Scripture that penitents could be assured of expiation and God's forgiveness. The annual Day of Atonement (Lev. 16), the daily sacrifices carried out by priests (e.g. Lev. 7) and the individual offerings of penitents, who showed their repentance by making restitution, all helped to reassure members of the covenant community that God had forgiven them.

In his book, *The Gospel and the Land*, W.D. Davies argues that the Fourth Gospel presents Jesus as the replacement of the Temple:

> The Shekinah is no longer there (in the Jerusalem Temple), but is now found wherever Christ is because later (10.36 makes this probable, if not unmistakably clear) Christ himself is the Sanctified One, the altar and Temple, the locus of the Shekinah (1974: 295).

The points which Davies makes in arguing this hypothesis may be briefly summarized.

1. The Johannine version of the cleansing of the Temple (2.13-22) signifies the arrival of a new order. The Temple is to be replaced by 'the temple of his body' (2.21) referring either to the resurrected Jesus or to the community of his followers. Holiness is no longer to be attached to a place but to a person.

2. Chapters 7 and 8 describe the manifestation of the messiah at the Temple during the Feast of Tabernacles. At the end of Jesus' discourse, 'I am light of the world', he departs from the Temple (8.59). This departure Davies takes to be symbolic of Jesus' rejection of Judaism. But since Jesus returns to the Temple in 10.22, Davies has to argue against the view that the departure in 8.59 is no more than a dramatic closure of the scene. This he does by suggesting differences between the scenes in chs. 7–8 and ch. 10:

a. In the former, Jesus issues a challenge to the 'Jews', in the latter, the 'Jews' challenge Jesus.
b. In the former, Jesus is involved in the Feast of Tabernacles, in the latter he seems disengaged, merely walking about in the Temple.
c. The colonnade of Solomon was outside the Temple proper, constituting the boundary of the latter (Acts 3.11).
d. Hence in 10.39 there is no reference to departure from the Temple as there was in 8.59.
e. The feast described in 10.22 is usually identified with Hanukkah which celebrated the Temple's rededication after it had been cleansed from pollution following the Maccabaean revolt against the Seleucids (1 Macc. 4.41-61). But Jn 10.22 calls the feast ἐγκαίνια, that is, Renewal, the term used in the Septuagint to describe the dedication of the original tabernacle (Num. 7.10-11), of the Temple of Solomon (1 Kgs 8.63; 2 Chron. 7.5), and of the Second Temple (Ezra 6.16). Davies interprets 10.22-39 as follows:

> But Jesus walking on the fringes of the Temple during this feast of reconsecration knows that the hour of true renewal has passed; the ἐγώ εἰμι ('I am he') has departed from the Temple and the real dedication is the dedication of himself by God to fulfil the role of Temple, that is, to mediate the presence of God to men. This is made explicit in 10.37 which speaks of the sanctification of Christ (p. 293).

f. Hence, the Fourth Gospel has no room for a cleansing of the Temple during Jesus' final visit to Jerusalem in ch. 12. It had already been made clear that Jesus replaced the Temple.

Davies includes in his argument a discussion of the significance of Jesus' ἐγώ εἰμι in the Fourth Gospel, which he takes to signify divine presence and to indicate the divinity of Christ (p. 295). The suggestion was developed by Brown, but has already been refuted (Chapter 3). Nevertheless, the broad outlines of Davies's thesis, that the Fourth Gospel pictures Jesus' life, death and resurrection fulfilling the expectations aroused by the Temple and its sacrifices and festivals, including its function of reassuring penitent sinners that God forgives them, are surely correct.

Davies's contention that 8.59 marks Jesus' final departure from the Temple and that the setting of 10.22 is merely on the periphery of the Temple is unconvincing, however. Jn 10.23 clearly states that Jesus is in the Temple (ἱερόν), in the colonnade of Solomon which was actually within the Temple precincts (e.g. Josephus, *Ant.* 15.396-401; 20.220-21). Two words are used in the Septuagint to refer to the Temple, ναός which sometimes refers to the sanctuary within the Temple courts, and sometimes to the whole Temple precinct, and ἱερόν, which occurs in Ezekiel and 1 Chronicles, 1 Esdras and the books of Maccabees, and which refers to the whole precinct. In Josephus and the Synoptics, both ναός and ἱερόν refer to the whole Temple complex. The Fourth Gospel uses ναός in 2.19, 20, 21 and ἱερόν in 2.14, 15, 5.14, 7.14, 28, 8.20, 59, 10.23, 11.56 and 18.20. This means that the Johannine account of Jesus' action in the Temple (2.13-22) places the incident in the ἱερόν, in line with the Synoptic accounts, but interprets the significance of the incident and of Jesus' statement (2.19) in terms of the ναός. Are we to understand a distinction here? Does ναός refer to the sanctuary only and ἱερόν to that sanctuary together with its surrounding courts? This seems unlikely because the 'Jewish' reply in 2.20 to Jesus' prophecy about the destruction and rebuilding in three days of the ναός asserts that it had taken 46 years to build the existing ναός, and this must refer to Herod's rebuilding of the whole Temple complex, not just the sanctuary within it. In the Fourth Gospel, then, ναός and ἱερόν are synonymous and refer to the sanctuary and its surrounding courts.

The great strength of Davies's argument lies in the fact that it explains why the Temple incident occurs at the beginning of the Fourth Gospel instead of at the end of Jesus' ministry, as in the Synoptics. The move has involved sacrificing historical veracity for a theological purpose. The offence which Jesus' outrageous behaviour, in driving out the people who sold animals and changed money and overturning the tables (2.14-15), would have caused pious Jews could actually have led to his arrest and trial, and the Synoptic accounts preserve a temporal connexion between the incidents. By placing the Temple incident at the beginning of Jesus' ministry, the Fourth Gospel connects it with Jesus' death and resurrection, but on a theological rather than a historical level. First of all, the incident is interpreted through the disciples' perception that it fulfilled Scripture: 'His disciples remembered that it was written, Zeal for your house will consume me' (2.17). There is a significant difference between the Septuagint version of Ps. 69.9 and its quotation here. In the Septuagint the verb 'consume' is in the aorist, whereas in the Johannine quotation it is future. The change suggests that Jesus' zeal for God's house, which can refer both to the Temple and to God's household, the community of those who belong to God's covenant, will destroy him, as the story relates that it does. But this could imply that Jesus will be concerned about safeguarding the Temple itself. This possible interpretation is corrected by what follows. The 'Jewish' request for a sign is met by Jesus' promise to raise up the destroyed Temple in three days (2.18-19). 'Jewish' astonishment at his answer (2.20) marks the end of the incident but not the end of the narrative. Jesus' statement is interpreted, 'He was speaking of the Temple of his body' (2.21), and this is immediately connected with Jesus' resurrection through the reference to the disciples' subsequent rememberance of and trust in the Scripture and Jesus' words, when he was raised from the dead (2.22). The whole incident, as depicted and interpreted in Jn 2.13-22, suggests that Jesus will fulfil the expectations which Scripture associates with the Temple.

One such fulfilment had already been prophesied of Jesus by John.

The Temple was the place where priests offered sacrifices to ask for God's forgiveness of sin. John's witness to Jesus describes him as 'the Lamb (ἀμνός) of God who takes away the sin of the world' (1.29 and 36). Commentators cite various passages from Scripture to explain the reference to the lamb of God. For example, Isa. 53.7-10 depicts the suffering servant of God as 'one like a lamb (πρόβατον) that is led to slaughter, and like a sheep (ἀμνός) that before its shearers is dumb... He bore the sin of many.' That the passage was familiar to the author and readers of the Fourth Gospel is suggested by the paraphrase of Isa. 53.1 in 12.38 where it is used to explain the people's failure to believe in Jesus. A second passage which may have a bearing on the meaning is the story of Abraham's decision to sacrifice Isaac, and of God's provision of a lamb (πρόβατον) which was sacrificed instead (Gen. 22). There may be echoes of the story in Jn 3.16, although there are no verbal parallels. A third passage is Lev. 7.1-7 (cf. 4.32), according to which a lamb (πρόβατον) may be sacrificed as a guilt offering. This passage and that from Isaiah 53 explain the second half of John's testimony, 'who takes away the sin of the world'. Finally, there may be an allusion to the Passover lamb (πρόβατον) which was sacrificed at the celebration of God's rescue of his people from slavery in Egypt (Exod. 12), in spite of the fact that this was not understood as a sin offering. Although Exodus 12 uses the word πρόβατον instead of the Johannine ἀμνός, Num. 28.19 calls the Passover lamb ἀμνός, and ἀμνός is also used in connexion with many other sacrifices (e.g. Exod. 29.38-41; Lev. 9.3; 12.6; 14.10). Later in the Gospel Jesus' death is interpreted in the light of allusions to the death of the Passover lamb in Exodus 12. Four features make the connexion. Jesus dies at the time when the Passover lamb was sacrificed in the Temple (19.14; Exod. 12.3, 6), hyssop is used (19.29; Exod. 12.22), Jesus' bones are not broken and the fact is noted as fulfilment of Scripture (19.36; Exod. 12.46), and his body is removed from the cross before the morning (19.31; Exod. 12.10). It is possible that the Fourth Gospel interpreted God's rescue from slavery as a rescue from the slavery of sin (8.34-38). Jesus, then, fulfils the hopes of those who obeyed God in sacrificing the Passover lamb in the Temple. He does this as a true Israelite who is the servant of God, and his death assures his followers that God forgives sinners. Those who follow Jesus must also freely sacrifice their lives, hating life in this world to keep it for eternal life (12.25), and loving as Jesus loved, laying down his life for his friends (15.12-13). Hence, Jesus' death, like that of the Passover lamb, inaugurates a new community, united in love of God and humanity.

In the light of this teaching in the first two chapters of the Fourth Gospel, Jesus is depicted explaining the nature of true worship to the Samaritan woman. She had raised the question about the places where Samaritans and Jews worshipped (4.20), to which Jesus replied,

> The hour is coming when neither on this mountain nor in Jerusalem will you worship the Father. You worship what you do not know; we worship what we know, for salvation is from the Jews. But the hour is coming, and now is, when the true worshippers will worship the Father in spirit and truth, for such the Father seeks to worship him. God is spirit and those who worship him must worship in spirit and truth (4.21-24).

Genuine and faithful worship, the worship appropriate to God, will be offered, when 'the hour' has arrived, that is, the hour of Jesus' death, neither on the mountain in Samaria nor in Jerusalem. When the woman thinks that Jesus' statement refers to the time of the messiah, Jesus declares that he is the messiah (4.25-26). The woman's fellow Samaritans who come to believe in Jesus therefore recognize him as the 'Saviour of the world' (4.42). But just how followers of Jesus will worship the Father 'in spirit' is left over till Jesus' explanation in ch. 7.

At the Feast of Tabernacles, Jesus declares:

> If anyone thirst, let him come [to me], and let he who believes in me drink. As the Scripture has said, out of his belly shall flow rivers of living water (7.37-38; see the earlier discussion of this passage, pp. 144-45).

The saying is interpreted (7.39) to refer to Jesus' bestowal of the Spirit on disciples, a promise which is fulfilled by the resurrected Jesus in 20.22. But why is this teaching linked with a scriptural passage, and to which passage does it refer? There is an association between water and spirit in Isa. 44.3 and an association between water and wisdom in Prov. 18.4 and Sir. 24.30-34. Moreover, Ps. 78.16, 'He made streams to come out of the rock and caused water to flow down like rivers', recalls God's miraculous provision of water in the wilderness, which followed his miraculous gift of food (Exod. 16–17; Num. 11 and 20). Since John 6 provides a discourse on the manna, John 7 is often interpreted in the light of the wilderness miracle of water flowing from the rock. This is possible, but a link with another rock may be suggested, the rock on which the Temple stood.

According to Zech. 14.8,

> On that day [a future day on which God would save Israel from the nations and come to Jerusalem], living waters shall flow out from Jerusalem, half of them to the eastern sea and half of them to the western sea; it shall continue in summer and winter.

This vision is associated with the celebration of Tabernacles in Zech. 14.16. It is a vision which parallels that in Ezekiel:

> Then he brought me back to the door of the Temple, and, behold, water was issuing from below the threshold of the Temple towards the east, for the Temple faced east; and the water was flowing down from below the south end of the threshold... And the man then led me through the water and it was ankle deep... it was knee deep... it was up to the loins... it was deep enough to swim in, a river that could not be passed through... And wherever the river goes every living creature which swarms will live, and there will be very many fish... so everything will live where the water goes (47.1-9).

Could it be that this vision of life-giving water issuing from the Temple is applied to Jesus and reinterpreted in the light of Isa. 44.3 to refer to Jesus' bestowal of the Spirit? The saying in 2.21 suggests this possibility. If it is correct, it helps to explain the theological significance of 19.34. The blood and water which flow from Jesus' side after his death on the cross reveals his death as a sacrifice for sin (the blood) and as the source of the Spirit which his disciples are to receive (the water).

The Johannine narrative continues to describe events at the Feast of Tabernacles. After discussions about Jesus' identity among the people and among the Pharisees (7.40-52), Jesus declares his own identity with the words: 'I am the light of the world' (8.12). No doubt the Gospel is interpreting Jesus' teaching in terms of wisdom which brings light (e.g. Prov. 4.18; 6.23; Wis. 7.26; Ps. 119.105) and Jesus speaks as personified Wisdom (e.g. Prov. 8.12-21). But once again a connexion with the Temple is possible. There are instructions in the law to keep a light perpetually burning before the veil of the tabernacle (e.g. Exod. 27.20; Lev. 24.2; Num. 4.16) and this was the practice in the Temple (2 Chron. 4.20; and see the depiction of the menorah on Titus's triumphal arch in Rome). That this light was understood metaphorically as an assurance of the presence of God's light is suggested by Pss. 89.15 and 104.1-2, and Ps. 43.3 petitions

God: 'Send out your light and your truth; let them lead me, let them bring me to your holy hill and to your dwelling'. Moreover, the prophecy already quoted from Zechariah 14 is introduced, 'And there shall be continuous day. . . for at evening time there shall be light' (Zech. 14.7 cf. Pss. 36.8-9 which also connects feasting with drinking from God's river and with God's light). The Johannine Jesus, as the light of the world, replaces the light in the Temple. Moreover, as God's servant, he is a light to the nations (Isa. 49.6).

The sign which signifies Jesus' role as the light of the world, the healing of the man blind from birth (ch. 9), leads into Jesus' teaching in 10.1-18 which depicts his mission as the model shepherd in contrast to that of the Pharisees, who are mere hirelings or thieves. The discourse leads to a division among the 'Jews', some pronouncing him possessed by a demon and mad, but others doubting that his words and his action in performing the miracle can be attributed to someone who is demon possessed (10.19-21).

Then the narrative notes the passing of time, and places Jesus once more in the Temple, in the colonnade of Solomon, at the winter feast of Renewal (10.22-23). Jesus' teaching is prompted by the 'Jewish' request to be told openly whether he is the Christ (10.24). He cites the works which he had performed in the Father's name, but suggests that they do not believe because they are not of his sheep (10.25-27). These sheep are gifts from the Father to Jesus and evidence the unity of purpose which Jesus shares with the Father (10.28-30). The 'Jewish' response to this claim is to try to stone Jesus for blasphemy because he seemed to be making himself equal to God (10.31-33). Jesus refutes the accusation by quoting Scripture and repeating the claim which he had actually made, not to be equal to God, but to be God's son acting as the Father's agent by effecting the Father's works (10.34-38). But this appeal to trust in his works only provokes another attempt to arrest him, and he is forced to withdraw (10.39-40). As part of Jesus' refutation of 'Jewish' misunderstanding, he refers to himself as a person whom the Father has consecrated and sent into the world (10.36). The passage in Numbers 7 which uses the verb 'to renew' in connexion with the dedication of the original tabernacle (Num. 7.10-11) also refers to Moses' consecration of the tabernacle and its furnishings in 7.1, using the same verb as Jn 10.36, ἁγιάζω. Jesus' discourse, therefore, argues that the present renewal is effected by God through Jesus, whom he has consecrated for the purpose. Effects previously associated with the Temple, like enlightenment and forgiveness of sin, are now associated with Jesus. The confession of Peter at the end of ch. 6, 'You are the Holy One of God' (6.69) provides a suitable introduction to the teaching of the chapters which follow in 7–10. Moreover, in Jesus' prayer at the end of his Farewell Discourses, he asks the Father to sanctify his disciples:

> Sanctify them in the truth; your λόγος is truth. As you sent me into the world, so I have sent them into the world. And for their sake I sanctify myself, that they also may be sanctified in truth (17.17-19).

In other words, Jesus' sanctification is shared with his disciples, who are to become a community dedicated to God.

It was noted in the introduction to this section that the Temple service was not only concerned with the forgiveness of sin but also with the removal of uncleanness. This is reflected in the 'Jewish' desire to purify themselves before the Feast of Passover (11.55) and to remain pure to celebrate the feast (18.28). The narrator of the Fourth Gospel shares this interest in purity, but reinterprets it metaphorically as the psalmist had already done (Ps. 51.2). The first of Jesus' signs (2.1-11) relates how Jesus changed the water of 'Jewish' purification into wine, and soon afterwards we are told that Jesus was baptizing (3.22, corrected in 4.2 with the statement that only his disciples baptized) at the same time as John was baptizing (3.23). It is in this context that a dispute arose between a disciple of John and a 'Jew' about purification (3.25). Probably we are to infer that baptism is understood as a purificatory rite, but we have to wait until the Farewell Discourses to read Jesus' explanation of the significance of purification.

In ch. 13 Jesus washes the disciples' feet and declares: 'He who has bathed does not need to wash, but he is *clean* all over' (13.10). Then he goes on to explain that what he has done is exemplary for the disciples, they ought to wash one another's feet (13.14-15). Finally, after the discussion about the person who would betray him and Judas's exit, Jesus meditates upon the honour which will be accorded the Son of man and gives his disciples a new commandment, to love one another as he had loved them (13.34). 'Cleanness', therefore, is interpreted metaphorically as a morality of love like Jesus' love. Judas is excluded (13.11) because his act of betrayal is not an act of love. The same connexion between purity and love is made in ch. 15. In the discourse on the vine, the Greek term for 'prune' (καθαίρει, 15.2) is interpreted in 15.3 by the adjective 'clean' (καθαρός): 'You are already *clean* through the λόγος which I have spoken to you'. This is explained in 15.9. The branches, the disciples, which remain attached to the vine, Jesus, are encouraged to 'remain in my love'. Jesus therefore reverts to the commandment he had given: 'This is my commandment, that you love one another as I have loved you. Greater love has no one than this, that a person lay down his life for his friends' (15.12-13). In other words, Jesus fulfils the Temple's function of ensuring purity by exemplifying a moral purity for a community united in a love like his own.

It seems fair to conclude, therefore, that the expectations engendered by the existence of the Temple and its festivals and sacrifices are fulfilled in Jesus' life, death and resurrection, according to the Fourth Gospel. This is why the Gospel includes Jesus' claim that when he is lifted up, he will draw all people to himself (12.32). The prophets looked forward to a time when all peoples would come to the Temple (Isa. 2.3; 60.6; Zech. 14.16). The λόγος becomes flesh, 'tabernacles' among the confessing community (1.14). And the disciples are to become a community sanctified in service to God (17.17-19).

4. *Salvation*

What, then, is the content of salvation? It releases people from the limited perspective of worldly selfishness, from sin, from lives which are murderous (3.20-21; ch. 8), to a conscious acknowledgement of the God who gives eternal life (3.16). This release brings to believers a fearless peace (14.27) and a fully realized joy (15.11). It enables them to live lives which express a love like that of Jesus who laid down his life (15.12-17). But it involves human dishonour, hatred, persecution and death in this world (15.18–16.3). The honour they receive from God is accorded to those consecrated to his work, living only from him (17.11-19). Belief in Jesus is acceptance that God has sent him to be a model for their lives (13.1-20) and salvation entails making his life their own (6.52-59). Love, peace and joy define the life of salvation. Such a combination of characteristics would have a wide appeal. Many people would like to live lives of love, peace and joy, in some sense of these words, although few have adopted enthusiastically the way of selfless dedication to God which the Fourth Gospel sees as the only route to this end. Moreover, the Gospel does not explain or explore the implications of this vision in concrete detail. It is possible that such a task was made unnecessary by the acceptance of Scripture as an authoritative guide, since Scripture contains just those details omitted from the Gospel. But it is also possible that the gap is deliberately left for another reason. The Gospel is an invitation to choose Jesus' way and follow him. Those who do so, it affirms, will discover peace, joy and love, and are themselves to fill in the details from their own experience of living in a loving community dedicated to God. The very lack of concrete detail has ensured the Gospel's appeal across generations and cultures.

The Johannine emphasis on the community's present experience of love, peace and joy in a world which is alienated from God and which hates that community, however, does not exclude the expectation of a future in which evil will no longer constrain its life. That future is not depicted in parables about the kingdom which God would establish at the parousia of Jesus, as it is in the Synoptics (e.g. Mk 13 and parallels). Rather, it is simply mentioned as an assurance already well known to its readers (3.3, 5; 5.28-29; 6.39, 40, 44, 54; 11.24-27; 12.24-25; 14.2-3; 17.24). Those who follow Jesus will walk along a way which leads through persecution and death to resurrection, and will join Jesus in the place prepared by him with God (14.3; 21.22). But the Johannine expansion of the Synoptic teaching about the present experience of Jesus' followers, before his parousia, means that its teaching encourages all those members of his community who continue to live in an unjust world.

Part III

Historical Reference in the Fourth Gospel

Chapter 11

THE IMPLIED AUTHOR: HIS IDENTITY, HIS SOURCES AND HIS STYLE

The existence of a text implies that, at some time or at different times, someone or some people wrote it. A text both implies an author or authors and supplies some information about him, her or them. It can tell us about the world-view, knowledge and writing skills of this 'implied author', but it cannot give us a full picture of the actual author. When we read several works by the same author whose biography is well known from other sources, we cannot but be struck by the fact that the 'implied author' of each individual text and the actual author of all of them do not share completely the same characteristics. For example, readers have often expressed difficulty in attributing *Mansfield Park* to Jane Austen who also wrote *Emma* and *Pride and Prejudice*, not least because the heroine of *Mansfield Park*, Fanny, represents a passivity and feebleness so out of character with the heroines of the other stories. A different value system seems to guide the 'implied author'.

Reliable evidence, external to the text itself, is required to discover the actual author. It will be clear from the title of this chapter that I think what evidence exists to link the Gospel with the apostle John is late and unreliable, but I shall set it out for the reader to make up his or her own mind. In the first and second centuries CE authors did publish works under their own name. For example, the Jewish historian Josephus published his books under his own name, although he did not provide a single title for the work which became known as *The Jewish War*. The canonical Gospels, however, appear to have circulated anonymously at first. The attribution of each to a particular author seems to have happened only when the four were well known in many churches and were brought together, so that distinguishing one from another became necessary. In the earliest period it is possible that only one Gospel was used by an individual church, so that it functioned as *the* Gospel, without qualification. And even later, when church fathers in the first half of the second century quote from or allude to material from the Gospels which have come down to us, they do not attribute the passage to a particular Gospel by mentioning the author (see Metzger 1987: Appendix III). Nevertheless, what evidence is available will at least help us to date the composition of the Fourth Gospel.

1. *The Identity of the Author*

I shall present the details under four headings: manuscripts which contain all or part of the Gospel; allusions to stories or sayings which are also found in the Fourth Gospel, and which show either that the Gospel already existed or that some elements which became part of the Gospel existed independently; clear references to the Gospel which do not attribute it to the apostle John; and, finally, references to the Gospel which do attribute it to the apostle John.

1.1. *Manuscripts*

The earliest manuscript of a fragment of the Fourth Gospel, 18.31-33, 37, 38 is Papyrus 52 (see Roberts 1935), a papyrus discovered in Egypt and dated on palaeographical evidence before 150 CE, perhaps as early as 125 CE (see Aland 1986). Third century Egyptian papyri contain more of the Gospel. $\mathfrak{P}^{66}$, the earliest of these, dated about 200 CE, contains most of the Gospel with some gaps, due to damage. Details about the contents of the rest are as follows:

$\mathfrak{P}^{5}$	fragments of chs. 1, 16 and 20
$\mathfrak{P}^{22}$	15.25–16.2, 21-32.
$\mathfrak{P}^{28}$	6.8-12, 17-22
$\mathfrak{P}^{39}$	8.14-22
$\mathfrak{P}^{45}$	fragments of chs. 10 and 11
$\mathfrak{P}^{75}$	chs. 1–12 almost complete, fragments of 13; 14.9-30; 15.7-8
$\mathfrak{P}^{90}$	18.36–19.7 (see Aland 1986)

The fourth century vellum codices, Sinaiticus and Vaticanus, contain the whole Gospel, as do the later manuscript (see Aland 1966). The survival of early manuscripts is a matter of chance and climatic conditions. But the discovery of $\mathfrak{P}^{52}$ gives us a date, before 150 CE, by which the Gospel must have been written and tells us that it was read in Egypt, even though it may not have been written there.

1.2. *Allusions to Stories and Sayings which also Appear in the Fourth Gospel*

Clement of Rome's First Epistle to the Corinthians 49.1 (about 96 CE) may allude to Jn 14.15: 'Let him who has love in Christ perform the commandments of Christ'. (For an English translation of this and all the other references below, see *The Ante-Nicene Christian Library*). Some of the epistles of Ignatius of Antioch (died about 115 CE) may also allude to passages in the Fourth Gospel, but there are no verbatim quotations, and Haenchen, for example, thinks none is a true parallel: *Phld.* 7.1 to Jn 3.8 and 8.14; *Phld.* 9.1 to Jn 10.7 and 9; *Rom.* 7.3 to Jn 6.33; *Magn.* 7.1 to Jn 5.19; *Magn.* 8.2 to Jn 1.1, 8.29 and 7.28. Justin Martyr (100-165 CE) may allude to Jn 6.34 and 52 in his discussion of the sacraments (*First Apology* 66.2, about 155 CE), and his reference to the serpent in the wilderness as a type of Christ (*Dialogue with Trypho* 91) could echo Jn 3.14 or both could reflect a common tradition based on Scripture and also represented by the *Epistle of Barnabas* 12.7 (first half of the second century). In addition, his statement about the baptist (*Dialogue with Trypho* 88.7) is like that in Jn 1.20.

None of these possible allusions is close enough to the wording of the Fourth Gospel to provide certain evidence of knowledge of that text.

1.3. *Clear References to the Written Gospel which do not Attribute it to the Apostle John*

Whether the following passages should be cited in this section or the previous one is a matter of judgment, but in mine they are clear references to the written text as we have it. The earliest come from the fragments of a previously unknown apocryphal gospel contained in the Egerton Papyrus 2 in the British Museum. It was found in Egypt and is dated from palaeographical evidence to the middle of the second century. C.H. Dodd's discussion of the gospel contains the Greek text and an English translation (1936). Dodd convincingly demonstrates that the first section of the fragments is based on Jn 5.39, 45, 9.29, that the second section is based on Jn 7.30, 32, 44, 8.20, 59, 10.31, 33, 39, and that the sixth section may be based on Jn 10.30-31.

He concludes that the Fourth Gospel was more popular in Egypt than the Synoptics before 150 CE. The second earliest comes from Justin Martyr's *First Apology* 61.4-5 (around 155 CE), 'Unless you are born again you will not enter the kingdom of heaven. Now it is clear to all that those who have once come into being cannot enter the womb of those who bore them.' The expression 'the kingdom of heaven' is Matthaean rather than Johannine, but the rough quotation and allusion to Nicodemus's misunderstanding draw on the text of Jn 3.1-5. The third example comes from the 170s, Tatian's quotation of Jn 1.51 in *Orations to the Greeks* 13.1. More general evidence for the existence of the Fourth Gospel is provided by the fact that Tatian's *Diatessaron* (about 175 CE) accords to the Fourth Gospel the same status as that given to the Synoptics (See Eusebius's *Ecclesiastical History* 4.29.6). From the same date, about 170 CE, comes Melito of Sardis's *Homily on the Passion* which alludes to the Fourth Gospel both in its recurring theme of Christ as the Paschal Lamb (e.g. 7 and 5.70-71) and in two particular passages: 78 mentions the raising of a man four days dead (see Jn 11.39-44) and 95, in describing Jesus' crucifixion, mentions the τίτλος (used only in John) and states that Jesus was lifted up (ὑψόω) on a cross (see Jn 3.14 and 19.19). Finally, Theophilus of Antioch (*Ad Autolycum* 2.22, around 180 CE) quotes Jn 1.1 in his discussion of Spirit-inspired people. He calls the author John, but does not specify whether he is an apostle.

These references confirm the manuscript evidence that the Fourth Gospel existed and circulated by 150 CE.

1.4. *References to the Fourth Gospel which Attribute it to the Apostle John*

Evidence for a biography of the apostle John is not only sparse but contradictory. The Synoptic Gospels tell the story of Jesus' call of the two sons of Zebedee, James and John (Mt. 4.21-22 and parallels) and later list them among the twelve (Mt. 10.2 and parallels). Matthew and Mark also relate Jesus' reply to their or their mother's request that they sit at Jesus' right and left hand in his glory or kingdom (Mk 10.35-45; Mt. 20.20-28): 'Are you able to drink the cup that I am to drink?' Their affirmation prompts Jesus' prophecy: 'You will drink my cup'. The passage can be interpreted as a prediction of the brothers' martyrdom, and Acts 12.2 asserts that James was killed by Herod. Some fifth-, sixth- and ninth-century references claim that

John was also martyred (see Barrett 1978: 103-104), but no account of John's death occurs in the New Testament. Both Acts 1–12 and Gal. 2.9 picture John alive and well in Jerusalem in the earliest period, but say nothing about what happened to him later. The Fourth Gospel never mentions James or John, although the appendix, 21.2, refers to 'the sons of Zebedee' without naming them.

According to Irenaeus (about 130–200 CE), John lived into the reign of the Emperor Trajan (96–117 CE) in Asia. In discussing the age of Jesus when he died, Irenaeus claims that 'those who were conversant in Asia with John, the disciple of the Lord, [affirmed] that John conveyed to them that information. And he remained among them up to the times of Trajan' (*Against Heresies* 2.22.5. See also the fourth-century church historian Eusebius, who also refers to Irenaeus in *Ecclesiastical History* 2.23.3-4; 4.14.3-8; 5.8.4 and 5.20.4-8). Irenaeus also cites Polycarp, bishop of Smyrna in the second half of the second century, as the authority for a story about John seeing the Gnostic Cerinthus in the baths at Ephesus:

> There are also those who heard from him [Polycarp] that John, the disciple of the Lord, going to bathe at Ephesus, and perceiving Cerinthus therein, rushed out of the bath-house without bathing, exclaiming, 'Let us fly, lest even the bath-house fall down, because Cerinthus, the enemy of truth, is within' (*Against Heresies* 3.3.4).

Unfortunately, Polycarp's letters do not mention John.

Irenaeus is the first writer clearly to attribute the Fourth Gospel to the apostle John: 'Afterwards [that is, after the writing of the Synoptic Gospels] John, the disciple of the Lord, who also had leaned upon his breast, did himself publish a gospel during his residence at Ephesus in Asia' (*Against Heresies* 3.1.1). Here Irenaeus identifies the apostle John with the beloved disciple who reclined on Jesus' bosom according to Jn 13.23. The identification of the beloved disciple as the author of the Fourth Gospel rests on an interpretation of Jn 21.24. Immediately after an account of the resurrected Jesus' conversation with Peter about the fate of the beloved disciple, the text reads: 'This is the disciple who bears witness concerning these things and who wrote or who caused to be written [cf. 19.19, 22] these things, and we know that his witness is true'. It is not unnatural to interpret this as an attribution of the Gospel to the beloved disciple by the authors (we) of 21.24, although this may mean no more than that the Fourth Gospel is based on the witness and writings of the beloved disciple, not that our present Gospel was written by him, but it is more likely that the beloved disciple bore witness to Jesus' statement about his fate in 21.22. Certainly, 21.24 was not written by him. Moreover, the beloved disciple is never identified with John in the Fourth Gospel, and his function is that of an ideal, perhaps Gentile, disciple (see Chapter 14).

Eusebius (about 260–340 CE) also quotes a letter of Polycrates, bishop of Ephesus (about 189–198 CE), who identifies John with the beloved disciple, calls him a priest and claims that he was martyred and buried at Ephesus (*Ecclesiastical History* 3.31.3), although he does not say that he wrote the Fourth Gospel. This connexion of John with Ephesus which is also mentioned in the gnostic *Acts of John* (dated about 150–160 CE, Hennecke 1965: II, 144-76) is puzzling since no earlier documents associated with that place mention John's presence there (Paul's epistle to the Ephesians, the Acts of the Apostles, Ignatius's *Epistle to the Ephesians*).

Earlier, Justin Martyr (about 100–165 CE), in his *Dialogue with Trypho* 8.4 (written after 155 CE), mentions the apostle John as the author of Revelation. Rev. 1.1-2 claims that a certain John received the revelation but does not identify him as the apostle. On stylistic grounds, the author of the Fourth Gospel and of Revelation must be distinguished.

Another account of how the Fourth Gospel came to be written, different from that of Irenaeus, is found in an index to the canon, discovered by Muratori and named after him, which is generally dated in the second century, but could be later:

> The Fourth of the gospels, that of John, one of the apostles. When his fellow disciples and bishops urged him, he said, 'Fast with me from today for three days, and what will be revealed to each one let us relate to one another.' In the same night, it was revealed to Andrew, one of the apostles, that whilst all were to go over it, John in his own name should write everything down. . . What wonder then if John so boldly sets forth each point, saying of himself in his epistle(s), What we have seen with our eyes and heard with our ears, and our hands have handled, these things we have written. For so he avows himself to be not only an eyewitness and hearer but also a writer of all the wonderful works of the Lord in order (*New Testament Apocrypha*, I).

By the second half of the second century, therefore, the Fourth Gospel is said to be the work of the apostle John, but the tradition cannot be traced to an earlier period. Papias, bishop of Hieropolis (about 130–140 CE), for example, does not refer to a Gospel written by John but emphasizes, according to Eusebius (*Ecclesiastical History* 3.39.3), that sayings which the presbyters passed on to their disciples from Jesus' disciples were of more worth than books. In this section both the apostle John, as the source of some of the presbyters' sayings, and a presbyter John are mentioned, but the line of tradition runs from original disciples to presbyters to their disciples to Papias. Irenaeus's claim that Papias was 'a hearer of John' (*Against Heresies* 5.33.3-4), therefore, telescopes history, whether it refers to the apostle or the presbyter. (For a discussion of these and other passages, see Barrett 1978: 100-15, and Haenchen 1984: I, 6-19.)

We know that when Irenaeus was writing against heretics, especially Gnostics, he was anxious to cite the four Gospels as authorities and to associate their origin with apostles. In the case of the Fourth Gospel, this could be done by identifying John with the beloved disciple and attributing the written Gospel to him. Irenaeus had no reliable external evidence for doing so, and his case rests on the ambiguous statement in Jn 21.24.

Moreover, Gnostics themselves favoured the Fourth Gospel. Irenaeus provides us with details of Gnostic interpretation of the Prologue, noting that they ascribed the Gospel to 'John, the disciple of the Lord' (*Against Heresies* 1.8.5). Heracleon (about 145–180 CE), a disciple of Valentinus, who lived in Rome between 136–165 CE, wrote a commentary on the Fourth Gospel to which Origen refers in his own commentary (185–254 CE) (Brooke 1891). Also the Valentinian *Gospel of Truth* from the Nag Hammadi library seems to be dependent on the Johannine Prologue (see Barrett 1984: ch. 4). There are other possible allusions to the Fourth Gospel in Gnostic texts (see Metzger 1987: 75-90). Perhaps it is surprising that a document which contains teaching at variance with Gnostic doctrine should have gained popularity in such circles. The Prologue sees the material world as the creation of God through the λόγος, and states that the λόγος became flesh. Moreover, the Gospel clearly depicts Jesus' dying on the cross. The references to 'glory' in connexion with the miracle stories, however, have sometimes led to Docetic interpretations, when 'glory' is understood not as 'honour' but as 'divine power', and the presence in the Gospel of words like 'truth' and 'life' would have been attractive to Gnostics. Once the Gospel was cut off from its scriptural roots, key terms could take on new meanings. Furthermore, if Irenaeus is correct in exemplifying Gnostic exegesis, it is clear that the Prologue could be read, rather against its grain, in the light of Gnostic teaching which could then be found in it. At the very least, the Prologue encourages a more detailed explication of cosmology (see Pagels 1973).

Another second-century heretical group, the Montanists, also favoured the Fourth Gospel. According to Hippolytus's account (*Refutations of all Heresies* 8.19.1-3, written about 200 CE; Montanus lived around 157 CE), Priscilla and Maximilla both claimed that the Spirit Paraclete inspired their prophecies.

Hengel's recent attempt to identify the author of the Fourth Gospel with the 'elder John' mentioned by Papias (1989) is unconvincing. For example, he argues that the Fourth Gospel was attributed to 'the disciple John' a generation before Irenaeus wrote, but the evidence is against this view. On p. 8 he suggests that Ptolemy, the disciple of Valentinus, attributed the Gospel to 'John, the Lord's disciple', citing Irenaeus's *Against Heresies* 1.8.5. But Irenaeus points out in his preface that he is particularly concerned to refute the teachings of Ptolemy's disciples, not those of Ptolemy himself. Hence, his quotation in 1.8.5 is a quotation of 'their' teaching not 'his'. In the Latin text of *Against Heresies*, but not in the Greek text, the section concludes with the statement: 'Such are the views of Ptolemy', but this is an explanatory gloss which divides Prolemaic teaching from that of other Gnostic schools. We can say, therefore, on the basis of Irenaeus's quotation, that Ptolemy's disciples and contemporaries of Irenaeus attributed the Gospel to 'John, the Lord's disciple', but not that Ptolemy did. Hengel goes on to cite Ptolemy's letter to Flora, which is quoted by the fourth-century writer against heresies, Epiphanius (*Panorian* 33.3.6), and which contains the statement: 'Moreover, the *apostle* says that the creation of the world was peculiar to him and that all things were made through him and apart from him nothing was made'. This quotation from Jn 1.3 is therefore attributed to an unnamed apostle. But Epiphanius's text is notoriously corrupt and has been subject to considerable emendation. Even so, it counts against Hengel's thesis, rather than for it, since it attributes the Gospel to an unnamed apostle, not to the elder John. Hengel's grounds for asserting that Ptolemy attributed the Gospel to John, the Lord's disciple and apostle, are therefore extremely shaky, and his inference that Valentinus, Ptolemy's teacher, knew the Fourth Gospel, is without warrant (p. 9).

Similarly, he accepts Irenaeus's view that Papias knew the elder John and plays down the fact that, according to Eusebius, Papias claimed to have interrogated the followers of the elder, not the elder himself (pp. 17-23). He explains Eusebius's disagreement with Irenaeus as an attempt to belittle Papias, but Eusebius actually quotes Papias. Later, Hengel even claims that Eusebius supports his view, namely that Papias knew the elder John, by translating Eusebius's *Ecclesiastical History* 3.39.14 as follows (p. 27): Papias 'gives accounts of the Lord's sayings obtained from Aristion or learnt directly from John the elder'. The Greek of this quotation is found only in the footnote, and is more appropriately translated: 'Papias gives us in his work accounts of the aforesaid Aristion of the sayings of the Lord, and *the traditions* of John the elder'. This is not a claim that Papias learnt directly from John the elder, but a repetition of the earlier statement that Papias had received the traditions of John the elder (because he had met his followers). Moreover, Hengel's suggestion that the order of the apostles listed by Papias is derived essentially from the order in Jn. 1.40-51 and 21.2 is unconvincing (pp. 17-21). Papias's order is Andrew, Peter, Philip, Thomas, James, John and Matthew. Jn. 1.40-51 has Andrew, Peter, Philip, Nathanael, and Jn 21.2 has Peter, Thomas, Nathanael, the sons of Zebedee and two others. The only correspondence in order is between Andrew, Peter, Philip in Papias and John 1. Otherwise, there are differences both in order and content.

But even if we were to accept Hengel's interpretation of the evidence, we would still be faced with a difficulty. We are being asked to accept the details of testimonies to the authorship of the Fourth Gospel from people who lived in the second century, but, at the same time, we have to reject their main contention that the author was John the son of Zebedee. Hengel argues that the Gospel could not have been written by John the son of Zebedee (p. 130), but was written by John the elder.

Again, if we were to accept this hypothesis, we would know only the name of the author, 'the elder John' and nothing more about him. Papias provides no details of his biography. In ch. 5 Hengel suggests that the name John makes it probable that the author was a Palestinian Jew, since the name was popular in Palestine, and that he was probably from a priestly family, since many high priests were called John. This allows him to accept Polycrates' testimony, quoted by Eusebius, that the author was a priest, but he rejects the other part of that testimony, that the author was martyred. The other points which Hengel adduces in support of his hypothesis, that the author knew Aramaic and was conversant with the cultural traditions and topography of Judaea and Jerusalem, will be considered in section 3 of this chapter and in Chapters 13 and 14, where it will be shown that the suggestions fail to explain the features of the Gospel. As far as the name 'John' is concerned, it became popular in Gentile Christian circles when Christianity became a largely Gentile religion.

1.5. *Conclusion*

The attribution of the Fourth Gospel to the apostle John is not found earlier than the second half of the second century. Irenaeus's claims were motivated by his opposition to heresies and are based on the obscure reference to the beloved disciple in Jn 21.24. The beloved disciple is pictured by the Fourth Gospel as close to Jesus, but is distinguished from Peter. The Synoptic Gospels give special prominence to Peter, James and John (e.g. Mt. 17.1; 26.37 and parallels), and Acts 12.2 tells of James's martyrdom. If all four Gospels are assumed to be describing the same historical characters straightforwardly and accurately, John is a likely candidate for identification with the beloved disciple as he is not otherwise mentioned in the Fourth Gospel. Jn 21.2 lists the sons of Zebedee and two other unnamed disciples amongst those present at the final resurrection appearance, and then goes on to mention the beloved disciple. Irenaeus must have assumed that the beloved disciple was a son of Zebedee, not one of the other unnamed disciples. The reference can, of course, be interpreted differently (see later, Chapter 14). Moreover, as Barrett notes (1978: 115), the paucity of references to the Fourth Gospel in the early period, outside of Gnostic circles, tells against any suggestion that it was published with apostolic authority.

Nevertheless, the survey has confirmed that the Gospel must have been written before 150 CE, and may have been written much earlier. The earliest possible date for its composition is difficult to determine. Irenaeus supposed that it was written after the Synoptic Gospels, and, if so, a date after 90 CE would have to be accepted. Those, like Barrett, who think the Gospel is dependent on Mark and Luke, would support such a date. Otherwise, we have to assume that enough time has elapsed to allow for considerable reflection on Jesus' significance, and, perhaps, for the death of the original disciples. Certainly, the fact of Peter's martyrdom is alluded to in 21.19 (cf. *1 Clem.* 5.4). Such considerations suggest any date after about 65 CE. Recently John Robinson has argued for the Fourth Gospel's independence from the Synoptics and for an early date (Robinson 1985).

We can come to no more certain conclusion about the Gospel's place of origin. The earliest manuscripts come from Egypt so it is just possible that it was written at Alexandria, although, if this were the case, we should expect it to show a far greater affinity with Platonism and Stoicism after the manner of Philo of Alexandria's writings. Barrett makes two further suggestions (1978: 128-30). It could have been written at Antioch, since Theophilus of Antioch (about 180 CE) quotes from it and is reputed to have written a commentary on it. Or it could have been written at Ephesus. If it was, this might account for the development of a tradition connecting John with Ephesus once he was identified as its author.

The Fourth Gospel tells its story of Jesus from the perspective of an omniscient narrator. The convention of the omniscient narrator is found in scriptural as well as classical Greek narratives. Its use does not imply that the author claimed to be omniscient, although it does impart to the narrative a sense of authority and unity. The actual author is limited to a human life in time and space, and hence to the limitations of language, cultural awareness, historical knowledge and theological perceptions which time and place impose. The text, then, should provide us with some information about the person or people who wrote it.

1.6. *Literacy*

Harris's study of literacy in the Graeco–Roman world (1989) explains the difficulties of discovering the extent and nature of literacy among different social groups. Could all males belonging to the higher orders read, and could they also write? It is likely that they could, but unlikely that more than a small percentage of women from the same social orders could. Moreover, any document which was to be read by others had to be written in a neat, legible hand, and scribes were employed for the actual labour of writing, so that, even when the rich could write, their documents were produced by professionals. In modern western society, too, documents are usually produced by secretaries at their employers' dictation, and, before the invention of typewriters and word processors, by professional scribes. But scribes could also work for members of the lower orders who could not themselves write. Scribes could draw up legal documents for commercial and civil transactions, write letters and produce texts for reading in public. No doubt, in Palestine, priests who were not on duty in the Temple could perform these useful functions. Josephus mentions that male Jewish children were taught 'letters' and 'learnt both the laws and the deeds of their forefathers' but this probably refers to the ability to read rather than write (*Apion* 2.204). In general, most peasants could neither read nor write. But how widespread was literacy among the middle orders? Paul is an interesting case. Was his detailed knowledge of the Septuagint based on reading or on memorizing? His lifestyle as an itinerant missionary makes it unlikely that he would have been able to refer to a written text when composing his letters, but his memory must have been based on study of actual texts of the Septuagint. Moreover, he could write too, although he normally dictated most of his letters to a scribe, sometimes adding a final note in his own hand (1 Cor. 16.21-24; Gal. 6.11-18; 2 Thess. 3.17-18; Phlm. 19-25; see also Col. 4.18).

Could the author of the Fourth Gospel read and write? It seems most probable that he could read. His quotations from and allusions to Scripture seem to have been based on memory, but his memory was probably based on study of the texts. His use of sources also suggests an ability to read. Whether he could write is less clear. The Fourth Gospel could have been dictated to a professional scribe and probably would have been even if the author himself could write. Whether he could write is therefore uncertain. Whether the members of the community for which the Gospel was composed could read is also uncertain. At least one of them must have been able to do so for the enterprise to be worthwhile, but it is possible that the author read his own work to the community. In any case, most members of the community would have heard public readings of the text rather than reading it for themselves. The nature of the text, with its leisurely, simple and repetitive style, makes it comprehensible to listeners.

1.7. *The Implied Author: Male or Female?*

The Pauline epistles sometimes refer to women who exercised responsibilities in the churches he founded and nurtured (e.g. 1 Cor. 1.11; 11.5; 16.19; Rom. 16.1-2, 3, 6, 7, 12, 15). We cannot assume, therefore, that an educated Christian woman could not have written the Fourth Gospel in the first century CE, although female literacy in the Graeco–Roman world was much rarer than male literacy, even among the élite (see Harris 1989). Nevertheless, it seems unlikely that the author implied by the text was a woman. In Chapter 10 it was noted that the women depicted in the Gospel are assigned the role of servants to men. There is no parallel to the account of the Canaanite or Syro-Phoenician woman who wins her argument with Jesus according to the Gospels of Matthew and Mark (Mt. 15.22-28; Mk 7.24-30). Moreover, the Johannine depiction of Mary Magdalene, who found the empty tomb, and to whom the resurrected Jesus first appeared, is marginalized (Jn 20.1-18, compare Mt. 28.1-10). She merely reports the disappearance of Jesus' corpse so that Peter and the beloved disciple can confirm that the tomb is empty, and the beloved disciple is the first to believe in the resurrection of Jesus. When the resurrected Jesus does appear to her, his message is for the disciples rather than for her. Like that of other women in the Fourth Gospel (the Samaritan woman, Martha and Mary) her function is to serve men, or, in the case of Jesus' mother, to be protected by a man. The author of the Fourth Gospel assumes the prophetic and inspired role of retelling the story of Jesus. It seems unlikely that a woman could have done this while, at the same time, assigning a subsidiary duty to women within the story.

In the first-century Graeco-Roman world, including the Jewish world, men were responsible for defending the security and relative political independence of communities through war and diplomacy. The superiority of male physical strength and their freedom from childbearing determined their duty. But the Fourth Gospel refuses to accord the male function of dominance to Jesus and his followers. As the representative of a humanity completely dedicated to God, Jesus is no warrior or political advocate. Rather, he is martyred by the military might of Rome. His role is that of a servant (13.3-17), and his example could be followed by women as well as men. It is a pity that the male myopia of the author prevented him from drawing out this implication more clearly. There is something of a parallel between the story of Mary of Bethany's anointing Jesus' feet (12.3-8) and the story of Jesus' washing the disciples' feet (13.3-10), but this is not followed through. Jesus' meeting with Mary Magdalene could have included a more positive appreciation of her.

2. *Sources Used by the Gospel*

2.1. *The Synoptic Gospels*

It is likely that the present Gospel takes up earlier sources about the life of Jesus. We can be certain that the Synoptic Gospels made use of earlier sources which they reproduced with surprising fidelity, although whether Mark in its present form was used by both Matthew and Luke, whether Matthew and Luke depended on another source, or Luke used Matthew, or whether Mark is an epitome of Matthew and Luke, remains uncertain. The relationships among the Synoptics are still problematic because no one solution accounts for all the evidence, in spite of the fact that we have three Gospels which exhibit many verbatim agreements. The Fourth Gospel is not related to the first three in the ways in which they relate to one another. In general, the vocabulary and style of the Fourth Gospel are distinctive, its ordering and timing of events are unique (although Mk 14.13-14 and Lk. 13.34 may suggest earlier visits by Jesus to Jerusalem), and many of the individual episodes are without parallel in the other Gospels.

Nevertheless, some of the individual Johannine stories are very similar to some found in the Gospels according to Mark and Luke: Jesus and John (Jn 1.29-34; Mk 1.7-11; Jn 3.24; Mk 1.14), the incident in the Temple (Jn 2.14-22; Mk 11.15-19), the healing from a distance (Jn 4.46-54; Lk. 7.1-10), the healing of the feeble man (Jn 5.2-9; Mk 2.1-12), the feeding of the five thousand (Jn 6.1-14; Mk 6.33-44 and 8.1-10), the walking on the water (Jn 6.16-21; Mk 6.45-51), the healing of the blind man (Jn 9.1-7; Mk 7.33 and 8.22-26), the anointing at Bethany (Jn 12.1-8; Mk 14.3-9; Lk. 7.37-38), the entry into Jerusalem (Jn 12.12-16; Mk 11.1-10), the passion narrative (Jn 18.1–19.30; Mk 14.43–15.41; Lk. 22.47–23.49), the burial of Jesus' corpse (Jn 19.38-42; Mk 15.42-46), the empty tomb (Jn 20.1, 11-12; Mk 16.1-8), the catch of fish (Jn 21.3-8; Lk. 5.1-11). These stories are similar in form and share some of the Greek vocabulary of the accounts in Mark or Luke, although not to the extent that the Synoptics agree with one another (see the list in Barrett 1978: 44-45).

If John were dependent on Mark and Luke for these parts of the Gospel, considerable freedom has been exercised in the retelling (see Bailey 1963; and on the passion narrative, Green 1988: ch. 4).

Could it be that the Fourth Evangelist was capable of even greater creative freedom in taking up traditions from the Synoptics? The stories of Martha, her sister Mary and their brother Lazarus in John 11–12 suggest this possibility. An incident involving the sisters Mary and Martha is related in Lk. 10.38-42, in which Mary sits at Jesus' feet listening to him, while Martha serves the dinner, as she does in Jn 12.2. Luke also records a parable about a rich man and a poor man called Lazarus (Lk. 16.19-31). In the parable both characters die and the rich man asks Abraham to send Lazarus to his living brothers to warn them of the torments that lie in store after death. Abraham's final refusal is expressed in these words, 'If they do not hear Moses and the prophets, neither will they be convinced if someone should rise from the dead' (Lk. 16.31). The story of the raising of Lazarus in John 11–12 demonstrates the truth of this assertion, since the incident leads the chief priests to plot the death of Lazarus as well as that of Jesus. Then Mary's anointing of Jesus' feet at Bethany (Jn 12.1-8) combines features of Mark's account of an unnamed woman at Bethany anointing Jesus' head (Mk 14.3-8) with Luke's account of an unnamed woman who weeps over Jesus' feet, wipes them with her hair and anoints them (Lk. 7.36-38). To suppose that the Fourth Evangelist has so freely elaborated the material in Mark and Luke throws doubt on the accuracy of historical particulars in the Fourth Gospel, but no more so than in the case of the Johannine Jesus' discourses which are largely free compositions. Moreover, the supposition explains why the Synoptics are ignorant of an extraordinary miracle, the resuscitation of Lazarus, Jesus' friend. Similarly, the footwashing in Jn 13.3-17 exemplifies the saying in Lk. 22.27 and 37.

Barrett has drawn attention to the fact that, although there are many differences in the order of events in Mark and John, there are also some striking parallels. His best examples come from comparing Mark 6–8 with John 6. The feeding of the five thousand (Mk 6.34-44; 8.1-10; Jn 6.1-13) is followed by the walking on the water (Mk 6.45-52; Jn 6.16-21), and these incidents help to prompt Peter's confession (Mk 8.29; Jn 6.68-69). In between, the 'Jews' ask for a sign (Mk 8.11-12; Jn 6.30), and Jesus and the disciples discuss bread (Mk 8.14-21; Jn 6.32-58).

Again, in spite of the differences, there are echoes of Jesus' teaching from Mark and Luke in John, for example: Mk 9.1 in Jn 8.51; Mk 10.45 and Lk. 6.40 in Jn 13.13-16; Mk 14.18 in Jn 13.18; Mk 14.22 in Jn 6.51; Mk 14.30 and Lk. 22.34 in Jn 13.38; Mk 14.41 in Jn 13.1; Lk. 10.16 in Jn 13.20-21; Lk. 11.9-10 in Jn 16.23; Lk. 13.24 in Jn 10.1. Moreover, Luke gives Jesus a farewell discourse at the supper table (22.14-38) which may have provided the basis for the Johannine expansion. Also, the Fourth Gospel, like the Third, names a second Judas, not Iscariot, as one of Jesus' disciples (Jn 14.22; Lk. 6.16), mentions Annas as a chief priest (Jn 18.13; Lk. 3.2), and explains Judas's betrayal as Satan possession (Jn 13.2, 27; Lk. 22.3). Occasionally, Johannine discourses seem to provide commentaries on sayings found in the Synoptics. For example, Jesus' statements about eating his flesh and drinking his blood in Jn 6.51-58 expound the significance of Jesus' identification of the bread and the wine in Mk 14.22-25, while Jesus' prayer in Jn 12.27-28 transforms the Gethsemane prayer in Mk 14.34-36. Again, Jesus' prayer in John 17 echoes petitions in the Lord's Prayer (17.1, 4, 11-12, 15 and Lk. 11.2, 4; cf. Mt. 6.10, 13). The same can be said about some of the parallel incidents recorded. For example, the Johannine account of John's recognition of Jesus (Jn 1.29-34) seems to presuppose the account of Jesus' baptism in Mk 1.7-11. (For fuller lists of parallels between John and the Synoptics see Solages 1979; and see the studies, Dodd 1963; Lindars 1971; Robinson 1985.)

Fewer instances of parallels exist between the Fourth Gospel and the First, but some details are shared by both, for example: Jn 1.27 and Mt. 3.11; Jn 4.53 and Mt. 8.13; Jn 6.3, 5 and Mt. 15.29b-30; Jn 11.49 and Mt. 26.3-4; Jn 12.14b-15 and Mt. 21.4-5; Jn 12.20, 25-26, 44 and Mt. 10.38-40; Jn 13.16 and Mt. 10.24-25; Jn 19.38 and Mt. 27.57. Most importantly, Matthew depicts a resurrection appearance to Mary Magdalene like John (Mt. 28.8-10; Jn 20.11-18 cf. Lk. 24.12 and Neirynck 1984), and mentions the doubt of at least some of the disciples about Jesus' resurrection (Mt. 28.17), a feature exemplified in the Johannine story of Thomas's doubt (Jn 20.24-29).

Given these striking parallels with the Synoptics, however, how are the differences to be explained? Jesus' itinerary, with several visits to Jerusalem, is determined by the Johannine conception that Jesus came to 'his own' and was rejected. The Synoptics already hint at earlier visits before the final one (Mk 13.13-14; Lk. 13.34) and the Fourth

Gospel actualizes them in order to present Jesus' confrontations with the 'Jews' and especially their leaders. The Fourth Gospel also dates Jesus' death to the time when the Passover lambs were being sacrificed in the Temple, and therefore excludes the possibility that his last meal with his disciples was a Passover meal, as the Synoptics depict it. But this connexion with the Passover meal is made only in the introductions to the Synoptic eucharistic narratives, not within the account of the meal. No connexions are made between the eucharistic meal and the main elements of Passover meals, lamb, bitter herbs and unleavened, not ordinary, bread. The introductions to the eucharistic meal in the Synoptics seek to make a connexion with the Passover so that a theological typology can be discerned between the Passover sacrifice and Jesus' death, symbolized by the interpretation of the significance of bread and wine. The Fourth Gospel makes the same theological connexion by timing Jesus' death to coincide with the Passover sacrifice and by allusions to Exodus 12. The other major difference between John and the Synoptics is to be found in the amount of space devoted to eschatological teaching and teaching about the gift of Spirit. The Synoptics illustrate their eschatological teaching in parables and contain 'apocalyptic' discourses. The Fourth Gospel merely refers to eschatological beliefs without illustration, and, instead, concentrates on the significance of Jesus' life, death and resurrection as a model for the life of a community which continues to live in an unjust world. Teaching about the Spirit explains how the community can remain faithful to Jesus. In this way it supplements Synoptic teaching without contradicting it.

There used to be a consensus among scholars that the Synoptics were unknown to the Fourth Evangelist, but that some traditions were common to the Synoptics and John. The use of a term like 'traditions' is, however, too vague. What the thesis requires us to posit is the existence of independent individual stories about Jesus, written in Greek, and inherited by Mark, Luke, Matthew and John. Barrett is certainly right in asserting that it is easier for us to assume that the Fourth Evangelist knew the Gospels of Mark and Luke, but that he used and transformed them with more freedom than the other Evangelists did their sources. Moreover, those who argue *both* that John drew on Synoptic-like material but not on the Synoptics, *and* that the material was modified, as most recently Green (1988) does in his study of the passion narratives, have no way of distinguishing

Synoptic-like material from the Synoptics. Barrett is not alone in recognizing Johannine dependence on the Synoptics. Neirynck (1979, 1982, 1984, 1990) argues that John knew all the Synoptics. Boismard's theory (1977) is more complicated since he argues that each of the four Gospels went through more than one stage of composition and that, at the second stage in the development of the Fourth Gospel, the redactor drew on the Synoptics at various stages in their development (see the criticisms by Neirynck 1979: Appendix V). Moreover, the Fourth Gospel is *re*telling a story already familiar to the audience (Part I, Chapter 1). If the audience was not familiar with the stories in the Synoptics, it was familiar with stories very like them in outline and in detail. Given the nature of the material, it cannot be proved that the Fourth Evangelist used the other three Gospels as sources, but it seems the most likely explanation of their literary relationships.

2.2. *Other Sources*

Nevertheless, the Fourth Gospel seems to have drawn on details independent of the Synoptics. There are many names of people and places in the Fourth Gospel without parallel in the others. Only John transliterates the Hebrew messiah (1.41) and the Aramaic Cephas (1.42). It calls Simon the son of John (1.42 contrast Mt. 16.17) and Judas the son of Simon Iscariot (e.g. 6.71). It mentions Nathanael (1.45; 21.2), Nicodemus (3.1-10; 7.50-52; 19.39-40); Malchus (18.10), Mary the wife or daughter of Clopas (19.25, see Lk. 24.18). It refers to places unknown in the Synoptics: Bethany beyond the Jordan (1.28), Cana (2.1), Aenon near Salim (3.23), Sychar (4.5), the place described in 5.2, the sea of Tiberias (6.1), the pool of Siloam (9.7; see Lk. 13.4), the portico of Solomon (10.23), the Kidron valley (18.1), Gabbatha (19.13). Also some Aramaic or Hebrew terms are translated in John but not in the Synoptics: rabbi (1.38; see Mt. 23.8) and rabboni (20.16; see Mk 10.51), messiah (1.41), Cephas (1.42), Siloam (9.7) and Thomas (11.16).

Is it possible to define other sources used by the Gospel? Bultmann (1971) suggested that the miracle stories were derived from a signs source. Although the Gospel has a remarkably unified style, the following sections give the impression that they are derived from sources: 2.1-10, 13-19, 4.46-53, 5.1-16, 12.1-8 and 12-15, three of which include miracles (see Ruckstuhl 1951: 217-19). Moreover, the miracle of changing water into wine is called 'the *first* of his signs' (2.11) and the healing of the royal official's son concludes with 'This was now the *second* sign that Jesus did when he had come from Judea to Galilee' (4.54). Between these two stories the Gospel notes that Jesus performed signs at the Passover feast in Jerusalem (2.23) but does not describe them. Bultmann therefore supposed that the enumeration of the two Cana miracles comes from the signs source, and that the summary in 2.23 is redactional. These two points are not, however, sufficient to warrant Bultmann's signs source. The arrangement of material can be explained differently. The changing of water into wine is the first of Jesus' miracles recounted in the Gospel and it is set in Cana in Galilee. The healing of the royal official's son is the second of Jesus' miracles in Galilee, also set at Cana (4.46). In other words, the enumeration makes sense in the present structure of the Gospel. The Gospel distinguishes Jesus' ministry in Galilee, where he met with initial success (4.45) until his rejection there (6.60), from his ministry in Judaea where he was opposed by most of the 'Jewish' leaders. He does perform signs in Judaea (2.23; 5.2-9; 9.1-7 and 11.39-44) but the last three are the occasions for opposition from the leadership, not acceptance. Moreover, Johannine stylistic characteristics are as frequent in most of the miracle stories as they are elsewhere. Recent attempts by Fortna (1970) and Nicol (1972) to define the signs source are not convincing (see Ruckstuhl 1977). Bultmann's second suggestion, that the discourses depend on another source, has met with even less interest (see Ruckstuhl 1951: 219). Haenchen's commentary (1980, 1984), written over a long period, never finally revised, and published posthumously, tries to distinguish tradition from redaction, but without the criteria for doing so. All these attempts fail because of the Gospel's impressive stylistic unity.

Only in the case of the Prologue have many scholars been convinced that a pre-Johannine hymn can be separated from its Johannine editing. There are two criteria which determine the procedure, poetic style and distinctive vocabulary. Nevertheless, these criteria are less weighty than has sometimes been supposed. It is appropriate to a Prologue about the eternal purpose of God that it should find expression in poetic parallelism. The juxtaposition of poetry about the eternal λόγος and prose about the earthly witness of John (1.6-8; 1.15), sections which are often labelled secondary, serves as a coherent introduction to John's and Jesus' ministries. The move from the eternal perspective to the historical is also signalled by the change of verb, from 'be' (εἰμι) to 'become' (γίνομαι). Moreover, poetic parallelism and prose are juxtaposed not only in the Prologue, but later in the Gospel (e.g. 6.37; 8.31-32).

It is true, however, that some of the vocabulary in the Prologue is not repeated in the rest of the Gospel. Each example needs to be assessed in turn. The Prologue tells of the eternal λόγος, and states that the 'λόγος became flesh' (1.14). In the rest of the Gospel Jesus refers to his teaching about himself as λόγος, which he has received from the Father and imparted to his disciples (e.g. 8.55; 14.24; 17.6, 14, 17; contrast 5.38), but he is not called the λόγος. Rather, he is called 'the Son'. The change, however, makes perfectly good sense. Once Jesus is identified as the embodiment of God's plan for humanity, it is reasonable to exemplify this man's relationship with God through the metaphor of son and father. More telling is the use of 'grace' (χάρις) in the Prologue, in the scriptural expression 'grace and truth' (1.14 and 17), and in the phrase 'grace instead of grace' (1.16). The word does not occur elsewhere in the Gospel, although it could easily have appeared in 6.29 or in the Farewell Discourses. It is found in the introductory formula in the second Johannine epistle (v. 3) and in a variant reading in the third epistle (v. 3). The Fourth Gospel uses the second of the scriptural pair, 'truth', to express its interest in fidelity and what is genuine. The failure to make use of 'grace' is the most significant of the arguments in favour of seeing parts of the Prologue as a pre-Johannine hymn. There is also one other word which occurs only in the Prologue, 'fullness' (πλήρωμα), in the confession, 'From his fullness we have all received' (1.16), but we might expect this word in a summary of the adequacy of faith in Jesus and not in the statements of partial faith which are found in the subsequent narrative. Only in the conclusion to the Gospel could it have recurred, in 20.30 or 21.25, but these final statements are apologies for the limitations of the narrative, together with an assurance that enough of the story has been told to justify belief in Jesus.

On the other hand, most of the key terms which the Gospel will explore are present in the Prologue: life, light and darkness, witness, to believe, true, truth, world, his own, to receive, children of God, flesh, honour, unique or only, and Father. Words important in the rest of the Gospel but absent from the Prologue include to lift up, the Son of man, the way, Paraclete, the Spirit, and to abide, but these would have been inappropriate at the beginning of the Gospel.

Parts of the Prologue, therefore, may have existed as a confessional hymn before the Gospel was written, but it is more likely that it was composed as an essential introduction to the story of Jesus which the Gospel relates. No doubt the Gospel takes up older material into its construction, but, without the existence of independent sources, it is now impossible to delineate them exactly. In the case of Mark, however, the Fourth Gospel seems to present revised versions of some of its stories. In the case of Luke and Matthew, it is possible that some of their traditions have also influenced John.

2.3. *The Unity of the Gospel*

The present form of the Gospel, with its abrupt transitions, corrections and additions gives the impression that it was written and rewritten but never finally revised. There is a sudden break at the end of ch. 5, Jesus' discourse in Jerusalem, without any lead into the opening of ch. 6, set in Galilee. Jn 6.1, 'After this Jesus went to the other side of the sea of Galilee, which is the sea of Tiberias', should follow a previous incident set near the lake. For this reason some commentators have reversed chs. 5 and 6. The previous incident would then be the healing of the official's son when Jesus was at Cana in Galilee (4.46-54). There is no manuscript support for the rearrangement, but the discourse in Jerusalem, chs. 7–10, does refer back to the healing of the feeble man in ch. 5 (7.21-24). The present order of the chapters, however, with 6 between 5 and 7, gives some relief from the disputes in Jerusalem, in spite of Jesus' rejection in Galilee at the end of ch. 6, and ch. 6 justifies Jesus' appeal to Moses at the end of ch. 5.

Again, chs. 15–17 seem to have been interpolated between the end of ch. 14, 'Rise, let us go hence', and the beginning of ch. 18, 'When Jesus had spoken these words, he went forth with his disciples'. Moreover, themes explored in chs. 13 and 14 are repeated in chs. 15–16, like Jesus' exemplary significance for his disciples (13.14-17 and 15.13), his imminent departure (13.33; 14.1-4 and 16.4-7, 16-24), his commandment to love one another (13.34-35 and 15.12-15), keeping Jesus' commandments (14.15, 21-24 and 15.7), and sending the Paraclete (14.16-17, 26 and 15.26; 16.7-15). Possibly, two versions of similar teaching have been included side by side instead of integrating them. Nevertheless, repetition is a feature of the Evangelist's style throughout the Gospel.

Occasionally, too, there are parenthetical corrections to statements in the text. For example, after the remark that Jesus was making and baptizing more disciples than John, a disclaimer is added, 'although Jesus himself did not baptize but only his disciples' (4.2). Similarly, after Jesus' statement 'Moses gave you circumcision' stands the correction 'not that it is from Moses, but from the fathers' (7.22). Perhaps these corrections were marginal glosses added by the original author or a later scribe and subsequently incorporated into the text, but there is no manuscript evidence to support their exclusion.

Finally, ch. 21 serves as an appendix to the main account, after a conclusion had been reached in 20.30-31. Because the resurrection narrative of ch. 21 is not placed before that conclusion, and a second, similar conclusion ends ch. 21, commentators have thought that the chapter was added later, and by a disciple of the original author. Unfortunately, stylistic arguments do not settle the question of authorship. There are some words used in ch. 21 which are not found in chs. 1–20, of which the following are most significant: ἀδελφοί (brothers for Christians); ἐξετάζω for ἐρωτάω (ask); ἰσχύω for δύναμαι (to be able); τολμάω (to dare); παιδία (children); ἀπό in a causative sense in v. 6; ἀπό for ἐκ in 'some of', v. 10; ἐπί for 'by' in v. 1; πλέον for μᾶλλον (more than); οὐ μακράν (not far) for ἐγγύς (near); and πρωΐα for πρωΐ (early). But most of the vocabulary and the themes are perfectly consonant with chs. 1–20, and Ruckstuhl (1951: 218) shows that the style is the same. It is clear, however, that the chapter was added some time after most of chs. 1–20 reached their present form. If the suggestion is accepted that the resurrection story in 21.1-14 is particularly concerned with the Gentile mission (see Chapter 14), it would make a suitable appendix to the main Gospel, set away from Jerusalem, as would the prediction of Peter's martyrdom and the discussion about the future of the beloved disciple. The Gospel would be impoverished by the removal of this final chapter. Whether by the same author or another, it provides a fitting conclusion.

These peculiarities can hardly elude any reader, but whether other additions to the Gospel can be discerned is less evident. Bultmann (1971) proposed that an ecclesiastical redactor added passages to an original Gospel in order to make its message more orthodox and less attractive to Gnostics. The additions are of two kinds, sacramental and eschatological. There are no stylistic reasons for distinguishing the passages as secondary, but the argument is advanced on the basis of contradictions in the message of the text. For example, there is no account of the institution of the eucharist when Jesus takes his last meal with his disciples, and no command from the resurrected Jesus that the disciples should baptize converts. Instead, it is suggested, the ecclesiastical redactor added eucharistic teaching at the end of the discourse on the bread of life (6.52-59), and incorporated a reference to baptism in the discourse to Nicodemus about rebirth (3.5). It is true that 6.52-59 meditates on the significance of Jesus' death for his disciples, and the passage provides the grounding for eucharistic practice in the church, but it is not an account of the institution of the eucharist. Similarly, if 3.5 is a reference to baptism, it is not explicit. Had an ecclesiastical redactor wanted to found these sacraments in the words and deeds of Jesus, he would have been better advised to place more explicit teaching in the Farewell Discourses or the resurrection narratives, as the First Gospel does. The Fourth Gospel shows no concern for sacramental practice, but great concern for understanding the point of Jesus' ministry, which is what occasions Christian sacraments.

Schnackenburg (1968, 1980, 1982) has followed Bultmann in viewing as secondary additions references to a future resurrection and final judgment. The refrain in ch. 6, 'I will raise him up at the last day' (6.39, 40, 44, 54), the statement in 5.28, 'For the hour is coming when all those who are in the tombs will hear his voice and come forth, those who have done good to the resurrection of life, and those who have done evil to the resurrection of judgment', and that in 11.25, 'He who believes in me, though he die, yet shall he live', all of which express a belief in a future resurrection at the end of history, are supposed to be additions because they encapsulate a horizontal perspective in contrast to the Gospel's dominant vertical perspective (e.g. 14.2-3). Moreover, 14.22-23, 'Lord, how is it that you will manifest yourself to us and *not* to the world? Jesus answered him, If a man loves me, he will keep my word, and my Father will love him, and we will come to him and make our home with him', has been read as a straightforward denial of a future parousia of Jesus. But the question is better understood as a reference to Jesus' resurrection appearances to the disciples and not to outsiders. Hence, Jesus' answer gives assurance that while the world exists, disciples can rely on the support of Jesus and the Father. Later, in 21.22-23, 'until I come' refers to a future parousia of Jesus, and it stands in the text without any apology. Whether the passage was written by the same author as 14.22-23 or not, no tension is perceived to exist between the two. Moreover, in 14.3 Jesus promises, 'I will come again and will take you to myself, that where I am, you may be also'. Bultmann and Schnackenburg insist that the vertical perspective excludes the horizontal, but this is true neither of apocalyptic literature like Daniel and *1 Enoch*, nor of the Fourth Gospel. Since neither manuscript evidence nor stylistic features require the separation of these passages, it is better to integrate them into the whole, as was attempted in Part II.

What picture of the 'implied author' emerges from these characteristics of the text? Certainly, he did not write the work all at once, but added subsidiary material at a later date. This is not an unusual procedure for writers. What is unusual is that the work should be circulated before its final revision. This probably implies that the author died before the text could be edited. If so, it is noteworthy that no disciple felt free to take on the role of editor, a matter which tells against any hypothesis involving a redactor. Just those parts which cry out for editorial revision are left as they are.

3. *Style*

Barrett (1978: 5, 7) succinctly and accurately characterizes the style of the Fourth Gospel:

> It is neither bad Greek nor (according to classical standards) good Greek. Solecisms are avoided; and so are all the fine and characteristic subtleties of the Greek language. In spite of the absence of these niceties the style remains not only clear but very impressive, charged with a repetitive emphasis and solemn dignity which are felt even in translation. John's vocabulary is very small, but even so many of his frequently used words occur comparatively rarely in the synoptic gospels. . . John can hardly be said to create a new vocabulary, yet his choice of words is undoubtedly distinctive. His Greek moves slowly and within narrow limits, which clearly distinguishes it from the other gospels; but it must be acknowledged to be an adequate instrument for the author's purpose. In spite of the small vocabulary, the reader never receives the impression of an ill-equipped writer at a loss for the right word; rather that of a teacher who is confident that his message can be summed up in a few fundamental propositions which he has learned to express with studied economy of diction.

The studies by E. Schweizer (1939) and E. Ruckstuhl (1951) make available the evidence for the unity of the Gospel's style. Johannine stylistic features are seen to be fairly evenly distributed throughout the Gospel. Ruckstuhl refutes Fortna's attempt to isolate a signs source (1970) and reasserts his earlier conclusions (1977), which are sound. Barrett (1978) provides a list of words, like ἀγαπάω (to love), ἀλήθεια (truth) and cognates, ζωή (life), Ἰουδαῖοι (Jews), κόσμος (world), μαρτυρέω (to bear witness) and cognates, μένειν (to remain), πέμπω (to send), τηρέω (to keep), φιλέω (to love) and φῶς (light), which are commonly found in the Fourth Gospel but seldom, if ever, in the other three (pp. 5-6), and a second list of common words in the Synoptics which are rarely or never used in John (p. 6). These two lists demonstrate the distinctive vocabulary of the Johannine presentation. There are also distinctive uses of otherwise common words. The particle οὖν has lost its force as 'therefore' and functions as a mere connective 'then' (e.g. 9.18). The demonstrative adjective ἐκεῖνος is used as a pronoun 'he' when οὗτος would have been expected (e.g. 5.35, 37, 38). The possessive pronoun ἐμός (my) is very common, and not simply in the genitive as often in the rest of the New Testament. The expressions ἀφ' ἑαυτοῦ (from himself) and ἀπ' ἐμαυτοῦ (from myself) also occur more frequently than elsewhere in the New Testament. Clauses introduced by ἵνα generally express no sense of purpose but are rather imperatival, 'Let such and such happen' (Turner 1965: 145-48). Finally, the construction οὐ (or μή). . . ἀλλά is more frequent in the Fourth Gospel than elsewhere. (For a complete list of the fifty stylistic characteristics used in Ruckstuhl's study, see Ruckstuhl 1951: 203-205.)

We should note that in spite of the limited vocabulary, however, synonyms are sometimes used for variety (e.g. ἀγαπᾶω/φιλέω; πέμπω/ἀποστέλλω) without any subtle distinctions. On the other hand, the Gospel usually presents its message by contrasting terms which are diametrically opposed: love/hate; light/darkness; life/death; truth/falsehood; above/below. This extremism, which may have been occasioned by the Gospel's Scripture, gives a kind of urgency and clarity which encourages the reader to choose life wholeheartedly.

One of the stylistic characteristics which helps to create the Gospel's slow dignity is the use of parataxis, that is, linking clauses and sentences with 'and' instead of making some subordinate to others. When 'and' is not used, often there is no connective (asyndeton), but sentences are simply set side by side (e.g. 1.40, 42, 45, 47). Both these features are common in Koine but not literary Greek. Verbs are often in the historic present, and the present and imperfect tenses are frequently periphrastic, that is, formed with the verb 'to be' and a participle (e.g. 3.23). Again, this gives the narrative a leisurely quality.

3.1. *Semitisms*

None of these stylistic features helps us to identify the author with any precision, except that he is a teacher, more intent on the profundity of the message than on the flourishes of stylistic elegance. But the presence of Semitisms, that is, Greek which reflects Hebrew or Aramaic idioms, has suggested to some commentators (e.g. Barrett, Lindars, Hengel) that the writer spoke Aramaic. The question is complicated by a number of factors, since the presence of Semitisms can be explained in quite different ways. First, they may be Septuagintisms, that is, expressions used in imitation of the Greek translation of the Hebrew Scriptures where the original Hebrew is sometimes translated literally, creating a new form in Greek. Such Septuagintisms are common in the Third Gospel and the Acts of the Apostles. Secondly, Semitisms may have been present in the traditions inherited by the Evangelist from the earliest Aramaic-speaking church. Thirdly, not only would natives of Palestine who spoke Aramaic be inclined to use Semitic idioms in Greek, but so would most of the inhabitants of the regions of the eastern Roman Empire, where some dialect of the Semitic family of languages was spoken (e.g. in Syria). The question is made even more difficult by the fact that some stylistic characteristics which are common in the Koine Greek of the papyri but not in literary Greek, like parataxis and asyndeton, could also be features of Semitic influence (see Moulton 1929: II, appendix, 411-85).

The following examples may reflect the influence of the Septuagint.

1. *The resumption of a pronoun after a relative with which it agrees (1.27, 33; 13.26).* This construction is common in the Septuagint but it may also be a feature of Koine Greek (Moulton 1929: II, 435).

2. *A verb with a cognate noun in the dative (3.29).* This could reflect the Hebrew infinitive absolute construction, as it does in the Septuagint, but it is also found in classical Greek (Moulton 1929: II, 443-44).

3. *The impersonal plural verb (15.6; 20.2).* This is common usage in Hebrew and Aramaic, and hence in the Septuagint, but it is also found in Greek (Moulton 1929: II, 447-48).

4. *The Son of man (e.g. 1.51; 3.14-15).* This expression would be foreign to Greeks. It is found without the article in Ezek. 2.1, 3.1, 17, Ps. 8.4, Dan. 7.13; cf. Jn 5.27. Its application with the article to Jesus was part of the tradition which the Gospel inherited. The Synoptics reserve it for Jesus' direct speech. Only the Fourth Gospel (12.34) and the Acts of the Apostles (7.56) place it on the lips of other people.

5. On two further occasions the Fourth Gospel uses the Semitism 'Son of... ' to express a character trait in terms of filial relationship, at 12.36 'sons of light' and at 17.12 'the son of destruction' who is Judas. In the Septuagint of Isa. 57.4 'children (τέκνα) of destruction' are mentioned and in Prov. 24.22 a 'son of destruction' is the indefinite form of the Johannine phrase. The form is common in the Septuagint but there is no exact parallel to 'sons of light'. The scrolls from Qumran use the Aramaic equivalent (e.g. 1QS 3.13; 14.25). We may explain the two Johannine instances as analogical formations, based on the Septuagint (e.g. 1 Sam. 14.52; 26.16; 2 Kgs 14.14). In Jn 17.12 there is a play on words in the Greek: 'None of them is lost (ἀπώλετο) but the son of destruction (ἀπωλείας)'.

6. It has sometimes been argued that the Gospel uses ὑψόω (e.g. 3.14) to refer to Jesus' uplifting on a cross because in Syriac and Aramaic the same verb means both to 'lift up' and to 'crucify'. It is more likely, however, that the Johannine ὑψόω and δοξάζω are dependent on the Septuagint of Isa. 52.13.

7. *The Fourth Gospel refers to the lake of Galilee as a sea* (θάλασσα) *(6.1; 21.1).* It is described as the 'sea of Chinnereth' in Num. 34.11. Matthew and Mark also refer to it as a 'sea'. Josephus, more appropriately, calls it a 'lake' (λίμνη, *War* 3.57; 4.456). Johannine usage may therefore reflect the Septuagint or Christian tradition, but there is also evidence that Greeks used θάλασσα to mean 'lake' (Bauer, Arndt and Gingrich 1957).

8. The idiom, 'to do the truth' (3.21) is found in the Septuagint (Gen. 32.10; 47.29; Isa. 26.10).

9. *Amen, amen, a transliteration of the Hebrew, introduces a solemn declaration (e.g. 1.51; 3.3).* The Septuagint sometimes transliterates the verb (1 Chron. 16.36; Neh. 5.13; 8.6; Tob. 8.8; 14.15) but more often translates it as γένοιτο. All 25 occurrences in the Fourth Gospel double the 'amen'. In the Synoptics it is never doubled. In Scripture it usually comes at the end of prayers, where it can be doubled (Num. 5.22; Pss. 41.13; 72.19 = γένοιτο; Neh. 8.6 = amen). Only in Jer. 28.6 does the single 'amen' introduce a declaration. Lindars's suggestion (1972: 48) that the Fourth Gospel's 'amen, amen' is not merely a stylistic device but, in nearly every case, points to the use of a traditional, Synoptic-type saying is unnecessary. Rather, it is a stylistic device which draws attention to crucial assertions. The doubling of 'amen', which goes beyond both Scripture and the tradition of the Synoptics, slows the discourse in a way which both adds to its impressiveness and ensures that the reader is alert to what follows.

10. *On three occasions the Gospel refers to 'angels' in the scriptural sense of divine messengers.* At 1.51 Jesus promises that the disciples will see heaven opened and the angels of God ascending and descending on the Son of man, picking up the imagery of Jacob's dream in Gen. 28.12. At 12.29 the heavenly voice saying 'I honoured it [the Father's name] and I will honour it again' is interpreted by some of the crowd as an angel speaking to Jesus (cf. Exod. 19.16 for a reference to the heavenly voice as thunder). Finally, in the story of the empty tomb, Mary Magdalene sees two angels in white who ask why she is weeping (20.12), a question taken up by Jesus himself (20.15). For an angel dressed in white, compare 2 Macc. 11.8; Dan. 10.5.

11. *The Gospel refers to the activity of Satan (13.27).* The Hebrew word is always translated in the Septuagint as 'the slanderer' (ὁ διάβολος e.g. Job 2.1; Zech. 3.1-2; 1 Chron. 21.1; see Jn 6.70; 8.44 and 13.2). The Gospel refers to a divine being who is God's adversary, as in 1 Chron. 21.1. In this one instance (13.27) the Gospel, unlike the Septuagint, transliterates the Hebrew. This transliteration is commonly used in Christian tradition (the Synoptics, Paul and

Revelation) and was probably inherited by the Fourth Evangelist (see especially Lk. 22.3).

12. The names of Jewish feasts are derived from the Septuagint: Passover (τό πάσχα) e.g. 2.23; Exod. 12.11, 21, 27, 43, 48; Tabernacles (ἡ σκηνοπηγία) e.g. 7.2; Deut. 16.16; 31.10; Zech. 14.16, 18, 19; Renewal (τά ἐγκαίνια) 10.22; Num. 7.10-11; 1 Kgs 8.63; Ezra 6.16; Sabbath (τό σάββατον) 5.9; 9.14; 2 Kgs 4.23; 11.5, 7, 9; 1 Chron. 9.32. Elsewhere, the Septuagint often has the plural, τὰ σάββατα.

13. The use of the terms 'above' (ἄνω) and 'below' (κάτω) is derived from the Septuagint (e.g. Exod. 20.4) and not from classical or Hellenistic Greek in which ἄνω means 'on the earth' and κάτω 'under the earth'.

14. The expression 'eternal life' (ζωή αἰώνιος) is taken from Dan. 12.2.

15. The idiom 'running/living water' (ὕδωρ ζῶν, 4.10) is derived from the Septuagint, e.g. Gen. 26.19; Lev. 14.5; Jer. 2.13; Zech. 14.8.

16. The expression 'one on either side' (ἐντεῦθεν καὶ ἐντεῦθεν) to explain the positions of the two men crucified with Jesus (19.18) comes from the Septuagint e.g. Num. 22.24.

17. The combination 'grace and truth' (χάρις καὶ ἀλήθεια) is used only in the Prologue (1.14, 17). The Septuagint often combines ἔλεος and ἀλήθεια (e.g. 2 Sam. 2.6; Ps. 25.10) but in later books χάρις and ἀλήθεια are found (Est. 2.9, 16, 17; Sir. 7.33; 40.17).

18. τό μάννα (6.31, 49), the miraculous food given to the fathers in the wilderness (Exod. 16), is transliterated exactly from the Hebrew by τό μαν in the Septuagint of Exod. 16.35, but by τό μαννα in Num. 11.6, 7, 9, Deut. 8.3, 16. The longer form seems to have been influenced by the Greek ἡ μάννα, 'a little grain'.

19. 'All flesh' (17.2) is a Septuagint idiom for 'all humanity' (e.g. Isa. 40.5).

20. Hyssop (ὕσσωπος), a transliteration found in the Septuagint, is mentioned in connexion with Jesus' crucifixion in 19.29. An allusion to Exod. 12.22, the use of hyssop when sacrificing the Passover lamb, is clearly intended.

21. σεμεῖα καὶ τέρατα (signs and wonders) is common in the Septuagint (e.g. Deut. 28.46; 29.2; Ps. 135.9; cf. Jn 4.48).

22. The expression 'to see death' (8.51) is found in Ps. 88.49 (see Lk. 2.26).

23. Human beings as 'children of God' (1.12; 11.52) is found in Hos. 11.1, referring to Israelites (see the contrary Isa. 30.1).

24. 'Heart' in the distributive singular rather than the normal Greek plural (14.1, 27; 16.6, 22) is found often in the Septuagint, for example in Isa. 6.10, paraphrased in Jn 12.40.

25. ψυχή for ordinary life (10.11, 15, 17; 12.25; 13.37-38; 15.13) parallels Septuagint usage, for example Exod. 4.19; 1 Kgs 19.10, 14; Isa. 29.8. It is also used as a reflexive pronoun (10.24; 12.27) as in Isa. 53.10; 58.3, 5.

26. The resurrected Jesus' greeting to the disciples, 'Peace to you' (20.19, 21, 26) also reflects such greetings in the Septuagint, for example Judg. 6.23.

27. In 9.31 the man cured from blindness asserts that 'if someone is θεοσεβής' (devout) God hears him. The adjective is found nowhere else in the New Testament, although it was common in Greek literature (θεοσέβεια is used in 1 Tim. 2.10). It is, however, found in the Septuagint, in Jethro's advice to Moses about the kind of leaders he should choose (Exod. 18.21), in the description of Job (Job 1.1, 8; 2.3) and in Judith's self description (Jdt. 11.17). It is therefore aptly used in Jn 9.31.

28. The term διασπορά (7.35) occurs in the Septuagint of, for example, Isa. 49.6, Ps. 147.2.

29. The expression in 7.19, 'do the law' (ποιεῖ τὸν νόμον) is found in Lev. 18.5 and Deut. 27.26 (see Mt. 5.19).

Some of these examples suggest that the Fourth Evangelist sometimes imitates the Septuagint's Semitic expressions. This is consonant with the fact that the writer is deeply indebted to Scripture's motifs and themes.

The following examples have been thought to prove that the Evangelist knew Aramaic.

1. In the Gospel there are some Aramaic words which are translated into Greek. (On the Greek form of Aramaic names, see Moulton 1929: II, 143-50.) The following examples can be cited: 'rabbi' which means 'teacher' (1.38, 49; 3.2, 26; 4.31; 6.25; 9.2; 11.8; 20.16); 'messiah' (also Hebrew) which means 'Christ' (1.41; 4.25 cf. Septuagint 1 Sam. 26.15; Ps. 2.2); 'Cephas' which means 'Peter' (1.42); 'Siloam' (also Hebrew) which means 'sent' (9.7 cf. Isa. 8.6; 2 Esd. 13.5 in Septuagint); 'Thomas' the 'twin' (11.16; 20.24; 21.2); 'the place of the skull' which is called in Hebrew (or Aramaic) 'Golgatha' (19.17). The translations, however, are not always strictly accurate. 'Rabbi' means 'my master' (but see Mt. 23.8 which gives the impression it means 'teacher'), as does the longer form 'rabbouni' (Jn 20.16; Mk 10.51). 'Siloam' is not the passive participial form of the Hebrew verb 'to send'. 'Golgatha' means 'skull' not 'the place of the skull', but Mark's interpretation corresponds with John's (Mk 15.22). Dependence on Mark may also explain the transliteration 'Hosanna' instead of the Septuagint translation 'save' in Ps. 118.25 (Mk 11.9; Jn 12.13).

Most of the Aramaic or Hebrew names of characters and places are not translated, however: for example, Simon, 1.41; Nathanael, 1.45; Joseph, 1.45 or 19.38; Moses, 5.45; Abraham, 8.39; Mary, 11.1 or 19.25; Martha, 11.1; Lazarus, 11.2; Judas, 6.71 or 14.22; or Caiaphas, 11.49; Nazareth, 1.45; Bethsaida, 1.44; Bethany, 11.1; Jerusalem, 2.13; Kidron, 18.1; or Arimathea, 19.38. Nothing is said about the meaning of 'Pharisees' (e.g. 1.24) or 'Levites' (1.19). Also Gabbatha (19.13), the name of the Pavement, is not translated and its derivation is uncertain.

Can a rationale be discerned, which would explain why some Hebrew or Aramaic terms are translated and others not? Certainly messiah, rabbi and Siloam have meanings which are important for the story but the other translations are no more crucial than those which are not supplied. For example, Nathanael means 'God has given' and the Gospel pictures the disciples as gifts from God (e.g. 6.37; 10.29), but the name is not translated. Similarly, Lazarus, the shortened form of Eleazar, means 'he whom God helps', a translation which would have formed an appropriate addition to ch. 11. The Matthaean interpretation of the name Jesus, 'he will save' (1.21), recognizes it as the Greek equivalent of Joshua, but the Fourth Gospel gives no such interpretation. The most likely explanation of the evidence is that the translation of only some of the Aramaic terms had been handed down in the tradition inherited by the Evangelist. In other words, the author did not know Hebrew or Aramaic but took up what tradition made available, in order to give colour and veracity to the narrative.

2. The Gospel defines the costly ointment (myrrh) of nard used by Mary of Bethany as πιστική (12.3). In the New Testament the word occurs only here and in Mark's story of the anointing (14.3). In second-century writers it is understood as a derivative of πιστός meaning 'genuine', which would make sense in the Johannine context. Alternatively, since Theophylactus Simocatta (7th century, *Patrologia Graeca* 123, 645B) offers another derivation, from a name of some kind, it is possible that it comes from the Aramaic *pistaca*. If so, the Syriac translator did not recognize it (Moulton 1929: II, 379-80), which makes such a derivation unlikely.

3. The Gospel often follows πιστεύω with εἰς (e.g. 1.12; 2.11, 23). In classical and literary Greek εἰς (into) expresses destination, whereas the Johannine phrase requires the sense 'to believe in'. This meaning is not impossible in Greek since εἰς has a wide range of meaning in the vernacular, but some commentators suppose that it translates the Hebrew or Aramaic b^e. In the Septuagint, however, πιστεύω is not found with εἰς. Moulton thinks the usage is appropriate to Christian belief and therefore distinctive of Christian literature (1906: I, 67-68). Derivation from Aramaic is both unlikely and unnecessary.

4. As in 2 above, some scholars have sought to explain a difficult reading in the Gospel by recourse to an Aramaic word which is supposed to lie behind it. Perhaps the best example is at 11.33 (cf.

11.38). The Greek text reads, 'When Jesus saw her (Mary) weeping...he *was angry* (ἐνεβριμήσατο) in spirit and *troubled*.' ἐμβριμάομαι means 'to snort' and is used of human beings to indicate anger. There have always been Christians who have been loathe to attribute anger to Jesus (see the attempt to replace another verb for 'to be angry', ὀργίζομαι, by 'to have compassion' in Mk 1.41) and naturally they find this reading in 11.33, 38 unsettling. Torrey (1923: 338-39) noted that the Aramaic root *rgz* could mean both 'to be angry' and 'to be deeply moved' (see also Black 1967: 240-43). Could the Greek expressions in Jn 11.33, 'to be angry in spirit' and 'to be troubled', be two alternative renderings of a single Aramaic verb in a source from which the story was taken? Certainly such a possibility is conceivable. Even if it happened, however, we do not know whether the Fourth Evangelist or an earlier translator of an Aramaic tradition was responsible for the doubling. In any case, the hypothesis is not required to make sense of the Greek text. The Evangelist obviously had no qualms about attributing anger at the death of a friend to Jesus (cf. Mark 1.43).

The Gospel, therefore, contains no convincing evidence that the writer knew either Aramaic or Hebrew. The use of Aramaic names is better explained by supposing that they were handed down in a tradition which sometimes also provided a translation. Moreover, the deliberate ambiguity of Jesus' remarks to Nicodemus, 'Unless one is born again/from above (ἄνωθεν) (3.3 and 7) depends on the Greek language and cannot be duplicated in Aramaic. The same can be said of the play on words 'his own home' (τὰ ἴδια) and 'his own people' (οἱ ἴδιοι) in 1.11 or 'he takes away' (αἴρει), 'he prunes' (καθαίρει) and 'you are clean' (καθαροί) in 15.2-3. The Gospel is a Greek Gospel, influenced by motifs, themes, style and vocabulary from its Scripture, and by the Christian traditions it inherited, but taking advantage of some of the resources the Greek language affords.

3.2. *Latin Loan Words*

The Gospel depicts a time when Palestine was part of the Roman Empire and the presence of Latin loan words helps to confirm that reality: φραγέλλιον for *flagellum* 'a whip' (2.15); δηνάριον for 'a small coin' (6.7; 12.5); σουδάριον for 'a handkerchief' (11.44; 20.7); λίτρα for 'a pound' (12.3; 19.39); λέντιον for 'a linen cloth' or 'towel' (13.4-5); πραιτώριον for 'Praetorium' (18.28, 33; 19.9); καῖσαρ for 'Caesar' (19.15) and τίτλος for 'title' (19.19-20). In the first century CE such words were common in Hellenistic Greek. Their presence indicates the accuracy of the tradition or the author's knowledge of the Greek of the Roman Empire.

Conclusion

The author of the Fourth Gospel adopted a style and vocabulary most suited to the purpose. Hebrew, Aramaic and Latin terms provide authentic local colour. Septuagintisms give the narrative a 'religious' aura. The leisurely and repetitive manner serves a didactic purpose and creates a respectful dignity and deliberate solemnity.

Chapter 12

GEOGRAPHY: THE IMPLIED AUTHOR'S KNOWLEDGE OF THE TOPOGRAPHY, THE FLORA, AND THE CLIMATE OF PALESTINE AT THE TIME OF JESUS

1. *Locations*

1.1

The Gospel sets Jesus' ministry in Galilee, Samaria and Judaea (on the Greek forms of Semitic place names, see Moulton 1929: II, 147-50) at the time when Pilate was governor (of Judaea and Samaria, 26-36 CE) and Caiaphas was high priest in Jerusalem (18-36 CE). How accurate are the geographical references for this period? On the most general level, the distinctions between Galilee, Samaria and Judaea are correctly depicted. Galilee is envisaged as a separate entity, although the Gospel never mentions that Herod Antipas ruled there. The direct route from Judaea to Galilee would pass through Samaria (4.3-4; see Lk. 9.52), a separate cultural area with its own holy mountain (4.20), and the journey would take about three days (11.6, 39; see Lk. 13.33 and Josephus, *Life* 269). Johannine knowledge of the relative positions of the political regions of Palestine is therefore superior to Lukan. Luke's depiction of Jesus' journey to Jerusalem from Lk. 9.51 onwards envisages Samaria and Galilee as adjacent territories, both bordering on Judaea (Lk. 17.11), which is a mistake the Fourth Gospel does not repeat. One of the regions where John baptized and to which Jesus withdrew is 'across the Jordan' but it is not called Peraea (1.28; 3.26; 10.40. See Isa. 9.1; Ezek. 47.18; Mt. 4.15; 19.1; Mk 3.8; 10.1).

1.2. *Jerusalem and Judaea*

Jerusalem in Judaea (always spelt Ἱεροσόλυμα as in 2–4 Maccabees and Matthew, Mark and sometimes Luke, and not Ἰερουσαλήμ as in most of the Septuagint and mostly in Luke) is the place where the

Temple is situated and hence is the pilgrimage centre at festival times (e.g. 7.1-9). Perhaps 2.13-22 contains a hint that the Temple would be destroyed, an event which happened during the Jewish War against Rome in 66-70 CE, about forty years after the period of Jesus' ministry.

The Gospel relates four visits of Jesus to Jerusalem at festival times (2.13, Passover; 5.1, an unnamed feast; 7.10, Tabernacles leading to 10.22, Renewal; 12.12, Passover) and includes various details about the Temple. On his first visit he drives out the men in charge of animals and overturns the tables of money changers (2.14-22; see Mt. 21.12-13; Mk 11.15-17; Lk. 19.45-46). The Gospel specifies the animals (oxen, sheep and pigeons) which were required for various sacrifices according to Scripture (Leviticus. Matthew mentions only pigeons, and Mark and Luke do not note the kinds of animals). None of the Gospels explains that animals were available for purchase by pilgrims who wished to offer sacrifices in the Temple because only animals without blemish were acceptable (Lev. 1–7), and purchasing them at the Temple would both guarantee their validity and obviate the need to take some on a journey. Pilgrims came not only from Galilee but from Jewish settlements throughout the Roman Empire and beyond. Nevertheless, it is unthinkable that oxen and sheep were kept for this purpose actually within the precincts of the Temple, since excrement would defile the Temple (Philo, *Spec. Leg.* 1.74-75). Moreover, ordinary people were never required to sacrifice an ox. At Passover, of course, lambs were offered for sacrifice by all the families of pilgrims. Otherwise, lambs and pigeons constituted the usual sacrifices of most people. Pigeons may have been sold in the Royal Portico (see Sanders 1992: Part II, ch. 6). It appears that the Fourth Evangelist elaborates the story in the Synoptics on the basis of scriptural references, and in ignorance of details about first-century practice at the Temple. Money changers were necessary because of the variety and debasement of local coinage which had to be exchanged for reliable Tyrian currency. Money was needed to pay the Temple tax (Exod. 30.13; 38.26). But the Johannine story is unconcerned about the realities of an incident in the Temple at Passover time. These it overlooks by focusing on the fate of Jesus. The Temple was an awesome, holy sanctuary. People who entered it had first to immerse themselves in pools to remove uncleanness (Lev. 12, 14–15; Num. 19.1-13). Large ritual baths have been discovered by archaeologists near the Temple site and in people's homes in Jerusalem (Avigad 1983: ch. 3; Mazar 1978). The Fourth Gospel later mentions Jews' purifying themselves (11.55) but never describes the ritual nor depicts Jesus undergoing it before entering the Temple. It is difficult for modern westerners to appreciate Jewish devotion to this holy site, but Josephus's descriptions of Jewish reactions to any threat against its sanctity (e.g. *War* 2.172-74) indicate how great is the gulf between first-century and some twentieth-century sensibilities. Since thousands of pilgrims visited the Temple for festivals, Temple officers (e.g. Jn 7.45. See Mt. 26.58; Mk 14.54, 65; Philo, *Spec. Leg.* 1.156) had to be skilled at crowd control. Moreover, religious fervour could and did lead to riots against Roman rule. Additional Roman troops were therefore brought into Jerusalem to deal with disturbances, and their Antonia fortress overlooked the Temple (Josephus, *Ant.* 15.406). The Roman governor also moved to Jerusalem from Caesarea at festival times for the same reason. Anyone upsetting tables of money or driving out the men who sold animals would quickly have been removed to prevent chaos. No sense of this situation is conveyed by any of the Gospels. In the Johannine version Jesus' outrageous behaviour is a mere backdrop to the saying about the Temple of his body.

The Jerusalem Temple which Herod the Great commissioned was a magnificent structure. Even the small section of the wall which has survived the centuries suggests its massive proportions. The Gospel notes that it had taken 46 years to build when Jesus was in Jerusalem (2.20). According to Josephus, Herod began the rebuilding in the eighteenth year of his reign (*Ant.* 15.380), that is, either 18 years from 40 BCE when he was appointed by the Romans, which would give a date of 22 BCE, or from 37 BCE when he captured Jerusalem, which would give a date of 19 BCE. But a reference in *The Jewish War* (1.401) dates the beginning of the project in the fifteenth year of his reign, that is either 25 BCE or 22 BCE. Josephus states that the Temple was not completed until 63 BCE (*Ant.* 20.219). Coordinating the Johannine statement with those of Josephus would give a date for the beginning of Jesus' ministry in 21, 24 or 27 CE. His ministry lasted at least two years. Either 24 or 27 CE would allow Pilate (26–36 CE) to be governor when Jesus reached Jerusalem on his final visit.

Two other details about the Temple buildings are mentioned in the Fourth Gospel. Jn 8.20 situates Jesus at or in (Greek ἐν) the treasury of the Temple (γαζοφυλακεῖον). According to 2 Esd. 22.44

(Neh. 12.44) and Josephus, *War* 5.200 and 6.282, the Temple housed several treasure chambers where money and other valuables were stored. Other passages refer to a single treasure chamber (1 Macc. 14.49; 2 Macc. 3.6, 24, 28, 40; 4.42; 5.18; 2 Esd. 23.5, 7 [Neh. 13.5, 7]). Archaeologists have discovered a large store room at the southeast corner of the Temple site, which may have functioned as one of the treasuries (Mackowski 1980: pl. 118). Not only the Jerusalem Temple but pagan temples too were used as safe deposits. It is possible that Jn 8.20 places Jesus at, rather than in, the site of one of the Temple treasure chambers. If so, the author could have gained this knowledge about the Temple precincts from Scripture. This, however, may not be the Johannine meaning. The word γαζοφυλακεῖον is used in the sense of 'contribution box' in the story of the widow's mite in Mk 12.41, 43 and Lk. 21.1. According to the Mishnah (*Šeq*. 6.5), there were thirteen shofar chests in the Temple, six of which were for free-will offerings (see Josephus, *Ant*. 19.294). If the Fourth Gospel is dependent on the Synoptics, it is likely that γαζοφυλακεῖον has the same meaning in Jn 8.20. Indeed, perhaps the Gospel writers did not distinguish one kind of treasury from another.

The second detail is recorded in Jn 10.23 which describes Jesus walking in the Temple, in the colonnade of Solomon. Josephus places this on the east side (*War* 5.184-85; *Ant*. 15.396-401; 20.220-21). This information must have been derived from tradition independent of the Synoptics (see Acts. 3.11; 5.12). These two references, because they are quite incidental to the main interest of the narrative, help to make it concrete, and, since they are accurate, the author must have had good information about the Temple as it existed before 70 CE. This information could have been derived from Scripture or the Synoptics in the first instance, but from another tradition in the second.

The Gospel does not mention where the chief priests and Pharisees assembled for their meeting (11.47). Josephus refers to a meeting room in the Temple precincts where a council (βουλή) met (*War* 5.144; 6.354), but the Fourth Evangelist knows nothing of such a place. The Synoptics can be construed as setting the meeting of the Sanhedrin in the high priest's house (Mt. 26.57 and parallels), and the Fourth Gospel seems to envisage Jesus' questioning by Annas in Annas's house (Jn 18.13).

The Gospel includes other details about Jerusalem. It sets the healing of the feeble man 'in Jerusalem, by the Sheep pool, that which is called in Hebrew Bethzatha [variant readings Bethesda, Belzetha and Bethsaida], which has five colonnades' (5.2). The Greek construction 'by the Sheep pool, that which is called' is rather rough, and this has tempted translators to supply another noun, either duplicating 'pool' to read 'by the Sheep pool, a pool which is called', or supplying 'gate' from Neh. 3.1, 12.39 to read 'by the Sheep Gate, a pool which is called' (κολυμβήθρα could be nominative or dative). The variant readings of the name, none of which can easily be explained as secondary, create further uncertainty. There is a reference in a copper scroll from Qumran which mentions a pool near the Temple at Bet Esdatayan, apparently the dual form of Bethesda (3Q15 11.12). Otherwise, Josephus locates a Bezetha to the northeast, on a hill outside the northern wall, opposite the Antonia (*War* 2.530; 5.151). Archaeologists have excavated a site in this area where there is a huge first-century double pool (Mackowski 1980: 79-83), and many commentators (e.g. Barrett, Brown, Lindars) follow Jeremias (1966) in identifying this place with that described in Jn 5.2. This identification depends on interpreting Jn 5.2 as a reference to two pools. Jeremias, however, seems to describe some of the archaeological evidence in a misleading way. The pillars which he sees as parts of the colonnades in Jn 5.2 (pp. 31, 33, 36) actually come from a fifth-century church (Robinson 1985: 54-59). Moreover, Robinson draws attention to the massive dimensions of the pools, especially their depth, which would make them unsuitable for the immersion of invalids.

For this reason, Robinson, following Mackowski, prefers to identify the site of Jn 5.2 with a place nearby, to the east, which was excavated by Duprez (1970). From the middle of the second century BCE to 70 CE, when it was destroyed by Titus's army (Josephus, *War* 2.530), this site consisted of small grottoes with steps leading down to them. Stone basins were also found from this period, but no pools or colonnades. From the third to the fourth century CE come relics of votive offerings which indicate that it was a healing sanctuary dedicated to Asclepius or Serapis. A Byzantine church was built over this whole area in the fifth century CE. In order to identify Jn 5.2 with this site, Robinson has to suppose that it was a Jewish healing sanctuary before 70 CE. But the absence of colonnades and a pool makes the identification extremely unlikely. Since archaeology has failed to discover at either site the five colonnades mentioned in Jn 5.2, since there is uncertainty over the name, and since the supposition of a double pool rests on one of two possible interpretations of Jn 5.2, it is more prudent to conclude that the site of Jn 5.2 cannot be identified on the basis of our present knowledge of Jerusalem before 70 CE. We know that the details could have been derived neither from Scripture nor from the Synoptics, but we cannot tell whether they are accurate.

The healing of the man blind from birth relates Jesus' instruction to the man to wash in the pool of Siloam (9.7). The place is mentioned in Scripture (Isa. 9.6; Neh. 3.15). Archaeologists place it within the first-century city walls, at the south of the Tyropean valley. Unlike the other details, this one is not incidental to the story since the interpretation of the name 'sent' reminds the reader of Jesus' mission.

The passion narrative also refers to places in Jerusalem. Jn 18.15-16 (see Mk 14.54) tells how Peter managed to get into the courtyard where Jesus was held, presumably the chief priest's house. Large houses with courtyards, probably belonging to chief priests, have been excavated near the Temple in Jerusalem (Avigad 1983: ch. 3). The praetorium (18.28; see Mk 15.16), Pilate's residence in Jerusalem, could be the Antonia fortress or Herod's palace in the southwest of the city. The incidental reference to Pilate at Herod's palace in Philo's *Leg. Gai.* 299 suggests the latter. Each of these buildings would have had a pavement outside, but the name Gabbatha (19.13) is not recorded elsewhere. The pavement recently discovered near the Antonia, however, dates from the second not the first century CE (Mackowski 1980: pl. 87).

Several places in the environs of Jerusalem are mentioned in the Fourth Gospel but we have no archaeological evidence which indicates their exact location. Jesus is crucified at Golgotha, (the place of) the skull (19.17, 20; see Mk 15.22) which must have been outside the city. He was arrested in a garden across the Kidron Valley (18.1), which runs along the east side of the city. The Kidron Valley is often mentioned in Scripture (e.g. 2 Sam. 15.23; 1 Kgs 2.37) but the exact location of the garden is unknown. John does not provide the names Gethsemane (Mk 14.32) or the Mount of Olives (Mk 14.26). Another garden is the place where Jesus was buried (19.41). The Synoptics do not define the area where the tomb was. Bethany, however, where Lazarus, Mary and Martha live, provides the setting for some of the incidents in chs. 11 and 12, and this could plausibly be El Azariyeh, southeast of the Mount of Olives. The modern name is derived from Lazarus. The Gospel mentions that it is 15 stadia (about 2 miles) from Jerusalem (11.18). Mk 11.1 sets Bethany near Jerusalem (see also Mk 14.3). Arimathaea, Joseph's place of origin (19.38; Mk 15.43) is usually but not certainly identified with Samuel's birthplace in the hill country of Ephraim (1 Sam. 1.1), that is, on the northern border of Judaea. No information is provided by the Gospel about the exact place in Jerusalem where Jesus ate his last supper with the disciples (13.1-2; see Mt. 26.17-19; Mk 14.12-16; Lk. 22.7-13) nor about the room where he appeared to them after his death (20.19, 26; see Lk. 24.33-49). The only other reference to Jesus' activity in Judaea pictures him baptizing somewhere in the area early in his ministry (3.22).

Much of this information could have been derived from the Synoptics. Other details could have been found in Scripture: the animals used in sacrifice, the prescribed rituals for uncleanness, the pool of Siloam and the Kidron Valley. Neither of these sources, however, could have provided details about the period taken to build the new Temple complex, the location of the colonnade of Solomon, the site at the pool where Jesus healed the feeble man, the name Gabbatha for the pavement outside the praetorium, the garden where Jesus was arrested, and the garden where he was buried. The two gardens may be no more than picturesque additions, but the other references suggest that the author had access to historical traditions independent of Scripture and the Synoptics.

1.3. *Galilee*

Some of the sites in Galilee can be located with more precision. Nazareth, Jesus' place of origin (1.45; see Mk 1.9) overlooks the Plain of Esdraelon. It is mentioned neither in the Septuagint nor in Josephus's writings. It was a small and politically insignificant settlement. Capernaum, also not mentioned in Scripture, is the place where Jesus stayed with his family (2.12; see Mt. 4.13) and later preached in the synagogue (6.17, 59; see Mk 1.21). It was on the north shore of the lake of Galilee, west of the Jordan river (Josephus, *War* 3.519; 5.403). Jn 2.12 and 4.51 indicate that Jesus 'went down' to Capernaum, a correct depiction of the descent necessary from the hills to the lake. Jn 6.17 shows knowledge that it can be reached by boat (Mk 1.16, 21). Tiberias (6.23), named incidentally as the place from which boats came, was also on the lake, in the west. It had been built by Herod Antipas as his new capital, around 19 CE (Freyne 1980: 122-34) and subsequently gave its name to the lake (6.1; 21.1). Magdala, Mary's place of origin (19.25; 20.1; see Mk 15.40; 16.1), was probably on the west coast of the lake too (Freyne 1988: 145). Cana (2.1; 4.46; 21.2) is mentioned in Josh. 16.8 and 19.28, and is situated by Josephus a night's march from Tiberias (*Life* 86 and 90). It is remarkable that the old capital of Galilee, Sepphoris, a flourishing city, is never mentioned in any of the Gospels.

The Fourth Gospel also places Bethsaida in Galilee (1.44; 12.21). The impression that it was in Galilee could have been gained from the Synoptics (Mt. 11.21; Mk 6.45; 8.22; Lk. 9.10; 10.13). It was, in fact, Philip the tetrarch's capital, on the east of the Jordan and north of the lake, in his territory rather than in Galilee. He rebuilt it and renamed it Julias early in the period of his rule (Josephus, *War* 2.168; 3.57, 515; 4.454; *Ant.* 8.28; 18.108). Pixner (1985) discusses the relative merits of three suggested sites and identifies et-Tell as the most likely since the others are too small. He suggests that the course of the Jordan river has moved slightly over the centuries. The location of Bethsaida in Galilee (12.21) is only possible if the city spanned both sides of the Jordan. It is more likely, however, that the Fourth Gospel has simply mistaken the location.

Of the places in Galilee mentioned by the Fourth Gospel, most could have been derived from the Synoptics. Cana is mentioned in Scripture but not in the Synoptics. The references to Tiberias suggest the use of another historical source.

1.4. *Peraea*

Bethany across the Jordan (1.28; 10.40, note the various spellings in different manuscripts), where John was baptizing, cannot be identified exactly, but seems to have been in Peraea (Murphy-O'Connor 1990). Aenon near Salim (3.23) could be in the southeast of Samaria or in Peraea. Aenon is situated in the wilderness according to Josh. 15.61 (Murphy-O'Connor 1990). Salim is mentioned only in manuscript B of Josh. 19.22. Once again, these names, without Synoptic parallels, suggest a separate historical source.

1.5. *Samaria*

Several places in Samaria are also named. Jesus meets the Samaritan woman in 'a city of Samaria, called Sychar, near the field that Jacob gave to his son Joseph. Jacob's well was there' (4.5-6). Sychar is mentioned neither in the Septuagint nor in the Synoptics. It is usually but uncertainly identified with the modern Askar, close to Shechem, and on the route between Judaea and Galilee (see the doubts expressed by Brown 1971: I, 169). Jacob's well is not mentioned in Scripture but 'the fountain of Jacob' is mentioned in the Hebrew, not the Septuagint, of Deut. 33.28. The land which Jacob gave to Joseph is apparently a reference to Gen. 33.18-20 and 48.22. John 4 also relates the woman's claim that 'our fathers worshipped on this mountain' as distinct from Jerusalem (4.20). Such information could have been derived from Scripture (e.g. Amos 4.1; 6.1; 8.14). The temple on Mount Gerizim had been destroyed in 128 BCE, but the site seems to have been used for rites even after that date (Josephus, *Ant* 13.255-56). In this section the reference to Sychar must have been derived from a source other than Scripture or the Synoptics. It is possible that Ephraim near the wilderness to which Jesus withdrew (11.54) was also in Samaria. Such a place, near Bethel, is mentioned in 2 Sam. 13.23, and this would situate it near the Judaean desert.

Conclusion

It is unfortunate that so many of the places referred to in the Gospel cannot be located with certainty, but of those which can, only Bethsaida is wrongly placed. When they carry no theological significance, these names give an air of realism to the story. How would the author have gained such information? It is likely that it was derived from Scripture, or the Synoptics or other traditions about Jesus on which the Gospel is based. Certainly, after 66-70 CE, when the land was devastated by war and Jerusalem with its Temple destroyed, no research in the area would have been profitable. Some commentators have suggested that the accuracy and detail of the Johannine depiction of Palestine indicates that the Gospel was written by a native of the country or an eyewitness to the events described (e.g. Robinson 1985). Some of the elements in the descriptions of settings, like the five colonnades (5.2), the grass (6.10), the names, Bethsaida, Cana, Capernaum, Bethany, Ephraim, the Kidron Valley, Gabbatha, Golgotha, are incidental and could have been replaced by general characterizations. Providing these details certainly makes the narrative less vague, but there are no elaborate descriptions (contrast the works of Josephus). The reader of the Fourth Gospel learns only the barest outline of the geography of Palestine. There are three named districts, Galilee, Samaria and Judaea, and another region across the Jordan; there are small towns dotted about; there is a festival centre in Jerusalem, Judaea, and an alternative cultic site in Samaria; there are hills and valleys, grass and desert, fishing on the lake in Galilee, harvesting of crops in Samaria. Apart from the mislocation of Bethsaida, the information which can be tested is accurate, but the presentation suggests not the report of an eyewitness, nor the reminiscences of a native of Palestine, but the availability of some historical traditions.

2. *Plants and their Products*

The Fourth Gospel occasionally refers to plants or their products (see Moldenke 1952). Below is a list with comments.

2.1
Jn 1.48 pictures Nathanael sitting under a fig tree (συκῆ). The tree grew both wild and cultivated throughout Palestine. It is often mentioned in Scripture (e.g. Gen. 3.7; Deut. 8.8; 1 Kgs 4.25; 2 Kgs 20.7; Ps. 105.33; Jer. 24.1-8; Amos 8.1-2; Zech. 3.10; Mic. 4.4), frequently as a sign of plenty. Reference to fig trees is also found in the Synoptics (Mt. 7.16-20; 21.1, 19-21; 24.32; Mk. 11.13, 20; Lk. 6.44; 13.6-9; 21.29-30) but there is no parallel to this particular account in John.

2.2
Jn 12.12-19 recounts Jesus' entry into Jerusalem just before Passover (11.55; 12.1, 12) when Jewish crowds went to greet him carrying palm branches (βαΐα τῶν φροινίκων) and crying, 'Hosanna. Blessed is he who comes in the name of the Lord, even the king of Israel' (12.13). The reason why they did this, according to 12.18, is because they had heard about Jesus' sign, bringing Lazarus back to life. The parallel account in Mk 11.1-10 makes no mention of Lazarus, devotes much of the narrative to details about the requisition of the colt, and notes that the crowds spread in Jesus' path garments and leafy branches (στιβάς) which they cut from the fields. Their greeting is

also slightly different: 'Hosanna. Blessed is he who comes in the name of the Lord. Blessed is the kingdom of our father David that is coming. Hosanna in the highest.' The Johannine text refers to the king rather than to the eschatological kingdom. Luke's account begins in parallel with Mark's (Lk. 19.28-40), but is closer to the Johannine version in its development in 19.37-40:

> The whole multitude of the disciples began to rejoice and praise God with a loud voice for all the mighty works that they had seen, saying, Blessed is the king who comes in the name of the Lord. Peace in heaven and glory in the highest. And some of the Pharisees in the multitude said to him, Teacher rebuke your disciples. He answered, I tell you, if these were silent, the very stones would cry out (see the Johannine reference to the Pharisees' consternation in 12.19).

The Fourth and First Gospels agree in citing the text from Zech. 9.9, although each quotation differs slightly from the other and from the Septuagint version. They also agree in including tree branches in the ceremony of greeting, although Matthew does not specify palm branches and pictures them spread on the ground.

The Johannine detail about the palm branches is noteworthy (see Farmer 1952). The term βαΐα (palm branches) is used in the description of Simon Maccabaeus's entry into Jerusalem (1 Macc. 13.51) and palm branches (φοῖνιξ) were a feature of the celebratory festival after the cleansing of the Temple accomplished by Judas Maccabaeus (2 Macc. 10.7). This text notes the similarity between the celebration and the Feast of Tabernacles. Lev. 23.40 commands that palm branches (Septuagint: κάλλυνθρα φοινίκων) be carried at the Feast of Tabernacles. Moreover, the Mishnah, which was written about 220 CE but which draws on older material, associates the shaking of the lulab, of which palm fronds formed a part, with the recitation of Psalm 118 (*m. Suk.* 3.9), and the crowd's greeting in Jn 12.13 echoes Ps. 118.26.

Since the Johannine account pictures Jesus as king and dates the incident near the Passover not Tabernacles, however, the palm branches probably symbolize Jesus' kingship and his victory over death. The Hasmonaeans, Herod, and the leaders of the first and second revolts against Rome used palms on their coins to symbolize their authority, and the *Testament of Naphtali* pictures Levi receiving twelve palm branches as a symbol of authority over Israel (5.4). Also, Jewish tombs and sarcophagi from the Graeco-Roman period are often decorated with palms probably to symbolize triumph over death. In fact, Jews shared this symbol with their Near Eastern and Graeco-Roman neighbours (e.g. Suetonius, *Twelve Caesars, Caligula* 32).

The meaning of the crowd's action, therefore, seems clear: Jesus is greeted as king and victor over death. But were palm branches available in Jerusalem at Passover time? The date palm needs a hot climate for its fruit to ripen and Jericho was famous for the quality of its dates which were used to make wine (Deut. 34.3; Pliny, *Natural History* 13.45). A letter, written near Jerusalem, by Simon Bar Kochba, who led the second revolt against Rome in 132–135 CE, contains an order to one of his lieutenants to bring palms from Engedi on the Dead Sea to Jerusalem, probably for the celebration of Tabernacles (Yadin 1961: 190). This suggests that, at that time, no abundant supply of palms was available near Jerusalem. Nevertheless, palm trees grew in Palestinian areas which were too cool for the fruit to ripen and Pliny seems to assume their existence around Jerusalem: 'The town of Engedi, second only to Jerusalem in the fertility of its land and in its groves of palm trees' (*Natural History* 5.73). Perhaps the war in 66–70 CE destroyed the palm groves along with the Temple and much of the city of Jerusalem. In other words, these details about palm branches in the Johannine account of Jesus' entry into Jerusalem show an appreciation of Jewish and Mediterranean symbolism and are consonant with conditions around Jerusalem at the time.

2.3

Jn 12.24 mentions a grain of wheat (κόκκος τοῦ σίτου) falling into the ground, dying and bearing much fruit. At least five kinds of wheat, some summer and some winter, grew wild and cultivated in Palestine. It is often mentioned in Scripture (e.g. Deut. 7.13; 2 Kgs 18.32; Neh. 5.2; Ps. 4.7; Prov. 3.10) and in the Synoptics (Mt. 3.12; 13.25, 29, 30; Mk 4.28; Lk. 3.17; 12.18; 16.7; 22.31). The Synoptics, however, refer to a grain of mustard as something very small (Mt. 13.31; 17.20; Mk 4.31; Lk. 13.19; 17.6), never to a grain of wheat, and they do not explain the significance of Jesus' death with this Johannine image.

2.4

Vines (ἄμπελος, Jn 15.1-11) grew well in Palestine. The fruit was eaten, dried as raisins or made into wine. Vineyards were surrounded by walls or hedges to keep out animals. Towers were built for security against thieves. Again, there are many references in Scripture, of which Isa. 5.1-7 gives the most details about the care such cultivation required. Coupled with fig trees, vines are signs of plenty (e.g. Zech. 3.10; Mic. 4.4). The fruit of the vine is mentioned in Mt. 26.29, Mk 14.25 and Lk. 22.18, and vineyards serve as subjects in parables (Mt. 20.1-16; 21.28, 33-46; Mk 12.1-12; Lk. 13.6; 20.9-19). The Johannine depiction of Jesus as the true vine develops this imagery.

Sour wine (ὄξος) is offered to Jesus on the cross (19.29; see Mt. 27.48; Mk 15.36; Lk. 23.36). This wine was popular because of its cheapness and its effectiveness in quenching thirst. Probably the Gospels are alluding to Ps. 69.21.

2.5

According to Jn 19.2, soldiers made a crown of thorns (ἄκανθα) and placed it on Jesus' head. Thorns are often contrasted with more useful plants in Scripture and the Synoptics (e.g. Gen. 3.18; Hos. 10.8; Jer. 12.13; Mt. 7.16; Lk. 6.44). The crown of thorns is also mentioned in Mk 15.17 and Mt. 27.29, Matthew's wording corresponding exactly with John's.

2.6

Hyssop (19.29) is used to hold the sponge of sour wine to Jesus' mouth. The identity of the plant is disputed, but the most likely candidate is marjoram. The reference is probably an allusion to Exod. 12.22.

2.7

Jn 19.39 mentions the mixture of myrrh (σμύρνα) and aloes (ἀλόη) which Nicodemus contributed to Jesus' burial. Neither Nicodemus nor the spices are found in the Synoptics at this point (Mk 16.1; Lk. 24.1 mention that the women went to the tomb with spices). Myrrh is a resinous aromatic substance, a luxury item, mentioned in Scripture (e.g. Song 3.6; 4.6, 14). Exod. 30.23 records God's command to Moses to use myrrh in a mixture of spices for anointing the tent of meeting, and Ps. 45.8 mentions myrrh as one of the fragrances with which the king's robes are perfumed. In the Synoptics, Mt. 2.11 includes it among the gifts offered to Jesus by the magi, and Mk 15.23 uses the verbal form to describe wine mixed with myrrh and offered to Jesus on the cross. Myrrh was a product of southern Arabia (Pliny, *Natural History* 12.70). Aloes is an aromatic substance made by drying the sap of a tree. It was imported from an island in the Red Sea. It occurs in Scripture only in Song 4.15, and is not mentioned in the Synoptics. The spices specified in Jn 19.39 seem to be appropriate to Jesus' burial because of the scriptural associations.

These few references accurately reflect the agricultural realities which Palestine shared with the rest of the Mediterranean world in the first century CE. All the information could have been gathered from Scripture or from the Synoptic Gospels, but the Fourth Gospel often uses the information to depict Jesus significance in its own way.

3. *Climate*

In the Fourth Gospel there are few references which indicate what the climate of Palestine was like. Mentioning the desert (1.23; 11.54; see Mk 1.3-4, 35; 6.31) suggests shortage of rain, and references to water, a well, pools and rivers (1.26, 31, 33; 2.7, 9; 3.23; 4.6-15; 5.2-9; 7.38; 9.7; 13.5; see Mk 9.41; 14.13; Lk. 7.44), more frequently than in the Synoptics, suggest the importance of this element for life in Palestine. 'Much grass' on the mountain by the sea of Galilee at Passover time (6.10; see Mk. 6.39) accurately reflects conditions in Galilee in the spring. Jn 10.23 records that 'it was winter' but nothing in the story which follows refers to conditions in Jerusalem at that time of year. Jn 18.1 also mentions incidentally the winter flow of water in the Kidron Valley (2 Sam. 15.23; 1 Kgs 2.37; Josephus, *Ant.* 8.17). The Gospel, however, explains the presence of a fire in the high priest's courtyard, 'because it was cold' (18.18). Mk 14.54 and Lk. 22.55 mention the fire, but without explanation. The explanation suggests that nights were cold in Jerusalem, even in the spring at Passover time.

In general, the weather is not a factor which interferes with Jesus' ministry. The information accurately reflects climatic conditions in Palestine, and most of it could have been gained from Scripture or the Synoptics. Only the explanation of the presence of the fire may or may not hint that these conditions, which Palestine shared with other countries of the Mediterranean world, were foreign to the Gospel's author or readers.

Chapter 13

CULTURAL HISTORY

The Gospel refers to various features of cultural life in first-century Palestine. It assumes a Jewish or Samaritan environment at the time when a Roman governor was responsible for the administration of Judaea. How detailed and how accurate is this cultural world?

1. *The 'Jews' and their Leaders*

1.1. *The 'Jews'*

The Gospel frequently mentions the 'Jews' but the exact nuance of the word varies from context to context. Sometimes the 'Jews' refers to the crowds who saw and heard Jesus, whether in Galilee (e.g. 6.41, 52) or in Judaea (e.g. 5.10, 16). These 'Jews', like Jesus himself, are distinguished from Samaritans (4.9, 20). But sometimes Galilaeans are distinguished from the 'Jews' who are Judaeans (e.g. 4.43-45; 7.1). The Gospel at first pictures the Galilaeans as enthusiastic followers of Jesus (4.43-45), until they reject him (6.52-60). But it is the Judaeans who are Jesus' own people, in spite of the fact that he is said to come from Nazareth in Galilee (1.45). The Prologue mentions that the light 'came to his own home and his own people received him not' (1.10), and Jesus testifies to the Galilaeans that 'a prophet has no honour in his own country', that is, in Judaea (4.44). Most of the narrative describes Jesus' rejection in Judaea.

Very often, then, the 'Jews' exemplify the world's rejection of Jesus (5.10, 18; 8.48, 52; 10.19, 31, 33, 39; 11.54; 18.35; 19.12, 15), although this bleak picture is sometimes tempered by suggestions that they were attracted to him, and even wondered whether he was the Christ (e.g. 7.11, 15, 25-26, 31, 40; 8.30; 10.41; 12.9, 11, 12). Nevertheless, 'fear of the Jews' is sometimes given as a reason why believers in Jesus do not declare their allegiance openly (7.13; 19.38;

20.19; cf. Est. 8.17). The context of the reference in 7.13 makes it clear how odd this usage is. Jn 7.11-13 records,

> *The Jews* were looking for him at the feast. . . While some were saying, He is a good man, others were saying, No, he is leading the people astray. Yet for fear of *the Jews* no one was speaking openly of him.

The first reference to the 'Jews' is to the Jewish crowds, and the second to the Jewish leadership (see also 7.30; 10.39). Elsewhere, 'fear of the Pharisees' is given as a reason for reticence (12.42).

In spite of the fact that Jesus and his disciples are Jews, therefore, the Gospel uses the name the 'Jews' to indicate the crowds in the historical environment in which Jesus lived, or, occasionally, their leaders, or 'the worldly' who failed to recognize him and even opposed him. The theological structure, made clear in the Prologue, is obscuring the full dimensions of the historical reality.

1.2. *Jewish Authorities*

Several groups of Jewish leaders are described. The most general term is 'ruler' (3.1; 7.48, see Mt. 9.18, 23; Lk. 8.41; 14.1; 18.18; 23.13, 35; 24.20). There are also priests and Levites in Jerusalem (1.19) who are sent to question John. Levites (see Lk. 10.32), a group subordinate to the priests who offered sacrifices, are never mentioned again in the Gospel. Chief priests (see the Synoptic passion narratives) are in control of officers in the Temple (7.32, see Mt. 26.58; Mk 14.54, 65) and are members of the council which condemned Jesus in his absence (11.47). They give orders about reporting Jesus' whereabouts (11.57). They plan to put Lazarus to death too (12.10), although the story does not relate whether the plan was executed. They send officers with Judas to arrest Jesus (18.3) and later hand him over to Pilate (18.35). Of the chief priests, two are named. Caiaphas is their leader (11.49; 18.13, 24, 28), and as high priest, he has the gift of prophecy (11.51; in Scripture Moses and Ezekiel are priests who prophesy. See also Levi in *Jos. Asen.* 26.6). Annas is his father-in-law (18.13), and it is Annas who questions Jesus after his arrest (18.19-23). When Pilate is cross-examining Jesus, the chief priests and their officers demand his crucifixion (19.6, see Lk. 23.21), and utter the Jewish blasphemy 'We have no king but Caesar' (19.15). They object to Pilate's title over Jesus' cross, 'the king of the Jews' (19.21). Unlike the Synoptics, the Fourth Gospel never calls the chief priests Sadducees.

The power the Gospel assigns to the chief priests in Jerusalem before the destruction of the Temple accurately captures the historical situation. The priests carried out the sacrifices required by Scripture for the people's welfare, and were supported in this role by the people's tithes and offerings (never mentioned in the Fourth Gospel; contrast Mt. 5.23-24; 8.4; 23.23). But their power was circumscribed by Roman rule. The Romans determined who should be high priest by keeping his robes and releasing them only to their nominee. The high priest had to safeguard the religious and social interests of the people without offending the Roman governor (see Sanders 1992: Part III, ch. 15). Josephus relates how Annas was deposed as high priest in 15 CE and succeeded by other appointees in quick succession (*Ant.* 18.35, 95). He does not tell us that Caiaphas was Annas's son-in-law. Caiaphas was unusually successful in holding on to the office from about 18–36 CE. He and Pilate must have found a way of working together. It was in the interests of the chief priests and the people that confrontations with Roman troops should be avoided. But does the Gospel make a mistake in describing Caiaphas as high priest 'that year' (11.49; 18.13)? The remark could be construed to imply that the Jerusalem high priesthood was an office held only for a year, like some pagan priesthoods, and if this is a correct interpretation, the Gospel mistakes the nature of the Jerusalem high priesthood. But this may not be the right inference. The expression can be read in the sense that Caiaphas was high priest 'that particular year when these events happened'.

In 11.47-53 the chief priests are said to call a *a council* in order to decide what to do about Jesus. The Mishnah tractate, the *Sanhedrin*, about 220 CE, describes the composition, powers and procedures of *the* Sanhedrin as if it were a permanent body. The Synoptic passion narratives also refer to *the* Sanhedrin as if it were a permanent body (Mt. 26.59; Mk. 14.55; Lk. 22.66). The Fourth Gospel, on the contrary, uses the indefinite, *a* council, and gives the impression that Jewish leaders called together an ad hoc assembly when they needed advice or support. This may reflect the historical situation more accurately (see Sanders 1992: Part III, ch. 21).

But why does the Fourth Gospel include this account of a meeting in ch. 11 and not in ch. 18? And why is it held without Jesus being present? The First Gospel refers to such a meeting (Mt. 26.3-5) but the Fourth places it earlier in the narrative. The structure of the

Johannine narrative makes it appropriate to place the meeting at the end of ch. 11. During the discussions between the officers, the chief priests and the Pharisees in 7.45-52, Nicodemus chides the others for judging Jesus without a hearing. Although he is silenced, in fact the Pharisees do give Jesus a hearing in chs. 8–10 and condemn him. The meeting at the end of ch. 11, after Jesus' final and impressive sigh, highlights the opposition of the 'Jewish' leadership at the end of Jesus' public ministry as a fitting introduction to the final events in Jerusalem. Hence, no trial before a Jewish council is necessary in ch. 18. The reader is reminded of the earlier meeting (18.14), and Jesus is simply questioned by a chief priest before being sent to trial by Pilate.

All of this helps to make historical sense of Jesus' crucifixion. As someone who attracted Jewish crowds by his preaching and healing, and who fired their hopes for a better life under his messianic leadership, he could be viewed by the authorities as an unsettling influence who had to be eliminated in the interests of peace and security (11.48-49). The Gospel, however, sees political motives as part of that 'worldliness' which inevitably leads to a rejection of God and God's son.

The other group of leaders depicted in the Fourth Gospel is the Pharisees. (There is no mention of 'scribes', in contrast to the Synoptics.) Like the chief priests, their centre is Jerusalem and they are not pictured living in Galilee. They often oppose Jesus (7.47-48; 8.13; 9.13, 15, 16, 40). They join the chief priests at the council which condemns Jesus (11.47) and are associated with them in sending officers to arrest him (7.32, 45; 18.3) and in taking steps to discover his whereabouts (11.57). They are exasperated by his popularity with the Jerusalem crowds (12.19). They seem to be able to exclude people from the synagogue (12.42), an exclusion which is elsewhere attributed to the 'Jews' in the sense of Jewish leaders mentioned above (9.22 compare 16.2 indefinite). Nicodemus is the only Pharisee who is prepared to offer Jesus any support (3.1; 7.50; 19.39-42).

This portrait of Pharisees is more difficult to square with realities in Judaism before 70 CE. The Gospel gives the impression that they represent the real power which influences what the priests do. But it is noticeable that the high priest guides the council meeting (11.47-53) and that the Pharisees are not mentioned after the arrest of Jesus (18.3). The Pharisees were in fact a small group of mostly laymen (Josephus numbers them at 6,000, *Ant.* 17.42), interested in studying, interpreting and putting into practice the Jewish Law, but the priests were a very much larger group of professionals (Josephus numbers them at 20,000, *Apion* 2.108), who determined the lives and wellbeing of the Jewish people through their administration of the Law in relation to the Temple. It was to the priests that people would go with tithes and offerings and in matters of uncleanness and sin. A Palestinian Jew could not avoid the influence of or contact with the priesthood, but could easily ignore the teachings of the Pharisees. Both priests and Pharisees were concerned with keeping the Law, but the priestly function guaranteed that their interpretations were determinative for every Jew's life. After the destruction of the Temple in 70 CE, the priests lost their function and therefore their power. As it gradually became clear that the Temple would not be rebuilt, after the Second Revolt of the Jews against Rome (135 CE), under the leadership of Bar Kochba, the Pharisees assumed a more crucial role in safeguarding Jewish tradition. It is therefore assumed by most commentators, following J.L. Martyn's lead (1968 and 1979), that the historical situation reflected in the Fourth Gospel is not that of Judaism before 70 CE, but that of Judaism after the destruction of the Temple. In particular, the importance of the synagogue and the power to exclude from the synagogue are seen as reproductions of the Johannine church's relation with the local synagogue dominated by the Pharisees.

In support of this hypothesis, commentators assert that the addition of the twelfth to the Eighteen Benedictions, about 85 CE, was designed to exclude Christians from synagogue worship. According to the Mishnah (220 CE, but containing some older traditions), Jews were required to recite the Benedictions or their substance three times a day, and if they attended the synagogue they could say them in public (*m. Ber.* 4.1-7). The twelfth, the *birkath ha-minim*, includes a curse on the *minim* and it is assumed that no member of the *minim* would curse himself or herself. If *minim* meant a particular, identifiable group, whose members would recognize the term as applying to themselves, this is a reasonable inference. But who were the *minim*? Kimelman (1981) cogently argues that *minim* means 'sectarians' without any more specific reference, and that, therefore, the *birkath ha-minim* could exclude from the synagogue only those who identified themselves as 'sectarian'. Moreover, even if in some places at some time, *minim* were understood to include Jewish Christians, this hardly throws light on the situation described in the Fourth Gospel. There believers are warned that they will suffer expulsion from the synagogue because of their belief in Jesus. Nothing is said about prayers or curses which would make their attendance difficult.

What, then, is the evidence that Jews in the first century CE excluded people from their synagogue, and, if they did, what were the grounds for expulsion? Horbury's essay on extirpation and excommunication (1985) tackles some aspects of this problem. It asks and answers a series of questions. How far were various forms of excommunication practised by the Jewish community during the Second Temple period? Does the fact that forms of excommunication are found at Qumran and amongst the Essenes, the early Christians and the 'associates' in the Mishnah suggest that it was practised by closely-knit minority groups rather than by the larger Jewish community? In the later Talmudic period (5th century CE), the synagogue ban seems to have been in use, although it is fully described only in even later sources. Are these regulations derived from earlier Jewish sectarian usage rather than from general Jewish practice? Are scholars correct in drawing attention to the facts that Jewish diversity was so great and communal organization so loose that expulsions could not have been effectively agreed upon and enforced?

Horbury demonstrates that two matters receive extensive treatment in the Scripture which became authoritative in the Second Temple period.

1. There is regulation of those who were admitted to or excluded from the Temple congregation (e.g. Deut. 23.1-8 treats the exclusion of physically defective Jews and aliens; Ezra 10.7-8 excludes those returned exiles who failed to respond to Ezra's summons to an assembly in Jerusalem). There is some evidence that the category of a physically defective Jew, who could be excluded from the congregation, was extended to include Jews with moral defects (Ezek. 44.6-9; Philo and Josephus).

2. Exclusion from the covenant community is expressed in curses (e.g. Lev. 26.14-39; Deut. 27.11-26; 28.15-68; 29.10-30; Neh. 10.29; 2 Chron. 15.12-15; cf. Ezek. 13.9). Idolatry is the main cause for such exclusion, and exclusion is effected by death, inflicted by God (e.g. Num. 25.9; Deut. 4.3) or through human agents (e.g. Exod. 22.20; Num. 25.4-8; Deut. 13.6-18; 17.2-7). Links in the vocabulary of exclusion—'they will not be written in the writing of the house of Israel'—can be traced from Ezek. 13.9 through Isa. 4.3 and Ps. 69.28

to the curse of the *minim* in the twelfth benediction.

In a detailed and complicated discussion of all the relevant passages, Horbury shows that in spite of the meagre evidence for the practice of exclusion or extirpation in the Second Temple period, there is continuity of concern, expressed in similar vocabulary. His conclusion (p. 38) reads as follows:

> Failure to uphold certain convenantal observances and beliefs has throughout incurred, according to biblical, pre-rabbinic and rabbinic evidence, a penalty which in theory and sometimes in practice is capital, but which is represented or prepared for by excommunication. . . The evidence for excommunication from the general Jewish body in the pre-rabbinic period is not plentiful, but it is enough to suggest the existence of a recognized custom. Groups such as the Qumran community and the 'associates' in the Mishnah would have been likely, from their limited and exclusive character, to implement the custom more frequently than the general body. Nevertheless, the evidence reviewed in Section III, from references to exclusion, their vocabulary, and their background in biblical law, suggests that the custom was familiar to non-sectarian Jews.

What is unfortunately absent from Horbury's discussion is a consideration of the following issue. The biblical references concern exclusion from the Temple not the synagogue. It is easy to see how they could be enforced by the priests and their officers during the Second Temple period, and there is ample evidence that they were so enforced. But at what stage were these Temple regulations extended to and observed by synagogue communities? Horbury assumes that Essene and Christian groups excluded members from their congregations (e.g. Josephus, *War* 11.143-44; 1 Cor. 5) in imitation of already existing synagogue practice, but this is not necessarily the case. Essenes and Christians could just as easily have applied biblical precedent about the Temple to their own congregations. On general grounds it seems most likely that non-sectarian Jews would have extended the Temple regulations to the synagogue only after the Temple was destroyed in 70 CE. But how long would it take after 70 for such a practice to become generally recognized? What kind of Jewish organization or authority would have linked the synagogues throughout the Roman Empire and beyond in such a manner as to make the practice general? Unfortunately, the Fourth Gospel was written at a time about which answers to these questions are impossible.

The reference to exclusion in Jn 16.2 links expulsion with persecution; 'They will put you out of the synagogue [ποιεῖν, 'make', ἀποσυνάγωγος; in 9.22 and 12.42, ἀποσυνάγωγος is used with γίνομαι, 'become', but ch. 9 explains that the man born blind was thrown out of the synagogue; he did not simply leave of his own accord]; indeed the hour is coming when whoever kills you will think he is offering service to God'. Elsewhere in the New Testament Jewish Christians are said to have been persecuted by Jews. In Acts Paul is reported saying, 'In every synagogue I imprisonned and beat those who believed in you [Jesus]' (Acts 22.19 cf. 26.11 where Paul's authority is said to come from the chief priests not the Pharisees). Paul himself mentions that he had persecuted the church, but gives no details about where, how, on what grounds and on what authority (1 Cor. 15.9; Gal. 1.13—perhaps the context implies that the place was Damascus). He does, however, claim to have been beaten by Jews when he was a Christian missionary: 'Five times I received at the hands of the Jews the 40 lashes less one' (2 Cor. 11.24 cf. 1 Cor. 6.4; Mt. 10.17 and Deut. 25.2-4, which forbids more than 40 lashes). But neither he nor Acts mentions that he was excluded from the synagogue. On the contrary, Acts pictures him excluding himself because of Jewish unbelief (18.6; 28.28). Moreover, Paul's letters to churches give the impression that the Christian communities founded by him were completely separate from synagogue communities and had no regular dealings with them, so the matter of exclusion could hardly arise.

The Johannine references to exclusion from the synagogue (9.22; 12.42 and 16.2) give belief in Jesus as the messiah as the grounds for exclusion. This is true of the account in ch. 9, in spite of the fact that the man excluded had confessed that Jesus was a prophet (9.17) not Christ. But belief in Jesus as the messiah could hardly have warranted exclusion from Jewish communities as long as the Torah was obeyed. Rabbi Akiba was not excluded from the synagogue in the second century CE because he believed Bar Kochba was the messiah. The story of the man born blind in John 9, however, links the exclusion with belief in a prophet, Jesus, who broke the Sabbath commandment. The grounds for exclusion, therefore, included a breach of the Torah. Horbury's study indicates that the most common reason for exclusion from the covenant community was the practice of idolatry, but he cites one example in which the accusation includes Sabbath breaking (Josephus, *Ant.* 11.346-47).

The Sabbath command in Exod. 20.8-11 and Deut. 5.12-15 forbids work on the Sabbath. Num. 15.32-36 relates the story of a man who was stoned to death because he worked on the Sabbath by gathering sticks. Lev. 4.27-31 stipulates a sin offering for inadvertent transgression of the laws. But nowhere in the Bible is 'work' fully defined. The most common-sense interpretation of the command would forbid everyday work like farming and baking. Jer. 17.19-27 forbids carrying burdens, which it construes as a form of work. Neh. 10.31 and 13.15-22 forbids trading on the Sabbath, even with Gentiles.

Sanders (1992: Part II, ch. 11) discusses Sabbath observance by first-century CE Jews. Apart from the references cited above, he draws attention to the fact that during the second century BCE Maccabaean Revolt, Jews resolved to fight on the Sabbath, but only in self-defence (1 Macc. 2.29-41), and that this resolution was kept in subsequent wars with the Romans (Josephus, *War* 1.145-47). Moreover, Gentiles could take advantage of Jewish holy days by pursuing court cases against Jews when they could not engage in business (Josephus, *Ant.* 16.45-46). Josephus also cites decrees from cities in Asia Minor that granted Jews the right to keep the Sabbath, among other privileges (e.g. *Ant.* 14.264).

But none of these biblical or extra-biblical references defines fully what constitutes the work forbidden on the Sabbath. The Covenant of Damascus (10.14–11.18) shows how the extreme wing of the Essenes defined work, and the Mishnah Tractate on the Sabbath (220 CE) shows how Pharisees elaborated lists. But we do not know whether all of the Pharisaic categories would have been applied in the first century CE. We can presume that the main categories of everyday work would have counted for sectarians and all Jews alike. Sanders concludes his discussion:

> We may be sure that Jews did not work (on the Sabbath) in any ordinary sense of the term and that they would not fight unless directly attacked. Exterior jobs (farming, selling and the like) and domestic work (such as baking and cooking) were treated alike: all were forbidden and the basic prohibition of work was observed. . . We cannot say much more than this with regard to common practice. . . What the details and modifications were in private observance of the Sabbath we cannot know (1992: 211).

In the accounts of Jesus' healing miracles in John 5 and 9, Jesus is accused of breaking the Sabbath. In ch. 5 nothing Jesus himself does could be construed as breaking the Sabbath, since he healed simply by word, and speaking was not construed as work even by the most extreme pietists. Nevertheless, his command to the man to take up his bed and walk caused the man to work by carrying a burden, according to Jeremiah's interpretation and that of the 'Jews' in the narrative (Jn 5.10). In ch. 9 Jesus makes clay and anoints the eyes of the blind man, and this could have been construed as work by some sectarians, as the Pharisees do in Jn 9.14-16. Nevertheless, Jesus' behaviour, even if some construed it as Sabbath breaking, could be defended, as Jesus does in Jn. 5.19-47, 7.19-24 and 9.39–10.21. Even if the Pharisees insisted that he had broken the Sabbath, therefore, his sin would have been inadvertent. The most they could have demanded of him was that he should make a sin offering (Lev. 4.27-31), but at the time of Jesus they had no power to enforce such a demand.

Did they have that power at the time when the Fourth Gospel was written? John 9 pictures the Pharisees in control of the synagogue. But Freyne (1988: 205) and Sanders (1992: Part II, ch. 11) show that in the first two centuries of the Common Era there is no evidence to suggest that Pharisees exercised such control. Moreover, John 9 does not mention the requirement of a sin offering, but specifies that the man healed was excluded from the synagogue. In order to accept the references to exclusion from the synagogue in John 9, 12.42 and 16.2 as a reflection of the practice of a Jewish synagogue known to the Johannine community, we would have to accept the following proposals: (1) that Pharisees controlled the synagogue; (2) that those Pharisees counted carrying a bed and making clay for anointing as work; (3) that they demanded for inadvertent transgression not what the law requires, a sin offering, but exclusion from the synagogue, for followers of such a transgressor; (4) that they applied biblical teaching about exclusion from the Temple to exclusion from the synagogue, and broadened the categories for such exclusion. These proposals cannot be supported by evidence from outside the Fourth Gospel. It is just possible that the Johannine community knew about a very exceptional synagogue, but the hypothesis is hardly compelling.

It is more likely that the Evangelist is not reflecting the practice of contemporary Jews at all, but is extrapolating from Scripture in order to justify the fact that the Christian community has nothing to do with the Jewish community. It is noticeable that in the teaching of Jesus which follows the incidents in ch. 9, Jesus is 'the good shepherd' who leads his sheep out of the fold (10.3) and he is 'the door' through which the sheep go in and out to find pasture or life (10.9-10). There is no suggestion that the sheep are expelled. The Pharisees are represented in the discourse, which is addressed to them, as 'thieves' (10.1, 8, 10) or 'strangers' (10.5) or 'hirelings' (10.12-13). The Evangelist could have read all those passages in Scripture which encourage God's people to form a community separate from sinners (e.g. Deut. 29.16-29; Ezra 6.21; 10.1-3; Neh. 10.28-30), and could have been influenced in depicting the drama in ch. 9 by this reference in Isa. 66.45: 'Your brethren who hate you and cast you out for my name's sake have said, "Let the Lord be glorified that we may see your joy" but it is they who shall be put to shame'. John 9 reads like an illustration of this text.

Moreover, if the Fourth Gospel is dependent on the Synoptics, the role it assigns to the Pharisees becomes comprehensible. It is possible to infer from the Synoptics that the Pharisees were equal to the priests in their control of Judaism at the time of Jesus' ministry (e.g. Mt. 12.9-14; 15.1; 16.6-12; 18.3; 21.45; 22.15, 34, 41; 27.62; Mk 2.16, 24; 3.6; 7.1; 8.11, 15; 10.2; 12.3; Lk. 5.17, 30; 6.2; 7.36; 11.42-43; 12.1; 14.1; 15.2; 16.14; 19.39). But the Synoptics do not list exclusion from the synagogue among the persecutions that disciples can expect in the future as the Fourth Gospel does. They refer rather to beatings in the synagogue (Mt. 10.17; Mk 13.9; Lk. 21.12 mentions only delivering up to the synagogue). Nevertheless, it is possible to infer from the story in Lk. 4.16-30 that those who caused offence could be forcibly removed and even put to death. According to this story, Jesus' preaching in the synagogue at Nazareth was so offensive to Jews present that 'they rose up and put him out of the city and led him to the brow of the hill on which their city was built, that they might throw him down headlong' (4.29). Again, the consternation Jesus caused by healing in a synagogue leads Jesus to withdraw and call the twelve, so forming his own community, just as he does in John 9–10 (Mk. 6.2-13; Lk. 6.6-16). Finally, one of the Lukan beatitudes (6.22) reads: 'Blessed are you when people hate you and when they exclude (ἐκβάλλω as in Jn 9.34) you and cast out your name as evil on account of the Son of man' (as in Jn 9.35). The story in John 9 exemplifies this beatitude.

Moreover, since the 'Jews' and their leaders exemplify the unbelieving world in the Gospel story, it is consistent to see them excluding

Christians from their community and putting them to death, in the way they had persecuted Jesus. The 'Jews' make concrete the world's hatred. They force believers to form their own community of mutual love. Often, the structure of a narrative takes on a dynamic of its own, irrespective of historical veracity.

2. *Jewish Beliefs*

The Gospel's dialogues of Jesus with the 'Jews' and the Pharisees reflect a knowledge of various Jewish beliefs. The 'Jews' see themselves as children of Abraham (8.33; see Lk. 3.8) and as sons of God (8.41; Exod. 4.22; Deut. 14.1). The Israelites in the wilderness were their fathers (6.31). They are disciples of Moses (9.28 cf. 5.45; not an expression commonly used by Jews, but see Mt. 23.2) who gave them the Law (7.19), and they read the Scriptures to discover how to live (5.39). They recognize the need to give precedence to one command over another when demands clash, as in the case of circumcision and the Sabbath (7.22—this knowledge could not have been derived from Scripture or the Synoptics). They believe that blasphemy deserves stoning in accordance with the Law (10.33 cf. 19.7: Deut. 18.20; Lev. 24.10-16). They accept what the Law teaches, for example, that at least two people are required as witnesses for their testimony to be accepted (5.31-38; 8.13; Deut. 19.15). Nicodemus is able to chide members of the council for abrogating the Law in condemning Jesus without a hearing (7.51; Deut. 1.16-17; 17.4-6) and the omission is rectified immediately afterwards and when he is arrested. They keep the laws of purity (2.6; 3.25; 11.55; 18.28; Leviticus).

These 'Jews' are interested in the kingdom of God (3.3, 5; Dan. 7) and expectant of a messiah (1.20-21; 3.28; 7.26-27, 31; 10.24; 11.21), who would be a descendent of David from Bethlehem (7.42; Mic. 5.2; Isa. 11.1) and who would reign for ever (12.34; see Ps. 72.5, 7; Dan. 7.13-14), or a prophet who would lead them (7.40, 52; 9.17; Deut. 18.15, 18). They require a claimant to justify himself by performing a sign (6.30; 7.31; Deut. 13.1-5), but they also believe that a man could be possessed by a demon causing madness (10.20; Zech. 13.2). They believe that God does not hear sinners (9.31; see Prov. 15.29), and that some people were born in sin (9.34; see Ps. 51.5). On the other hand, they listen to religious leaders and call them 'rabbi' (1.38, 49; 3.2, 26; 4.31; 6.25; 9.2; 11.8; 20.16; and the Synoptics, e.g. Mk 9.5;

10.51). They believe in a future resurrection from the dead (5.25; 6.39, 40, 44; 11.24; Dan. 12.2).

This picture of first-century Jews, familiar with their Scripture, anxious to put its insights into practice, and expectant of its promises, seems accurate in very general terms. There is, however, no sense of the variety of first-century Jewish belief. Judaism is treated as a unified body. Not even the difference between Pharisees and Sadducees over the resurrection is noticed (contrast the Synoptics, Mt. 22.23-33 and parallels). Most importantly, the Gospel views Judaism negatively. It suggests that the 'Jews' did not in fact keep the Law (7.19) or honour Moses as they should (5.45-47), that they could not recognize Jesus' genuine claims because they sought honour from others and not from God. Indeed, they are sons of the devil, would-be murderers, not sons of God (8.44). They are condemned because they do not believe in Jesus. Belief in Jesus is the sole criterion which interests the author. No other distinctions seem to be worth making.

What do these features tell us about the author? They suggest that he knew something about Jewish beliefs at the time of Jesus. How was such knowledge acquired? Was he a Jew who became a Christian? That the author was a converted Jew seems unlikely since no sympathy is wasted on the 'Jews' nor is there much respect for their life-style. Johannine attitudes contrast with those of Paul (e.g. Phil. 3.4-6; Rom. 9-11). The 'Jews' of the Fourth Gospel are treated as alien (see the reference to *their* law in the context of Jesus' discussion about the world's hatred 15.25). Could he have come by such knowledge from aquaintance with Jews? It has been suggested that disputes between Jesus and the 'Jews' in the Gospel are transcriptions of disputes between the Johannine community and its local synagogue (e.g. Martyn 1968, 1979). If this were true, should we not expect more convincing and pertinent arguments instead of the general accusations the Gospel contains? If Moses bears witness to Jesus as the messiah, where exactly does he do so? Why should Jews object to Jesus calling himself God's son when they claim that sonship for all Jews? What justification from Scripture could be adduced to show that Jesus and his followers were more obedient sons than other Jews?

Justin's *Dialogue with Trypho*, although it represents Trypho the Jew as a straw man who always plays into the hands of his Christian opponent, at least provides some sense of the basis of Jewish–Christian dialogue, with its constant reference to passages from Scripture and their interpretation. The Fourth Gospel could have done the same, for example, by citing Moses' prophecy of a future prophet like himself (Deut. 18.15, 18) or his teaching about the ideal king (Deut. 17.14-20), but such opportunities are missed.

Moreover, the Gospel makes mistakes in its characterization of Jewish belief. In 7.52 the Pharisees counter Nicodemus by saying, 'Are you from Galilee too? Search and you will see that no prophet is to rise from Galilee.' But the following saying is attributed to Rabbi Eliezer (about 90 CE), 'You have no single tribe in Israel from which a prophet has not come forth' (*b. Suk.* 27b). What is more, the scriptural prophet Jonah, the son of Amittai (2 Kgs 14.25), came from Gath-hepher in Galilee. Again, the suggestion, placed on the lips of the Pharisees, that a man who is a sinner could not perform a sign like giving sight to the blind man (9.16), is contradicted by Scripture (Deut. 13.1-5). But most important of all, the Gospel attributed to 'Jews' beliefs about the messiah which only Christians held. Both the Synoptics and the Fourth Gospel see Jesus as the messiah who is also the prophet like Moses, performing miracles which the Fourth Gospel calls signs. Contemporary Jews did not expect the messiah to perform miracles. Rather, they distinguished the role of the messiah like David from the role of the prophet like Moses (see Martyn 179: ch. 4). But the 'Jews' of the Fourth Gospel make no such distinction. In ch. 6 those who witness Jesus' feeding miracle respond by trying to make him king (6.15). Soon afterwards, in 7.31, people ask, 'When the Christ appears, will he do more signs than this man has done?' Again, in ch. 9, the man cured of blindness testifies to Jesus as a prophet (9.17) and is thrown out of the synagogue (9.35), but the reason given for exclusion from the synagogue in 9.22 is belief in Jesus as the Christ.

The Gospel does not give the impression that it is formed out of real disputes between Jews and Christians. Rather, it suggests that what knowledge of Judaism it contains is derived from Scripture or from traditions about Jesus, not from first-hand experience. There is no attempt to enter into the world of Jews in order to convince them of Jesus' importance but rather an attempt to convince Christians about the characteristics of their own separate identity (see Freyne 1985). The author, then, is a Christian who sees Christianity as a religion distinct from Judaism. Moreover, the general portrait of the 'Jews', as a religiously disobedient and rebellious people, is very much like that of the Israelites in the Jewish Scriptures which Christians had taken over (see, for example, the whole of Deuteronomy). Those Scriptures do not idealize Israel's past. Even David does not emerge with an untarnished record. Only the prophets, like Moses or Elijah, are truly obedient to God, and they suffer rejection. The 'Jews' in the Gospel murmur against Jesus (e.g. 6.41) just as the Israelites murmur against Moses. It is Scripture which exerts more influence on the author than contemporary Judaism. (See Isa. 53.1 and 6.10 quoted at the end of Jesus' public ministry, Jn 12.37-43.)

3. *Samaritan Beliefs*

The Gospel acknowledged that Samaritans formed a religious group separate from Jews (4.9), with its own cultic centre (4.20), and that Jews denigrated Samaritans (8.48; see Sir. 50.25-26). If συγχρῶνται in 4.9 is rightly translated 'have dealings with', the statement 'for Jews have no dealings with Samaritans' is an exaggeration. Daube's alternative translation (1950), 'use (vessels for food and drink) together', is more specific, but it is doubtful whether it reflects the historical situation at the time any more accurately (see *m. Ber.* 7.1). Little else in Jesus' discussion with the Samaritan woman or in the Samaritans' response to Jesus reflects genuine Samaritan concerns. The Samaritan woman perceives that Jesus is a prophet (4.19) and believes in the future advent of the messiah (4.25) and the Samaritans confess that Jesus is the saviour of the world (4.42). Actually, the Samaritans derived their beliefs from the teachings of the Pentateuch and therefore looked forward not to a messianic descendent of David but to a prophet like Moses. They accepted the prediction of Deut. 18.15, 18 that God would raise up a prophet like Moses to give the people his commands (Macdonald 1964).

It seems that the author of the Fourth Gospel was not very fully informed about Samaritan beliefs. Nevertheless, no difficulty is felt about Samaritan converts (contrast Acts 8.14-17) because the story looks beyond the time of the Jerusalem Temple to a new community distinct from both the Jewish and the Samaritan.

The story about Jesus and the Samaritan woman, however, does reflect accurately the social conventions which constrained relations between men and women in first-century Palestine. The text relates that the disciples 'marvelled that he was talking (alone) with a woman, but none said, What do you wish? or Why are you talking with her?' (4.27). We may gather that individual men and women did not normally converse together without company (Sir. 9.9).

4. *Jewish Practices*

Various Jewish customs form the background to stories about Jesus in the Gospel. How far are they accurately depicted? The fact that annual Jewish festivals in Jerusalem provide the setting for some of Jesus' miracles and the themes for discourses has already been discussed in Part I, Chapter 2, where it was indicated that the festivals are mentioned in the correct order—Passover (in the spring), 2.13, 23; an unspecified feast, 5.1; Passover, 6.4 (note the abundance of grass in Galilee, 6.10); Tabernacles (in the autumn), 7.2; Renewal (in the winter, a fact noted), 10.22; Passover, 11.55. Since three Passovers are mentioned, it is clear that this festival is most significant for the narrative. It sets the time for Jesus' action in the Temple and the saying about raising the temple of his body (2.13-21), for Jesus' feeding of the five thousand, his walking on the water and the discourse on the bread of life (6.1-71), which is both the climax of his Galilaean ministry and the cause of his rejection there, and for his death at Jerusalem. The account of Jesus' death makes one explicit reference to the depiction of the death of the Passover lamb in Exodus 12, namely that no bone is broken (Jn 19.33, 36; Exod. 12.46) but there are also implicit allusions. Jesus dies on the day when the Passover lambs were sacrificed (Jn 19.14; Exod. 12.6), hyssop is used (Jn 19.29: Exod. 12.22), and his body is not allowed to remain on the cross overnight (Jn 19.31; Exod. 12.10). It is noteworthy that the Fourth Gospel refers to this festival simply as Passover, and, unlike the Synoptics (Mt. 26.17; Mk 14.1; Lk. 22.1), never mentions Unleavened Bread. Presumably this is because the death of the Passover lamb was the important feature of the festival as far as the Fourth Evangelist was concerned. Nevertheless, in Scripture the sacrifice of the Passover lamb is understood to safeguard the survival of Israelite first-born makes when God slayed Egyptian first-born males. It is not understood as a sacrifice for sin. The Fourth Gospel, however, seems to understand Jesus' death as a sacrifice for sin (1.29). It is unclear whether the expression of this belief by connecting Jesus' death with that of the Passover lamb is effected by combining Exodus 12 with other references in Scripture to sacrifices for sin (e.g. Lev. 7), or is a misunderstanding on the part of the Evangelist.

In connexion with the final Passover, the Gospel accurately notices the need for Jews to purify themselves in order to participate in the Temple festival (11.55 cf. 3.25), but when it states that they would not enter the praetorium 'so that they might not be defiled, but might eat the Passover' (18.28), it is mistaken. The positioning of Jews outside while Jesus is inside allows dramatic scene changes when Pilate moves from one to the other, but any uncleanness incurred could have been removed by bathing in the evening and the setting of the sun, before the Passover meal was eaten. It was only corpse impurity which required a seven-day ritual and there were no graves in Jerusalem. The Gospel also explains the requests for the corpses to be removed 'to prevent the bodies remaining on the cross on the Sabbath, for that Sabbath was a high day' (19.31). The prohibition of corpses remaining beyond nightfall (Deut. 21.22-23) does not mention the Sabbath, and would have applied whether the following day was a Sabbath or not. This may be a slight misunderstanding on the part of the author.

Tabernacles, with its celebration of God's gifts, especially of water and light, provides the themes of Jesus' discourses in chs. 7–9, on water and the Spirit (7.37-39) and the light of the world (8.12), which leads into the healing of the man blind from birth (9.1-12) and the discourse about the good shepherd (10.1-18). Brown (1966) suggests that these themes can be explained only on the basis of an intimate knowledge of the celebrations of Tabernacles in the Temple at the time of Jesus (p. 326), but he himself cites scriptural references in 1 Kings 8 and Zechariah 9–14 (see especially 11.7; 14.7-8, 16-17) which are sufficient to explain the Johannine treatment. The Gospel sets Jesus' teaching 'on the last day of the feast, the great day' (7.37). Lev. 23.39 picks out the first and final days of the feast as special days of rest.

The only other feast mentioned, Renewal (10.22), uses the name which is found in reference to the dedication of the tabernacle or the Temple in Scripture, and develops the theme of Jesus' dedication to the Father.

Information about these festivals would have been available to the Evangelist from the Jewish Scriptures which the church had inherited. Only a few of the annual festivals receive mention. In particular, it is noteworthy that the Day of Atonement (Leviticus 16), which could have prompted the development of important theological themes, plays no such role. Those which are referred to function both to explain Jesus' significance and to account for the presence of crowds in Jerusalem, except in the case of the second Passover (6.1), when Jesus remains in Galilee.

The weekly celebration of the Sabbath is the setting of two of Jesus' healing miracles and leads to criticism of Jesus' behaviour. According to the first (5.1-47), Jesus instructs the healed man to 'take up your pallet and walk'. Since the Decalogue (Exod. 20.8-11 and Deut. 5.12-15) states that no work should be undertaken on the Sabbath, carrying a pallet would break the Sabbath law and the man is criticized for his action (5.9-10; Jer. 17.19-27). Because he was following Jesus' instructions, however, Jesus is involved in the illegality in spite of not breaking the Sabbath himself. Healing by word was not a breach of the Sabbath because it required no work. Between the account of the healing and Jesus' discourse, moreover, a statement is made in the iterative imperfect which shows that Jesus' behaviour on this one occasion is typical: 'This is why the Jews used to persecute Jesus, because he used to do these things on the Sabbath' (5.16). The summary allows the narrative to introduce Jesus' discourse 'My Father is working still and I am working'. Without the intervening generalization, Jesus' remarks would have had no obvious connexion with the actual Sabbath healing described. The second healing on a Sabbath (9.1-12) provides a better introduction to Jesus' claims in ch. 5 because in this account his action in making clay could be construed as work (9.6 and 14). The story also and uniquely shows interest in healing techniques used by Jews and Gentiles in the first century and known from the Gospel according to Mark (7.33-34; 8.23) and from the magical papyri. The spittle of a great man was thought to be particularly efficacious (Tacitus, *Histories* 4.81; Suetonius, *The Twelve Caesars*, *Vespasian* 7). This second breach of the Sabbath leads to the controversy over Jesus' identity between the Pharisees and 'Jews' who think he is a sinner (9.24) and the cured man who thinks he is a prophet (9.17, 31-33). The man is excluded from the synagogue (9.22 and 34) but believes in Jesus as the Son of man (9.35-38. See the earlier discussion under Jewish authorities.)

Because the Law forbade Jews from working on the Sabbath, preparations had to be made on the preceding day. The day before the Sabbath, therefore, came to be called παρασκευή (preparation;

Mt. 27.62; Mk 15.42; Lk. 23.54; Jn 19.31; Josephus, *Ant.* 16.163. This usage is not found in the Septuagint). Alternatively, it was referred to as προσάββατον (Mk 15.42; Jdt. 8.6; 2 Macc. 8.26; Josephus, *Ant.* 3.255). The Fourth Gospel uses παρασκευή in this sense in 19.31 and later refers to the same day as 'the preparation of the Jews' (19.42). Earlier, however, in 19.14, the expression 'the preparation of the Passover' is used. Since the same day is meant in all three references, it is not clear whether the Evangelist supposed the three expressions to be interchangeable, or whether, uniquely, παρασκευή is applied to the day before a feast, perhaps on the basis of a misunderstanding of the Synoptics.

The existence of Jewish synagogues is taken for granted in the Gospel, although little indication of their function is given. Jesus' preaching in 6.25-58 is set in the synagogue at Capernaum in Galilee (6.59; see Mk 1.21), which suggests that it was a place where Jews were allowed to gather to listen to teaching, but nothing is said about the liturgy and the readings from Scripture. The synagogue, which became the most important public place for celebrating and inculcating Jewish traditions after the destruction of the Temple, is therefore of no particular concern to the author of the Gospel (see Sanders 1992: Part II, ch. 11). It is an institution of an alien community.

The Jewish practice of circumcision is mentioned once in the Gospel, as an instance in which the Sabbath law is abrogated (7.22). The law that a male child should be circumcised on the eight day (Lev. 12.3) was allowed to take precedence over the law forbidding work on the Sabbath, in spite of the fact that circumcision required work (*m. Šab.* 18.3; 19.2). In the Gospel this is the clearest instance of knowledge of post-biblical practice, since Scripture does not explain which law should be followed when they clash. The reference forms part of Jesus' justification of his own practice, but it is not a very convincing argument. Both circumcision on the eighth day and Sabbath observance were required by the Law, whereas Jesus' healings, which did not prevent death, could easily have been postponed to the following day. The argument would therefore have convinced no Jew, but suggests that the author saw no contradiction between the Sabbath command as he interpreted it and Jesus' healings. How the Sabbath was interpreted and whether keeping it was a practice of the author, however, is not clear from the narrative. But it is reasonable to assume that circumcision formed no part of the Christian initiation ceremony, since it is never mentioned in connexion with the disciples' mission. It is likely that baptism, understood as bestowal of the Spirit, had replaced circumcision in Johannine circles (1.33; 4.2; 20.22-23).

On three occasions, Jesus is present at meals which form the background to his words and actions. The first of Jesus' miracles is set at a wedding in Cana, but only the mention of the bridegroom (2.9) makes this feast different from any other, and he plays no part in the action. The setting appropriately evokes a time of joyful celebration. The steward (2.8), literally the man in charge of three couches, a Greek term with no Aramaic equivalent, is distinguished from other servants (2.5). Barrett (1978: 192-93) therefore thinks the story may be of Hellenistic origin, but our knowledge of meals in Galilee in the first century is too slight to warrant firm conclusions. That meals were sometimes eaten while the guests reclined on couches is again indicated in the Johannine account of Jesus' supper with his disciples (13.25; Mt. 26.20; Mk 14.18; Lk. 22.14), but on that occasion no servant or steward is present. On the contrary, Jesus performs the role of a servant in washing the disciples' feet (13.4-17), although the service would normally have been offered when guests arrived from a journey, not during the meal (e.g. Gen. 18.4; 19.2; 24.32; 43.24; Judg. 19.21; all these references picture people washing their own feet, but see the reference to Abigail washing David's servants' feet in 1 Sam. 25.41, and see Lk. 7.44). The detail that Jesus dipped a morsel and gave it to Judas (13.26; see Ruth 2.14) implies that bowls of food were shared by all the guests and that they ate with their hands. Barrett (1978: 447) thinks this reference to dipping a morsel must be to the Jewish custom of dipping bitter herbs into a sauce at Passover meals, but, if so, the Evangelist was ignorant of the custom, since the meal is dated before the Passover and bitter herbs are not specified. In neither of these accounts of Jewish meals is reference made to the Jewish custom of giving thanks to God for the bread and wine, although Jesus does so at the feeding miracle in 6.11 (see Mt. 14.13-21; Mk 6.32-44; Lk. 9.10-17). One final detail from the account of the wedding at Cana needs to be noticed. The presence of six stone water jars for purification (2.6) shows knowledge of purificatory rites, like those described in Scripture. Jews regarded stone as better than other materials presumably because stone vessels are not mentioned in the scriptural passages about the impurity of vessels (Lev. 11.32; 15.19; *Mishnah*: 802; see *m. Par.* 3.2; *Kel.*). But whether the Evangelist knew this is not clear. The only place where stone vessels are mentioned in Scripture is in the account of Moses' instructing Aaron to hold his rod over the waters of Egypt so that they change to blood (Exod. 7.19). This is likely to be the source of the Johannine reference.

Another custom associated with welcoming guests, no doubt less common than footwashing, was anointing (cf. Ezek. 16.9). Jn 12.1-8 relates the story of Mary, the sister of Martha and Lazarus, who anointed Jesus' feet and wiped them with her hair, when he arrived at their home in Bethany. A similar but different story about a woman who came to the house of Simon the leper in Bethany to anoint Jesus' head introduces the passion narrative in Matthew and Mark (Mt. 26.6-13; Mk 14.3-9). The Johannine story precedes rather than follows Jesus' entry into Jerusalem (Jn 12.12-19; Mt. 21.1-11 and parallels). A story about a woman who was a sinner crying over Jesus' feet, wiping them with her hair and anointing them is found in Lk. 7.36-50. The Johannine anointing story serves two purposes. It pictures Judas the betrayer as a thief (12.4-6), and it presents Jesus' anointing as preparation for burial (12.7) rather than for a triumphal messianic role. But what does Jesus' comment 'That she may keep it for the day of my burial' mean? How can Jesus say that she has kept it, when she has just used it all? Presumably, it means that she has kept it instead of selling it and giving the proceeds to the poor, as Judas suggests (12.5). The normal translation interprets ἵνα with the subjunctive as a purpose clause, which is often but not always its function. In this instance, Lindars (1972: 419) is probably right in understanding it as epexegetical, in effect stating, 'the reason she did not sell it and give the money to the poor was that she might keep it for the day of my burial'. Not that the action took place on the day of his burial, since it is dated six days before the Passover (12.1), but it is understood as proleptic. Later Joseph of Arimathaea and Nicodemus actually anoint the corpse and prepare it for burial (19.38-39; contrast the Synoptics). That Mary wiped Jesus' feet with her hair further emphasizes her devotion to him.

Two stories in the Gospel refer to Jewish burial customs. Lazarus is buried near Bethany (11.34) in a cave covered by a stone (11.38), and his corpse, including the head, is bound in grave clothes (11.44, κειρίαις, plural, and a σουδάριον). Later, Jesus' corpse is bound in linen clothes (ὀθονία, plural, cf. Lk. 24.12, and a σουδάριον, 20.5-

7), with spices, 'as is the custom of the Jews' (19.40), and is placed near Jerusalem in a new tomb in a garden (19.41-42), with a stone covering the entrance (20.1). Such tombs have been excavated outside Jerusalem (see Tzaferis 1970). Matthew and Mark describe Jesus' corpse buried in a σινδῶν, that is, a single piece of linen. Only Lk. 24.12 and Jn 20.5-6 use the plural ὀθονία. The Mishnah refers to a coffin and wrappings (*m. Šab* 23.4). A story in the Babylonian Talmud (*b. M. Qat.* 27b, fifth century CE) refers to a perfuming pan placed under the bier and tells the story of Gamaliel II who was dressed in a linen shroud instead of expensive vestments for burial. 2 Chron. 16.14 describes the burial of Asa: 'They buried him in a tomb which he had hewn out for himself in the city of David. They laid him on a bier which had been filled with various kinds of spices prepared by the perfumer's art, and they made a great fire in his honour', but this makes no reference to the fact that tombs had to be outside cities and villages to avoid corpse impurity, or to binding the body. Although spices were used, Jewish burial customs did not involve embalming, as is clear both from Martha's anxiety that after four days Lazarus' corpse would smell (11.39) and from the external evidence. Mk 14.1 and Lk. 24.1 mention that the women brought spices to the tomb to anoint Jesus' corpse. Jewish customs were therefore different from Egyptian, as well as from the Roman practice of cremation. From the evidence available, the Johannine depiction of Jewish burial practice seems to be accurate. Similarly, mourning customs are assumed, though little detail is provided. The story of the raising of Lazarus mentions that 'Jews' went to the house to console the sisters (11.19, 31) and they joined Mary in weeping (11.33), as did Jesus (11.38) (see 2 Sam. 18.33, David weeping over the death of his son Absalom, and *b. M. Qat.* 27b, which condemns excessive mourning. See also Mt. 9.23; Mk 5.38; Lk. 8.52). Mary Magdalene also wept at Jesus' tomb, but because of the disappearance of Jesus' corpse (20.11, 13-15). These references to mourning are not specific enough to distinguish them from those of other cultures, since weeping is universally a response to bereavement.

Finally, in the Gospel's account of Jesus' trial, Pilate refers to the Jewish custom of releasing a prisoner at Passover time (18.39, '*You* have a custom'). All four canonical Gospels tell the story of Barabbas's release but each understands it differently: Matthew states that 'the governor was accustomed' (27.15), Mark that 'he [Pilate] used to release for them one prisoner' (15.6), Luke represents it as a spontaneous demand by the people (23.18). Neither Roman nor Jewish sources refer to such a custom (see Barrett 1978: 538-39), so no decision about the relative accuracy of these accounts can be made.

Conclusion

Of the Jewish practices referred to in the Gospel, most could have been known from a reading of Scripture or the Synoptics, but one suggests independent knowledge: circumcision taking precedence over the Sabbath (7.22). As far as we can tell from the evidence available, the Gospel makes one mistake about Jewish practice. Fear of defilement which would exclude Jews from eating the Passover is offered as the reason for their remaining outside the praetorium (18.28), but any such uncleanness was removed by bathing and the sun setting, which would happen before the Passover meal was eaten. The evidence indicates that the author was not a Jew but inherited traditions about Jewish life in Palestine, most of which reflected Jewish customs at the time.

5. *Roman Rule in Judaea*

The Gospel never formally introduces its readers to the political situation in Palestine. Herod Antipas, the tetrarch who ruled Galilee, is not mentioned, and Pilate's status as prefect is never defined. Caesar is referred to in the Jewish taunt (19.12) but who he was is not explained. There are no stories about tax collectors or centurions. Nevertheless, Roman rule in Judaea is taken for granted. Roman soldiers and their colonel (χιλίαρχος) are involved in Jesus' arrest (18.3, 12; contrast the Synoptics, but Mt. 27.27 and Mk 15.16 involve them later in the mockery scene). Had Roman soldiers arrested Jesus, they would undoubtedly have taken him straight to Pilate, not to the chief priests. The reference is probably an attempt to present the passion narrative as a coherent whole. Four soldiers carry out the crucifixion (19.23-25; see Mt. 27.35-36; Mk 15.24; Lk. 23.33-34). They divide Jesus' clothes between them, and this may have been a prerogative given to executioners (Sherwin-White 1963: 46). Roman power over the Jewish people is encapsulated in Caiaphas's prophecy, 'It is expedient for you that one man should die for the people, and that the whole nation should not perish' (11.50), and by the 'Jewish' statement to Pilate that 'it is not lawful for us to put any man to death' (18.31).

It is not, however, quite clear whether the assertion made by those who took Jesus from the high priest to Pilate—'It is not lawful for us to kill anyone' (18.31)—is historically correct. Scripture demanded the death penalty for a whole range of offences, but at the time when Rome ruled Judaea through a prefect, it is likely that the death penalty had to be confirmed by the prefect before it could be carried out. This is suggested by Josephus's account of the execution of James the brother of Jesus (*Ant.* 20.200-202) which happened on the orders of a sanhedrin in the absence of the governor. The new governor, however, threatened vengeance in a letter to Ananas, the high priest responsible, who was then deposed by King Agrippa. On the other hand, Gentiles who entered the inner courts of the Temple were executed on Jewish orders (Josephus, *War* 5.124-26; *Ant.* 15.417 and see the footnote in the Loeb edition which gives the text of the inscription found by archaeologists, which forbids Gentiles to enter the inner courts on pain of death). The only other evidence comes from the New Testament, but both the attempted stoning of the woman taken in adultery (Jn 8.3-11) and the stoning of Stephen (Acts 7.58-60) can be read as mob reactions rather than judicial executions. All this suggests that Jn 18.31 is right, with the exception of Gentiles who entered the Temple's inner courts. Nevertheless, Jesus is executed as king of the Jews, a claim that would have been Pilate's direct concern.

Pilate is introduced when Jesus is taken to him for trial (18.28-29; Mt. 27.2; Mk 15.1; Lk. 23.1). Roman trials were normally conducted in public (the Synoptics; Josephus, *War* 2.301) but the Fourth Gospel achieves a more dramatic effect by shifting scenes between Pilate and the crowds outside and Pilate and Jesus alone inside. Pilate sits on the tribunal in public, however, to pronounce judgment (19.13; Mt. 27.19; Josephus, *War* 2.172-76).

The Gospel records a number of other events involving Pilate and his soldiers during Jesus' trial and crucifixion: scourging when Pilate had declared Jesus innocent (19.1; Mt. 27.26; Mk 15.15; Lk. 23.16), mockery at the hands of the soldiers (19.2-3; Mt. 27.27-31; Mk 15.16-20), Jesus bearing his own cross (19.17; contrast the Synoptics, Mt. 27.32 and parallels, but see Lk. 14.27), the notice Pilate placed over the cross (19.19-22; Mt. 27.37; Mk 15.26; Lk. 23.38), vinegar offered to Jesus (19.29; Ps. 69.21; Mt. 27.48; Mk 15.36; Lk. 23.36), breaking the legs of victims to hasten death (19.32), piercing Jesus' side with a spear (19.34), Pilate giving Jesus' corpse to Joseph of Arimathaea (19.38; Mt. 27.57-59; Mk 15.42-45; Lk. 23.50-52), Jesus' hands pierced by nails but referred to only subsequently (20.20, 25, see Lk. 24.39 which refers to the piercing of hands and feet, and Ps. 22.16).

Josephus tells of the scourging and torture which preceded the crucifixion of Jews caught by Titus's army (*War* 5.449). Plutarch indicates that prisoners carried their own crosses to the place of crucifixion (*Morals* 554). The Fourth Evangelist may have omitted the reference to Simon, however, to avoid distracting readers' attention from Jesus, or to fulfil Lk. 14.27, making Jesus' action exemplary. Recently, archaeologists discovered near Jerusalem the skeleton of a first-century crucified man. It shows an iron nail through the heel bones, the effects of the shins being broken by a heavy blow and the marks of a nail through the forearm (Haas 1970).

As far as the notice over the cross is concerned, we have no evidence about such a custom, and the fact that Pilate directly authorizes it (19.19, contrast the Synoptics) serves to make clear that in spite of Pilate's protestations of Jesus' innocence, he was in fact responsible for executing him as 'king of the Jews'. Commentators sometimes refer to an incident related by Suetonius, according to whom Gaius Caligula ordered a slave convicted of theft to be paraded at a banquet after his hands had been cut off and hung around his neck. A placard was to explain his punishment (Suetonius, *The Twelve Caesars*, *Caligula* 32), but the incident is one of a series illustrating Caligula's brutality and tells us nothing about normal Roman practice. Only the Fourth Gospel tells us that the notice was in three languages, Aramaic, Latin and Greek (the variant reading in Lk. 23.38 is influenced by Jn 19.20). It was not uncommon in the Roman Empire for public notices to be written in both Latin and Greek (e.g. Josephus, *Ant.* 14.191; *War* 6.125). This Johannine detail adds to the verisimilitude of the account.

The Fourth Gospel could have derived most of this information from the Synoptics. It goes its own way in depicting Jesus' bearing his own cross. It mentions the breaking of the victims' legs, which may have been customary, but the piercing of Jesus' side was probably dictated by theological considerations.

The Fourth Gospel agrees with the Synoptics in its depiction of Pilate out-manoeuvred by the 'Jewish' crowds. In spite of Pilate's three assertions of Jesus' innocence (18.38; 19.4, 6; Mt. 27.18, 19, 24;

Mk 15.10, 14; Lk. 23.4, 14-15, 20, 22), he condemns him to crucifixion. Quite a different impression of Pilate emerges from the descriptions of Josephus and Philo. Josephus's *Jewish War* (2.167-77) discusses incidents during Pilate's governorship, one of which depicts his treatment of Jewish crowds:

> On a later occasion he provoked a fresh uproar by expending upon the construction of an aqueduct the sacred treasure known as *Corbonas*; the water was brought from a distance of 400 furlongs. Indignant at this proceeding, the populace formed a ring round the tribunal of Pilate, then on a visit to Jerusalem, and besieged him with angry clamour. He, foreseeing the tumult, had interspersed among the crowd a troop of his soldiers, armed but disguised in civilian dress, with orders not to use their swords, but to beat any rioters with cudgels. He now from his tribunal gave the agreed signal. Large numbers of the Jews perished, some from the blows which they received, others trodden to death by their companions in the ensuing flight. Cowed by the fate of the victims, the multitude was reduced to silence.

Similarly, Philo describes Pilate as 'naturally inflexible, a blend of self-will and relentlessness', and accuses him of bribery, insults, robberies, outrages and wanton injuries, executions without trial constantly repeated, ceaseless and supremely grievous cruelty (*Leg. Gai.* 28.299-305). These Jewish accounts are apologetic, but, then, so is the Johannine. It served the interests of Christians living in the Roman Empire to exonerate the Romans and blame the Jews for Jesus' death. Moreover, theological concern predominates to such an extent that the Johannine account of Jesus' trial and execution has become a dramatic exploration of the confrontation between the Son's obedient fulfilment of God's will and worldly reactions to him.

Chapter 14

NAMED CHARACTERS, THE MOTHER OF JESUS, AND THE BELOVED DISCIPLE

It seemed appropriate to treat the Gospel's information about Caiaphas, Annas and Pilate in the previous section, under cultural history, and to reserve for this chapter a discussion of those who, in various ways, bear witness to the author's conception of reality, most of whom are more or less 'insiders' rather than 'outsiders'. About most of these named characters, little or no information is available apart from the four Gospels, and about some of them, nothing is known apart from the Johannine portrait. Nevertheless, it may still be possible to assess the extent and accuracy of the implied author's knowledge.

1. *John*

The Fourth Gospel, unlike the Synoptics, does not call John 'the Baptist'. Although it refers to his activity as a baptist (1.25, 28, 31; 3.23), the text does not state explicitly that he baptized Jesus. The First Gospel (Mt. 3.14-15) offers an apologetic explanation of why Jesus was baptized by John. The Fourth Gospel avoids the difficulty by backgrounding baptism (Jn 1.31) and foregrounding John's role as witness to Jesus. He testifies that Jesus ranks before him (1.15, 30), that he is the lamb of God who takes away the sin of the world (1.29, 36), that he will baptize with the Holy Spirit (1.33), and that he is the chosen one (or son) of God (1.34). Indeed, his baptismal ministry serves the sole purpose of revealing Jesus to Israel (1.31), making explicit what the Synoptics imply. Since he is given this crucial but limited function, he is not identified with Elijah (1.21, contrast Mt. 11.10-14; 17.11-12 and the Markan parallel, but not Luke). The Synoptics do not attribute miracles to John (see Jn 10.41), but they do make clear that he suffered persecution as Elijah did. The Fourth Gospel, however, does not include the story of John's martyrdom at the hands of Herod Antipas, as a foreshadowing of Jesus' martyrdom, in the manner of Matthew and Mark (Mt. 14.1-12; Mk 6.14-29; see the different account in Josephus, *Ant.* 18.116-17). It does refer to John's imprisonment, however, as if it is a well-known fact: 'For John had not yet been put in prison' (3.24). Nor does it provide instances of John's preaching of repentance to the crowds, as Matthew and Luke do (Mt. 3.7-10; Lk. 3.7-14), although it represents people calling him 'rabbi' (3.26) and recognizes that he has a following (1.35; 3.25). Even Jesus testifies to him, 'He was a burning and shining lamp and you were willing to rejoice for a while in his light' (5.35; see Ps. 132.16-17; Sir. 48.1). Perhaps the form of the testimony implies that John had already died at this point in Jesus' ministry.

Nevertheless, like the Synoptics and using similar imagery, the Fourth Gospel depicts John's testimony to Jesus as someone greater than himself who will baptize with the Holy Spirit (1.26-27, 32-33; Mt. 3.11; Mk 1.7-8; Lk. 3.16). This theme, that Jesus is greater than John, is further expanded and dramatized in the Fourth Gospel (3.22-36). The two ministries are set side by side, and whereas in ch. 1 only two of John's disciples follow Jesus (1.37), by ch. 3 'all are going to him' (3.26 and see 4.2), an impression which John confirms by implying that Jesus is the Christ (3.28), calling himself the friend of the bridegroom and Jesus the bridegroom (3.29), and by admitting that 'he must increase but I must decrease' (3.30). The 'must' implies that this accords with God's purpose. Jn 3.31-36 explores Jesus' superiority in terms of the metaphor of 'above' and 'below' which had been expounded in the first part of the chapter, in Jesus' conversation with Nicodemus. The section could be construed either as part of John's testimony or as the comment of the narrator.

The Fourth Gospel, however, does not simply repeat and expand the Synoptic account of John's testimony. Readers are probably to infer from John's rejection of the roles, Christ, Elijah and the prophet (1.20-21; see Lk. 3.15-16), that Jesus is to perform those roles, and this is confirmed by the rest of the story. Moreover, John defines Jesus' destiny by calling him 'the lamb of God who takes away the sin of the world' (1.29), indicating both the fact and the significance of Jesus' death. Probably John also calls Jesus 'the chosen one of God' (1.34 see the variant 'son'), which recalls God's choosing the messiah

(Deut. 17.15; 1 Sam. 16.12). Here John has become the spokesman of the implied author.

The Fourth Gospel could have derived most of this material from the Synoptics, reforming and expanding those traditions to suit its own theological structure. But perhaps the Evangelist also inherited independent information about the location of John's activity. It sets him in 'Bethany across the Jordan' (1.28; 10.40) and in 'Aenon in Salim'. These names are not derived from the Synoptics, which set his ministry in the wilderness of Judaea at the Jordan (Mt. 3.1, 5; Mk 1.4-5; Lk. 3.2-3).

2. *Jesus of Nazareth*

Few scholars who attempt to discover historical information about Jesus of Nazareth use the Fourth Gospel as a major source. Nevertheless, the Gospel itself purports to be giving information about Jesus' life and work, and about what happened to him. One of the reasons for neglecting the Fourth Gospel and concentrating on the other three is that, since the Synoptics are verbally related to one another, comparison provides insights into the history of tradition. Accounts of some incidents in John, like the feeding of the five thousand, the walking on the water and the passion narrative, because they are sufficiently close to those in the Synoptics, can be used in the same way, but most of the material stands alone, whether miracles and other incidents in his life, or the style and content of his teaching. John Robinson (1985) has most recently argued for the authenticity of Johannine information and has tried to coordinate it with that of the Synoptics, but even he has to admit that the discourses are Christian reflections on the significance of Jesus, rather than the *ipsissima verba* of Jesus.

Some of thc distinctive information in the Fourth Gospel may well represent accurate history. For example, it is very probable that Jesus' ministry lasted more than two years, not the few months which the Synoptics encompass. It is possible that Jesus embarked on a ministry of baptism parallel to John's (3.22, see 4.1). It is likely that Jesus restricted his activity to Palestine and did not go to Tyre and Sidon, perhaps not even to Philip's territory (Caesarea-Philippi). Nor is it possible to suppose that he abrogated the Jewish Law by declaring all foods clean. It is likely that Jesus was questioned by a chief priest, without a formal Sanhedrin trial, and that Pilate finally decided his fate. The intriguing detail (8.57) that Jesus was 'not yet fifty years old' could, but may not, imply that he was in his forties rather than his thirties (Lk. 3.23). Moreover, the general outlines of Jesus' career which the Fourth Gospel shares with the other three are most probably correct: that he came from Nazareth, that his parents were known and that his father was Joseph (the Fourth Gospel never alludes to the virgin conception), that he had brothers who did not follow him during his ministry (the Fourth Gospel does not include their names), that he was baptized by John, that he pursued a ministry of preaching and healing, attracted crowds, handed on his work to his twelve disciples, was believed to be prophet and messiah, was crucified by the Romans, and that his disciples survived to relate what they knew of him. The Gospels also no doubt reflect history in portraying Peter's denial and Judas's betrayal although what he betrayed and why is unclear. But scholars are right in doubting that much more can be gathered from the Fourth Gospel. It situates Jesus in history, but it concentrates on theology. Its combination of history and theology gives priority to theology and provides just enough history to prevent its readers from understanding the story as myth. And in comparing the Fourth Gospel with the other three and with the writings of Paul, we meet with the difficulty that these other sources are also combinations of history and theology. Were we in the fortunate position of having accounts of Jesus' life from sources independent of the New Testament, like Roman or Jewish descriptions, we would be better able to assess the reliability of the various New Testament portraits, but Roman histories largely ignore Jesus (Tacitus mentions that Christ was executed in Judaea under Pontius Pilate when Tiberias was Emperor, *Annals* 15.44.4), while references to Jesus in the Babylonian Talmud (5th century CE) rely on Christian accounts and do not represent independent historical information. The testimony to Jesus in Josephus's *Jewish Antiquities* (18.63) has, very unfortunately, been rewritten by Christian scribes. The apocryphal Gospels are also more valuable in telling us about later Christian interests than in supplementing the history which can be gleaned from the New Testament.

Certainly, it is reasonable to suppose that the author of the Fourth Gospel inherited historical traditions about Jesus of Nazareth, probably including those in the Synoptic Gospels, and some of these provide plausibly reliable information about what Jesus did and what happened to him. On the basis of the details examined in previous chapters and of the general tenor of the narrative, however, it is impossible to think that the Evangelist was an eyewitness to the events or that he was a Jew. But it is clear that the author had good reason for believing that Jesus was a man who lived, worked and died in Palestine at the time when Caiaphas was high priest and Pilate governor of Judaea, and that this is the presupposition of the theological interpretation of Jesus' significance which the Gospel presents. (For a detailed reconstruction of the life of Jesus, see Sanders 1984.)

3. *The Disciples*

The first chapter of the Fourth Gospel relates how Jesus attracted a small band of five disciples. The first two, disciples of John who respond to his testimony that Jesus is the lamb of God, follow Jesus (1.35-38). One of these is never named, but the other is Andrew who is defined as Simon Peter's brother and who tells his brother Simon that he has found the messiah (1.40-41). Jesus renames Simon, the son of John (see 21.15, 16, 17 and contrast Mt. 16.17, 'the son of Jona'), Cephas, which is translated from the Aramaic into the Greek, Peter (1.42). When Jesus goes to Galilee, he himself calls Philip to follow him (1.43). Philip, Andrew and Peter are all said to come from Bethsaida (1.44). Philip's testimony to Nathanael, that Jesus of Nazareth, the son of Joseph, is the one of whom Moses and the prophets wrote, meets with scorn, and it is left to Jesus to convince Nathanael that he is Son of God and king of Israel (1.45-49). These confessions summarize Jesus' role, so that, unlike in the Synoptics, the Johannine disciples know whom they are following from the beginning, although they only gradually and through repeated misunderstandings, come to realize what the confessions really mean. No more call narratives are included in the Gospel, but we are led to infer that Jesus attracted others from general remarks like 'the Pharisees heard that Jesus was making and baptizing more disciples than John' (4.1).

This narrative first dramatizes the effect of John's witness to Jesus by depicting two of his disciples leaving to follow Jesus (1.35-37). It then names one of these, Andrew, but defines him as Simon Peter's brother, as if Simon Peter is already well-known to the reader. It is Andrew not Jesus who calls his brother. Jesus then gives Simon Peter the nickname Peter which had already been used (see Mt. 16.18 which does not include, however, the Aramaic form Cephas, and Matthew's version interprets the significance of this naming whereas John's does not). Later Philip calls Nathanael. The Fourth Gospel does not relate the story of the disciples' mission during Jesus' ministry in quite the form adopted by the Synoptics (Mt. 10.5-42 and parallels) but prefers to encapsulate something of their missionary responsibility in this introductory chapter, so that their testimonies can define Jesus' significance. Hence, Jesus' statement in 4.38, 'I sent you (the disciples) to reap that for which you did not labour' is not quite without warrant in the Johannine narrative (see 17.20).

The Fourth Gospel also provides the detail that Philip, Andrew and Peter came from Bethsaida (1.44). The Synoptics do not indicate their place of origin, except that Peter is a Galilaean (Mt. 26.73; Mk 14.70). They set the call narratives on the shore of the lake at an unspecified place (Mt. 4.18-19 and parallels) and later imply or state that Peter's house is in Capernaum (Mk 8.5, 14 and parallels), but that does not necessarily imply that Capernaum was where he was born. We have no way of knowing whether the Johannine information is correct.

Jesus' disciples almost always accompany him, to the marriage at Cana (2.2, 11), to stay with his mother and brothers at Capernaum (2.12), perhaps to the Temple in Jerusalem (2.17), to Judaea (3.22), through Samaria (4.8, 27) and in Galilee (6.3, 8, 12, 16, 22, 24). During the first part of Jesus' ministry, only on his second visit to Jerusalem (5.1-47) is their presence not noted. But at the end of Jesus' discourse on the bread of life, in the synagogue of Capernaum, many disciples take offence (6.60) and withdraw (6.66). Jesus is left with 'the twelve', one of whom, Judas, is to betray him (6.67-71). The Fourth Gospel therefore agrees with the Synoptics in counting Jesus' close band of disciples as twelve, presumably representing the twelve tribes of Israel, but, unlike the Synoptics, never lists their names. 'The twelve' are mentioned again at 11.9 and 20.24. From the end of ch. 6 we are probably supposed to construe all the references to the disciples as references to the twelve (see the references to those whom Jesus chose: 6.70; 13.18). They are people who openly follow him and become his associates. Others, like Joseph of Arimathaea (19.38), are only secret disciples (12.42).

Curiously, the disciples are not said to accompany Jesus to

Jerusalem in ch. 7. On the contrary, Jesus goes alone and secretly (7.10). Nevertheless, they appear at his side to ask whether it was the man blind from birth or his parents who sinned (9.2). Again, they are not mentioned in connexion with Jesus' withdrawal across the Jordan (10.40), but he informs them of his intention to return to Judaea (11.7), and they misunderstand his reference to Lazarus's death as a reference to sleep (11.12). They respond to Thomas's call to go with him, that they may die with him (11.12) and so accompany him to Bethany. When Jesus next withdraws, to Ephraim in the wilderness, they go with him (11.54). We should probably understand that, later, they were invited to the supper at the house of Martha, Mary and Lazarus, since Judas criticizes Mary's use of the ointment (12.4), and also that they witness his entry into Jerusalem (12.16). They are present at Jesus' final meal and individual disciples question him about his teaching (13.22, 35; 15.8; 16.17, 29). Judas, however, leaves the supper (13.30). Afterwards, they accompany Jesus across the Kidron Valley to the garden, where he is betrayed by Judas and arrested (18.2-3). Jesus secures their freedom from arrest (18.8, contrast the Matthaean and Markan statement that they flee, Mt. 26.57, parallel, but see Jesus' prediction that they shall be scattered, Jn 16.32). Only the beloved disciple is mentioned at the crucifixion (19.26-27), a matter which contradicts Jesus' prophecy (16.32) and suggests that the beloved disciple is the ideal disciple not a historical character. After the resurrection Mary Magdalene is sent by Jesus with a message for the disciples (20.17-18), and he himself appears to them that evening when they are assembled in a room behind locked doors (20.19; John, like Luke, sets the appearance stories in ch. 20 in Jerusalem). It transpires that Thomas was absent (20.24), but he is present a week later when Jesus appears to them again (20.26). The third resurrection story involves perhaps seven disciples, Simon Peter, Thomas the Twin, Nathanael, the sons of Zcbedee (not mentioned before) and two other disciples (21.1-14). The rest of ch. 21 concerns the fates of Peter and the beloved disciple.

A was noted in Chapter 2, two of the references to the disciples tell how they came to understand the significance of events in the story at a later time, when Jesus was raised from the dead (2.22) or when he was honoured (12.16). Within the story they often fail to understand Jesus (e.g. 4.31-38; 6.6; 11.12; 14.8, 9, 22). Moreover, they are never portrayed as courageous associates. Alone in the boat, they are frightened (6.19). After Jesus' crucifixion they gather behind locked doors 'for fear of the Jews' (20.19). The promises of Thomas (11.16) and Peter (13.37), to die with or for Jesus, turn out to be empty. Peter denies Jesus (18.25-27) and Judas betrays him (18.2). Nevertheless, Jesus commissions them as the Father had commissioned him, endows them with the Holy Spirit, and gives them authority to forgive or retain sins (20.21-23). This critical portrait means that the only characteristic which distinguishes the disciples from other Jews is their belief in Jesus. By contrast, the beloved disciple, who is not named, represents the ideal disciple who is close to Jesus, even when he is on the cross.

Only seven of Jesus' twelve disciples are named in the Gospel: Simon Peter, son of John, his brother Andrew, Philip, Nathanael, Thomas the Twin, Judas, the son of Simon Iscariot, and another Judas. Matthew and Mark list the twelve as Simon Peter, his brother Andrew, James and John, the sons of Zebedee, Philip, Bartholomew, Thomas, Matthew, James, the son of Alphaeus, Thaddaeus (or Lebbaius in some manuscripts of Matthew), Simon the Canaanean, and Judas Iscariot (Mt. 10.2-3; Mk 3.16-19). Luke gives a slightly different list, calling the Canaanean 'the zealous one' and replacing Thaddaeus by Judas, the son of James (Lk. 6.14-16). The Fourth Gospel never names James and John and never mentions Bartholomew, James the son of Alphaeus, Simon the Canaanean or Thaddaeus. It agrees with Luke's inclusion of a second Judas, but also includes Nathanael, whose name does not occur in the Synoptics. From this evidence it appears that traditions accorded Jesus twelve intimate disciples but agreed on the names on only some of them. The Johannine omission of James and John, the sons of Zebedee, except in 21.2 where they are not named, is surprising, since James's martyrdom is mentioned in Acts 12.2, and both Acts and Galatians picture John as a leading member of the earliest church, alongside Peter (Acts 1–12; Gal. 2.9). The Fourth Gospel, however, does agree with the other three and the Pauline writings in assigning Simon Peter a leading role.

3.1. *Simon Peter*

Simon is the brother of Andrew, the son of John, and like Philip, comes from Bethsaida, which the Gospel locates in Galilee (12.21), but which was in fact in Philip the tetrarch's territory. The Fourth

Gospel does not mention the Markan detail that Simon and Andrew had a house in Capernaum (Mk 1.29). On their first meeting, Jesus gives Simon the name Cephas in Aramaic, or Peter in Greek, that is, 'the Rock'. What prompted this nickname, either here or in the Synoptics, is not entirely clear, since he rarely exhibits rock-like qualities. It is true that he is spokesman of the twelve in expressing allegiance to Jesus after the discourse on the bread of life had resulted in other disciples leaving. In typically Johannine terms, Peter confesses, 'Lord, to whom shall we go? You have the words of eternal life; and we have believed and have come to know that you are the Holy One of God' (6.68-69, compare Mt. 16.13-20 and parallels). Also, at the last supper, he finally submits to Jesus' washing his feet, after some misunderstanding (13.6-10). Subsequently, he signals to the beloved disciple for him to discover to whom Jesus refers as the betrayer (13.24) and he promises to lay down his life for Jesus (13.36-37; Lk. 22.33), but Jesus immediately predicts his future denial and he is seen fulfilling the prophecy (18.25-26; Lk. 22.34). Before his denial, however, he does show more courage than the other disciples, albeit mistakenly in drawing a sword and cutting off the right ear of the high priest's servant (18.10; the Synoptics do not attribute this action to Peter, but the Johannine account shares much of the vocabulary of the Lukan account), and in following Jesus with another disciple into the courtyard of the place where Jesus is questioned by Annas (18.15-18; Mt. 26.58, 69-75 and parallels), but this boldness is only the prelude to his denial. After Mary Magdalene's report that Jesus' tomb is empty, he runs to inspect it, and sees the grave clothes, but, unlike the beloved disciple, he does not immediately believe in Jesus' resurrection (20.2-10; see Lk. 24.9, 34). Like the other disciples, however, he is endowed with the Holy Spirit and commissioned to forgive and retain sins (20.21-23; see Lk. 24.48-49).

Jesus' commission here at the end of the Fourth Gospel differs from that placed in the middle of Jesus' ministry by the Synoptics (Mt. 10.5-42 and parallels). There the disciples are sent to announce the nearness of the kingdom and to heal. The expectations of persecution which are mentioned, however, find echoes in the Johannine Farewell Discourses. Matthew's final scene of Jesus' commission to his disciples focuses on baptism and teaching all the nations (Mt. 28.19-20) and assures them of Jesus' continuing presence with them, the second and third features also finding expression in the Farewell

Discourses (17.20; 14.18-19). The Johannine version of the final commission, though differently worded, is most like that given to Peter after his confession in Mt. 16.19 and given to all the disciples in Mt. 18.18. 'Forgive sins' in Jn 20.23 could include a healing ministry, since sin and illness are connected in the Gospel (5.14). Moreover, Jesus had promised in the Farewell Discourses,

> He who believes in me will do the works that I do; and greater works than these will he do, because I go to the Father. Whatever you ask in my name I will do it, that the Father may be honoured in the Son; if you ask anything in my name, I will do it (14.12-14).

This promise encompasses more than healing miracles but certainly includes them.

In the third resurrection story Peter responds to the beloved disciple's identification of Jesus by swimming ashore (21.7) and hauling in the catch of fish (21.11). The detail about the charcoal fire (21.9) reminds the reader of the charcoal fire in the courtyard (18.18) where Peter denied Jesus. He is finally rehabilitated by professing that he loves Jesus; in response to Jesus' three questions, the three declarations of love revoke his earlier three denials (21.15-17; Lk. 24.34 records an appearance of Jesus to Simon without providing details). This is the only instance in the Gospel of character development, if it can be called that: Peter who had denied Jesus becomes his devoted disciple. Jesus' command, 'Feed my sheep' implies that Peter is to imitate Jesus as the good shepherd. Jesus then predicts his future captivity, which is interpreted as a prophecy about his martyrdom, by which he honours God (21.18-19). The ambiguous statement does not necessarily imply that Peter was crucified (see *1 Clem.* 5.4 which does not know the form of Peter's martyrdom). These statements imply that Peter became a faithful follower of Jesus and so help to explain how others, including the author and his community came to be followers too. The final conversation between Peter and Jesus (21.20-23) concerns the fate of the beloved disciple, who may be spared martyrdom. The Fourth Gospel does not imply that Peter, or any of the other disciples, is married, whereas the Synoptics include the story of his mother-in-law's healing (Mt. 8.14-15 and parallels). Unlike the Synoptics (e.g. Mt. 10.35-38 and parallels), John includes no statements about the effects of discipleship on family life.

Insofar as the Gospel provides a characterization of Peter, he is impetuous, but accepts the responsibilities of leadership. He is, however, less close to Jesus than the beloved disciple. He is too fearful to be completely reliable, but, like the others, is entrusted with Jesus' commission. How are we to understand this portrait of Peter? Is he, as the representative of the original historical disciples, being denigrated, especially in comparison with the beloved disciple? Is the Fourth Gospel marginalizing the original twelve and their leader in favour of its own ideal (see Quast 1989)? In a sense yes, and in a sense no. The Gospel shows that neither Peter nor the other named disciples live up to the ideal of discipleship, whereas the shadowy figure of the beloved disciple does. In describing the historical disciples as fearful and slow to understand Jesus, the Fourth Gospel has much in common with the First and Second. The disciples are not portrayed as religious virtuosi but as people who are completely dependent on Jesus. They are the kind of people with whom readers can sympathize but whom they should not imitate. They are not idealized and transformed into characters worthy of imitation, as they are in Luke–Acts. Alongside this realistic portrait of the historical disciples, the Johannine description of the beloved disciple presents a reassuring ideal because it emphasizes that Jesus loved the disciple, not that the disciple loved Jesus. The beloved disciple's closeness to Jesus is determined by Jesus' love. The difference between the ideal and the historical is the difference between the disciple who accepts and the one who only partially accepts that love.

In comparison with the Synoptics' portrait, Simon Peter plays the same role of leader and spokesman of the twelve. There are parallel stories of the confession, Jesus' prediction of his denial in response to his promise of fidelity, his denial, and Jesus' resurrection appearances to the disciples, including Peter, in the Gospels of Matthew and Luke. The Synoptic stories which pick out Peter, together with James and John, at the transfiguration and in Gethsemane, however, are not repeated in the same form by the Fourth Evangelist. The assurance given by God to the disciples in the transfiguration story is generalized throughout the Fourth Gospel, which repeatedly asserts that the Father sent Jesus as his agent. The Johannine parallel to the Gethsemane story, 12.27-36, is set in the presence of crowds and all the disciples rather than in the presence of three sleeping disciples. The Synoptics also picture Peter, James and John accompanying Jesus to the scene of his healing Peter's mother-in-law and his raising of the ruler's daughter. The Fourth Gospel tells no stories of female healings, but the raising of Lazarus happens in the presence of all the disciples and crowds. Mark also names Peter, James, John and Andrew as the disciples who ask Jesus privately about the destruction of the Temple and the sign when all these things are to be accomplished (13.3; Matthew attributes the question to all the disciples, 24.3). The Fourth Gospel, however, merely refers to the eschatological raising of the dead and the future arrival of Jesus without expanding these references into an apocalyptic discourse. Peter's rebuke of Jesus after he had predicted his suffering and death in Jerusalem, and Jesus' rebuke of Peter (Mt. 16.21-23 and Markan parallel) is dramatized in the Johannine story of the footwashing (13.1-20).

Since none of the Synoptic stories about James and John (their call, the transfiguration, the healing of Peter's mother-in-law, the raising of the ruler's daughter, their request to sit at Jesus' right and left hands in his glory, the question about the eschatological events, the Gethsemane story) finds an exact parallel in the Fourth Gospel, they are never named. In 21.2 the sons of Zebedee are among those present at Jesus' resurrection appearance in Galilee, a story which transforms Lk. 5.1-11, in which the sons of Zebedee appear. The omission of their names is still surprising, since other disciples besides Peter are named, but the omission of the particular forms of the Synoptic stories in which they are named and the lack of references to them elsewhere allow Simon Peter to appear as the sole leader and representative of the twelve, and he can then be compared the more easily with the disciple whom Jesus loved.

3.2. *Andrew*

Andrew, originally a disciple of John who follows Jesus because of John's testimony about the lamb of God (1.35-40), draws his brother Simon into the group by confessing Jesus' messiahship (1.41). He comes from Bethsaida and has a Greek rather than an Aramaic name, although this does not imply that he is not Jewish. Perhaps because of his Greek name, Andrew is told about the Greeks who approached Philip with a request to see Jesus (12.22). In response to Jesus' concern about the crowds in Galilee, he draws his attention to the lad with five barley loaves and two fish, but adds the question, 'What are they among so many?' (6.9; in the Synoptic versions, the disciples mention the bread and fish). Otherwise, he is not singled out from the other disciples. His name does not appear in the list of disciples in 21.2. We have to infer that he is commissioned to forgive and retain sins in 20.22-23, and the role which he is given is that of leading people to Jesus.

In comparison with the Synoptics' references to Andrew, he is given a more significant individual role: in responding to John, first by following him and then by accepting his testimony to Jesus, in calling his brother Simon Peter, and in being particularly associated with Gentiles. This association, however, may have been prompted by his Greek name rather than by independent historical tradition. He is not referred to by name in 21.2, but it is possible that we are to understand that he is one of the unnamed disciples.

3.3. *Philip*

Philip, also from Bethsaida, and also with a Greek name, is called by Jesus and persuades the unimpressed Nathanael to meet him. He describes Jesus as the one of whom Moses in the Law and also the prophets wrote (1.43-47). He is questioned by Jesus about feeding the crowds in Galilee (6.5) but his reply simply highlights the immense quantity of food required, 'Two hundred denarii would not buy enough bread for each of them to get a little' (6.7; this is similar to the question put by all the disciples in Mk 6.37). At the Passover feast he receives the request of the Greeks to see Jesus (12.20-26) but when he takes Andrew to tell Jesus, Jesus replies with a meditation on the significance of his own death, implying that Greeks will become followers only after his historical mission is completed. At the last supper Philip requests Jesus to 'Show us the Father and we shall be satisfied' which Jesus interprets as a statement of unbelief, 'Have I been with you so long and you do not know me Philip? He who has seen me has seen the Father.' (14.8-9). Like the other disciples, then, Philip misunderstands Jesus, but is commissioned together with them (20.22-23).

In comparison with the Synoptics' references to Philip, then, the Fourth Gospel dramatizes and individuates what they generalize. He is called by Jesus and immediately becomes a missionary in calling Nathanael, and he also plays the useful role of Jesus' interlocutor. Like Andrew, he is associated with Gentiles, but perhaps only because of his Greek name. It is surprising that he is not named among the seven in 21.2, unless we are to infer that he was one of the unnamed disciples present then.

3.4. *Nathanael*

Nathanael makes a striking appearance at the beginning of the Gospel. He replies to Philip's confession, 'Can anything good come out of Nazareth?' But he is brought to a new respect for Jesus when he is identified as 'an Israelite in whom is no guile' (1.45-47). Since later (1.51) Jesus seems to give Nathanael the role of Jacob in seeing heaven opened and the angels ascending and descending (Gen. 28.12), Nathanael's lack of guile can be understood as the antithesis of Jacob's cunning. In Scripture the name Nathanael often appears in lists (Num. 1.8; 2.5; 7.18-23; 1 Chron. 2.14; 15.24; 24.6; 2 Chron. 17.7; 35.9; Ezra 10.22; Neh. 12.21). In 1 Chron. 2.14 he is listed as the fourth son of Jesse (in Jn 1 he is the fourth of the named disciples). In 1 Chron. 24.6 he is the fifth son of Obededom in a list of gatekeepers (in Jn 1 he is the fifth disciple to follow Jesus). In all the references, whether to princes or priests or gatekeepers, Nathanael is among Israelites whose actions are praised. The name, then, if it carried any scriptural associations for the readers of the Gospel, would suggest someone who was praiseworthy.

Nathanael's confession forms the final climax to the disciples' testimonies, 'Rabbi, you are the Son of God, you are the king of Israel' (1.49). The only other occasion when Nathanael's name occurs is in the list of disciples in 21.2, where we are told for the first time that he came from Cana. It is surprising that this detail is unnoticed in connexion with the two miracle stories at Cana (2.1-11; 4.46-54; contrast 10.40; 12.1). We have to assume that Nathanael is at the last supper, although no questions or requests are attributed to him, and that he is also commissioned (20.22-23). It is a pity that the author missed the opportunity to translate his name ('God has given') since the Gospel sees Jesus' disciples as gifts from the Father (e.g. 6.37).

3.5. *Judas*

This Judas is mentioned only once in the Gospel, when a question is attributed to him at the last supper, 'Lord, how is it that you will manifest yourself to us and not to the world?' (14.22). The question can be understood as a denial of belief in Jesus' parousia, but it is more likely to refer to Jesus' resurrection appearances to the disciples only. If this is correct, there is no contradiction of Jesus' statement about his future coming in 14.3 and 21.22-23. In spite of any misunderstanding, however, Judas is commissioned with the others (20.22-23).

3.6. *Thomas*

Thomas, whose name is translated as 'twin' (not in the Synoptics), first emerges from obscurity by encouraging his fellow disciples, 'Let us also go [to Judaea] that we may die with him' (11.16). This brave summons, however, does not prevent the escape of the disciples when Jesus is arrested. During the Farewell Discourses he questions Jesus, 'Lord, we do not know where you are going: how can we know the way?' and elicits Jesus' reply, 'I am the way, the truth and the life' (14.5-6). He is unaccountably absent when the resurrected Jesus gives the disciples the Spirit and commissions them, and he refuses to believe their testimony to Jesus' resurrection (20.24-25). He represents disciples who doubt the reality of the resurrection (see Mt. 28.17). Only when, a week later, he is with the others and Jesus encourages him to put his finger in his side and see the marks of the nails in his hands, does he make the confession, 'My Lord and my God' (20.26-28). The incident leads to Jesus' beatitude, 'Blessed are those who have not seen and yet believe', a blessing which is meant to include the readers of the Gospel (20.29-31). Hence, a clear distinction is made between the original disciples and witnesses of the resurrection, and later believers. Thomas is finally present at the third resurrection appearance (21.2). Like Judas, Thomas plays the simple roles of Jesus' interlocutor and witness. No information about either their place of origin or their fathers is supplied. They are useful in prompting Jesus' clarifying declarations, or in voicing the author's belief in Jesus.

3.7. *Judas, the Son of Simon Iscariot*

Judas is introduced to the reader from the first as the betrayer, 'Jesus answered them, Did I not choose you, the twelve, and one of you is a devil?', which the narrator explains, 'He spoke of Judas the son of Simon Iscariot, for he, one of the twelve, was to betray him' (6.70-71; see Mt. 10.4 and parallels). The Gospel envisages Jesus as someone who knows the characters of those he meets (e.g. 1.47-48; 2.24; 4.16-18), and here he knows that Judas, one of the twelve whom he has chosen, will do the work of the devil. In other words, Jesus is neither surprised nor deceived by Judas's betrayal. On the contrary, he even instructs him to get on with it (13.27). Moreover, he prepares the other disciples for the shock, so that it does not lead them to doubt him (13.19). In this conversation at the supper Jesus states that he knows those whom he has chosen (13.18) and, by implication, that he chose Judas in order that the Scripture might be fulfilled, 'He who ate my bread has lifted his heel against me', an inexact quotation of Ps. 41.9 (see the allusion to the psalm in Mk 14.18). He then challenges the disciples with the clear saying that one of them will betray him (13.21; see Mt. 26.20-25 and parallels), which leads them to wonder whom he means, and Peter to signal to the beloved disciple to discover the traitor's identity. But when Judas leaves, they suppose that he is going to buy necessities for the Passover meal or to give money to the poor (13.21-30). The Synoptic Jesus' saying about one who dips the dish with him (Mt. 26.23; Mk 14.20) is transformed in the Johannine account into an action which identifies Judas as the betrayer, but only to the beloved disciple: 'It is he to whom I shall give this morsel when I have dipped it. So when he had dipped the morsel, he gave it to Judas, the son of Simon Iscariot' (13.26).

This story and Judas's part in the account of Mary's anointing Jesus (12.1-8) contain an intriguing detail which, if accurate, gives the only glimpse we are ever afforded into how Jesus and the disciples managed their lifestyle. Judas objects to Mary's use of the ointment by asking, 'Why was this ointment not sold for 300 denarii and given to the poor?' (12.5; see Mk 14.5, where the objection is attributed vaguely to 'some people'), and the narrator explains, 'This he said, not that he cared for the poor but because he was a thief, and as he had the money box he used to take what was put into it' (12.6). The references to the money box (see 13.29) suggest that Jesus and the disciples shared a common life, that they pooled their money, that Judas was responsible for it, and that Jesus gave instructions for its use. Unfortunately, nothing is said about the source of the money. Perhaps Judas's remarks to Mary and the narrator's comments imply that the group depended on gifts from friends. Lk. 8.3 mentions a group of women 'who provided for them [him] out of their means'.

In this story the Fourth Gospel gives Judas a blacker character than does any of the Synoptics. He is a thief. That he is avaricious might have been gathered from the story that he accepted money from the chief priests for betraying Jesus (Mt. 26.14-16 and parallels), but John does not relate that story. In keeping with the black and white rhetoric of the Fourth Gospel, however, Judas is simply caricatured as a bad lot.

In both 6.71 and 13.26 Judas is called 'the son of Simon Iscariot'. (In 12.4 and 13.2 he is called Judas Iscariot.) The Synoptics do not mention his father's name. Some manuscripts add 'from Karuotos' at 6.71, 12.4, 13.2, 26. Whether Iscariot means 'man of Kerioth', a place in southern Judaea mentioned in Scripture (Jer. 48.24, 41 and Amos 2.2), or comes from the Hebrew root for 'falsehood' is uncertain. The Synoptics call him Judas Iscariot, but if the name originally indicated that he was a betrayer, its significance has been lost.

Chapter 18 recounts the fulfilment of Jesus' prophecy of betrayal, when Judas brings a band of Roman soldiers and Jewish officers to arrest Jesus in the garden known to him as a place where Jesus often met his disciples (18.2-3; see Lk. 22.39). The text can be read to imply that this information is what Judas betrayed (cf. 11.57). The Synoptics are even more vague about the nature of Judas's betrayal. Mark and Luke's detail that Judas kissed Jesus (Mk 14.45; Lk. 22.47-48) may suggest that he identified which of the group was Jesus. None of the Gospels attempts to explain why he became a betrayer, although John and Luke attribute his behaviour to Satan or the devil (13.2, 27; see Lk. 22.3). Matthew and the Acts of the Apostles provide different accounts of his death (Mt. 27.3-10; Acts 1.18-19). The Fourth Evangelist's depiction of Jesus' relations with Judas, like that of the other Gospels, offers an apology for what was obviously an awkward fact, namely, that one of the twelve disciples, called by Jesus, turned out to be a traitor. The Fourth Gospel sees the betrayal as a fulfilment of Scripture, and therefore consonant with God's purpose.

3.8. *Conclusion*

Apart from those of Simon Peter and Judas, there is no real portrait of an individual disciple in the Fourth Gospel, and even these two are very little more than flat caricatures. Attributing questions and comments to the others serves to break up and enliven the narrative by specifying and countering possible misunderstandings. And the Fourth Gospel prefers to place questions in the mouths of individual disciples, rather than the disciples as a group. Only in 9.2 and 16.17 is a question attributed to a group of disciples. Nevertheless, the Gospel does create a general impression of discipleship as dependence upon

Jesus who expresses God's love for the world, and it helps to define the future responsibilities of those disciples who are to remain faithful to Jesus. In creating this impression, does the Gospel also indicate what kind of knowledge the Evangelist possessed about Jesus' original associates? It tells us that the author knew the names, patronyms or places of origin of some of the twelve, but very little more. Peter's future martyrdom is mentioned in 21.9, but there are no details about the fates of the rest. Like the Synoptics, John envisages a group of twelve led by Peter and including Judas the betrayer, and agrees on some of the other names, but the nature of the material excludes the possibility that the Evangelist was one of the twelve. Rather, he has used what came down in tradition to communicate a sense of mission to the readers of the Gospel. It seems to be important to the narrative, however, that Jesus' original associates did come to understand his significance and engaged in a mission to make him known. Not that the link between the Gospel's witness and that of the twelve is traced in historical detail, but it is assumed.

4. *Other Named Followers of Jesus*

4.1. *Mary, Martha and Lazarus*

Various other followers of Jesus are named in the Fourth Gospel. Mary and Martha at Bethany are Jesus' friends to whose house he is invited when their brother Lazarus is ill (11.1-3), and when Jesus returns from Ephraim (12.1). On the first occasion, Martha expresses her belief that Jesus' presence earlier would have saved her brother from death (11.21), her belief in the eschatological resurrection (11.24), and she goes on to confess Jesus' messiahship (11.27), but she does not expect him to bring her brother back from the dead (11.39). Mary similarly is confident that Jesus could have healed her brother before he died (11.32). On the second occasion, they give a supper at which Martha serves and Mary demonstrates her devotion to Jesus by anointing his feet and wiping them with her hair. The roles of the sisters are not unlike those given them in the story Luke relates about Martha distracted by preparations for the meal and Mary seated at his feet (10.38-42), but Luke does not identify the village where they live, nor attribute to Mary either the anointing of Jesus, which is not recorded in the Third Gospel, or the act of penitence by a prostitute at Bethany (7.36-38), and nowhere outside the Fourth Gospel is their brother Lazarus mentioned as a historical character. Luke's parable of Dives and Lazarus (16.20-31), however, provides the name and the theme of someone coming back from the dead, while Matthew and Mark's accounts of the anointing provides the place, Bethany (Mt. 26.6; Mk 14.3) and the fact that Jesus stayed in Bethany (Mt. 21.17; Mk 11.12). The Synoptics also tell other stories about Jesus' raising the dead (Mt. 9.18-26 and parallels; Lk. 7.11-17). The Fourth Gospel seems to have combined all these elements into a single story which forms the climax of Jesus' public ministry.

The raising of Lazarus is Jesus' seventh and final miracle (11.1-44). It illustrates Jesus' love (11.3), even endangering his life by his return to Judaea, and his claim to be the resurrection and the life (11.25-26), prefiguring his own resurrection. But Lazarus is resuscitated to an ordinary mundane existence which is vulnerable to death, not resurrected to a transformed life. Moreover, the interest the miracle occasions places Lazarus's life in the same kind of jeopardy as Jesus' (12.9-11, 17-19). This, however, is the last mention of Lazarus, so it is unclear what happened to him. The Evangelist uses these named characters, Martha, Mary, Lazarus, for dramatic effect and as witnesses of Jesus' activity, but shows no other interest in their biography. The traditions inherited all centred on Jesus himself and included no further information about most of the people who came in contact with him.

4.2. *Mary and Mary Magdalene*

Two other female followers of Jesus are named in the Gospel. Mary, the wife or daughter of Clopas, is one of the women standing by Jesus' cross (19.25). The statement mentions Jesus' 'mother, and his mother's sister, Mary the wife or daughter of Clopas and Mary Magdalene'. It could refer to two people, his mother and his mother's sister, who are then named, Mary the daughter of Clopas (Jesus' mother, elsewhere unnamed in the Gospel, must have been the wife of his father, Joseph), and Mary Magdalene. But it could refer to three or four women. Matthew describes women observing the crucifixion from afar, amongst whom are Mary Magdalene, Mary the mother of James and Joseph, and the mother of the sons of Zebedee (27.55-56; see also 20.20). Presumably, Mary the mother of James and Joseph is also the mother of Jesus (Mt. 13.55). Mark replaces Matthew's 'the mother of the sons of Zebedee' with Salome (15.40), Luke with

Joanna (23.49, 55-56; 24.1-11). In each of the Gospels the women are witnesses of Jesus' death, his burial (not in John), and his empty tomb (only Mary Magdalene in John). Their presence as witnesses, in the absence of the disciples, serves to guarantee that Jesus died and was buried, and that it was his tomb which was empty. The general improbability of friends being allowed near the victim of crucifixion (Josephus, *Life* 420-21) makes the Johannine depiction historically unlikely. The Synoptics place them at a distance. Mary, the wife or daughter of Clopas, is not mentioned by the other Gospels. Brown (1966: 905-906) tries to coordinate the four accounts but admits the uncertainty of his conjectures. Luke names one of the disciples to whom Jesus appeared on the Emmaus road Cleopas, which is like but not the same as Clopas (24.18). It is intriguing that the Fourth Gospel names a woman who is otherwise unknown as a witness to the crucifixion, but there is no way of telling how far the information is reliable.

Mary Magdalene, from Magdala, possibly on the sea of Galilee, is a witness to the crucifixion and the empty tomb according to all four Gospels, but John includes no indication of how she knew where Jesus was buried. Only Luke (8.2) tells of her earlier association with Jesus, that he exorcized seven devils from her, and that she was one of the women who provided for Jesus from her means. The Johannine story of her dramatic meeting with the resurrected Jesus (see Mt. 28.9-10, without parallel in Mark and Luke), when she takes him to be the gardener until he calls her by name (20.11-18), exemplifies Jesus' identification of himself as the good shepherd who calls his sheep by name (10.3) and knows and is known by them (10.14). Mary is given the task of taking a message to the disciples but she is not included with them in Jesus' commission. Again, it would be interesting to know how much of the story is traditional and how much the work of the Evangelist. Its present form and emphases are certainly Johannine in the sense that they cohere perfectly with other parts of the Gospel. Moreover, it would be typical of the Fourth Gospel to individuate a response attributed to a group in the Synoptics. It could be, therefore, that the Evangelist freely elaborated Matthew's account of the appearance to the women, choosing Mary Magdalene from the two named there.

4.3. *Malchus, Joseph of Arimathea and Nicodemus*

Three other named characters play parts in the Fourth Gospel. One, Malchus (the name is a Hellenistic form of the Hebrew word for 'king', but is not translated), is assigned only the passive role of suffering the loss of his right ear, cut off by Peter's sword during Jesus' arrest (18.10). The other Gospels record the incident but name neither the assailant nor the victim (Mt. 26.51 and parallels). Luke and John specify that it was the right ear (Lk. 22.51) and Luke has Jesus heal the man. Providing the names gives the Johannine narrative more dramatic and concrete force but whether the names are reliably recorded cannot be decided. Malchus's kinsman later recognizes Peter in the courtyard (Jn 18.26), and this provides a link between the story of Jesus' arrest and that of Peter's denial.

Joseph from Arimathaea in Judaea (see 1 Sam. 1.1), described in Matthew as a disciple (27.57) and in John as a secret disciple 'for fear of the Jews' (19.38; contrast Mk 15.43; Lk. 23.50-51), takes upon himself the task of obtaining and burying Jesus' corpse. Normally this would be a family responsibility. Presumably, the other disciples were too far away to perform the service, or perhaps 'fear of the Jews' inhibited their devotion, and similar qualms could explain the absence of Jesus' family, including his mother, who was present at the crucifixion. The Johannine account differs from the other three in a number of respects. Apart from the details about the grave clothes, the Johannine version places the new tomb in a garden near the site of the crucifixion. Matthew's version says that the tomb belonged to Joseph and was hewn from rock. Both Matthew and Mark mention the great stone set at the entrance, a detail referred to only in the Johannine account of the empty tomb. Mark and Luke identify Joseph as a member of the council which condemned Jesus, although Luke exonerates him from blame (23.50-51). Mark has Pilate check that Jesus is dead by summoning a centurion before granting Joseph the corpse (15.44). Only Mark fails to specify that the tomb was new. There is no way of judging the accuracy of each of these details, none of which is contradictory. The Gospels' agreement in attributing the burial to Joseph must rest on historical tradition since Joseph is an unlikely candidate who plays no other part in the events.

Only in the Fourth Gospel is Joseph joined by another character, Nicodemus, who brought a huge quantity of spices, myrrh and aloes, and assisted with the burial (19.39). The text refers back to the earlier occasion when Nicodemus visited Jesus at night (3.1-2). There he is described as a Pharisee and ruler of the Jews, and his questions highlight the difficulty of rebirth, but there is little to suggest either here or when he defends Jesus' right to be heard (7.50-52) that he became a follower of Jesus, unless he is to be counted among the authorities who believed in Jesus but did not confess their faith openly out of fear that the Pharisees might exclude them from the synagogue (12.42). If so, he is included in the Gospel's harsh judgment, 'they loved the praise of men more than the praise of God' (12.43). Perhaps we should assume that, as one of the rulers of Israel, he was present at the council addressed by Caiaphas in Jerusalem (11.47-53), but, if so, he is silent on that occasion. It would make sense of the part he plays if he were present and agreed with Caiaphas's advice, since he honours Jesus with spices for his burial when he is dead and safely out of the way, sacrificed to ensure the security of the people and Jerusalem within the Roman Empire. Nicodemus, then, remains an 'outsider'. Along with Caiaphas, Annas, Pilate and Malchus, he provides an 'outsider's' view of Jesus. His witness to the fact of Jesus' death, by participating in his burial, is therefore all the more valuable.

Are we to suppose that the Fourth Evangelist inherited this story of the ruler of the Jews, a Pharisee, from traditions which came to him, and, if so, do we possess those traditions in the Synoptics? The story of Nicodemus's visit to Jesus at night reads like a Johannine exposition of the story of the ruler in Lk. 18.18-30 (see Mt. 19.16-30; Mk 10.17-31; and see Lk. 14.1 for a ruler who was a Pharisee). The Lukan ruler asks Jesus what he should do to inherit eternal life. Like Nicodemus, he respects Jesus as a good teacher. When Jesus replies by citing the Commandments, the ruler claims to have observed them from his youth. Jesus then goes on to instruct the ruler to sell all that he has and give to the poor so that he will have treasure in heaven, and to follow Jesus. But the ruler becomes sad at this demand for such a radical change, because he is very rich. Jesus recognizes the difficulty, but asserts: 'What is impossible with people is possible with God' (18.27). The story follows Jesus' saying about the kingdom belonging to children: 'Truly I say to you, whoever does not receive the kingdom of God like a child shall not enter it' (Lk. 18.15-17; see Mt. 19.13-15; Mk 10.13-16). The Fourth Gospel highlights both the difficulty of the change and the fact that only God can accomplish it in Jesus' discourse about being born from above. It also makes

Nicodemus a representative of those who believed in Jesus when they saw the signs, but to whom Jesus did not trust himself (2.23). Hence, in the dialogue with Nicodemus, Jesus speaks of 'we' (Jesus and the disciples) as opposed to 'you' (plural, those who are attracted to him only superficially, see 3.7, 11-12).

But if this is the Johannine version of the Synoptic story, where did the name 'Nicodemus' come from? It was a common Greek name, used also by Jews in the Hellenistic world (e.g. Josephus records that Aristobulus's envoy to Pompey was called Nicodemus, *Ant.* 14.37). The name means 'victory of the people' and perhaps readers would understand this meaning, since it captures the character's representative role. Supplying the name allows the Johannine development of the character's representative story in the other incidents.

4.4. *Conclusion*

The Gospel's depictions of its named characters are not very fully developed. Mostly, it is only their names which individuate them. They serve to dramatize events and dialogues, allowing Jesus to explain misunderstandings or to unfold his teachings. Some of them provide valuable testimony to Jesus, and some of the disciples act as his missionaries during his ministry, a role they are to continue after his resurrection. Only in the case of Simon Peter is there any kind of character development. The use of names probably indicates that the author inherited them in the traditions about Jesus, but we are in no position to judge exactly either how he used and elaborated those traditions or whether the traditions themselves were reliable. Comparison with the Synoptic stories suggests a fairly free elaboration in the interests of an arresting drama which effectively communicates the author's perceptions. The characters' words and actions fit coherently into the present Gospel and, apart from the account of the group near Jesus' cross, into what we know of Palestinian life in the first century. The fidelity of some of Jesus' associates after his death and resurrection helps in general to explain how the author and his community came to believe in Jesus, but no explicit historical links are provided.

5. *The Mother of Jesus*

The mother of Jesus is never named in the Fourth Gospel, unless the reference to the women near the cross in 19.25 is taken to indicate two rather than three or four women. Nor does the Fourth Gospel refer to the virgin conception nor to other events associated with Jesus' birth as the First and Third do. Nevertheless, the mother of Jesus is with him on three occasions during his public ministry. She is present at the wedding in Cana (2.1-11), where she draws Jesus' attention to the lack of wine. Jesus' reply, 'Woman, what have you to do with me? My hour has not yet come' distances her from his mission, as the Synoptics do through a different story (Mt. 12.46-50 and parallels), but also alerts the reader to the fact that his hour, that is the hour of his death when his mission will be completed, has not yet arrived. But the reply causes his mother no offence and she is confident enough to tell servants to carry out Jesus' instructions (2.5). No more is heard of her, however, in this story. She is not included among those who respond to Jesus' sign by believing in him (2.11).

Immediately following, the narrative relates that Jesus stayed with his mother, together with his brothers and disciples, at Capernaum (2.12). Perhaps we are to infer that Capernaum was where Jesus lived or where he and his family lived. Like the Synoptics, the Fourth Gospel recognizes Nazareth as Jesus' place of origin (1.45-46; Mt. 2.23; Mk 1.9; Lk. 1.26; 2.4, 39, 51; although Matthew and Luke place the actual birth in Bethlehem), but Jesus' discourse on the bread of life is set at the synagogue in Capernaum (6.17, 24, 59), and on that occasion, the 'Jews' remark, 'Is not this Jesus, the son of Joseph, whose father and mother we know' (6.42). In the following chapter a conversation between Jesus and his brothers takes place in Galilee without any more definite indication of location (7.1-9). The Fourth Gospel could have gained the impression from Matthew and Mark that Jesus or he and his family lived in Capernaum during his adult ministry. The First Gospel explains that Jesus left Nazareth to live at Capernaum (4.13). Later it sets Jesus in a synagogue 'in his own country' where his family is known to his listeners (Mt. 13.53-58 and Mk 6.1-6), but does not specify Nazareth as Luke does (Lk. 4.16). Moreover, the incident in which Jesus' mother and brothers call for him from outside a crowded house is set at Jesus' home by Mark

(Mk 3.19, 31-35). Matthew, Mark and John, therefore, create the impression that Jesus lived in Capernaum, probably with his family.

Finally, the mother of Jesus is close enough to his cross during the crucifixion for Jesus to address her (19.25-27). This is 'the hour' which Jesus had mentioned to her in 2.4. Now she is accompanied by the beloved disciple, not by the other disciples nor by Jesus' brothers. Jesus' instructions, 'Woman, behold your son' and, to the beloved disciple, 'Behold your mother', and the narrative statement, 'From that hour the disciple took her to his own home' serve to draw a parallel between Jesus and the beloved disciple. He it is who takes Jesus' place in the world. Whether this is the only significance of the narrative, or whether we are also supposed to gather that Jesus' mother was cared for by his disciple or disciples is difficult to determine. Acts 1.12-14 pictures Jesus' mother and brothers with the disciples in Jerusalem, and both Acts and Galatians give to his brother James an authoritative role in the Christian community at Jerusalem (Acts 12.17; 15.13; 21.18; Gal. 1.19; 2.9, 12). His mother, however, is not connected with arrangements for his burial in any of the Gospels.

These Johannine stories about Jesus and his mother suggest more filial contact, respect and concern than Jesus' teaching in the Synoptics allows (Mt. 8.22; 10.35-38; 12.46-50 and parallels). The Fourth Gospel is less offensive than the Synoptics to Jewish and Graeco-Roman family piety.

6. *The Beloved Disciple*

One of Jesus' disciples is never named but is described as 'the disciple whom Jesus loved' (ἀγαπάω or φιλέω which are used synonymously in the Gospel; 13.23; 19.26; 20.2; 21.7, 20). According to the rest of the Gospel, Jesus loves his disciples (e.g. 13.34; 15.12) as the Father loves Jesus (e.g. 3.16, 35; 5.20; 10.17; 14.21). According to Scripture, God loves Israel (e.g. Ps. 47.4; Hos. 2.23; 14.4; Isa. 43.4; 44.2; 51.2; 60.10; Jer. 12.7). Naturally, Israel and the disciples are supposed to respond to the love they enjoy by loving God and one another, but the primary perspective is God's and Jesus' love for them. 'The disciple whom Jesus loved' exemplifies this perspective.

The stories about the beloved disciple in chs. 13 and 20 depict him as somewhat apart from the other disciples. In 13.12-30, at the supper table, when he is lying next to Jesus, Peter signals to him to find out the identity of the betrayer, and Jesus does identify Judas to the beloved disciple, but Peter and the other disciples remain in ignorance, a matter which is stressed at the end of the story when Judas leaves:

> Now *no one at the table* knew why he [Jesus] said this to him [Judas]. Some thought that, because Judas had the money box, Jesus was telling him, Buy what we need for the feast, or that he should give something to the poor (13.28-29).

But the beloved disciple was in a position to understand the real meaning of Jesus' command to Judas. The story creates the impression that the beloved disciple is not a historical character like the other disciples.

A similar impression is made by the story in 20.1-10. When Mary Magdalene reports to Peter and the beloved disciple that Jesus' corpse had been taken from the tomb, they run to the tomb, the beloved disciple arriving first (see the parallels in vocabulary with Lk. 24.23, 24). From the entrance he sees the grave clothes but waits for Peter to enter first. The presence of the grave clothes and the absence of the corpse are sufficient to prompt the beloved disciple's belief in the resurrection of Jesus (20.8), yet the narrative continues in a curious fashion: 'For as yet they did not know the Scripture, that he must rise from the dead' (compare Lk. 24.27, 32, 44-47). Again, the beloved disciple's insight is not communicated to Peter who remains unaware of the significance of the empty tomb until he hears Mary Magdalene's message (20.17-18).

These odd characteristics of the stories involving the beloved disciple and the fact that he is described and not named suggest that he is a dramatized representative of the ideal disciple, an example for the reader rather than a historical character like the unexemplary historical disciples. Understanding the beloved disciple in this way helps to explain why he is present at the foot of the cross. In 16.32 (see Mk 14.27) Jesus tells his disciples, 'The hour is coming, indeed it has come, when you will be scattered, everyone to his own home, and will leave me alone'. Jesus' prediction is fulfilled in the case of all but the beloved disciple. Jesus' instruction to him from the cross (19.26-27) encapsulates the function of the disciple, to replace Jesus in the world after his death. Like all Jesus' disciples, he is Jesus' brother (20.17).

His responsibility is to accept the mission which God had entrusted to Jesus (e.g. 17.14-19; 20.22-23).

In the final chapter, an appendix to the original Gospel, the beloved disciple is present at the third appearance of the resurrected Jesus to the disciples, when he joins them at a meal, as in Luke (21.1-14; Lk. 24.30-31, 35, 41-43). The incident is set by the Sea of Tiberias like the feeding miracle in 6.1-13, and, like that miracle and the meal in Luke's resurrection narrative, fish and bread are eaten. Matthew and Mark, but not Luke and John, contain a second feeding miracle, of the four thousand, during Jesus' ministry (Mt. 15.32-39; Mk 8.1-10), which is usually interpreted as a proleptic intimation of the Gentile mission. It would have been inappropriate for the Fourth Gospel to include the story during Jesus' ministry since it restricts that ministry to 'his own', the Jews. Only Jesus' conversion of the Samaritans hints at the wider scope of God's purpose before Jesus' crucifixion. But it would be appropriate to treat the subject of the Gentile mission in an appendix, after Jesus' resurrection, and this seems to be the subject of the story in Jn 21.1-14. The reasons for interpreting the story in this way are as follows:

1. The allusions to the feeding miracles already mentioned.

2. The involvement of seven disciples, seven symbolizing universality, as in the seven baskets of fragments in the feeding of the four thousand miracle in Matthew and Mark. Of course, the number of disciples listed in 21.1 adds up to seven only if it is assumed that there are two sons of Zebedee, but this is a reasonable assumption if the Synoptic Gospels were known to the author and readers.

3. Fishing is a metaphor for missionary activity. The Fourth Gospel does not mention that some of the disciples were fishermen before they followed Jesus, but it does take up here Jesus' interpretation of the disciples' future role: 'I will make you fishers of men' (Mt. 4.18-22; Mk 1.16-20). The Johannine story also alludes to the Lukan parallel to these call narratives (Lk. 5.1-11), according to which, Jesus joins Simon in the boat to preach to the crowds on the shore and then commands Simon to take the boat out into the lake to catch fish. Simon asserts that they had toiled all night without success (see Jn 21.3) but that they would obey Jesus' command. They are then so successful that their nets begin to break and they have to call for assistance from their partners in the other boat, the sons of Zebedee. Both boats are filled with fish (compare Jn 21.4-6, 8, 11). Simon Peter's response to

Jesus, 'Depart from me, for I am a sinful man, Lord' is appropriate to the disciple who denies him (compare Jn 21.15). The Lukan narrative ends with Jesus' assurance, 'Do not be afraid; henceforth you will be catching men'. Understanding the Johannine account in 21.1-14 as an extended metaphor about the disciples' missionary work removes what would otherwise be a difficulty. It is impossible to suppose that the disciples who had heard Jesus' Farewell Discourses and received the Spirit should go back to an ordinary life of fishing in Galilee. Moreover, the verb πιάζω ('take hold of' 21.3, 10) is not normally used for catching fish.

4. The Johannine story states with unusual precision that the catch consisted of 153 large fish. We can speculate about the significance of the number but without reaching a definite conclusion. Since it does not state 'about one hundred and fifty', it is unlikely to mean 'a large number'. It would fit in with the symbolism of the story if the number represented the different kinds of fish then known to exist, but no evidence for this interpretation has yet been discovered. Augustine noticed that 153 is the sum of the numbers from one to seventeen. If this is the reason why such an exact figure is given, the number seventeen can be interpreted as the sum of ten, representing Jews, and seven, representing Gentiles, to indicate the world-wide mission. The net which is not torn would then suggest the unity of Jews and Gentiles in the Christian community, as in 10.16 and 17.20-21. The only place in Scripture in which the number 153 occurs is in 2 Chron. 2.17, where Solomon's census of the aliens within the land of Israel is given as 'a hundred and fifty-three thousand and six hundred'. It is just possible that the figure 153 in Jn 21.11 alludes to this number and represents 'aliens', that is non-Jews, who will come into Jesus' community in response to the disciples' mission.

5. This interpretation helps to explain why the appendix was added to the original Gospel. Chapters 1–20 had looked forward to the time, after the completion of Jesus' historical ministry, when Gentiles would join Jews in following Jesus, but ch. 20 gives no indication that the disciples obeyed Jesus' instructions to become missionaries. We know from Paul's epistle to the Galatians that the terms on which Gentiles should enter the church were hotly debated by the earliest Christian communities. The story in Jn 21.1-14 assures readers of the disciples' obedience and of the resurrected Jesus' support for the Gentile mission.

But what is the role of the beloved disciple in this narrative? His role in relation to Peter and the other disciples has changed. In the earlier narratives, he is distanced from the other disciples, but in this story he identifies the figure on the shore as Jesus, and Peter responds, typically, by jumping into the sea and gaining the shore before the others. The beloved disciple is therefore given the task of discerning Jesus' presence in the Gentile mission and communicating that insight to Peter and the other disciples, who finally accept it. We may infer that the beloved disciple represents not only the ideal disciple, but the ideal Gentile disciple. This helps to explain both the nature of the narratives in chs. 13, 19 and 20, which separate him from the historical disciples, and the rest of the narrative which concerns him in ch. 21.

After Jesus' questioning of Peter, Peter's response, his commission as shepherd and the prediction of his martyrdom, Peter raises the topic of the fate of the beloved disciple (21.20-24). The reader is reminded that the beloved disciple had been next to Jesus at the supper table and had asked who the betrayer was (21.20). This also reminds the reader that it was Judas, not the beloved disciple, who was identified by Jesus as the betrayer. In the context Jesus' reply to Peter's question, 'If it is my will that he remain until I come, what is that to you? Follow me', implies that the beloved disciple may not suffer martyrdom before Jesus' parousia, in distinction from Peter who will. The Farewell Discourses had emphasized that disciples would be hated by the world and would have to be prepared to lay down their lives as Jesus did. This stress on martyrdom gives the impression that all disciples who remain faithful to Jesus will suffer that fate. But not all followers of Jesus in the first century were martyrs. Were those who were not martyred nevertheless faithful to Jesus, or had they betrayed their calling? This story about the beloved disciple suggests that, contrary to the extremism of earlier statements, a disciple could remain faithful and yet not be martyred. But the statement by Jesus only raises that possibility. It does not entirely exclude the fate of martyrdom. The supposition that the beloved disciple would certainly not die is countered by repeating Jesus' words (21.23), and the narrator refers to the testimony of the beloved disciple himself in support of this view (21.24).

But why does 21.24 go on to describe the beloved disciple as the one 'who wrote these things' or 'who caused these things to be written' (see 'Pilate wrote or caused to be written', 19.19).

Generations of readers have interpreted the statement as a claim that the whole Gospel, or at least ch. 21, was written by the beloved disciple. But this interpretation is prompted by the desire to attribute the Gospel to a disciple of Jesus, an attribution which the nature of the narrative precludes. Dodd (1953: 212-13) is surely correct in proposing that 21.24 refers back to Jesus' statement in 21.22-23, and no further. The ideal Gentile disciple continues to bear witness (present) and wrote or caused to be written Jesus' prediction that he might not suffer martyrdom. Then the beloved disciple's witness is supported by the confession of the chorus which had appeared in the Prologue (1.14, 16), 'We know that his testimony is true' (21.24). Here 'true' probably means accurate, but the nuances 'genuine' and 'faithful' are also appropriate.

The Fourth Gospel concentrates on Jesus' mission to Jews in Palestine and looks forward to a wider mission only after Jesus' resurrection. The 'Jews' of the Gospel, therefore, have to be used to represent 'worldly' opposition to Jesus, and exclusion from the synagogue is associated with future persecution of the disciples (16.2). Unlike the Synoptics' Jesus (e.g. Mt. 10.18 and parallels), the Johannine Jesus never predicts that the disciples will be brought before governors and kings and will give their testimony to Gentile persecutors. There is good evidence that some Jews persecuted some Jewish Christians in the earliest period of the church's existence. Paul admits that he had violently persecuted the church and tried to destroy it before his call to be a Jewish Christian missionary to the Gentiles (Gal. 1.13; 1 Cor. 15.9), and he describes his own sufferings at the hands of some Jews when he was a Christian missionary (2 Cor. 11.24 and see Rom. 12.14 and 1 Thess. 2.14-16). Josephus relates how the high priest Ananus II took advantage of the Roman governor's absence to stone James, Jesus' brother, along with other Jewish Christians, for transgressing the Law, itself an illegal act in Roman eyes, for which he was deposed (Josephus, *Ant.* 20.200). Eusebius refers to the later Emperor Domitian's persecution of Jewish Christians in 96 CE, although the people concerned were probably Jews, not Jewish Christians (*Ecclesiastical History* 3.17-20).

The earliest evidence that Christians suffered persecution at the hands of the Roman authorities, rather than at the instigation of some Jews, is in 1 Thess. 2.14-16 and in Paul's account of his sufferings in 2 Cor. 11.25-26, where he specifically mentions 'three times I have been beaten with rods' and 'in danger from Gentiles'. But he gives no indication of charges or circumstances. During Nero's reign, however, both Tacitus and Suetonius relate that Nero blamed Christians for the fire in Rome and had them burned as arsonists and executed in other ways in 64 CE (Tacitus, *Annals* 15.44.2-8; Suetonius, *Nero* 16.2). Paul's epistle to the Romans suggests that the Roman church included Gentiles (especially Rom. 1.18–2.16; 11.17-36), so Gentile Christians must have been included among Nero's victims. Once the Roman authorities could distinguish Christian groups from Jewish communities, as they could have done from the foundation of Pauline Christian churches, which clearly formed completely separate social units, these Christian groups could be subject to Roman persecution because they had no right of assembly and no exemption from pagan worship, rights that Jews had won for their own communities from Rome in the first century BCE (see Josephus, *Ant.* 14.213-67). Tacitus describes Christians as 'a class hated for their abominations', and he calls Christianity 'a deadly superstition'. He describes the crime for which they were convicted as 'not so much of arson as of hatred of the human race'. Suetonius calls Christians 'a class of men given to a new and wicked superstition'. The Fourth Gospel depicts a Christian community completely separate from Judaism and therefore in danger from the Roman authorities.

At the beginning of the second century CE, Pliny became governor of Bithynia in about 112 CE and wrote to the Emperor Trajan (98–117 CE) to ask about the proper treatment of Christians (*Epistles* 10.96). He asks whether he should make any distinctions of age or relative weakness among Christians, and whether he should pardon those who recant, that is, whether the crime relates to being a Christian or to secret crimes involved in that religious practice. He goes on to show, however, that he had already made up his mind on this second issue and had acted accordingly. He reports that those who refused to recant he caused to be executed, unless they were Roman citizens, in which case he had them despatched to Rome. Those who claimed that they were not nor had ever been Christians, he required to prove their allegiance to Rome by reciting a prayer at Pliny's dictation, by making an offering of incense and wine to the Emperor's statue, and by cursing Christ. Their compliance had secured their freedom. Pliny then informs Trajan that Christians met to recite words to 'Christ as a god' and to bind themselves by an oath not to commit theft, robbery or adultery, or break their word. He notes that they had given up meeting to share a meal since Pliny's edict forbidding clubs. Pliny characterizes Christianity as a 'perverse and extravagant superstition' which had infected many people of all ages and rank, both in the countryside and in the cities of Bithynia. He ends his account by noting the effectiveness of his measures in restoring the ceremonies at pagan temples.

It is clear from this letter that Christians who refused to join in pagan worship when they were required to do so but preferred to meet together for their own 'superstitious' religious observances were considered traitors by the Roman government. But not all Roman governors were as conscientious as Pliny, and not all pagan worship in the Roman Empire suffered noticeably because so many people in the area were Christians. We have no evidence of persecution in other parts of the Empire during Trajan's reign. Most Christians at the end of the first century CE were free to live lives which did not end in martyrdom. But the possibility of martyrdom was not removed until Constantine converted to Christianity in the fourth century CE. Hence the Fourth Gospel's insistence that the beloved disciple, the ideal Gentile disciple, would not certainly but might possibly survive until the return of Jesus.

The Fourth Gospel, however, is careful not to invite Romans to persecute Christians. It emphasizes Pilate's three declarations of Jesus' innocence and pictures Pilate as a weak governor, giving in to the local population, that is, as the kind of governor that others should not imitate. It explicitly defines Jesus' kingdom as 'not of this world' to avoid any suggestion of subverting Roman authority. It also pictures the followers of Jesus as the faithful representatives of the ancient Israelite tradition rather than as a new religion. These elements could help to offset Roman contempt for Christianity.

7. *The 'Implied Author' of the Fourth Gospel*

The 'implied author' of the Fourth Gospel was not a Jew nor an eyewitness to the events described. He knew no Hebrew or Aramaic, but was in possession of traditions about the life of Jesus in Palestine which show a mostly accurate if general knowledge of the geography, culture, belief and practices when Pilate ruled Judaea. He pictures Judaism, however, as an alien religion, and the Christian community as completely separate. Information about named characters is sufficient to individuate them but is related only insofar as it bears on Jesus' words and deeds. The portrait of Jesus is historical in the sense that it is reasonably situated in history, but the emphasis of the Gospel is upon the theological significance of Jesus' life, death and resurrection, to which other issues are subordinated. The 'implied author' was a Christian with an original theological perspective, distinct from the Synoptics and from all other New Testament writings except the Johannine epistles, with which the Gospel is connected, probably not by common authorship but by community association (see Brown 1983). The text does not allow us to determine his place of origin except that it was outside Palestine. Probably, he lived in the second half of the first century, but certainly not later than the first half of the second century. The 'implied author' was clearly a teacher who was able to communicate profound insights in simple language. The impressive style and the imitations of the Septuagint, as well as the subject matter, effectively create an all-encompassing vision of reality. Why the teaching took the form of a Gospel instead of an epistle or homily is probably to be explained by his possession of traditions about Jesus, interpreted in a work which owes much to its Scripture but more to the Christian traditions and experience it reflects. On the one hand, the Fourth Evangelist has simplified these traditions, making them more general and typical, rather than particular, as in the case of 'the Jews' and their leaders, and in the case of the miracles. Moreover, the discourses are repetitive, picking out central themes, like the honour God accords to martyrs and the relation of death to love, as reflections on the particular, concrete instances of Jesus' teaching in the Synoptics. On the other hand, the Fourth Evangelist greatly expands the stories he has chosen to tell, dramatizing them into a series of scenes, individuating responses for dramatic effect. The Fourth Gospel is therefore better able than the Synoptics to appeal to and move Gentile Christians, sharpening their understanding and encouraging them to remain faithful followers of Jesus in an unjust and threatening world.

Only once does the author write of himself in the first person singular. In the conclusion to ch. 21 he muses: 'But there are also many other things which Jesus did; were every one of them to be written, *I suppose* that the world itself could not contain the books that would be written' (21.25). Here the author reflects, for the benefit of the reader, on the limitations of the task he has accomplished. Elsewhere he includes himself in the chorus of the believing community which occasionally confirms the truth of the Gospel's perceptions in confessions expressed in the first person plural (1.14, 16-17; 21.24). Like the author of the Fourth Gospel in 21.25, every author becomes aware of the manifold limitations of his or her work when it is finished and reflects with him on the seemingly infinite number of books which could be written. Also like him, every author finds consolation as a member of a community engaged in similar pursuits.

Chapter 15

The Implied Reader or Listener

1. *The Act of Reading*

No matter what the intentions of the author, no matter how potentially interesting a work may be, communication takes place only with the active participation of a reader. It is the reader who *makes* sense of the text, who understands what is read. At the most basic level, combinations of letters have to be construed as words and combinations of words as phrases, clauses and sentences. One sentence has to be related to the next, then the next. The reader gains expectations which are either fulfilled or thwarted.

> The activity of reading can be characterized as a sort of kaleidoscope of perspectives, pre-intentions, recollections. Every sentence contains a preview of the rest and forms a kind of viewfinder for what is to come; and this in turn changes the 'preview' and so becomes a 'viewfinder' for what has been read (Iser 1974: 279).

'There was a man sent from God whose name was John' (Jn 1.6). Nothing in the Prologue's meditation on God and the λόγος, light and darkness, the coming into existence of all things, had prepared the reader for this statement about an individual human being. Indeed, commentators see it as a secondary intrusion into a hymn about creation and enlightenment. Something of the surprise, however, is reduced by immediately bringing John into relation with the God whose activity had been described in previous verses; John has been sent from God. John's role is then defined: 'This man came as a witness, that he might bear witness to the light, so that all might believe through him' (1.7). John, then, provides a link between God and humanity. He is sent from God, like the prophets in Scripture, and his is a witness to the light which shines in the darkness (1.5), to the life which is in the λόγος (1.4). And this witness is directed not to one group but to the whole of humanity. But the nature of human response is belief not commonplace knowledge. Hence, humanity is in need of this witness. Readers have to construe the information about John in the light of previous statements in the Prologue as well as apprehending the new perspective it occasions. In doing so, however, they could identify John, the witness, with the light to which he bears witness. But this understanding is excluded by the next sentence, 'He was not the light, but (he came) that he might bear witness concerning the light' (1.8).

Readers may now expect more details about John and his testimony, but the Prologue reverts instead to a description of the light's fate in the world. It relates the fact that the world failed to recognize the light, that even 'his own' did not receive the light (1.9-11). These statements create tension. How is it that the man John can be sent to bear witness to the light in a world which has completely failed to perceive that light? Worse, how can anyone bear witness, when the light's own people did not receive him? Does 'the light's own people' include John? Did John, after all, fail to bear witness? And if the light suffered such a fate, what could the earlier statement in the Prologue, that the darkness did not overcome the light (1.5), possibly mean? Readers have to proceed to the next sentence to resolve the contradiction: 'As many as received him, he gave to those who believed in his name the authority to become children of God' (1.12). So, in spite of stating bluntly that the world and even the light's own people did not receive enlightenment, actually some did and John must be one of them. Readers now appreciate that general statements can be modified by particular exceptions.

Those excepted from the general rule, the next clause tells its readers (1.13), 'were born not from blood, not from the will of the flesh, not from the will of man, but from God'. Are these exceptions, then, non-human? Are they perhaps angelic beings? They cannot be so, since no such distinction had been made earlier in the Prologue and, if John is to be counted among them, he certainly was a man (1.6). Moreover, the next sentence goes on to state that 'the λόγος became or was flesh' (1.14), and this implies that the Prologue is concerned with only two kinds of existence, divine and human. But this declaration that the λόγος became flesh is completely unexpected. Again it modifies what had immediately preceded it. Those who received the light or λόγος are said to be born not of the will of the flesh, but the λόγος became flesh nevertheless. The distinction envisaged, then, is not that between human and angelic, but that between humanity rejecting God's will and humanity expressing God's will.

Even so, 'the λόγος became flesh' introduces a completely new idea to the readers, new not just in terms of what the Prologue had previously related but also in terms of what Scripture had prepared readers to expect. They know, however, that this description cannot refer to John because he was not himself the light (1.8) but must refer to someone else as yet unnamed. This someone else 'dwelt among us and we perceived his honour, honour as the unique one from the Father, full of grace and truth' (1.14). Readers are made aware, for the first time, that they are to read about someone whose vulnerable human existence has been perceived by those amongst whom he lived (by 'us') as an embodiment of the λόγος of God that existed eternally, as someone whose relationship to God is like that of only son to father, and as someone who is therefore full of grace and truth, an example of complete fidelity to God. At this point readers expect to be told the name of this person and to be introduced more fully to his life and work.

Not so, however. Instead, the next sentence returns to John and explains his role in relation to the person who instantiates God's λόγος. At last, John's testimony is summarized, 'This man was he of whom I said, He who comes after me has been and is before me, because he was before me' (1.15). The testimony can be read as a straight contradiction: I said he came after me and he came before me. But the contradiction is removed if 'before' and 'after' are construed in two different ways, in relation to time and in relation to status. John's precedence, in the Prologue and in history, is a matter of time but not of dignity. Here John's limited witness confirms the reader's impression that John, the witness, though introduced first, serves only to point towards a second person, still unnamed. John's witness is to God's λόγος, to the light (1.7-8), but to that light as it is focused in a particular human being (1.15), whose name is eventually given to the reader in the concluding confession, 'Jesus Christ' (1.17).

In coming to understand the Prologue, readers have been initiated into some of the skills required for reading the rest of the Gospel. For example, they have been encouraged to view humanity from the perspective of the Creator God's purpose in giving 'life' and 'light', and have learned to be patient enough to read on when puzzled, since enigmas and contradictions will be resolved and expectations fulfilled, even if in startling ways. My sketch of what readers have to do in order to construe the Prologue, however, exhibits a great many unexpressed presuppositions. In particular, it assumes that the Prologue's opening verses are to be read against the background of scriptural passages like Genesis 1 and not in terms of Gnostic cosmologies. Part of the competence the reader must bring to the text, in my exposition, is knowledge and acceptance of a Scripture which controls the construal of this new version. Familiarity with Scripture's literary repertoire, and with the theological perspectives these express, allows readers an initial grasp of the new text which repeats them, but that new text also rearranges the old patterns of meaning into new configurations, as when it states, 'the λόγος became flesh and dwelt among us' (1.14).

2. *Readers' Competence and Context*

Every reader brings to the text some competence. Construing written signs as letters and words is a prerequisite of all reading, knowing Hellenistic Greek is necessary to read the Fourth Gospel. But much more than these elementary requirements are needed to make sense of the Gospel. When we, in twentieth-century western society, enter a library and select a book from a shelf to read, we are helped in a great many ways to know what to expect from a text. Books are normally arranged in an orderly manner, under subjects like 'philosophy' or 'fiction', and are further subdivided by authorship, title and genre. When we take from the shelf a copy of Wittgenstein's *Philosophical Investigations*, we already know the book is unlikely to contain a fictional account of events in the nineteenth century or a collection of recipes. We may not know exactly what it will contain, but its subject will be philosophy, and we can expect it to address philosophical issues in the tradition of western philosophy. Those readers familiar with other works by Wittgenstein will be better prepared for reading this one than those whose experience of philosophical discourse has been limited to reading Plato's dialogues, but even readers of Plato will be better prepared than those whose previous reading has included only detective stories and letters.

In what circumstances, however, could first- or second-century readers be expected to come across the Fourth Gospel? Are we to imagine that they would also enter a library, arranged according to subject, and pick from a shelf of religious writings or even of Gospels a scroll or codex of the Fourth Gospel? Should we suppose that the potential reader was helped in anticipating what the work contained by its title and author's name? Cities in the Roman Empire did build libraries for their citizens, and some children were taught to read and write, were introduced to important texts and encouraged to appreciate them. Lexica existed to help with reading. Texts were read in public and copies were available for purchase. Rich individuals even had their own libraries at home (Kenyon 1932). But the scale of text production and distribution, and therefore the availability of texts, was much smaller than it is today. Texts were written and copied by hand on expensive material like papyrus or parchment. Apart from short business notes, personal letters and legal agreements, therefore, only important longer works were written, copied and circulated. Classical Greek works like the epics of Homer, the histories of Thucydides and Herodotos, the plays of Sophocles and Euripides and the philosophical writings of Plato and Aristotle might be found in public and private collections, but the majority of people, those who did not belong to the privileged orders of society, probably never handled copies of such works, even if they could read, but were dependent on public readings or performances. Within subcultures of the Roman Empire, however, particular texts would be preserved because of their importance to the group. Thus, Jewish synagogues would have copies of Jewish Scriptures to be read and expounded when Jews gathered together. Christian groups, too, must have possessed texts important for their lives, perhaps through the patronage of the more wealthy individual members. The author of the Fourth Gospel had come to know the Jewish Scriptures in their Greek translation, and those who first read and heard the Gospel were undoubtedly familiar with them too. (On levels of literacy in the Graeco-Roman world, see Harris 1989.)

2.1. *Scripture*

The reason for making this supposition is that knowledge of those Jewish Scriptures is required for understanding the text of the Fourth Gospel. It does not explain, for example, what the Jewish Festivals it mentions celebrated, but knowing that Tabernacles looked back and forward to God's gifts of water and light prepares the reader for

Jesus' statements about streams of living water (7.38), and about himself as the light of the world (8.12), which are set in the context of the feast (7.2, 10). Again, details about Jesus' crucifixion, its timing (19.14), the use of hyssop (19.29), the fact that his bones were not broken (19.32-33), and that his corpse did not remain until the morning (19.31, 38), take on the significance of a Passover sacrifice only if Exodus 12 is already well known to readers; so with the other feasts. On the other hand, the Law's prohibition of work on the Sabbath is made explicit in both accounts of Jesus' healings on the Sabbath, so perhaps the earliest Christian readers had to be reminded of this Jewish interpretation because they no longer kept the Sabbath law in the ways Jews did (5.10; 9.14-16).

Throughout the Gospel references to Scripture punctuate the narrative (e.g. 2.17; 5.39, 46-47; 6.31; 7.22, 38, 42; 12.38-41) and these encourage readers to notice allusions to Scripture in other parts of the Gospel, like those to Ezekiel 34 in the discourse on the good shepherd (10.1-18), or those to Exodus 16 and Numbers 11 in Jesus' discourse on the bread of life and reactions to it (6.26-71). More than this, however, the very language of the Gospel, its vocabulary and some of its idioms, its focus through the omniscient narrator, its theological presuppositions, its themes and motifs, are all reminiscent of Scripture. It is Scripture which provides the familiar literary stock from which the Gospel grows. Readers who come to the Fourth Gospel without a knowledge of this Scripture will be very much more perplexed than those whose reading of Scripture has determined their outlook and expectations.

What, for example, would readers ignorant of the first verses of Genesis, of Exodus and of some of the Psalms, make of Jn 6.16-21? 'When evening came, his disciples got into a boat and started across the sea to Capernaum.' The opening reads like so many Hellenistic romance stories of adventures at sea: 'It was now dark and Jesus had not yet come to them'. This statement marks the passing of time from evening to night and reinforces what had already been implied, that Jesus had been left in the mountain and the disciples were alone. 'The sea rose because a strong wind was blowing.' This reads like an introduction to a disaster story. The disciples seem to be in peril. 'When they had rowed about twenty-five or thirty stadia', that is, when they were far from the place where Jesus had left them, 'they saw Jesus walking on the sea and drawing near to the boat'. This is certainly an unanticipated development. Jesus, a normal human being like the disciples, needed a boat to cross the water. How is it that the disciples think they see him walking on the sea? Are they hallucinating? 'They were frightened' is their natural response to this abnormal experience. But the next statement affirms that this is no disturbed vision of threatened disciples, but a true perception of Jesus, 'He said to them, It is I, do not be afraid'. Reassured, 'they were willing to take him into the boat, and immediately the boat was at the land to which they were going'. Their acceptance of Jesus brings them to the completion of their journey.

How are readers to understand this depiction of Jesus as someone who can walk across the rough sea? Should they doubt their previous conception of him as a human being and, if so, how should they reconstruct their image? Is Jesus not a human being at all, but an angelic being who only appears to be a man? Those readers who adopt this option, however, will find the rest of the Gospel quite incomprehensible. Later Jesus does not behave like an angel. In particular, he does not disappear when the soldiers come to arrest him and he goes on to suffer and die on a cross. The story seems to be anomalous. But is there a way of understanding it which would retain the integrity of Jesus' humanity?

There is a way, but only if readers remember some passages from Scripture and information which the Gospel has already supplied about Jesus. The incident, like that which immediately precedes it, is set at Passover time (6.4). The account of the Passover related in Exodus 12–15 records the celebration of the Passover feast, the exodus, and the crossing of the Red Sea. Readers who knew this story might therefore expect John 6 to contain accounts of a meal and a sea crossing. But the details of the sea miracle are different in each case. The Johannine passage is much more reminiscent of another part of Scripture, the opening of Genesis 1: 'In the beginning, God created the heavens and the earth. The earth was without form and void, and darkness was upon the face of the deep; and the Spirit of God was moving over the face of the waters.' (Gen. 1.1-2). Darkness and movement across the surface of the waters connect this depiction of God's creative activity with the story of Jesus. But why should the Gospel present Jesus in terms reminiscent of God's creative Spirit? The answer is supplied by the Gospel's account of John's inspired testimony to Jesus, 'He on whom you see the Spirit descend and remain, this is he who baptizes with the Holy Spirit' (1.33). Jesus is therefore to be understood as a man whose whole life encapsulates God's creative purpose and hence one who can impart the gift of God's Spirit to his followers. The Johannine story of Jesus walking across the sea pictures the disciples' perceiving this truth about Jesus, and encourages its readers to adopt the same viewpoint. It is not so much an account of an 'incident' as of a recognition. Moreover, Scripture often treats 'the sea' as a symbol not only of formlessness, as in Genesis 1, but also of danger. In the Psalms God is praised as the one who rules the raging of the sea and stills its waves when they rise (Pss. 89.9; 135.6; 139.9), who 'is mightier than the thunders of many waters, mightier than the waves of the sea' (Ps. 93.4). As Israelites in the Psalms were protected from the sea's dangers by the Creator God, the disciples are protected by the presence of Jesus who embodies God's Spirit. They are reassured in a time of danger by recognizing Jesus' presence with them.

2.2. *A Familiar Story*

Time and again, the Fourth Gospel gives the impression that it is retelling a story already familiar to its audience. When Andrew is first mentioned, he is defined as Simon Peter's brother, as if Simon Peter were already known by both his name and his nickname (1.40). But only as the story proceeds are we told that Andrew brought his brother into the group of Jesus' followers and that Jesus gave him the nickname (1.41-42). When the Gospel reintroduces John who was baptizing at Aenon near Salim (3.23), an explanation of his continuing activity is offered: 'For John had not yet been put in prison' (3.24). We have to infer that readers and listeners were aware of his imprisonment and must have wondered how he could still be active. The Gospel, however, does not describe his subsequent imprisonment and execution. In ch. 11 Lazarus is introduced as 'Lazarus of Bethany, the village of Mary and her sister Martha' (11.1), as if Mary and Martha are familiar characters. Mary is then identified: 'It was Mary who anointed the Lord with ointment and wiped his feet with her hair, whose brother Lazarus was ill' (11.2). Mary's anointing is not related till the following chapter (12.1-8), but in ch. 11, Mary is identified as responsible for an action about which readers and listeners already knew. Lazarus is then defined as her brother.

The basic story which the Fourth Gospel tells, then, is one known to its readers and listeners. The text helps them to orientate their understanding by reminding them of what they already accept from another version of the story. The most plausible explanation of this phenomenon is that readers and listeners were already familiar with the Synoptic Gospels, or at least with the Gospels according to Mark and Luke. From those Gospels they would have come to know Simon Peter as the leader of Jesus' disciples. They would have understood that he often acted as spokesman for the group of 'twelve', who could be mentioned without further elaboration (6.67). They would have heard about John's imprisonment and execution and would therefore have required an explanation of his reappearance after the beginning of Jesus' ministry (3.24). They would have recognized Martha and Mary, but would need to be told that they came from Bethany, that Mary was the woman who anointed Jesus, that she anointed his feet not his head, and that Lazarus was her brother. We cannot prove that the Fourth Gospel is a new version of the other three because the Fourth Evangelist has made the story his own and has expressed it in his own distinctive vocabulary and style, but the nature of the narrative requires us to suppose that the Johannine version is a re-telling of an older story, and links can be made between it and the Synoptics at every point. If the Fourth Gospel was not revising the Synoptics' stories, it was revising a story which was remarkably like those in the Synoptics.

The readers implied by the text of the Fourth Gospel, therefore, were Christians who already knew the basic story of Jesus. But if this is so, why was a new version required? It was necessary so that many of the theological implications of those earlier versions could be spelt out more clearly. The Gospel focuses attention on Jesus, the Christ, rather than on the kingdom, although, once more, teaching about the kingdom seems to be taken for granted (3.3, 5). It expresses the exemplary significance of Jesus, God's son, so that readers can conform their lives to his and become sons, living from God in faithful obedience to him as recipients of his Spirit, laying down their lives for their friends in a new community united in love. The story is retold by picking out, coordinating and emphasizing what is crucially important for followers of Jesus, by meditating on the significance of his words and works which are completed in his death on a cross. It accords Jesus the honour of martyrdom in obedience to God's purpose, sees his death as a sacrifice which inaugurates a new community, and encourages its readers to understand his life as the true way to live in a world created by God but alienated through immorality, unfaithfulness and disobedience.

The author addresses his implied readers or listeners as 'you' in the original ending of the Gospel, 20.30-31 (compare 19.35), which explains the purpose of the work:

> Jesus did many other signs in the presence of his disciples which are not written in this book. But these are written in order that you may believe [or may continue to believe] that Jesus is the Christ, the Son of God, and that, continuing to believe, you may have life in his name.

The manuscripts of the Gospel which have survived provide two alternative readings: 'you may believe' (aorist, in the majority of manuscripts) and 'you may continue to believe' (present, in $\mathfrak{P}^{66}$ apparently, the original reading of Sinaiticus, altered to the aorist by a corrector, Vaticanus, Koridethi and two minuscules). Reading the present tense would make sense in the context, since the Gospel is addressing Christians who have already committed themselves to belief in Jesus. Reading the aorist would also make sense, however, in urging belief on readers and listeners, belief which has to be reaffirmed even by those who have made an initial commitment. The text supposes believing in Jesus, as the Son and messiah of the Creator God, to be crucial to the audience's life, not only determining their present temporal and mundane existence in a community united by love, but also their continuing existence after death.

3. *Readers and Narratees*

The Fourth Gospel's original readers and listeners would not have picked it off a shelf in a public library but would have become acquainted with it through readings in a Christian community which valued it, and this community would also have read the Scriptures they had inherited from Jews as well as other versions of Jesus' story. Since context influences all readings, this context would have determined theirs. Perhaps the author was even known to them, but the author is less important than the believing community which, even in the text, confesses its beliefs in God's purpose (1.14, 16-18). Texts sometimes indicate the nature of the audience anticipated by explicitly including 'narratees' within their compass. For example, stories about

'Lord Jim' are related by Marlow to dinner companions who were not experienced sailors like himself (Conrad 1949: 31, 76, 91, 107, 241, 253), and in Anthony Burgess's *The End of the World News* (p. 387), the tale of the earth's destruction is told to young people who were descendants of those who escaped. The Fourth Gospel does not define its narratees as clearly as these novels do, but it includes them nevertheless (see Staley 1988). This is the point of mentioning the community whose members believe that Jesus is the Son of God: 'So the λόγος became flesh and dwelt among *us*, and *we* perceived his honour, honour as the unique one from the Father, full of grace and truth' (1.14), 'that from his fullness *we all* received, grace instead of grace' (1.16). Later Jesus identifies with this believing community when he speaks in the first person plural to Nicodemus, 'Truly, truly, I say to you, *we* speak of what *we* know and *we* bear witness to what *we* have seen, and *our* witness you do not receive' (3.11). At the end of the Gospel its readers are specifically admonished to play the same role as its narratees, 'These things are written that you may believe [or continue to believe] that Jesus is the Christ, the Son of God, and that, continuing to believe, you may have life in his name' (20.31; and see 19.35).

It would be invaluable if we had detailed external evidence about these earliest Christian contexts in which the Gospel was read. Unfortunately, we have to fall back on a general knowledge that can be gleaned from other New Testament books and from Pliny's letters. We know that some Christian groups met together regularly to celebrate the eucharist (1 Cor. 11.17-34) and to pray, and to listen to prophecy and preaching (e.g. Acts 2.42; 15.30-32; 18.7-11; 20.7-12; 21.17-25; 1 Cor. 14.23-40). Pliny's correspondence, from Bithynia at a later period, about 112 CE, describes the testimony of former Christians to the Christian practice of assembling before dawn, reciting a form of words to 'Christ as a god', and binding themselves not to commit adultery or theft of any kind or to break their word. Later they would share a common meal (*Epistle* 10.96). Pliny makes it clear that Christian assembly had not been authorized by Rome in the way that Jewish assembly in synagogues had (Josephus, *Ant.* 14.213-67), so that Christians could come under suspicion as a possible threat to state security, and could suffer persecution. They seem to have been brought to the notice of the magistracy only exceptionally, however, if we are to judge from Pliny's questions. We may suppose that most

Christian communities in most places in the earliest periods assembled and pursued their interests without being molested. And the Fourth Gospel would have been read and heard at such gatherings.

But how much of the Gospel and how often would it have been read and heard? Unlike the Synoptics, the Fourth Gospel is not easily divided into the short sections which we are accustomed to hear as part of modern Christian liturgies. There are some short and relatively self-contained passages like the miracles at Cana (2.1-11; 4.46-54), and some longer sections, like chs. 5 or 6, which would make sense on their own, but chs. 7–10 have to be read as a single unit, as does the passion narrative, chs. 18 and 19. Best of all would be to read and hear the whole Gospel at once, which would take only a few hours. Modern churchgoers are unused to listening to such long readings but some actors have recently recited individual Gospels to appreciative audiences in the theatre. The simplicity of language, the repetition, the gradual building of a comprehensive perspective on Jesus' life, makes the Gospel the kind of work which can be assimilated by an audience prepared to spend the time listening to a complete reading. It does not make impossible demands on a group of listeners as Wittgenstein's *Philosophical Investigations* would. Nevertheless, we can get no further than conjecture in these matters.

The situation of later readers is similar in some respects but different in others. By the time of Irenaeus (about 130–200 CE), copies of the Gospel had circulated outside the original community to churches which knew the versions of other Gospels, as well as other Christian writings, some of which were finally collected and arranged into the New Testament by the fourth century CE. The churches which Irenaeus represents also read these writings in the light of their Scriptures, taken over from Jews, which became their Old Testament. But the Johannine version would have become one among many. Also, by the time Irenaeus wrote, the Gospel was known outside his circles, by Gnostics, who did not value the Jewish Scriptures but favoured and elaborated alternative cosmologies, and who read the Gospel in the light of their own insights, hearing quite different meanings. Moreover, we can imagine that an educated Greek, who knew nothing of Jewish traditions, but who was well-read in the dialogues of Plato and the plays of Sophocles, and who happened upon a copy in the library of a Christian acquaintance, would find it an alien work. He would miss the fullness of characterization, the subtlety of rational argument, the dramatic development, the sophisticated style of the classical Greek masters. And he would find the Gospel's teachings about creation, redemption and resurrection not only strange but probably offensive. Christian teachings had to be presented to educated Greeks by apologists like Justin, Clement of Alexandria and Origen in forms quite different from that of the Fourth Gospel.

4. *The Implied Readers*

But to return to the original readers, implied by the strategic rhetoric of the Gospel, what kinds of competence would they require in order to make sense of the text? It has already been suggested that, for a full appreciation of the Gospel, they would need to be well versed in Scripture, familiar with the story of Jesus, and should be part of a confessional community living out the insights of the Gospel. These qualifications would enable readers to fill out in detail the practical implications of teaching which the Gospel only hints at in the most general terms. In ethics the Gospel's single commandment to love one another as Jesus loved in laying down his life for his friends (15.12; 13.34) does not explain what should or should not be done in practical everyday matters to give expression to that love, but Scripture and the Synoptics do and so should the ethos of the community (13.35). Nor does the Gospel discuss in detail the effects of commitment to Jesus on family relationships. It does depict Jesus as a dutiful son in so far as he makes arrangements for the welfare of his mother just before he dies (19.26-27), if the passage is to be understood in that way, but nothing is said about responsibilities to spouses and children. Again, Scripture, the Synoptics and community tradition could have provided guidance. The question of whether the community practised the rites of baptism and eucharist is, however, more contentious. If it did so in anything like the manner of, for example, Pauline and Matthaean communities, the Gospel's teaching about birth from above in ch. 3 and the significance of Jesus' death in ch. 6 would make sense of those rites at a fundamental theological level.

Scripture, the story of Jesus, and community life would resonate through the reading of the Gospel. On the other hand, the very existence of the community is founded and fostered by the Gospel. Hence, parts of the Gospel, like the Prologue or the Farewell Discourses, could easily have provided passages for liturgical use, while shorter excerpts could have become the subjects of homilies. In all reading there is a dialectical relationship between text, context and readers, the text by its strategies encouraging readers to understand it in the terms dictated, and the readers bringing to the text understandings which inform its interpretation.

What other kinds of competence do the strategies of the Gospel's rhetoric require of the reader? It demands a number of skills and attitudes, without always explaining what they are. These will be treated under separate headings in what follows.

4.1. *Opposing Views and Irony*

The Prologue, the testimony of John and Jesus' disciples' confessions, all in the first chapter of the Gospel, inform readers who Jesus is, and they do so in a way which encourages people to see his life as the exemplification of the Creator God's plan for humanity in fulfilment of scriptural expectations about God's son and messiah. Indeed, readers are even made aware of the narratees' belief that he is now in the bosom of the Father (1.18). This orientation of readers allows them to discern an opposition between the interpretation of Jesus' significance which the narrative encourages, and the actual interpretation which some characters give to it.

Nicodemus's question to Jesus about being born again, 'How is a man able to be born again when he is old? Can he enter his mother's womb for a second time and be born?' (3.4), alerts the reader to the magnitude and difficulty of a change as fundamental as rebirth. Nicodemus's literal interpretation of Jesus' metaphor is, on one level, a mistake which readers can correct by remembering the Prologue's statement about the children of God (1.12-13), but it also urges them to realize that rebirth is as miraculous as a second ordinary birth, which can only be brought into effect by the Creator God's Spirit (3.5-8). They can also sympathize with the Samaritan woman's reluctance to identify Jesus as the messiah to her fellow Samaritans on the basis of Jesus' extraordinary knowledge (4.29). Her earlier question, 'Are you greater than our father Jacob who gave us the well, and he drank from it and his sons and his cattle?' (4.12), had been left unanswered, but readers were in a better position than the Samaritan woman to supply an affirmation, since they could drink from the 'living water' (4.10), which is the Spirit (7.38-39; 20.22). The crippled man, healed by Jesus in Jerusalem, on the other hand, probably irritates readers by his utter feebleness, having to be prompted to acknowledge even a desire to get well (5.6), failing to notice the identity of his healer (5.13) and, when Jesus makes himself known to him (5.14-16), telling Jesus' opponents. Again, the crowd's request for a sign from Jesus (6.30), after they had just witnessed his feeding of the five thousand and could have deduced his miraculous crossing of the sea, makes them appear to be slow in the eyes of readers. In chs. 7–10, too, 'Jewish' crowds and leaders repeatedly demonstrate their denseness in their conversations. They claim to know whence Jesus comes and suppose this disqualifies him from being the messiah (7.27), when readers perceive that he has been sent from God; they wonder whether he intends to go to the Dispersion, or even to kill himself, when he speaks of his departure to God (7.33-35; 8.21-22); some insist that a person from Galilee cannot be the messiah because the messiah must be a descendent of David from Bethlehem, when Jesus' credentials as prophet and Christ sent from God are shown to be better than David's (7.41-42, 52; see 1.46). In the passion narrative the 'Jews' show themselves to be fastidious about avoiding uncleanness by refusing to enter the praetorium, so that they can eat the Passover, when they have handed Jesus, the Passover lamb, to Pilate in the praetorium (18.28). The misunderstandings encourage readers to identify with the believing community in discerning the importance of Jesus which the characters miss.

When Jesus goes to Jerusalem on his final visit, crowds meet him because they had heard of his resuscitation of Lazarus (12.17-18). Commenting on Jesus' popularity, the Pharisees remark to one another, 'See, the whole world has gone after him' (12.19). Within the story theirs is an expression of frustration, but readers know that it also justly describes the appropriate response to Jesus. Hence the comment leads into the story of the Greeks who wish to see Jesus (12.20-22), and of Jesus' meditation on the effects of his imminent death (12.23-24, see 10.11-16).

Later, in the passion narrative, a number of statements and actions carries this double sense. The soldiers crown Jesus and dress him in purple so that they can hail him mockingly as king of the Jews (19.2-3), but their actions remind readers of Jesus' true identity. Pilate's title (19.19) functions in the same way. It summarizes the reason for which Jesus suffered the penalty of crucifixion, 'Jesus of Nazareth, the king of the Jews', but, at the same time, it rightly describes Jesus' status. The chief priests' attempt to have it reworded, 'He said, I am the king of the Jews', and Pilate's refusal, serve to reinforce the point (19.21). Finally, Jesus' last statement from the cross as he died, 'It is finished' (19.30), also denotes the successful completion of his mission.

Duke's study of irony in the Fourth Gospel (1985) treats all these examples as evidence of a pervasive irony (chs. 4 and 6; see also O'Day 1986). It does this because it recognizes an opposition between the narrative's views of Jesus' significance and the views of some of the characters in the story. Certainly, the narrative encourages its readers to adopt its own interpretation and reject that of the opposition, but it is inappropriate to call this rhetoric irony. Irony requires that the reader should be amused by the character's ignorance and should feel superior to it. Inasmuch as the readers are Christians, it can be assumed that they would be predisposed to accept the narrator's standpoint, but it is doubtful whether they could feel altogether superior to that of the opposition. To accept the narrator's view, they have to be prepared to lay down their lives as Jesus did, and they could hardly feel entirely secure in the self-knowledge that this is the option they would take. They cannot be amused by the views of Jesus' opponents, who raise real issues about the interpretation of Scripture and about Jesus' relationship with God.

Similarly, they cannot feel superior to the attitude of the disciples, expressed in their queries and misunderstandings (Duke 1985: chs. 3 and 5). With the disciples, they would have wondered what Jesus meant by 'a little while' and why he did not manifest himself to the world. Sometimes they would have doubted whether Jesus had shown them the Father and walked the only way which leads to him. They would have sympathized with Peter when he denied Jesus rather than face the consequences of affirming allegiance. They would be led to consider whether they were truly faithful or more like Judas, the betrayer. And many of them could have been impressed by Jesus as a wonder-worker, failing to see the significance of his signs, placing themselves alongside those whom Jesus did not trust. Some might have found their security in belonging to a special community with its own superior tradition, like the 'Jews' of the Gospel, instead of finding it solely in God. Any members of the community who exercised political power would find it easy to identify with Caiaphas and Pilate.

Nevertheless, the Fourth Gospel does include examples of irony, which Duke discerns (ch. 3). Jesus often asks ironical questions, that is questions which undermine the validity of implied claims. For example, Jesus asks Nicodemus, 'Are you a teacher of Israel and yet you do not understand these things?' (3.10). Similarly, he asks the 'Jews', 'If on the Sabbath day a man receives circumcision, so that the law of Moses may not be broken, are you angry with me because on the Sabbath I made a man's whole body well?' (7.23). A little later he states ironically, 'You know me and you know whence I come', but destroys the claim by countering, 'But I have not come of my own accord; he who sent me is true, and him you do not know' (7.28). In 10.32 he meets the 'Jewish' attempt to stone him with the challenge, 'I have shown you many good works from the Father; for which of these do you stone me?' He even disabuses Peter, when he promised to lay down his life for him, 'Will you lay down your life for me? Truly, truly, I say to you, the cock will not crow till you have denied me three times' (13.38). Finally, he undermines the disciples' confidence in their knowledge, 'Do you now believe? The hour is coming, indeed it has come, when you will be scattered, everyone to his own home, and will leave me alone' (16.31-32).

Moreover, one story in the Gospel explains the double meaning of a statement made by a character opposed to Jesus. At the assembly of 'Jewish' leaders (11.47-53), Caiaphas's advice is explained in this way:

> You know nothing; you do not understand that it is expedient for you that one man should die for the people and that the whole nation should not perish. This he did not say from himself, but, being high priest that year, he prophesied that Jesus was about to die for the nation, and not for the nation only, but that the scattered children of God might be gathered into one (11.50-51).

Caiaphas's statement makes perfect sense within the story. It offers 'Jewish' leaders advice about instigating Jesus' execution in order to prevent trouble with Rome. The narrator, however, explains how the statement takes on a much broader significance in the context of the Gospel's theology. Jesus' death will fulfil God's purpose in bringing all peoples into a unified relationship with him. Later, when Jesus is arrested, readers are reminded of Caiaphas's prophecy (18.14). But we should notice that Caiaphas is not placed on a par with the Pharisees and 'Jews' in the rest of the Gospel. His advice expresses a profound theological truth, according to the Gospel, because he is inspired by God to speak as a prophet.

The implied reader of the Fourth Gospel is encouraged by its rhetoric to accept its view of Jesus' significance and to lead a life characterized by a love like Jesus'. But this very fact of encouragement suggests that the implied reader is uncertain, even when he or she has made an initial commitment. Indeed, fidelity to God and to Jesus is ensured only by the presence of God's Spirit. The Gospel's rhetoric encourages fidelity but supposes that only the Paraclete can create it.

4.2. *Double Meanings and the Play on Words*

Competent Greek readers of the Fourth Gospel would notice what has to be explained to people reading a translation of the Gospel, that some words have two meanings, both of which are relevant for construing the development of the story, and that some passages play on the similarity of Greek words with slightly different meanings. In the dialogue between Jesus and Nicodemus, for example, Jesus warns that 'unless someone is born again/from above (ἄνωθεν), he is unable to see the kingdom of God' (3.3 and 7). Both 'again' and 'from above' are important for understanding. Later, Jesus' elaboration of his teaching contains two instances of the same word, each exemplifying one of the two possible meanings, 'the wind (τό πνεῦμα) blows where it wills, and you hear its voice, but you do not know whence it comes or whither it goes. So is everyone who is born of the Spirit (τό πνεῦμα).' (3.8).

In the dialogue with the Samaritan woman, Jesus again expresses himself ambiguously, intending one of two possible meanings while the woman understands the other (4.10). ζῶν, the present participle of ζάω, 'living', also means 'running' when used with 'water'. The woman understands Jesus to refer to the latter and asks how he can claim to provide 'running water' when he has no vessel and the well is deep (4.11), but readers are aware of the alternative meaning, 'living water' and can construe Jesus' offer metaphorically, as a reference to the life God gives through him. Hence, Jesus' further claim comes as no surprise: 'Whoever drinks from this water will never thirst again, since the water will become in him a spring welling up to eternal life' (4.13-14). The woman, however, remains unenlightened and thinks she is only to be saved the burden of drawing water from the old well (4.15). Those who continue to read the narrative, however, discover that 'water' is a reference to the Spirit (7.38-39).

In dialogue with the 'Jews' in Jerusalem, Jesus once more plays on the double meaning of a word. In response to a question about his identity (8.25), he promises that 'when you lift up (ὑψόω) the Son of man, then you will know that I am he' (8.28) Jesus will be lifted up physically on a cross (see 3.14), but readers may discern that this is to be Jesus' exaltation (12.32-33).

Finally, Greek readers would not be surprised by the development of Jesus' teaching from 15.2 to 15.3. Jesus describes the fate of the vine's branches at the hands of the gardener, 'Every branch which bears fruit he prunes (καθαίρει) that it may bear more fruit' (15.2) and goes on to apply the image to the disciples by saying, 'Already you are clean (καθαροί) on account of the λόγος which I have spoken to you' (15.3).

These ambiguities force readers to puzzle over possible meanings, to engage self-consciously in the act of construal, and they enjoy a sense of achievement when their efforts are rewarded with confirmation. But they can only come to a correct understanding by accepting the role of the narratees, by understanding Jesus from the perspective of belief. Competent readers are forced to play the role, and in doing so, they experience its insights as their own. It is this requirement and this experience which makes reading texts like that of the Fourth Gospel both a risky and a rewarding endeavour. Readers do not simply stand back from the text and take or leave what it says, as if they are objects separate from it. Their active participation in creating meaning affords them, as long as they continue reading, new experiences, which are not only cerebral but emotional. Their effects may be short-lived, but they can be profound.

4.3. *Explanations*

The Fourth Gospel, however, does not always make its readers work so hard to gain understanding. Its narrator not only uses its characters' misunderstandings as an opportunity for Jesus to explain his teaching more fully, but offers explanatory glosses of his own.

Some of these explanations supply translations of Hebrew or Aramaic words: rabbi, 1.38; messiah, 1.41; Cephas, 1.42; messiah, 4.25; Siloam, 9.7; Gabbatha, 19.13; Golgotha, 19.17; rabboni, 20.16; Thomas, 20.24. This implies that readers were interested in reading Hebrew and Aramaic words, which give local colour to the narrative, but could not supply translations. Not all the Hebrew and Aramaic names in the Gospel are interpreted, however, but this tells us more about the implied author than the implied reader.

Occasionally the narrative also explains local customs which were unfamiliar to readers. Explanations of 'Jewish' belief about the Sabbath have already been mentioned. In addition, the six stone water jars at the wedding in Cana are 'for the Jewish rites of purification' (2.6). Later, 4.9 explains, 'For Jews have no dealings with Samaritans'. 'Jewish' reluctance to enter the praetorium is also elucidated: 'They themselves did not enter the praetorium so that they might not be defiled but might eat the Passover' (18.28).

The narrator is also careful to distinguish those who believe in Jesus from those who only superficially believe or do not believe at all, so that the implied readers are left in no uncertainty about the people with whom they should align themselves, namely, with the narratees (e.g. 2.11; 2.23-24; 7.5; 8.31-38; 12.37-43; 16.29-33).

By offering such help to readers, the narrator gains their confidence. He can be relied upon as a guide to be followed. His view is not partial or limited, and he gives readers just the kind of information which enables them to comprehend the sense of the narrative. In accepting his guidance, readers are also seduced into accepting his world-view.

4.4. *Recognition of Metaphors and Themes*

One of the skills necessary for readers of the Fourth Gospel is the ability to relate parts of the narrative to the whole, to see one episode in terms of what precedes and follows, and, most importantly, to judge mundane events in the light of God's purpose. By shifting from an everyday to a theological perspective, Jesus' statements, about his origin, about his destiny, about the gifts he brings, so often construed by his listeners in a trivial sense, are understood by competent readers in a new way. The Prologue and the testimonies to Jesus provide the reader with this theological dimension and their importance cannot be overestimated. Jesus' enigmatic actions and declarations are, for the readers, windows through which God's plan can be perceived, as Jesus had promised the disciples at the end of the first chapter: 'You will see heaven opened and the angels of God ascending and descending upon the Son of man' (1.51). Moreover, metaphors like 'living water', 'bread of life', 'true vine', 'good shepherd', and, most pervasively, 'father' and 'son', have to be recognized for what they are (see Part

II). Particular incidents and discussions may dominate readers' awareness, but each serves to exemplify the theological themes which the Gospel expounds, each is a microcosm of the whole, highlighting certain aspects of the total picture. There is little historical development in the narrative. Jesus sometimes attracts crowds who later fall away in disbelief (e.g. 4.45 and 6.66; 12.18-19 and 37), but from the beginning only his disciples have an inkling of the honour due to him (2.11), while representatives of worldly interest always oppose or misunderstand him. The certainty of Jesus' death and the effects it would bring are never far from the surface (e.g. 2.4, 21; 3.14-16; 4.21, 42; 5.21, 27-28; 6.51-58). Development is not in the story but in the readers. Each section adds to the readers' understanding, so that by the end of the Gospel they are in a position to decide whether to believe in Jesus as the Christ, the Son of God. Moreover, by engaging in this exercise of comprehension, they are predisposed to accept rather than reject the Gospel's contentions.

The story of Jesus' raising of Lazarus, for example, draws on what precedes and prepares for what follows by adding a new facet to the reader's configuration. 'Now when Jesus came, he found that he [Lazarus] had already been in the tomb four days' (11.7). Jesus, far from Bethany, across the Jordan (10.40), had heard of Lazarus's illness, the illness of someone he loved (11.3), but had remained where he was for two days before making the time-consuming journey to Bethany (11.6). Lazarus's death comes as no surprise in 11.17, however, since Jesus had already told the disciples about it (11.11-14), but the information creates a tension in the story because Jesus had at first declared that Lazarus's illness 'is not unto death; it is for God's honour, so that the Son of God may be honoured by means of it' (11.4). The opportunity has been lost, and the assurance contradicted.

'Bethany was near Jerusalem, about fifteen stadia off, and many of the Jews came to Martha and Mary to console them concerning their brother' (11.18). These 'Jews' from Jerusalem will witness what happened next and this will affect what they do afterwards (12.9-19). 'When Martha heard that Jesus was coming, she went and met him while Mary sat in the house' (11.19). The first scene, then, involves only Martha and Jesus, not Mary and the 'Jews'. (The disciples are ignored.) It is Martha who opens the conversation, 'Lord, if you had been here, my brother would not have died. And even now, I know that whatever you ask of God, God will give you.' Martha confirms the reader's impression that Jesus' presence would have saved Lazarus, as it had saved the royal official's son, the feeble cripple, the hungry crowds, the threatened disciples and the man born blind, because he received whatever he asked from God (see 11.41 and 9.31-33). But now that Lazarus is dead, what can Jesus ask? Perhaps that the sisters be comforted in their distress. Jesus' reply offers comfort, 'Your brother will rise again'. It presupposes the scriptural hope of resurrection (Dan. 12.2; see Jn 6.39, 40, 44). Martha responds by confirming her belief in the future resurrection, 'I know that he will rise again in the resurrection at the last day' (11.24). But Jesus goes on to make a declaration about himself, 'I am the resurrection and the life; he who believes in me, though he die yet shall he live, and whoever lives and believes in me will never die' (11.25-26a). Belief in Jesus is what will determine whether someone will be resurrected. Moreover, Jesus claims to *be* the resurrection and the life. In other words, those who believe are the ones who participate in his life (6.35-58). Martha therefore confesses that she believes Jesus to be 'the Christ, the Son of God' (11.27). The conversation sums up teaching which had been given earlier in the Gospel: Jesus is the Christ (1.41; 4.25-26), the Son of God (1.49; 5.19-23), who gives eternal life to whom he will (e.g. 5.21, 24), who exercises God's judgment (5.22, 27), whose voice the dead hear (5.25) and come out of the tomb to the resurrection of life or the resurrection of judgment (5.28-29); those who believe in Jesus and who participate in his life will be raised on the last day (6.35-38). All this Jesus does and will do as God's agent (5.17-47).

The scene now changes with Martha's departure to call her sister. When Mary meets Jesus, however, she is accompanied by the 'Jews' who follow because they suppose she is going to Lazarus's tomb to weep there (11.28-31). Mary expresses her respect for Jesus by falling at his feet and confessing that his presence would have saved her brother from death (11.32). Jesus is so angered by Lazarus's death and so moved by the mourning of Mary and her neighbours that he asks where the tomb is and weeps there himself (11.33-35). This prompts the 'Jews' to discern his love for Lazarus, reminding readers of earlier information which could have been forgotten since nothing in Jesus' behaviour up to this point had confirmed it (11.36 and 3). These 'Jews' also wonder whether what Martha and Mary had previously confessed could be true, 'Could not he who opened the eyes of the blind man have kept this man from dying?' (11.37). The readers, however, are in a better position to make that connexion than these characters in the story. We are not told that they were present at the healing miracle in ch. 9.

This rhetorical question, to which readers may answer 'Yes', leads into the final scene, with its brief introductory setting, 'Then Jesus, again angered in himself, came to the tomb; it was a cave, and a stone lay upon it' (11.38). Jesus' anger is appropriate as a response to the fact of death and, in the context, as the expression of an act of judgment. But this is all the preparation the text offers the characters or the readers for Jesus' next command, 'Take away the stone' (11.39). Martha's reaction (apparently she was there too), is only too comprehensible: 'Lord, by this time there will be an odour, for he has been dead for four days' (11.39). Readers are left in no doubt that Lazarus was well and truly dead. Jesus' rebuke, 'Did I not tell you that if you would believe you would see God's honour' (11.40), is not quite fair, however, because Jesus had said no such thing to Martha. His remarks had been directed to the disciples before he set out for Bethany (11.4). It is the reader who can make this connexion, not Martha. Moreover, even the reader must develop the earlier statement from 'this illness is not unto death; it is for the honour of God' into 'even this death is for the honour of God'. When the stone is removed Jesus is depicted praying to God in confirmation to the characters and the readers that the Father always hears him. It confirms what Martha had said earlier (11.22) but in an unexpected way. The miracle about to be related is intended to show that the Father sent Jesus (11.41-42), and hence to fulfil Jesus' promise that the Son would be honoured (11.4). Jesus then calls Lazarus from the tomb and the dead man responds by emerging in his grave clothes. Jesus' final command is to unbind him and let him go, that is, to release him from the last fetters of death (11.44).

Readers may understand the story as a demonstration of Jesus' authority over death, and, therefore, as a guarantee of the truth of his identification of himself as the resurrection and the life. It is, however, proleptic and not final, since Lazarus is resuscitated to a mortal existence and will die later, an interpretation confirmed by references to the chief priests' plot to kill him as well as Jesus (12.9). Only at the end of the Gospel, when Jesus is resurrected from the dead to a transformed existence, is Jesus' claim finally shown to be true. The story focuses and dramatizes Jesus' earlier teaching but also points forward to a final fulfilment. It leads readers into a more complete appreciation of Jesus' mission but makes them wait till the last chapters for full comprehension.

Conclusion: The Ideal Readers of the Fourth Gospel

The ideal readers of this narrative are those who can play the role of the narratees in believing that Jesus is the Christ, the Son of God, resurrected and living in the bosom of the Father, whose life, death and resurrection inaugurates a new community of mutual love in which to live their lives of obedience to God. Those who cannot play this role, even for the duration of their reading, are unlikely to continue the task the text sets them. Platonists, for example, would be inclined to spend their time refuting the opening statements of the Gospel about creation, upon which the rest depends, and would proceed no further. Stoics might be willing to read on because of their familiarity with the λόγος concept, but would soon be alienated by the provincial milieu and the Jewish conceptions. Cynics would be offended by the claim that Jesus is a king, albeit of an unworldly kingdom, as they would discover if they pursued the argument as far as Jesus' discussion with Pilate (18.33-38), and by Jesus' willing submission to the power of his enemies (18.4-11). Jews would be inclined to identify with those who bore their name in the story, but would soon be frustrated by their incompetence in questioning Jesus, preferring, no doubt, to furnish their own more pertinent arguments.

Modern readers who are not completely alienated from the Christian tradition and who are prepared to make the effort involved in any attempt to read a text written in Greek and coming from a society so different from their own, may perform the role of the ideal reader and be affected by the experience the narrative evokes. But even if they are believing Christians, they cannot remain in the world their reading creates. With the benefit of hindsight, they can see that the Gospel raises as many questions as it answers. Is it conceivable that the world is the creation of a loving God? How is it that the life, death and resurrection of a vulnerable human being can give knowledge of God? In what ways is the inspiration of the Paraclete who leads disciples into all truth to be distinguished from false promptings? Is resurrection a coherent conception of personal survival? What does the love command require of those who would obey it in an unjust world?

How far does the failure of Christians to love one another invalidate their claims and distort their experience? The Fourth Gospel provides the inspiration for Christian living but not the final word. What it does is to remind and encourage all its readers to understand their mundane existence in the light of God's purpose in sending his son. It spurs them into action and into further reflection by its power to move them.

And the Fourth Gospel has the power to do this even for modern western women whose potential roles are so different from those of the women depicted in the Gospel. To be moved rather than infuriated by the Fourth Gospel, they have to recognize their own identity with 'the disciple whom Jesus loved', with Jesus himself, and with the narratees of the Gospel, so that they can receive God's Spirit, conform their lives to Jesus', and accept the responsibilities which rebirth entails. And many of them have one obvious advantage over most western men. They are not entirely blinded by society's macho, competitive spirit, which judges success in terms of the power of money and the social status it brings. They have experienced the destructive effect of that pervasive ethos, and some of them have glimpsed the freedom that comes from loving service to fellow human beings. They can identify more readily with the Jesus of the Fourth Gospel who is crucified. But I do not want to suggest that this justifies in any way western society's denigration and persecution of women. There is a complete difference between an enforced subordination and a free perception and implementation of alternative values. Rather, it highlights the extreme gulf between the ethos of modern western society and the ethos of the loving community envisaged by the Fourth Gospel. Women as well as men who accept the responsibility of living from the God whom the Fourth Gospel sees as the Creator of life and light, have their parts to play in creating new kinds of communities in which love, not the power of money, gives value to human existence. But this requires a social revolution more fundamental and far reaching than any that human history has so far witnessed. And it involves moving from the general to the particular, a move which the Fourth Gospel does not make. It requires an understanding of our political, social and economic history, both within churches which accept the Fourth Gospel as Scripture and outside them, in order to engage effectively in a struggle which will create genuine communities.

Another of the benefits which hindsight has brought modern

Christians is the recognition that the Fourth Gospel's depiction of Judaism, like that of the other Gospels, is partial and polemical. We are in a position to read the literature which Jews wrote at the time when the Fourth Gospel was written, and to appreciate its profound religious and moral perceptions, and the debt which Christianity owes to it, not least in Christianity's adoption of Jewish Scriptures. We can also recognize that the caricature of Judaism by the Fourth Evangelist served two purposes. First, the caricature presented readers with a simple depiction of the kinds of false securities to which its own religious tradition was prone. This depiction functions as a necessary warning against a 'worldliness' which prefers honour from fellow human beings to honour from the transcendent God. Secondly, the caricature served to define the Christian community as separate from Judaism.

These functions, however, had far-reaching consequences for the history of Christianity, for those who identified with the implied readers of the Fourth Gospel. In acknowledging the separate identity of Christian communities, Christians lost the privileges that Judaism had won for itself within the Roman Empire. As soon as Roman emperors and governors could identify Christians as a separate religious group, Christianity became subject to Roman persecution, and various Christian communities suffered persecution and martyrdom during the first four centuries of the church's existence. But with the conversion of the Emperor Constantine to Christianity in the fourth century, the situation changed. In the centuries which followed, Christian scriptures and teachings could influence the policies of emperors in Europe and the Middle East. And the Gospel's caricatures of Judaism could and did fuel Christian anti-Semitism. The Fourth Gospel's positive depiction of a loving community, dedicated to God who sent his son to save the world by laying down his life, did not prevent Christians from violently persecuting Jewish communities. We may think that the Fourth Gospel would have been a more accurate historical version of Jesus' ministry if it had provided a less polemical picture of Judaism, but we can hardly hold the Gospel responsible for the violence and hatred of subsequent Christians who cited it in support of their viciousness. Nor, however, can we who call ourselves Christians escape the responsibility of acknowledging this history as that of our own churches.

BIBLIOGRAPHY

Only those books and articles mentioned in the argument of the book are listed in the bibliography.

Primary Sources

Achilles Tatius (trans. S. Gaselee; LCL; London: Heinemann, 1917).

The Ante-Nicene Christian Library (ed. A. Roberts and J. Donaldson; 10 vols.; repr. Grand Rapids: Eerdmans, 1951–1956 [1885–1897]).

The Apocryphal Old Testament (ed. H.F.D. Sparks; Oxford: Clarendon Press, 1984).

The Babylonian Talmud (London: Soncino Press, 1969).

Corpus Hermeticum (ed. A.D. Nock and A.J. Festugière; Paris: Budé, 1945).

Diodorus Siculus (trans. C.H. Oldfather; LCL; Cambridge, MA: Harvard University Press, 1967), I–X.

Epictetus, *Dissertations* (trans. W.A. Oldfather; LCL; 2 vols.; London: Heinemanns, 1928).

Euripides, *Bacchae* (trans. A.S. Way; LCL; Cambridge, MA: Harvard University Press, 1979), II.

Eusebius, *The Ecclesiastical History* (trans. K. Lake and J.E.L. Oulton; LCL; 2 vols.; Cambridge, MA: Harvard University Press, 1926–1932).

The Gospel of Philip (ed. and trans. R.McL. Wilson; London: Mowbrays, 1962).

The Greek New Testament (ed. K. Aland *et al.*; London: United Bible Societies, 3rd corrected edn, 1966).

Josephus, *Works* (trans. H.St.J. Thackeray, R. Marcus, A. Wikgren and L.H. Feldman; LCL; 10 vols.; Cambridge, MA; Harvard University Press, 1965).

The Mishnah (ed. H. Danby; Oxford: Oxford University Press, 1933).

New Testament Apocrypha (ed. R.McL. Wilson; 2 vols.; London: SCM Press, 1963, 1964).

Ovid, *Metamorphoses* (trans. F.J. Miller; LCL; 2 vols.; London: Heinemann, 1916).

Pausanias, *Description of Greece* (trans. W.H.S. Jones; LCL; 4 vols.; London: Heinemann, 1918).

Philo, *Works* (trans. F.H. Colson and G.H. Whitaker; LCL; 10 vols.; Cambridge, MA: Harvard University Press, 1929–1932).

Philostratus, *The Life of Apollonius of Tyana* (trans. F.C. Conybeare; LCL; Cambridge, MA: Harvard University Press, 1912).

Plato, *Republic* (trans. P. Shorey; LCL; 2 vols.; Cambridge, MA: Harvard University Press, 1982).

Pliny the Elder, *Natural History* (trans. H. Rackham; LCL; Cambridge: Harvard University Press, 1952), I–IV.

Pliny the Younger, *Letters* (trans. W. Melmoth; rev. W.M.L. Hutchinson; LCL; 2 vols.; London: Heinemann, 1915).

Plutarch, *Lives* (trans. B. Perrin; LCL; 11 vols.; London: Heinemann, 1914).

Plutarch, *Moralia* (trans. P.H. De Lacy and B. Einarson; LCL; Cambridge, MA: Harvard University Press, 1959), VII.

Septuaginta (ed. A. Rahlfs; 2 vols.; Stuttgart: Württembergische Bibelanstalt, 1935).

Suetonius, *The Lives of the Caesars* (trans. J.C. Rolfe; LCL; 2 vols.; Cambridge, MA: Harvard University Press, 1913).

Tacitus, *The Annals* (trans. J. Jackson; LCL; 3 vols.; Cambridge, MA: Harvard University Press, 1931).

Modern Studies

Abrams, M.H.
1971 *A Glossary of Literary Terms* (London: Holt, Rhinehart and Winston).

Aland, K.
1986 'Der Text des Johannesevangeliums im 2. Jahrhundert', in W. Schrage (ed.), *Studien zum Text und zur Ethik des Neuen Testaments* (Berlin: de Gruyter).

Avigad, N.
1983 *Discovering Jerusalem* (Oxford: Basil Blackwell).

Bailey, J.A.
1963 *The Traditions common to the Gospels of Luke and John* (Leiden: Brill).

Balsdon, J.P.V.D., and J. Ferguson
1974 *Social Life in the Early Empire* (Milton Keynes: The Open University Press).

Barr, J.
1961 *The Semantics of Biblical Language* (Oxford: Oxford University Press).
1983 *Holy Scripture* (Philadelphia: Fortress Press).

Barrett, C.K.
1950 'The Holy Spirit in the Fourth Gospel', *JTS* NS 1: 1-15.
1975 *The Gospel of John and Judaism* (London: SPCK).
1978 *The Gospel according to St John* (London: SPCK, rev. edn).
1982 *Essays on John* (London: SPCK).

Bauer, W., W.F. Arndt and F.W. Gingrich
1957 *A Greek–English Lexicon of the New Testament and Other Early Christian Literature* (Chicago: University of Chicago Press).

Bindley, J.
1950 *The Oecumenical Documents of the Faith* (London: Methuen, rev. edn).

Black, M.
1967 *An Aramaic Approach to the Gospels and Acts* (Oxford: Clarendon Press, 3rd edn).

Boismard, M.-E., A. Lamouille and G. Rochais
1977 *L'évangile de Jean* (Paris: Cerf).

Borgen, P.
1968 'God's Agent in the Fourth Gospel', in Neusner 1968: 137-48.

Boring, M.E.
1979 'The Influence of Christian Prophecy on the Johannine Portrayal of the Paraclete and Jesus', *NTS* 25: 113-23.

Brooke, A.E.
1891 *The Fragments of Heracleon* (Texts and Studies, 1.4; Cambridge: Cambridge University Press).

Brown, R.E.
1966 *The Gospel of John* (AB; 2 vols.; Garden City, NY: Doubleday).
1971 'Jesus and Elisha', *Perspective* 12: 85-104.
1979 *The Community of the Beloved Disciple* (London: Cassell; New York: Paulist Press).
1983 *The Epistles of John* (AB; Garden City, NY: Doubleday).

Buchanan, G.W.
1968 'The Samaritan Origin of the Gospel of John', in Neusner 1968: 149-75.

Büchsel, F.
1964 'ἄωνθεν', *TDNT*, I, 378.

Bultmann, R.
1955 *The Theology of the New Testament* (London: SCM Press), II.
1971 *The Gospel of John: A Commentary* (Oxford: Basil Blackwell).

Burchard, C.
1985 'Joseph and Asenath', in J.H. Charlesworth (ed.), *The Old Testament Pseudepigrapha* (Garden City, NY: Doubleday), II, 177-247.

Cadman, W.H.
1969 *The Open Heaven* (ed. G.B. Caird; Oxford: Basil Blackwell).

Casey, P.M.
1987 'General, Generic and Indefinite: The Use of the Term "Son of Man" in Aramaic Sources and in the Teaching of Jesus', *JSNT* 29: 21-56.

Cassem, N.H.
1973 'A Grammatical and Contextual Inventory of the Use of Kosmos in the Johannine Corpus', *NTS* 19: 81-91.

Charles, R.H.
1893 *The Book of Enoch* (Oxford: Oxford University Press).

Charlesworth, J.H. (ed.)
1972 *John and Qumran* (London: Geoffrey Chapman).

Childs, B.S.
1974 *Exodus* (OTL; London: SCM Press).

Conrad, J.
1949 *Lord Jim* (Harmondsworth: Penguin Books).

Culpepper, R.A.
1983 *Anatomy of the Fourth Gospel: A Study in Literary Design* (Philadelphia: Fortress Press).

Daube, D.
1950 'Jesus and the Samaritan Woman: The meaning of συγχράομαι', *JBL* 69: 137-47.

Davies, W.D.
1974 *The Gospel and the Land* (Berkeley: University of California Press).

Dodd, C.H.
1936 'A New Gospel', *BJRL* 20: 56-92.

1953 'Note on John 21.24', *JTS* NS 4: 212-13.
1963 *Historical Tradition in the Fourth Gospel* (Cambridge: Cambridge University Press).
1968 *The Interpretation of the Fourth Gospel* (Cambridge: Cambridge University Press).

Duke P.D.
1985 *Irony in the Fourth Gospel* (Atlanta: John Knox).

Duprez, A.
1970 *Jésus et les dieux guérisseurs à propos de Jean V* (Cahiers de la Revue Biblique, 12; Paris: Gabalda).

Falk, Z.W.
1974 'Jewish Private Law', in S. Safrai, M. Stern, D. Flusser and W.C. van Unnik (eds.), *Compendia Rerum Judaicarum ad Novum Testamentum* (Assen: Van Gorcum), I, 504-34.

Farmer, W.R.
1952 'The Palm Branches in John 12.13', *JTS* NS 3: 62-66.

Fortna, R.
1970 *The Gospel of Signs: A Reconstruction of the Narrative Source underlying the Fourth Gospel* (SNTSMS, 11; Cambridge: Cambridge University Press).

Freed, E.D.
1965 *Old Testament Quotations in the Gospel of John* (NovTSup, 11; Leiden: Brill).

Freyne, S.
1980 *Galilee, from Alexander the Great to Hadrian* (Wilmington, DE: Michael Glazier).
1985 'Vilifying the Other and Defining the Self: Matthew's and John's Anti-Judaism in Focus', in J. Neusner and E. Frerichs (eds.), *To See Ourselves as Others See Us* (Brown Studies in the Humanities; Chico, CA: Scholars Press).
1988 *Galilee, Jesus and the Gospels* (Dublin: Gill and Macmillan).

Genette, G.
1980 *Narrative Discourse* (Oxford: Basil Blackwell).
1989 *Narrative Discourse Revisited* (Ithaca, NY: Cornell University Press).

Glasson, T.F.
1963 *Moses in the Fourth Gospel* (SBT, 40; London: SCM Press).

Gombrich, E.H.
1972 *Symbolic Images* (London: Phaidon).

Goodenough, E.R.
1962 *An Introduction to Philo Judaeus* (Oxford: Basil Blackwell, 2nd edn).

Grayston, K.
1981 'The Meaning of Paracletos', *JSNT* 13: 67-82.

Green, J.B.
1988 *The Death of Jesus: Tradition and Interpretation in the Passion Narrative* (WUNT, 2.33; Tübingen: Mohr [Paul Siebeck]).

Haas, N.
1970 'Anthropological Observations on the Skeletal Remains from Giv'at ha-Mivtar', *IEJ* 20: 33-37 and plates.

Haenchen, E.
1984 *John* (Hermeneia; 2 vols.; Philadelphia: Fortress Press).

Harner, P.B.
1973 'Qualitative Anarthrous Predicate Nouns: Mark 15.39 and John 1.1', *JBL* 92: 75-87.

Harris, W.V.
1989 *Ancient Literacy* (Cambridge, MA: Harvard University Press).

Harvey, A.E.
1976 *Jesus on Trial* (London: SPCK).
1987 'Christ as Agent', in L.D. Hurst and N.T. Wright (eds.), *The Glory of Christ in the New Testament* (Oxford: Oxford University Press).

Hengel, M.
1989 *The Johannine Question* (London: SCM Press; Philadelphia: Trinity Press International).

Hennecke, E.
1963–1965 *New Testament Apocrypha* (ed. W. Schneemelcher; 2 vols.; London: SCM Press).

Hick, J.
1966 *Evil and the God of Love* (London: Macmillan).

Horbury, W.
1985 'Extirpation and Excommunication', *VT* 35: 13-38.

Isaac, E.
1983 '1 Enoch', in J.H. Charlesworth (ed.), *The Old Testament Pseudepigrapha* (London: Darton, Longman & Todd), I.

Isaacs, M.E.
1976 *The Concept of Spirit* (Heythrop Monograph, 1; London: Heythrop College).

Iser, W.
1974 *The Implied Reader* (Baltimore: The Johns Hopkins University Press).
1978 *The Act of Reading: A Theory of Aesthetic Response* (Baltimore: The Johns Hopkins University Press).

Jeremias, J.
1966 *The Rediscovery of Bethesda* (New Testament Archaeology, 1; Louisville: Southern Baptist Theological Seminary).

Johnston, G.
1970 *The Spirit-Paraclete in the Gospel of John* (SNTSMS, 12; Cambridge: Cambridge University Press).

Käsemann, E.
1968 *The Testament of Jesus* (London: SCM Press).

Kenyon, F.G.
1932 *Books and Readers in Ancient Greece and Rome* (Oxford: Oxford University Press).

Kilpatrick, G.D.
1957 'The Religious Background of the Fourth Gospel', in F.L. Cross (ed.), *Studies in the Fourth Gospel* (London: Mowbrays).

Kimelman, R.
1981 'Birkath ha-Minim and the Lack of Evidence for an Anti-Christian Jewish

Prayer in Antiquity', in E.P. Sanders, A.I. Baumgarten and A. Mendelson (eds.), *Self-Definition* (London: SCM Press), II, 226-44.

Lakoff, G., and M. Johnson
1980 *Metaphors we Live by* (Chicago: University of Chicago Press).

La Potterie, I. de
1986 'The Truth in St. John', in J. Ashton (ed.), *Interpretation of John* (Philadelphia: Fortress Press; London: SPCK).

Liddell, H.G., and R. Scott
1968 *A Greek–English Lexicon* (Oxford: Clarendon Press).

Lindars, B.
1971 *Behind the Fourth Gospel* (London: SPCK).
1972 *The Gospel of John* (NCB; London: Oliphants).
1983 *Jesus, Son of Man* (London: SPCK).

Loader, W.
1989 *The Christology of the Fourth Gospel: Structure and Issues* (Beiträge zur biblischen Exegese und Theologie, 23; Bern: Peter Lang).

MacDonald, J.
1964 *The Theology of the Samaritans* (London: SCM Press).

Mackowski, R.M.
1980 *Jerusalem, City of Jesus* (Grand Rapids: Eerdmans).

Maddox. R.
1974 'The Function of the Son of Man in the Gospel of John', in R.J. Banks (ed.), *Reconciliation and Hope* (Exeter: Paternoster Press): 186-204.

Malatesta, E.
1978 *Interiority and Covenant* (Rome: Biblical Institute Press).

Marsh, J.
1968 *The Pelican Gospel Commentary on St. John* (Harmondsworth: Penguin Books).

Martyn, J.L.
1968 *History and Theology in the Fourth Gospel* (New York: Parthenon Press).
1979 *The Gospel of John in Christian History* (New York: Paulist Press).

Mazar, B.
1978 'Herodian Jerusalem in the Light of Excavations South and South-West of the Temple Mount', *IEJ* 28: 230-37.

Meeks, W.A.
1967 *The Prophet-King* (Leiden: Brill).

Metzger, B.M.
1987 *The Canon of the New Testament* (Oxford: Oxford University Press).

Miranda, J.P.
1972 *Der Vater, der mich gesandt hat* (Bern: Peter Lang).

Moldenke, H.N., and A.L. Moldenke
1952 *Plants of the Bible* (New York: Stechert–Hafner).

Moloney, F.J.
1978 *The Johannine Son of Man* (Rome: Bibliotea di Scienze Religiose 14, 2nd rev. edn).

Moule, C.F.D.
1962 'The Individualism of the Fourth Gospel', *NovT* 5: 171-90.

Moulton, J.H., W.F. Howard and N. Turner
1906, 1929, 1963, 1976 *A Grammar of New Testament Greek* (4 vols.; Edinburgh: T. & T. Clark).

Murphy-O'Connor, J.
1990 'John the Baptist and Jesus: History and Hypothesis', *NTS* 36: 359-74.

Neirynck, F. *et al.*
1979 *Jean et les synoptiques* (BETL, 49; Leuven: Leuven University Press/Peeters).
1982 'John and the Synoptics', in F. van Segbroeck (ed.), *Evangelica: Gospel Studies—Etudes d'évangile* (Leuven: Leuven University Press).
1984 'John and the Synoptics: The Empty Tomb Stories', *NTS* 30: 161-87.
1990 'John 21', *NTS* 36: 321-36.

Neusner, J. (ed.)
1968 *Religions in Antiquity* (Studies in the History of Religions, 14; Leiden: Brill).

Neyrey, J.H.
1989 'I said, "You are Gods": Psalm 82.6 and John 10', *JBL* 108: 647-63.

Nicholson, G.C.
1983 *Death as Departure: The Johannine Descent–Ascent Schema* (Missoula, MT: Scholars Press).

Nickelsburg, G.W.E.
1972 *Resurrection, Immortality and Eternal Life in Intertestamental Judaism* (Harvard Theological Studies, 26; Cambridge, MA: Harvard University Press).

Nicol, W.
1972 *The Semeia in the Fourth Gospel: Tradition and Redaction* (NovTSup, 32; Leiden: Brill).

O'Day, G.R.
1986 *Revelation in the Fourth Gospel: Narrative Mode and Theological Claim* (Philadelphia: Fortress Press).

Odeberg, H.
1968 *The Fourth Gospel* (Amsterdam: B.R. Gruner).

Pagels, E.H.
1973 *The Johannine Gospel in Gnostic Exegesis: Heracleon's Commentary on John* (SBLMS, 17; Nashville, TN: SBL).

Pamment, M.
1982 'Eschatology and the Fourth Gospel', *JSNT* 15: 81-85.
1985 'Path and Residence Metaphors in the Fourth Gospel', *Theology* 88: 118-24.
1985 'The Son of Man in the Fourth Gospel', *JTS* NS 36: 56-66.

Pixner, B.
1985 'Search for the New Testament Site of Bethsaida', *BA* 48: 207-16.

Quast, K.
1989 *Peter and the Beloved Disciple: Figures for a Community in Crisis* (JSNTSup, 32; Sheffield: JSOT Press).

Rengstorf, K.H.
1964 'ἀποστέλλω (πέμπω), ἐξαποστέλλω, ἀπόστολος, ψευδαπόστολος, ἀποστολή', *TDNT*, I, 398-447.

Roberts, C.H.

1935 *An Unpublished Fragment of the Fourth Gospel in the John Rylands Library* (Manchester: John Rylands Library).

Robinson, J.A.T.

1985 *The Priority of John* (London: SCM Press).

Rowland, C.

1982 *The Open Heaven* (London: SPCK).

Ruckstuhl, E.

1951 *Die literarische Einheit des Johannesevangelium: Der gegenwärtige Stand der einschlägigen Forschungen* (Studia Friburgensia, NS, 3; Freiburg: Herder).

1977 'Johannine Language and Style: The Question of their Unity', in M. de Jonge (ed.), *L'évangile de Jean: Sources, redaction, theologie* (BETL, 44; Leuven: Leuven University Press/Peeters).

Sanders, E.P.

1985 *Jesus and Judaism* (London: SCM Press).

1990 *Jewish Law from Jesus to the Mishnah: Five Studies* (London: SCM Press; Philadelphia: Trinity Press International).

1992 *Judaism: Practice and Belief, 63 BCE–66 CE* (London: SCM Press; Philadelphia: Trinity Press International).

Sanders, J.N.

1943 *The Fourth Gospel in the Early Church* (Cambridge: Cambridge University Press).

Sasse

1964 'ἐπίγειος', *TDNT*, I, 680-81.

Schnackenburg, R.

1968, 1980, 1982 *The Gospel according to St. John* (3 vols.; London: Burns and Oates).

1984 *Das Johannesevangelium* (Freiburg: Herder), IV.

Schneider, C.

1964 'ἀναβαίνω', *TDNT*, I, 519-22.

Schweizer, E.

1939 *Ego Eimi* (FRLANT, 56; Göttingen: Vandenhoeck & Ruprecht).

Sevenster, G.

1970 'The Humanity of Jesus in the Gospel and Letters of John', in *Studies in John* (NovTSup, 24; Leiden: Brill).

Sherwin-White, A.N.

1963 *Roman Society and Roman Law in the New Testament* (Oxford: Clarendon Press).

Solages, B. de

1979 *Jean et les synoptiques* (Leiden: Brill).

Soskice, J.M.

1985 *Metaphor and Religious Language* (Oxford: Clarendon Press).

Staley, J.L.

1988 *The Print's First Kiss: A Rhetorical Investigation of the Implied Reader in the Fourth Gospel* (SBLDS, 82; Atlanta: Scholars Press).

Sternberg, M.

1985 *The Poetics of Biblical Narrative: Ideological Literature and the Drama of Reading* (Bloomington: Indiana University Press).

Sundberg, A.C.

1964 *The Old Testament of the Early Church* (Harvard Theological Studies, 20; Cambridge, MA: Harvard University Press).

Taub, H.

1967 'ἐπουράνιος', *TDNT*, V, 538-42.

Teeple, H.M.

1957 *The Mosaic Eschatological Prophet* (SBLMS, 10; Philadelphia: Scholars Press).

1964 *Theological Dictionary of the New Testament* (ed. G. Kittel; 10 vols.; Grand Rapids: Eerdmans).

Thompson, M.M.

1988 *The Humanity of Jesus in the Fourth Gospel* (Philadelphia: Fortress Press).

Torrey, C.C.

1923 'The Aramaic Origin of the Gospel of John', *HTR* 16: 305-44.

Turner, N.

1963 'Syntax', in Moulton 1963: III.

1965 *Grammatical Insights into the New Testament* (Edinburgh: T. & T. Clark).

Tzaferis, V.

1970 'Jewish Tombs at or near Giv'at ha-Mivtar, Jerusalem', *IEJ* 20: 18-32 and plates.

Vermes, G.

1973 *Jesus the Jew* (London: SCM Press).

1975 *Post-Biblical Jewish Studies* (Leiden: Brill).

1983 *Jesus and the World of Judaism* (London: SCM Press).

Wheelwright, P.

1962 *Metaphor and Reality* (Bloomington: Indiana University Press).

Wiedemann, T.

1989 *Adults and Children in the Roman Empire* (London: Routledge).

Wiles, M.

1960 *The Spiritual Gospel* (Cambridge: Cambridge University Press).

Windisch, H.

1968 *The Spirit-Paraclete in the Fourth Gospel* (Philadelphia: Fortress Press).

Wolfson, H.A.

1948 *Philo* (2 vols.; Cambridge, MA: Harvard University Press).

Yadin, Y.

1961 'More on the Letters of Bar Kochba', *BA* 24: 86-95.

INDEXES

INDEX OF REFERENCES

OLD TESTAMENT

APOCRYPHA

PSEUDEPIGRAPHA

CHRISTIAN AUTHORS

OTHER ANCIENT SOURCES

INDEX OF AUTHORS

JOURNAL FOR THE STUDY OF THE NEW TESTAMENT

Supplement Series

25 THE UNDERSTANDING SCRIBE:
MATTHEW AND THE APOCALYPTIC IDEAL
David E. Orton

26 WATCHWORDS:
MARK 13 IN MARKAN ESCHATOLOGY
Timothy J. Geddert

27 THE DISCIPLES ACCORDING TO MARK:
MARKAN REDACTION IN CURRENT DEBATE
C. Clifton Black

28 THE NOBLE DEATH:
GRAECO-ROMAN MARTYROLOGY
AND PAUL'S CONCEPT OF SALVATION
David Seeley

29 ABRAHAM IN GALATIANS:
EPISTOLARY AND RHETORICAL CONTEXTS
G. Walter Hansen

30 EARLY CHRISTIAN RHETORIC AND 2 THESSALONIANS
Frank Witt Hughes

31 THE STRUCTURE OF MATTHEW'S GOSPEL:
A STUDY IN LITERARY DESIGN
David R. Bauer

32 PETER AND THE BELOVED DISCIPLE:
FIGURES FOR A COMMUNITY IN CRISIS
Kevin Quast

33 MARK'S AUDIENCE:
THE LITERARY AND SOCIAL SETTING OF MARK 4.11-12
Mary Ann Beavis

34 THE GOAL OF OUR INSTRUCTION:
THE STRUCTURE OF THEOLOGY AND ETHICS
IN THE PASTORAL EPISTLES
Philip H. Towner

35 THE PROVERBS OF JESUS:
ISSUES OF HISTORY AND RHETORIC
Alan P. Winton

36 THE STORY OF CHRIST IN THE ETHICS OF PAUL:
AN ANALYSIS OF THE FUNCTION OF THE HYMNIC MATERIAL
IN THE PAULINE CORPUS
Stephen E. Fowl

37 PAUL AND JESUS:
COLLECTED ESSAYS
Edited by A.J.M. Wedderburn

38 MATTHEW'S MISSIONARY DISCOURSE:
A LITERARY CRITICAL ANALYSIS
Dorothy Jean Weaver

39 FAITH AND OBEDIENCE IN ROMANS:
A STUDY IN ROMANS 1–4
Glenn N. Davies
40 IDENTIFYING PAUL'S OPPONENTS:
THE QUESTION OF METHOD IN 2 CORINTHIANS
Jerry L. Sumney
41 HUMAN AGENTS OF COSMIC POWER
IN HELLENISTIC JUDAISM AND THE SYNOPTIC TRADITION
Mary E. Mills
42 MATTHEW'S INCLUSIVE STORY:
A STUDY IN THE NARRATIVE RHETORIC OF THE FIRST GOSPEL
David B. Howell
43 JESUS, PAUL AND TORAH:
COLLECTED ESSAYS
Heikki Räisänen
44 THE NEW COVENANT IN HEBREWS
Susanne Lehne
45 THE RHETORIC OF ROMANS:
ARGUMENTATIVE CONSTRAINT AND STRATEGY AND PAUL'S
DIALOGUE WITH JUDAISM
Neil Elliott
46 THE LAST SHALL BE FIRST:
THE RHETORIC OF REVERSAL IN LUKE
John O. York
47 JAMES AND THE Q SAYINGS OF JESUS
Patrick J. Hartin
48 TEMPLUM AMICITIAE:
ESSAYS ON THE SECOND TEMPLE PRESENTED TO ERNST BAMMEL
Edited by William Horbury
49 PROLEPTIC PRIESTS:
PRIESTHOOD IN THE EPISTLE TO THE HEBREWS
John M. Scholer
50 PERSUASIVE ARTISTRY:
STUDIES IN NEW TESTAMENT RHETORIC
IN HONOR OF GEORGE A. KENNEDY
Edited by Duane F. Watson
51 THE AGENCY OF THE APOSTLE:
A DRAMATISTIC ANALYSIS OF PAUL'S RESPONSES
TO CONFLICT IN 2 CORINTHIANS
Jeffrey A. Crafton
52 REFLECTIONS OF GLORY:
PAUL'S POLEMICAL USE OF THE MOSES–DOXA TRADITION IN
2 CORINTHIANS 3.12-18
Linda L. Belleville

53 REVELATION AND REDEMPTION AT COLOSSAE
Thomas J. Sappington
54 THE DEVELOPMENT OF EARLY CHRISTIAN PNEUMATOLOGY WITH SPECIAL REFERENCE TO LUKE–ACTS
Robert P. Menzies
55 THE PURPOSE OF ROMANS: A COMPARATIVE LETTER STRUCTURE INVESTIGATION
L. Ann Jervis
56 THE SON OF THE MAN IN THE GOSPEL OF JOHN
Delbert Burkett
57 ESCHATOLOGY AND THE COVENANT: A COMPARISON OF 4 EZRA AND ROMANS 1–11
Bruce W. Longenecker
58 NONE BUT THE SINNERS: RELIGIOUS CATEGORIES IN THE GOSPEL OF LUKE
David A. Neale
59 CLOTHED WITH CHRIST: THE EXAMPLE AND TEACHING OF JESUS IN ROMANS 12.1–15.13
Michael Thompson
60 THE LANGUAGE OF THE NEW TESTAMENT CLASSIC ESSAYS
Edited by Stanley E. Porter
61 FOOTWASHING IN JOHN 13 AND THE JOHANNINE COMMUNITY
John Christopher Thomas
62 JOHN THE BAPTIZER AND PROPHET: A SOCIO-HISTORICAL STUDY
Robert L. Webb
63 POWER AND POLITICS IN PALESTINE: THE JEWS AND THE GOVERNING OF THEIR LAND 100 BC–AD 70
James S. McLaren
64 JESUS AND THE ORAL GOSPEL TRADITION
Edited by Henry Wansbrough
65 THE RHETORIC OF RIGHTEOUSNESS IN ROMANS 3.21-26
Douglas A. Campbell
66 PAUL, ANTIOCH AND JERUSALEM: A STUDY IN RELATIONSHIPS AND AUTHORITY IN EARLIEST CHRISTIANITY
Nicholas Taylor
67 THE PORTRAIT OF PHILIP IN ACTS: A STUDY OF ROLES AND RELATIONS
F. Scott Spencer
68 JEREMIAH IN MATTHEW'S GOSPEL: THE REJECTED PROPHET MOTIF IN MATTHAEAN REDACTION
Michael P. Knowles
69 RHETORIC AND REFERENCE IN THE FOURTH GOSPEL
Margaret Davies